TOURISM CONSUMPTION AND REPRESENTATION

Narratives of Place and Self

Tourism Consumption and Representation

Narratives of Place and Self

Edited by

Kevin Meethan
Social Research and Regeneration Unit, University of Plymouth, UK

Alison Anderson
School of Sociology, University of Plymouth, UK

and

Steve Miles
University of Liverpool, UK

www.cabi.org

CABI is a trading name of CAB International

CABI Head Office
Nosworthy Way
Wallingford
Oxfordshire OX10 8DE
UK

Tel: +44 (0)1491 832111
Fax: +44 (0)1491 833508
E-mail: cabi@cabi.org
Website: www.cabi.org

CABI North American Office
875 Massachusetts Avenue
7th Floor
Cambridge, MA 02139
USA

Tel: +1 617 395 4056
Fax: +1 617 354 6875
E-mail: cabi-nao@cabi.org

A catalogue record for this book is available from the British Library, London, UK.

Library of Congress Cataloging-in-Publication Data

Tourism consumption and representation : narratives of place and self / edited by Kevin Meethan, Alison Anderson and Steve Miles.
    p. cm.
  Includes bibliographical references and index.
  ISBN 0-85199-678-7 (alk. paper)
  1. Tourism--Social aspects. 2. Tourism--Economic aspects. 3. Geographical perception. 4. Consumption (Economics) 5. Economics--Sociological aspects I. Meethan, Kevin. II. Anderson, Alison. III. Miles, Steven. IV. Title.

G155.A1T58963 2006
306.4'819--dc22

                    2006015906

ISBN-10: 0 85199 678 7
ISBN-13: 978 0 85199 678 3

Typeset in Baskerville by Columns Design Ltd, Reading, UK
Printed and bound in the UK by Biddles, Kings Lynn

Contents

Contributors

Alison Anderson is Principal Lecturer in Sociology, School of Sociology, Politics and Law, University of Plymouth, UK. She is author of *Media, Culture and the Environment* (University College London and Rutgers University Press, 1997) and co-editor, along with Kevin Meethan and Steven Miles, of *The Changing Consumer* (Routledge, 2002). Recent articles on journalistic portrayals of environmental issues, genetics and war have appeared in *Sociological Research Online*, *Science Communication*, *Knowledge Technology & Society* and *New Genetics & Society*. Alison is currently conducting an ESRC-funded study on Nanotechnology and News Production.

Hazel Andrews is Senior Lecturer in Tourism and Leisure in the Centre for Tourism, Consumer and Food Studies, Liverpool John Moores University, UK. She has a masters in International Tourism Policy and her doctoral thesis was an ethnographic study of British character tourists to Mallorca. Hazel is interested in constructions, representations and consumption practices relating to identities, with particular focus on space, the body, food and drink, and folklore.

Stacey Lynn Camp is a doctoral candidate in the Department of Cultural and Social Anthropology and Archaeology Program at Stanford University, USA. Her dissertation ties together a suite of data sets – archaeological, archival and oral history research – to comprehend how Mexican immigrants' consumption habits were transformed upon crossing the border in late 19th and early 20th century California. Recently she has been actively involved in Californian historical and public archaeology projects, including San

Jose's Market Street Chinatown Archaeological Project and San Francisco's Tennessee Hollow Watershed Project. Her current research interests include the consumption and presentation of history in California and Ireland, and incidents of culture contact and exchange between immigrants and settlers in post-Mexican–American War California.

Torun Elsrud holds a PhD in sociology and works as a lecturer in Sociology at the Department of Humanities and Social Sciences at Kalmar University in Sweden. Her main research interests involve the social and cultural construction of 'self' and 'otherness', 'cross-cultural' communication processes, travel, migration, eurocentrism, mythologies in the media, gender and ethnicity.

Anabel Ford is the Director of the ISBER/MesoAmerican Research Center at the University of California, Santa Barbara (marc.ucsb.edu), USA and president of the non-profit Exploring Solutions Past: The Maya Forest Alliance (espmaya.org). Anabel is an anthropological archaeologist whose interests are widely interdisciplinary, working with rural development, conservation and related sciences that impact the understanding of the Maya.

Amy Hale teaches Humanities for St Petersburg College in Florida, USA. Research interests include the links between culture and economic regeneration, cultural tourism, and identity politics with a specialization in Cornwall.

Megan Joy Havrda, as a consultant with Counterpart International had the honour of developing and implementing the El Pilar Forest Garden Network from 2003–2005 with Dr Anabel Ford and local governmental and non-profit entities in Belize and Guatemala. She is now an advisor to the project. Megan also owns two companies specializing in urban revitalization, community development and green building, and currently lives in northern New Mexico, USA.

Diane Lee is a Senior Lecturer in the Tourism Programme at Murdoch University, Perth, Western Australia, the coordinator of the Western Australia Network of the Sustainable Tourism Cooperative Research Centre and is on the executive committee of the Forum Advocating Cultural and Eco Tourism (FACET) which is a Western Australian tourism community interest group. The concept of sustainable tourism development, incorporating the environment in all its aspects, underpins all areas of Diane's research interests. This covers the areas of host community attitudes and social representations of tourism. Her research on sustainable tourism development includes local area models for tourism planning and assessment of resources for tourism where tourism resources are 'valued' in the same manner as the resources of other industries. Tourism marketing using the societal approach to marketing research is viewed as a tool that encourages sustainable tourism development.

Kevin Meethan is Academic Director of the Social Research and Regeneration Unit at the University of Plymouth, UK. His research and publications have focused on tourism, cultural change and globalization, and include *Tourism in Global Society* (2001). Along with Alison Anderson and Steven Miles, he co-edited *The Changing Consumer* (2002). More recently he has been researching the relationship between genealogy tourism, identity and new technologies, the effects of new technologies on social memory, and the role of culture and the creative industries and tourism in relation to regeneration policies.

Jacqueline McGibbon completed her PhD in anthropology and comparative sociology at Macquarie University in Sydney, Australia. She was employed as a lecturer in the School of Tourism and Hospitality Management at Southern Cross University in Lismore, Australia for several years before temporarily leaving academia to care for her young children. Currently she lives in Austria, where she continues with her research as well as working as a translator. Her interests include the consumption of sport, tourism and leisure, the anthropology of work, issues of gender and the European Union.

Steven Miles is Reader in Sociology at the University of Liverpool, UK. He is the author of several books including *Consumerism as a Way of Life* (1998) and *Youth Lifestyles in a Changing World* (2000), co-editor of *The Changing Consumer* with Alison Anderson and Kevin Meethan, and co-author of *Consuming Cities* (2004) with Malcolm Miles. Steven is currently lead investigator on the Liverpool Model, designed to research the social, cultural, economic and environmental impacts of European Capital of Culture 2008 on the city of Liverpool. He recently co-edited a Special Edition of *Urban Studies* on 'culture-led urban regeneration'.

Nigel Morgan is a Reader in Tourism Studies at the Welsh Centre for Tourism Research at the University of Wales Institute, Cardiff, UK. His research interests embrace the political dimensions of tourism and destination marketing and critical tourism studies, and his latest book is the second edition of *Destination Branding*, published by Elsevier-Butterworth in 2004.

David Newsome is a Senior Lecturer in the School of Environmental Science at Murdoch University, Perth, Western Australia. David holds degrees in botany, soil science and geomorphology. His principal research interests are geotourism, human–wildlife interactions and the biophysical impacts of recreation and tourism. David's research and teaching, and the activities of his research group, focus on the sustainable use of landscapes and the assessment and management of recreational activity in protected areas. David is the lead author of the recently published books *Natural Area Tourism: Ecology, Impacts and Management* and *Wildlife Tourism* and is co-editor of *Geotourism*, a book which lays the foundation for the emergence of geotourism as a distinct discipline within the area of natural area tourism.

Caroline Oliver has recently joined the Faculty of Education at the University of Cambridge having worked as a lecturer in the School of Geography, Politics and Sociology for the last 3 years. She received her PhD in sociology and social anthropology from the University of Hull researching migration and ageing identities amongst older people retiring from Northern Europe to southern Spain. Aspects of this research have been published in journals including *Mortality* and the *Journal of Mediterranean Studies* whilst the main findings were recently published as a monograph by Routledge.

Celmara Pocock is a Postdoctoral Research Fellow in Cultural Heritage Tourism at the University of Tasmania, Australia. She completed her doctoral research on changing visitor experiences of space and place at the Great Barrier Reef at James Cook University, Australia. Her research interests include: environmental history and anthropology; history of travel and tourism; and photography and representation

Annette Pritchard is a Reader in Tourism Studies and Director of the Welsh Centre for Tourism Research at the University of Wales Institute, Cardiff, UK. Her research interests focus on the relationships between tourism, representation and social structures, experiences and identities, and her latest book is *Discourse, Communication and Tourism* (Channel View, 2005).

Jonathan Skinner is Lecturer in Social Anthropology at The Queen's University Belfast, UK. He has carried out fieldwork on the island of Montserrat in the Eastern Caribbean where he investigated colonial and post-colonial relations as expressed through tourism, carnival and political debate (*Before the Volcano: Reverberations of Identity on Montserrat*, Arawak Publications, 2004). He also has interests in salsa and jive dances, and dance communities. He is editor of the journal *Anthropology in Action*, and serves as EASA Publications Officer.

Amanda J. Smith is a Research Fellow for the Sustainable Resources research programme of Sustainable Tourism CRC in Western Australia and resides at the School of Environmental Science at Murdoch University, Perth, Western Australia. Her research interests include: the environmental and social impacts of tourism and recreation in protected areas; campsite impact monitoring; natural area tourism; wildlife tourism; and minimizing visitor impacts through resources and visitor management techniques. More recently she has been working in the fields of recreation ecology, visitor management including the review of user-pays systems, sustainable tourism and natural area management at

Murdoch University, Perth, Western Australia and Curtin University. Her research conducted for her doctoral thesis (2003) contributes to the current understanding of recreation impacts, both social and biophysical, in temperate eucalypt forests and improves procedures in impact assessment. It also provided a means, for the first time, of objectively monitoring designated, developed campsites where it is inappropriate to judge impacts against an undisturbed control.

Natalie Stoeckl is a Senior Lecturer in economics at James Cook University, Australia. She holds a BEc from the Australian National University, Townsville (ANU), an MEc from JCU and a PhD from ANU. Her primary research interests concern economic aspects of environmental and natural resource management problems – particularly in the area of tourism. She has participated in research projects in many regional areas (including Karumba, Port Douglas, Hervey Bay, Monkey Mia, the Australian Alps and Hinchinbrook Island) looking at topics such as: the community costs and benefits of tourism in remote areas, methods of measuring and monitoring sustainability in small communities; the private (business) costs and benefits of environmental self-regulation tourism; and the economic value of tourism.

Mika Toyota is a Research Fellow at the Asia Research Institute, National University of Singapore. She obtained her PhD from the University of Hull, UK in 1999 and subsequently lectured at the University of Hull for 3 years before taking up a Postdoctoral fellowship at the Asian MetaCentre for Population and Sustainable Development Analysis, National University of Singapore (2002–2004). She is currently engaged in various projects which examine international retirement migration, international marriages, and transnational care workers in ageing societies in the Asia-Pacific region.

Richard Voase is a Senior Lecturer in tourism at the University of Lincoln, UK. Prior to entering academia, he held practitioner posts in resort marketing and arts management. Central to his research interests is the relationship between consumer culture and cultural change. His last book *Tourism in Western Europe* is also published by CABI.

Tim Winter is currently Research Fellow at the University of Sydney, Australia. He is the author of two forthcoming books on Cambodia. The first examines cultural economies of tourism and heritage politics at Angkor within a framework of globalization, post-conflict reconstruction and post-colonial relations. The second, *Expressions of Cambodia; the Politics of Tradition, Identity and Change* (co-edited with Leakthina Ollier, RoutledgeCurzon Press 2006) critically examines contemporary Cambodia 25 years after the fall of the Khmer Rouge.

Preface

This volume addresses some new developments in approaches towards tourism analysis that focus on the interface between the production and consumption of tourist space, the narratives that are created around specific sites and specific forms of tourist activity, and the ways in which these are created, picked up, modified and incorporated into the narratives of self-hood that we all weave around our lives and the identities of the places in which we live.

Tourism research itself is continuing to develop away from early business and geographical models towards approaches more informed by other social sciences, in particular anthropology and sociology. In many ways, what we are seeing in tourism studies, if one can coin that term, is a replication of what is happening 'out there'. The boundaries of disciplines, like the boundaries of cultures, are becoming more open, more permeable and more mobile. At the same time, we also have to be aware that tourism itself as both an activity and subject matter for academic enquiry is too broad to be encompassed in one specific approach. The chapters in this volume then, regardless of the disciplinary backgrounds of the individual authors, conceive of tourist space not as a passive container through which the consumer simply passes, and in so doing absorbs the dominant meanings that are presented to them, but rather as an arena in which the meanings are contested not just at an abstract level, but through the active involvement of the consumer as a reflexive agent. They reflect important shifts that have occurred in contemporary society and the tourism studies field. Processes of globalization have led to increased flows of people and cultures around the globe and, at the same time,

individualism and consumerism have become more pronounced, and
new information technologies have accelerated the shrinking of time
and space. Moreover, the rapid growth of the public relations industry
has led to extensive resources being devoted to place marketing, and
the consumption of images has become increasingly significant. For
example, the United Nations designated 2002 as the International Year
of Ecotourism, and recent years have seen a growing spin around
marketing 'environmentally friendly' tourism, particularly as it is seen to
have greatest appeal among those social groups with higher spending
power. Cultural symbols are manipulated to exploit our experience of
the 'natural world'. However, we need to consider the complexity of
factors involved in the production of images and the reception of
meanings.

Although tourism involves spatial and cultural mobility, it is also
irreducibly associated with the specificity of places, with the processes by
which tourist sights are demarcated and set apart from the mundane.
The processes involved can be viewed as a form of commodification;
tourists not only travel to consume, but what they consume is in many
respects the destination itself. Paradoxically, however, the reflexive
consumer may have less of a say and may indeed feel less at home in a
world characterized by the commodification of place. In this context,
place is arguably bound up with the construction of image and
symbolism around that place rather than any localized meanings that
could be regarded as being inherent in the place itself. This
commodification of place as spectacle has constructed a situation which
raises the age old issue of choice: does the appeal of tourism promote
the essence of a place or the essence of a version of what place should be
in an idealized sanitized world of consumption? In part, the production
of tourist space is often the creation of tourism professionals, which
present official and sanctioned narratives of place and culture aimed at
a mythicized consumer. In this sense, it is possible to view such
production as the 'encoding' of dominant value systems, the production
of the 'tourist gaze'.

There are a number of problems with such approaches. First is the
assumption that representations in and of themselves are a form of
power and dominance that are somehow 'read' and reproduced. In
turn, we are left then with the possibility that tourists are 'duped' into
accepting a set of dominant values as the natural and given state of
affairs, with the only form of resistance or challenge being to adopt a
world-weary and rather cynical posture of postmodern ironic
detachment.

In turn, such approaches relate to the second problem, that of
conflating production with consumption, in assuming that gazes or
narratives are simply passively accepted and 'read' by consumers.
Although this may occur in certain circumstances, more recent theoretical

and empirical work has called into doubt such assumptions. Studies on the nature of biography and life histories, for example, draw attention to the fact that structure of personal narratives does not necessarily mirror other forms of literary discourse or public forms of narration. Similarly, the recent literature on consumption draws attention to its dynamic nature, and the ways in which consumption can be considered as a form of reflexive practice through which narratives of the self are actively constituted. For this reason, the dynamic interaction between production and consumption, between the public commodification of the tourist gaze and the personalized worlds of consumption needs to be the subject of serious enquiry. No one place is subject to the same processes under the same conditions; the market pressure for uniqueness is never far from the safety of uniformity.

Drawing on a variety of examples from Australia, Asia, Europe, the Caribbean and Central America, the chapters in this volume examine this interplay between the production and consumption of tourist spaces, placing an emphasis on the practices of public/private narrative, the tensions and overlap between them, and their relationship to the formation of place-identity and self-identity. Individually, they will also address a number of relevant subthemes which mediate the practices of consumption such as age, gender, sexual orientation, and perceptions of place, history, nature and the environment.

Kevin Meethan, Alison Anderson and Steve Miles

Introduction: Narratives of Place and Self

1

Kevin Meethan

Social Research and Regeneration Unit, University of Plymouth, UK

Tourism, Globalization and Mobility

The term globalization offers us not only a label to describe a particular state of affairs, however contested that may be, but also a powerful metaphor that evokes flux, change, movement and flows, the breaking down and transgression of boundaries and borders, the emergence of new forms of being and identity that are transcultural, cosmopolitan, new and dynamic. Travel and mobility then is an inherent quality of globalization, and tourism, as one variety of such mobility, brings to the fore a number of central issues surrounding the creation and consumption of commodities, places, cultures and identities in the context of global mobility.

Mobility, though, had always been a characteristic of human populations, yet significant changes to the scope and scale of such movement have been unprecedented in history; we are now connected and bound in a myriad of networks and relationships which less than a lifetime ago would have been the stuff of science fiction. With such changes must come new ways of behaviour as we adapt to our social world, and as social scientists must also force us to rethink our analytical frameworks, and to challenge the assumptions of the grand narratives of modernity. It is not my intention here to assess the full sweep of theoretical developments within the social sciences over the past two decades, and the forms which these challenges have taken. Rather, what I wish to draw attention to are a number of broad issues that are of particular relevance. First is that, in what we now like to term a globalized world, the old certainties of identity, the boundaries and markers as it were of place, culture and society, are more permeable and open to change than was previously the case. Secondly, we can no longer assume with certainty that any given society or culture is necessarily co-terminous with the boundaries of an existing or nominal nation state. As goods, information and monies flow in global circuits, so too do people, not only tourists as temporary migrant consumers, but also the more or less permanent economic migrants and others, refugees perhaps from wars or natural catastrophes, who have little choice in the matter (Robertson *et al.*, 1994; Cohen, 1997; Held *et al.*, 1999; Castells, 2004). We also have to consider the possibility that people's lives may be spread over a number of different locations and places, and may also incorporate elements derived from elsewhere (Beck, 1992, 2000; Martinez, 1998; Rapport and Dawson, 1998; Welsch, 1999; Morley, 2000; O'Reilly, 2000; Beck and Gernsheim, 2002).

There has always been an element of the global within tourism, yet, in common with many other forms of economic activity, the reach and spread of tourism have increased significantly over the past two decades. This geographical spread has also been complemented by increased market niching and specialization which has seen the traditional markets of the mass 'triple S' mode being superseded by more flexible patterns of tourism consumption. Yet this is consumption with a difference, because unlike other cycles of production/consumption, tourism requires people to travel to the point of production in order to consume. Linked as it is to specificity of places, the tourist product itself is not movable; it is people rather than goods which are imported and exported. To be a tourist then is to be mobile and transient and also to become involved, even if only superficially, in the worlds and lives of others (Smith, 1989; Rojek and Urry, 1997; Crouch, 1999; Coleman and Crang, 2002).

Such contact between 'hosts' and 'guests' has long been the subject matter of tourism analysis, and inevitably raises a number of issues relating to control over the process of cultural creation and maintenance (Appadurai, 1990; Miller, 1994; Allbrow *et al.*, 1997; Lovell, 1998; Featherstone and Lash, 1999; Meethan, 2003). Of course there is no denying that cultures have always adapted elements from each other, while at the same time seeking to preserve some notion of essentialism that differentiates them from each other. What globalization does is to speed up the rate of movement and hence the rate at which cultural practices are both challenged and changed by contact with 'others', so that we can point to a shift from cultures as being delimited and place-bound to ones that are more translocal in orientation. Such changes and adaptations are a response to, and an engagement with, the processes of globalization, in which we see both material goods as much as cultural practices being redefined and used in new contexts (Friedman, 1994, 1997; Miller, 1994; Howes, 1996; Clifford, 1997; Gurnah, 1997;

Edwards, 2000). What these examples indicate is that that despite Friedman's assertion that it is people and not cultures that travel (1997), there is no denying that cultural practices are to some extent mobile, and less rooted in specific localities, as may be expected, even if the notion of 'home' in some form or another still remains (Sarup, 1994).

Such a reworking or reordering of the world also requires a conceptual reorientation that consists of two basic elements. First is the way in which we conceptualize globalization itself, in terms of mobility, networks and interconnectedness, on approaches that focus on how new forms of boundaries, new forms of belonging and new forms of identity are emerging which challenge and cut across the old parameters of place, culture and society. This is more than just an empirical issue, as the concepts of networks and connections can also act as overarching metaphors and tropes around which we can organize our analysis (Clifford, 1997; Rapport and Dawson, 1998; Urry, 2000; Castells, 2004; van der Duim, 2005). The second is a consequence of the demise of the grand narrative of modernity and its apparent fragmentation which has resulted in a shift from focusing on the collective to the particularistic, from structure to agency, and consequently an interest and concern with the ways in which individuals actively engage in their social environments, and the construction of their individual biographies (Giddens, 1991; Beck, 1992, 1994, 2000; Evans, 1993; Cavarrero, 2000; Chamberlayne *et al.*, 2000; Mathews, 2000; Miller, 2000; Beck and Beck-Gernsheim 2002; Roberts, 2002; Misztal, 2003). Identity, no longer viewed as that which is given, becomes instead something that has to be actively worked at.

One way to approach this is through the notion of reflexive modernity, as derived from the works of Beck (1992, 2000) and later developed as 'institutionalized individualism' in Beck and Beck-Gernsheim (2002) (see also Bauman 1991, 1997; Giddens, 1991). Beck's writings bring to the fore two themes mentioned above: the changing nature of the institutional context in developed societies; and the role of reflexivity and biography which assume central importance in individual's lives. In what he terms advanced modernity, Beck argues that the individual has become removed from traditional supports and commitments, which have been replaced by the constraints of labour markets and consumption patterns. Take, for example, the role of social class and the family:

> People with the same income level, or put in the old fashioned way, within the same 'class', can or even must choose between different lifestyles, sub-cultures, social ties and identities. From knowing one's 'class' position one can no longer determine one's personal outlook, family position, social and political ideas and identity.
>
> (Beck, 1992, p. 131)

It is as if, in the past, an individual biography would be linear in nature, and socially prescribed by occupation, family role and social class; they are now self-produced and producing, to the extent that 'each person's biography is removed from given determinants and placed in his or her own hands' (Beck, 1992, p. 131). Beck is not arguing that this is some form of unfettered freedom; family roles, for instance, have not disappeared, but are now more fluid, and for many women opportunities for work also have to be reconciled with issues of childcare. In other cases, access to material resources, or a lack of them, makes the idea of free choice much more problematic and aspirational rather than realized. Such caveats aside, in general we can say that, in the developed economies at any rate, we now live in a milieu which offers us more choices and more freedoms than we have had in the past. Increasing choice, coupled with the forms of mobility that are implicit in globalization, means that the condition of contemporary society is one in which a sense of personal biography becomes the point around which we organize a coherent sense of who we are. The power of institutions has not faded but has changed; any choices that an individual can make have to be taken within a specific social, economic and cultural context. It is not a case of there being no restrictions; paradoxically, it is a case of the parameters within which we live compelling us to choose; as Bauman cautions, the apparent choice of contemporary society may be an illusion with 'no option to escape' (2002, p. xvi).

Institutional change no longer takes place solely within the confines of nation states; indeed it is a central tenet of Beck's argument that such changes are now global in scale and nature, and the crossing of boundaries, in both literal and metaphorical senses, adds further complexity, because mobility also leads to situations where people's lives may be spread over a number of different locations and places, so that a biography may be multi-locational and even transnational. At the risk of reductionism, one can say that globalization is not what happens out there, somewhere else, and to others, but rather is what we directly experience in our day to day lives to the extent that '… the world's oppositions … occur not only out there but also in the centre of people's lives' (Beck, 2000, p. 73). Yet for all that, people's lives are still rooted in specific places.

Narratives of Place

Tourism reconfigures and remakes socio-spatial relations in a number of ways, not the least being the fact that tourist space needs to be symbolically differentiated from the world of work, to be marked out as distinct and different (MacCannell, 1976; Böröcz, 1996; Urry, 2000; Meethan, 2001). In addition, places are invested in a variety of meanings that encompass notions of home, belonging, shared culture, shared language and history, and forms of personal and collective identity (Lefebvre, 1991; Cohen, 1997; Rapport and Dawson, 1998; Mathews, 2000; Morley, 2000; Meethan, 2001, 2003, 2004; Cattell and Climo, 2002; Bærendholt *et al.*, 2004). It is the values that are inherent to specific places, or the values ascribed to activities that are undertaken in such places, together with a bundle of associated services that comprise the tourist product sold in the marketplace.

These spaces, set apart from the mundane world of work for the tourists, are in part spaces of the imaginary, of fantasy and dreaming (Selwyn, 1993; Dann, 1996; Urry, 2000). Whatever the form of tourism indulged in, people always travel with a set of expectations derived from various media such as brochures, TV programmes, the Internet and the popular genres of travel writing. Much of this prior information removes uncertainty and reduces risk on the one hand, yet on the other can also be seen in both popular writing and academic analysis as a form of control which channels tourist experiences into pre-determined forms. The spaces of tourism are constructed, more or less consciously, to fulfil – or attempt to fulfil – such expectations. What they provide, through visual and other sensory cues, for example the production of guide books and the role of intermediaries, as much as the kinds of activities on offer, is a matrix of possibilities out of which tourists can construct a narrative of their wish fulfilment. In this sense, we can see the production of tourist space as the creation of socio-spatial forms which, by referring to common discourses and imagery, provide a framework within which experiences can be organized.

The dominant approach towards such issues in tourism has largely been derived from Foucualdian notions of the gaze (Urry, 1992, 1999, 2000; Rojek and Urry, 1997; Edensor, 1998) which draws attention to the social and controlled aspects of discourse and representation within modernity. Although such approaches have yielded insights regarding the social construction of tourist space, they nevertheless display a tendency to overemphasize the processes of production at the expense of consumption, as if consumers simply accept what is presented as a form of dominant ideology (Ritzer and Liska, 1997; Warren, 1999; Ritzer, 2000). There is no doubt that certain forms of tourism attempt to prescribe what is seen, yet overall the deployment of such paradigms displays a tendency to downplay the practical accomplishments of creating meaning, while at the same time overemphasizing the normative and controlling elements involved in tourism production.

In his discussion of tourist gazing, Crang argues that the practices involved are not just strategies to accumulate images, or simple mimetic activities, and that the practice of photography itself is more than the translation of an ideology on to film (1997, p. 367). If we see gazing as an active rather than a passive process, and as with other forms of production/consumption, it is incorrect to assume that the intentions of producers are simply absorbed whole and unmediated by passive consumers. Advertisers and marketing people attempt to imbue products with numinous power and social meaning that make them attractive, yet however effective this may be, there is no guarantee that beyond the point of acquisition a commodity may be used and thought of in ways that the original producers intended (see, for example, Clifford, 1997; Mathews, 2000) as commodities do not possess essential and authentic meanings that travel with them (Meethan 2001, 2003) but derive their meaning from use in context. One way of illustrating this latter point is to look at the production and consumption of souvenirs. Hanefors and Selwyn (2000), for example, draw our attention to the multiple 'public meanings' involved in both the production and consumption of souvenirs, while Mars and Mars (2000) examine the different aspects of 'private' meanings that can be ascribed to them (see also Kopytoff, 1986; Friedman, 1997; Linnekin, 1997). Similarly, Gable and Handler (2000), in their analysis of the heritage museum at Colonial Willamsburg (USA), note that the production of memory among the visitors is not the simple acceptance of one dominant 'reading' (see also Mellor, 1991; Raz, 1999) but instead is produced through a complex process of interaction, often involving family, memories of past visits and the purchase of souvenirs (see also Löfgren, 1999, p. 97). To argue over the authentic then is to engage in arguments of categorization and value systems that encompass more than a simple reading of places as text. Kopytoff (1986, pp. 79–80) argues that in complex societies, 'public' commodification coexists with other schemes of valuation such as those held by individuals, social categories and groups and that one significant aspect of the material aspects of culture is the ways they are '… culturally redefined and put to use' (Kopytoff, 1986, p. 67; see also Bourdieu, 1984; Howes, 1996). We can see that there is then a need to account for individual actions, other than seeing them as mere reflections of discourse, the simple reproduction of a dominant value system which prescribes what may or may not be viewed, and what is therefore truly authentic and of value.

Although control in terms of both production and consumption is clearly an issue to be addressed, the contributions to this volume suggest that it is a more contested area than has hitherto been acknowledged in the literature. In short, the producers of various narrativized spaces or gazes may attempt to control but, like the producers of other commodity forms, they have no final say over how narratives are perceived or acted on (Böröcz, 1996; Frow, 1997; Meethan, 2001). To accept the latter point does not in itself diminish the role of the producers of tourist space, rather it means focusing on the relationships between production and consumption as they are enacted as a set of practices, and, in turn, this may involve more active forms of participation than have previously been recognized; we do not simply inhabit space, but we interact with it, and through such interactions we embody and enact social relations (Coleman and Crang, 2002; Crouch

2002, 2004; Suvantola, 2002; Harrison, 2003; Bærenholdt *et al.*, 2004; van der Duim 2005). In short, the processes and practices through which meanings are attached to, and derived from, the places of tourism are more open and fluid than is often realized; they do not simply carry a prescribed set of essential 'authentic meanings' with them which are unproblematic and passively accepted (Appadurai, 1986; Gurnah, 1997; Edwards, 2000; Miles *et al.*, 2002).

The term narrative allows us to get away from the notion that tourism is an activity that is solely governed by and privileges visual consumption. To use the term narrative also implies a more active engagement with the social world than that of gazing. This is not to downplay the significance of the visual, rather it is to argue that other aspects of tourism which encompass forms of performance and embodiment, of self-reflection and personal autonomy are also elements worthy of further attention, the social world and being in it is more than a discourse, and place is more than just a passive container within which activities occur. By looking at the narratives of place, the stories, histories and myths that are associated with people and place, and by acknowledging the complexities involved in the ways in which people actively engage with their environment, together with the tensions between expectations and realization, we can arrive at a more nuanced understanding of the production and consumption of tourist spaces.

Narratives of Self

As I noted above, one of the challenges posed by the demise of the grand narratives of modernity has been a subsequent refocusing on the role of the individual, and in particular on the ways in which they negotiate their life course and identity through the complexities of our contemporary world. As Cavarero writes, 'Every human being, without even wanting to know it, is aware of being a *narratable self* – immersed in the spontaneous auto-narration of memory' (Cavarero, 2000, p. 33, emphasis in original). As noted above, it is through such processes of creating a biography, a self-narrative, that we as individuals produce a sense of who and what we are, whatever the specific combination of mediating factors such as ethnicity, religion, nation, work, class, gender, market relations and so on (Giddens, 1991; Evans, 1993; Rapport, 1997; Ahmed, 1999; Bal, 1999; Beck, 2000; Mathews, 2000; Miller, 2000; Beck and Beck-Gernsheim, 2002; Bell, 2003; Mistzal, 2003). The intention here is to focus on the ways in which experiences of travel and other places involve the active engagement of people in 'memory work'.

There is little doubt that many travellers and tourists love to regale their friends with tales of their adventures or misadventures away from home (Bruner, 1993; Elsrud, 2001). On a more mundane level too, the narratives that are constructed from the practices of consumption that tourism entails are ways of organizing both experiences and expectations, of working with them to produce coherent accounts reflexively (Giddens, 1991). Whatever the form or type of tourism indulged in, spending time away from one's day to day routines offers the individual the chance to reflect on and assess who they are in the world, and also to accumulate memories which arc then accommodated into the narrative accounts of their lives (Desforge, 2000; Gable and Handler, 2000; Galani-Moutafi, 2000; Elsrud, 2001, 2004; Coleman and Crang, 2002; Stephenson, 2002; Suvatanola, 2002; Harrison, 2003; Bærenholdt et al., 2004; Coles and Timothy, 2004; Meethan, 2004).

On the surface it may appear that this is no more than the reproduction of certain dominant discourses or metaphors, the idea of travel itself as a rite of passage, as a quest for a form of existential authenticity of the kind identified by Wang (1999), an inalienable condition, even if it is mediated through commodified forms. As with the gaze, what we are dealing with is a number of cultural elements which frame representational forms and expectations (Robertson et al., 1994; Clifford, 1997; Galani-Moutafi, 2000; Hall, 2000). Yet as Skultans convincingly demonstrates, self-narratives do not passively reflect the structure or content of discourses or literary texts, and that while narratives are '… undoubtedly a vehicle for shared cultural representations' they also involve '… imaginative truth and creativity' (Skultans, 1998, p. 27). In order to be intelligible, narratives, like other forms of experience, must be rendered into forms that are both culturally specific and common, and this ordering and accounting for experiences is an active, rather than a passive process in which people interpret, negotiate and create their own particular meaning (Skultans, 1998, p. 63).

As Desforge, drawing on the work of Giddens, argues, the importance of biography in relation to self-identity has both internal and external elements. The former refers to the ways in which an individual constructs a dialogue with themselves, and the latter the ways in which this is presented to the outside world (Desforge, 2000, p. 932). By analysing interviews with long-haul tourists, he shows how they used the opportunity of travel as a way to both narrate and represent their own sense of identity. Although Desforge is dealing with a particular niche market which may be seen as comprising independent travellers, Li (2000, p. 876) also shows that even within the confines of package tours, the potential for the re-imagination of the self through the experience of travel still exists. The combination of particular localities and forms of local knowledge with the mobile and transient narratives of travel, otherness and leisure create forms of tourism in which the narrative component is not bought off the shelf as it were, but rather takes the forms of an active construction of a personal narrative.

The mobility of globalization and the challenges that this poses also opens up the possibility that people's lives may be spread over a number of different locations and places, so that a biography may be multi-locational, transnational and/or multi-cultural, and may also incorporate elements derived from elsewhere (Martinez, 1998; Rapport and Dawson, 1998; Beck, 2000; Morley, 2000; O'Reilly, 2000). What these examples, and the chapters in this volume demonstrate, is that the dominant metaphors, discourses and gazes, the narratives of place created and sold by tourism professionals are not the end-point, rather they are the first step which remains to be confirmed, disconfirmed or modified by subsequent experience (Dann, 1996, p. 79), providing the means by which tourists can 'work at' creating their own personal narratives of place (Crang, 1997, p. 368). To acknowledge that a sense of the self is produced through processes of biographical narration is also to acknowledge that such processes involve elements of performance (Crouch, 2002, 2004). We are perhaps used to thinking of tourism as involving staged performances and events for the tourists, which often carry with it, as Coleman and Crang note, all the associated notions and problems of 'authenticity' (Coleman and Crang, 2002, p. 11). However, they argue that to see performance not as the simple consumption of a spectacle, but as a form of interaction between people and place is an acknowledgement that tourism is about, among other things, processes of transformation. However, there is a need to be cautious here, for this is not to claim that we can ascribe causation and agency to place and space, because after all, it is people who act – because, neither space, as an abstract concept, nor place as specific socialized manifestations, does not and cannot possess essential and inherent human attributes. To think otherwise is to commit the anthropocentric fallacy of assuming both nature, and the built environment, are capable of agency. Neither, however, is place an empty container, because it is the actions of people that animate it and ascribe specific meanings to it; space becomes the medium within which a more or less defined set of activities takes place which consist of both material and metaphorical elements (Coleman and Elsner, 1998). To think in terms of performance then is to think of ways in which we, as individuals, engage with the world around us in both sensual and social ways.

To sum up so far, the situation of contemporary society, in the developed economies of the West at any rate, is one where individuals exercise more control over who they can claim to be. In part, this is a consequence of structural changes that have shifted us to a position where identities are not wholly prescribed by virtue of birth, occupation or place of residence, but rather are more flexible and malleable. Coupled with the forms of mobility that are implicit in globalization, the condition of contemporary society is one in which a sense of personal biography, a narrative of place and self becomes the anchor around which we organize and narrate a coherent sense of who and where we are, should we chose to exercise that option, because, as many of the chapters in this volume show, while on the one hand we need to question the assumed passivity inherent in many analyses of tourist consumption, we should also be aware that its polar opposite, the notion of unfettered free choice, is just as problematic. The solution does not lie somewhere half way between these so much as in the complexity of relationships involved in the wider social milieu in which we live.

Structure of the Book

The first three chapters in this volume directly address a number of issues relating to the past and the rediscovery, or appropriation perhaps, of archaeological heritage. All of these deal with sites that are of international significance, two of which are also designated by UNESCO as World Heritage Sites. The fact that such sites and tourist destinations are multi-vocal and open to different forms of interpretation should come as no surprise; the question is how the complexity of these overlapping and perhaps exclusive narratives of place, which often involve an element of performance as much as passive consumption, can be accounted for (see also Crouch, 2002).

Lynn Camp's chapter focuses on the Brú na Bóinne complex that comprises the three prehistoric sites of Newgrange, Knowth and Dowth, located on the north bank of the River Boyne in the Irish Republic, and which are regarded by UNESCO as being Europe's largest and most important concentration of prehistoric megalithic art. By these criteria, the authenticity of the sites is beyond reproach, yet as Lynn Camp shows, the discovery and presentation of these sites owes more to the sensibilities of a 19th century romantic narrative used both to mythologize and justify the claims of nationalism. This leads, she argues, to a situation where the sites and the stories that have been woven around it contain many narrative contradictions. In addition, there are also a number of alternative ways in which the history and significance of these sights can be experienced and interpreted, that can, for example, emphasize Druidism, Celticism or Catholicism. Yet visitors do not simply absorb and regurgitate the dominant readings portrayed and presented to them. The nationalist narratives presented in the visitor centre are so blatant, she argues, as to invite criticism and challenge, but that in itself may well reflect wider changes within Irish society as a whole; the narrative that is presented might no longer have the resonance it once did.

A similar set of concerns are found in Tim Winter's chapter on Preah Khan, part of the temple complex of Angkor, Cambodia. He also finds the long shadow of romanticism and the valorization of the ruined and the picturesque. Built in the 12th century, the complex had fallen into disuse some 300 years later and was engulfed by the forest, only to be 'discovered' by Henri Mohout in 1860. The site itself, whose appeal as a partial ruin owes much to the loss and decay caused by vegetation, is also shrouded in competing and contradictory narratives which, as Winter notes, are being continually embellished and commodified for a global tourist market, and this too involves forms of practice and embodiment that, while based in a dominant narrative of lost ancient civilizations, none the less requires the active and at times conscious participation of the tourists themselves. There are a number of similarities to, but also some differences from the situation described by Ford and Havrda in Chapter 4. Like Winter's study, the subject is another set of 'lost' and 'discovered' ancient ruins deemed to be of global significance, in this case those left by the Maya of Central America, which straddle the borders of Belize and Guatemala.

As in the example of the Angkor Wat complex, the Maya ruins were also discovered in the 19th century, and the subsequent reconstruction and opening up of these sites for tourism calls into question the authenticity of the narratives through which such sites are presented to the outside world. The more notable sites of the Maya civilization such as Chichén Itzá have been painstakingly 'rescued' from the enveloping jungle and packaged for tourist consumption in a narrative of romantic lost civilizations that is the Maya story. The El Pilar site, however, is unique in many ways, not least being that as it was only rediscovered in the 1980s, its history is not linked to the romanticized narratives of the 19th century that encompass the other Maya sites in the region; instead what we see emerging here is a rather different narrative of place that is more in tune to the sensibilities of the 21st century. Ford and Havrda note that unlike the other Maya sites which have been cleared of the jungle vegetation, most of El Pilar has not. It is this that not only marks it off as unique among other sites in the region, but also calls for a more active engagement on behalf of the tourists, with the help of local guides, in order to interpret the site. There are two significant differences here. The first is that the jungle, instead of being viewed as a destroyer in a struggle between nature and culture, is seen instead as an ecosystem which informed the Maya system of belief as well as providing their sustenance. The second difference is the existence of everyday Maya residential areas which shift the narrative away from the grand, monumental aspects of Maya architecture back to the mundane aspects of daily existence of those who once inhabited El Pilar. This example serves to highlight the point made by Wang (1999) that there is more than one form of authenticity, but also that these are not mutually exclusive; the precise recording, dating and ascription of origins that is the basis of archaeology, and represents the museum definition of authenticity can also exist side by side with a more existential authenticity provided by a sense of personal discovery and empathy with the surrounding environment.

Moving on from the ruins of past civilizations, yet still with the theme of adventure and discovery, is Pocock's chapter on the Australian Barrier Reef. Renowned as one of the natural wonders of the world, and as such a designated World Heritage Site, the Reef has been a tourist attraction, or at least has attracted visitors as both scientists and sightseers, since it first came to the notice of the West. Although current narrative portrayals of the reef owe much to the European dream of a tropical paradise, this was far from the case for the early visitors. Recordings of the trips made in the 1920s for instance note the physical hardships of the environment as much as its unique beauty, which meant that experiences of the Reef were not just visual but were rather fully embodied experiences, and ones that also related to the wider historical narratives of early Reef exploration and were shared with other travellers. Such early tourists bear a number of similarities to contemporary backpackers who shun the contrived safety of the package tour in order to reach out for an 'authentic' experience, one that, because it is perceived to be unmediated and 'untainted', is also unique and unalienable. It was arguably the formalization of the tourist industry in the latter half of the 20th century, and the provision of bars, hotels and restaurants with air-conditioning, that has mediated and to some extent controlled the consumption of the Reef to the extent that in some areas, coconut palms were planted to meet the expectations of the visitors. Other technological changes have also had a significant impact on the ways in which the Reef is consumed, in particular advances in both diving and photographic equipment have resulted in an emphasis on the visual aspects of consumption; clearly we are dealing here with a specific form of gaze, yet this in itself raises a number of issues concerning how technology both mediates experiences and by so doing contributes towards the creation of tourist spaces and experiences.

Also dealing with the natural environment in Australia, and set in another World Heritage Site, but with a different perspective, is Chapter 6 by Smith *et al.* This examines the phenomenon of viewing dolphin feeding at Monkey Mia in Western Australia, dealing with a number of issues relating to the management and control of tourist space. As the authors point out, certain species have more attraction and indeed charisma than others, such as dolphins which feature in the mythology of many cultures across the world. The popularity of these aquatic mammals can be gauged by the fact they draw in 100,000 visitors to the area each year. The spectacle of the dolphins being fed is a practice that dates back to the 1960s, when local fishermen began to feed them in the shallows near the shore. Visitors began to arrive, and the site developed from a caravan park to a fully fledged visitor centre, from a spontaneous gesture by the fishermen into a carefully orchestrated and timed display that in turn requires careful management. The central dilemma according to the authors is that those wishing to view wildlife expect a degree of unpredictability and spontaneity in their encounters, yet are unlikely find it in the controlled environment of Monkey Mia.

Jacqueline McGibbon's chapter takes us from Australia to the Tirolean ski resort of St Anton am Alberg, another site given over to the singular pursuit of leisure. Once the preserve of a wealthy elite, skiing is now a mass participatory sport with associated support services, products and specialized equipment. Although rooted in place and dependent on the seasonal weather, skiing and other associated snow sports are, as McGibbon argues, a complex and transnational field that not only relies on a narrative of Alpinism, but also generates its own forms of social interaction and consumption groups such as the Teppich-Swingers and the skibums. The former tend to be long-standing and regular visitors, most of whom are from Germany and Austria, whose social relations are formalized by membership of a ski school. This is exemplified by the Teppich-Swinger Verein, a club that promotes the practice of a particular kind of formation skiing. This ritualized and formalized practice contrasts sharply with the skibums, a more heterogeneous and international collection of people who also work in the resort in order to cover the costs of their skiing and who are, in effect, a mobile and low paid transient workforce. Like the Teppich-Swingers, the skibums also have their preferred ways of skiing and different ways of socializing, both of which mark them out as easy going, offering perhaps images of an itinerant and 'alternative' lifestyle that seeks self-hood through the single-minded pursuit and consumption of leisure.

Other forms of cross-national relationships are addressed by Mika Toyota who focuses on the phenomenon of young single female Japanese tourists in Bali. Rejecting simple models of social causation in terms of host–guest relationships, Toyota argues that the interaction between both has in itself become a central component of Balinese identity, which in turn has a number of consequences for the tourists. As she points out, it is only in recent years that changes to Japanese legislation and employment patterns have resulted in the creation of a salary-earning, urban female cohort who embrace a number of distinct consumption patterns, including overseas travel. The marketing of destinations, most commonly through magazines, presents Bali as an island apart, the home of the 'authentic other' where the humdrum and routinized work of the office worker can be forgotten. Of course, such dreams of paradise have long been a stock in trade of the travel industry yet, as Toyota argues, this also requires the active involvement, rather than the passive consumption of the tourists, for just as much as the tourists gaze on the locals, the locals too gaze on the tourists. Unlike Japanese tourists who travel outside Asia, those who visit Bali are not seen by the Balinese as exotic others so much as familiar others, and the sense of familiarity can also extend to intimate relations. There is a tendency that Toyota identifies which sees sex tourism in terms of power and exploitation of the hosts by the guests, and by men over women. In the cases she discusses, the gender roles are reversed, and the people with whom the tourists interact are cultural intermediaries and brokers who also act as informal guides. Such relationships may also extend beyond the single visit, as many of the tourists become repeat visitors, some also marrying the locals; the tourist encounter then turns from the fleeting and transient to something more permanent.

Both the skibums referred to by McGibbon and the Japanese women that are the subject of Toyota's chapter could be seen as people in search of adventure. This theme is elaborated in Torun Elsrud's chapter which looks at the idea of adventure and risk taking among backpackers. Beginning with the observation that women are as likely as men to go backpacking, she also notes that dominant narratives which frame adventure are predominantly masculine; the adventuress therefore is a transgressive figure who, by virtue of her gender alone, is viewed as exceptional. An adventure though, is more than just travel, to use the terminology of marketing, it is a package, complete with associated imagery. The adventuress then is the person who, clad in worn cotton clothes that speak of distance and experience, travels to find the mythical other – the primitive, the poor and the native – and the closer the encounter, the better. It is not only dress but actions that mark out the adventuress, and such actions are consciously woven into autobiographical accounts that are told and exchanged with fellow backpackers as well as eagerly consumed by those at home.

The adventuress crosses more that the boundaries of space; the act of travel is seen in these cases as an 'identity project' but one where the adventuress crosses the boundaries from feminine modes of behaviour to modes of behaviour more generally thought of as masculine. By doing so, Elsrud notes that the act of journey itself, as time away from the usual norms, acts as a period of reflexivity and an arena in which the norms and expectations that accrue to gendered roles can be challenged, even if the challenge is concealed under a protective layer of irony. Such considerations allow Elsrud to examine some aspects of hegemonic and gendered narratives that surround the notion of travel for adventure, suggesting that the gendered dimensions of tourism in general are under-researched.

Adventure seeking is arguably a young person's pursuit, and some illuminating contrasts can be drawn between the backpacker's desire to court risk, and the apparent risk aversion of older people. Caroline Oliver's chapter on migrant retirees on Costa del Sol, Spain, examines the ambiguous position these people occupy in relation to narratives of ageing and tourism. These retirees, mostly of north European origin, inhabit a space alongside Spanish second home owners in what is a heavily, if not overdeveloped, tourism space. While some of these are seasonal migrants, many of them are also permanent residents, or 'woopies', i.e. well off older people. In common with many of their peers, there is a growing trend in Western societies for such people to move into segregated retirement communities, where life can be lived as if on vacation. In some respects, such developments are difficult to square with the established and generally accepted definitions that tourism comprises of temporary movement from both home and the workplace. The situation that Oliver describes is a bit more nuanced than such definitions allow for. As retirees, the distancing from paid work is a permanent condition, and their behaviour is, to all intents and purposes, the same as that of tourists. It is, however, the home–away, host–guest distinction that is more ambiguous; on the one hand they are guests, yet on the other they suffer and complain about the same problems that the other permanent Spanish residents do at the hands of 'tourists' during the height of the season, for whatever else these retirees may be, they are not tourists. Despite this liminal status, the narratives which these people construct are those of positive ageing rooted in a mythical imagery of Spain as a place of warmth and community, a place where the elderly are treated with a sense of respect that has been lost elsewhere. The status of permanent residence then is narrated in almost utopian terms. Such narratives are counterposed with an equally mythical 'other', the dystopian world of negativity and work that has been left behind, because, in common with other migrants, the past is always another country. However, in a globalized world, such transnational or hybrid forms of identity and consumption are becoming more commonplace; the ambiguities that are being played out here are the result of wider social and indeed political changes that allow for the freer movement of people across Europe. The ambiguity lies more in the fact that the ways in which these people can narrate themselves as situated social beings, the resources at their disposal, have not yet caught up with the actuality of their lives.

The chapter by Hazel Andrews offers another contrasting example from Spain by examining the ways in which space is conceptualized, commodified and consumed in the Spanish resorts of Palmanova and Magaluf situated on the Balearic Islands in the Mediterranean. These resorts cater mostly for the young British charter market and, while Palmanova tends to be regarded as the more 'upmarket' and family oriented of the two, both resorts abound in the display of signs of Britishness. In terms of food and drink for example, tourists are faced with not only fish and chips, but also the ubiquitous 'Full English Breakfast', a culinary phenomenon that is no doubt familiar to anyone who has holidayed in the Mediterranean, and which has also been recently sighted in Cambodia (R. Stirrat, personal communication). It is not only food but also brand name alcoholic drinks served in imperial measures, rather than the standard Spanish metric measures, consumed in bars and cafes, whose names are redolent with a sense of Britishness.

As already noted, the two resorts rely on charter package tourists, and the roles of the operators and reps are crucial in both creating and maintaining the dominant patterns of consumption. Under the guise of fun and games, organized bar crawls, ostensibly designed to show new arrivals around the town, are occasions to channel and control expenditure as well as patterns of behaviour which are both gendered and dominated by heterosexist assumptions. It is these patterns of consumption as much as the spaces in which they are performed that mark Palmanova and Magaluf as part of the pleasure periphery of Europe, where the narratives of place are those of infantile excess and abrogation of responsibility.

Annette Pritchard and Nigel Morgan also tackle the issue of sex and tourism, but start from a different viewpoint. Specifically, their focus is on sexual differences, control and use of space in the context of seeing Manchester's Gay Village as a contested space. Beginning with an acknowledgement that the terms gay and lesbian both refer to heterogeneous and different groups of people, they also point out the importance of space in defining the ways in which individuals can interact and present themselves, and by so doing construct forms of sexual and social identity. In the past, to be either lesbian or gay has meant concealment and the confining of sexual identity to the private realm; any overt and public display of such differences from the heterosexual norm would have been, and in some places still is, a high risk activity. The importance then of specific gay and lesbian spaces is as arenas in which 'other' sexualities can be expressed safely without fear of physical threats or social sanctions. The story of Manchester's Gay Village however, parallels that of many other tourist destinations – that success brings with it overcrowding – yet the difference here is that the overcrowding is not from gays or lesbians, but from heterosexuals who tended to see the area as an exotic theme park, in which 'the other' can be gazed upon, which is, as the authors note, evidence of the continually contested nature of place itself. What further complicates the issue here are the ways in which many lesbians find that the attitudes of some gay men are little better than those of some heterosexual men, that even among those of 'different' sexualities commonality is still a matter of gender. Contemporary sexualities are, they suggest, an aspect of tourism analysis that has generally been ignored and subsumed into a heterosexual and masculine norm which, in turn, equally underplays heterosexual tourism experiences.

Issues of commodification are of central importance in all of the chapters, and these are thrown into sharp relief in Jonathan Skinner's chapter about the Caribbean island of Montserrat, a place which capitalizes on its symbolic likeness as well as more tangible and historical connections to Ireland. Sometimes referred to as the 'Emerald Isle of the Caribbean', both the culture and the ethnicity of the islanders have been exoticized and commodified. Yet there is more at work here than the simple machinations of the tourist industry because, as Skinner shows, the creation of the Montserattians as the 'black Irish' perhaps owes more to the Islanders' own attempts to carve out a form of post-colonial identity for themselves. The Irish connections are in themselves a remnant of both colonialism and slavery, and while the Catholic church on the island had always celebrated St Patrick's Day, it was not until 1985 that a transformation occurred which turned it from a religious event to a 6-day festival with nationalistic overtones. In part, this was due to the claim that on St Patrick's Day in 1768, there was a failed slave revolt on the island; the celebrations of 17 March were then appropriated to serve the needs of an indigenous cultural awareness that began in the 1970s.

Such accounts are, however, disputed by both academics and the ways in which the Montserratians themselves construct their own narratives of belonging. While conceived as an expression of a unique and Caribbean heritage, the 'Irishness' of Montserrat also becomes the commodity that singles the island out as different among its neighbours. The tensions that exist between these competing but not exclusive narratives are those between insider and outsider forms of knowledge. Skinner refuses to fall into the obvious trap of seeing this as an instance of contrived authenticity, arguing instead that the 'modernist position' which draws a sharp line between the authentic and the inauthentic is no longer a tenable position. The celebrations are contested, and have no doubt also been influenced by tourism, yet are still shaped by the internal needs and demands of the islanders, while still remaining indigenous narratives of place and self.

The insider–outsider distinction is also the main concern addressed in Amy Hale's chapter which looks at Cornwall, the westernmost county of England, long a favourite tourist destination. Cornwall, however, is more that just a county in the way that Montserrat is more than just a Caribbean Island. Cornwall is distinct, not only because it is geographically remote from the economic and political centre of the UK, but also because of the claims that to be Cornish is to have a distinct ethnic identity. Certainly it is the only English county that has a distinct language, albeit one that was recovered in the warm glow of 19th century nationalist romanticism that emphasized the Celtic nature of Cornish identity. It is such ethnicity which has, as Hale argues, become incorporated, or perhaps appropriated, into marketing strategies. Hale also describes a variety of goods and services which span diverse markets, for both internal and external consumption. This difference has always been present since the early days of tourism, when the coming of the railways enabled wealthy metropolitans to experience the 'otherness' of Cornwall which in more contemporary times has been replaced with 'New Age' interpretations of Cornishness, often not shared by the inhabitants themselves. What Hale shows is that notions of Cornwall as a place that is 'other' and 'Celtic' are multi-faceted and complex narratives, and that the diversity of Cornwall's heritage and natural attractions is perhaps admirably suited to current patterns of consumer demand that move us from the provision of mass producer-defined products into more niche and bespoke consumer-led products.

Richard Voase's chapter provides a fitting coda to this collection. In part drawing on his own biographical account of life as a destination marketer, Voase argues that there is a fundamental paradox in terms of analysing tourism consumption and marketing. Certain forms of narrative or discourses are related to socio-economic differences and preferences which seek to reject the contrived in favour of the authentic, and are favoured by the service class (see also Maitland and Newman, 2004). Yet the paradox is that the 'authentic' is only ever defined as something 'new' or 'undiscovered', in contrast to the 'contrived' and the 'known'; the more that the unknown is sought for, the more it ceases to be the unknown and becomes in turn the familiar, the mundane. As Voase argues, while certain forms of narratives and discourses, and marketing strategies derived from them frame expectations of place, they are often no more than reflections of the consumption preferences of certain social classes and cultural intermediaries, and that to seek out novelty only results in more contrivances that are swiftly labelled 'false'. The logic of this argument indeed leads perhaps to the final paradox of consumption, that the most successful destination will be the one that does not market itself.

Conclusion

The values and meanings that are both derived from and imposed on forms of tourist space indicate that different interests create and consume different forms of knowledge perhaps built on wider cultural, social or group forms of consensus, perhaps as a more existential, unique and individual condition, or even combining elements of both. Overall, the main thrust of the arguments advanced by the contributions in this volume is that the practices involved in tourism, the production and consumption of tourism experiences and places is not simply a matter of dominant discourses or gazes prescribing what may be experienced, thus reducing the consumer to the status of a passive entity devoid of agency. Rather, what is examined is the complex and dynamic interplay between the producers and consumers of tourist space.

In turn, this needs to be set in the context of globalization, because despite arguments surrounding this often contentious term, there is no denying the empirical fact that people, commodities and cultural forms are now circulating more widely and more rapidly than they have before. Seeing mobility – of which tourism is one variety – rather than stasis as a condition of the contemporary world also necessitates an examination of the dynamics of place construction as a continually shifting interplay between local residents, the producers of tourist space and the tourists. Although such changes may seem to challenge the authenticity and purity of cultures, to acknowledge that cultures both give and take from each other is simply to acknowledge the creativity of people to engage with, and respond to, the changing circumstances in which they find themselves. In order to arrive at a more nuanced account of tourism, attention needs to be focused on the relationship between the production of the gaze or discourse on the one hand, and the practices of consuming on the other, and the contradictions, anomalies and paradoxes that this entails. In particular, attention should be paid to the ways in which values, meanings and forms of knowledge can be altered, changed and renegotiated at all points in the production–consumption chain, from prior expectations to point of purchase and beyond, and the ways in which different forms of knowledge are constructed out of the matrix of possibilities that narrativized spaces offer.

References

Ahmed, S. (1999) Home and away: narratives of migration and estrangement. *International Journal of Cultural Studies* 2, 329–347.

Albrow, M., Eade, J., Dürrschmidt, J. and Washbourne, N. (1997) The impact of globalization on sociological concepts: community, culture and milieu. In: Eade, J. (ed.) *Living in the Global City*. Routledge, London, pp. 20–36.

Appadurai, A. (ed.) (1986) *The Social Life of Things: Commodities in Cultural Perspective*. Cambridge University Press, Cambridge, UK.

Appadurai, A. (1990) Disjuncture and difference in the global cultural economy. In: Featherstone, M. (ed.) *Global Culture: Nationalism, Globalisation and Modernity*. Sage, London, pp. 295–310.

Bærenholdt, J.O., Haldrup, M., Larsen, J. and Urry, J. (2004) *Performing Tourist Places*. Ashgate, Aldershot, UK.

Bal, M. (1999) Introduction. In: Bal, M., Crewe, J. and Spitzer, L. (eds) *Acts of Memory: Cultural Recall in the Present*. University Press of New England, Hanover, New Hampshire, pp. vii–xvii.

Bauman, Z. (1991) *Modernity and Ambivalence*. Polity Press, Cambridge, UK.

Bauman, Z. (1997) *Postmodernity and its Discontents*. Polity Press, Cambridge, UK.

Bauman, Z. (2002) Foreword: individually, together. In: Beck, U. and Beck-Gernsheim, E. *Individualization: Institutionalized Individualism and its Social and Political Consequences*. Sage, London, pp. xiv–xxv.

Beck, U. (1992) *Risk Society*. Sage, London.

Beck, U. (2000) *What is Globalisation?* Polity Press, Cambridge, UK.

Beck, U. and Beck-Gernsheim, E. (2002) *Individualization: Institutionalized Individualism and its Social and Political Consequences*. Sage, London.

Bell, D.S. (2003) Mythscapes: memory, mythology and national identity. *Sociology* 54, 63–81.

Böröcz, J. (1996) *Leisure Migration: a Sociological Study*. Pergamon Press, Oxford, UK.

Bourdieu, P. (1984) *Distinction: a Social Critique of the Judgement of Taste*. Routledge and Keegan Paul, London.

Bruner, E. (1995) The ethnographer/tourist in Indonesia. In: Lanfant, M.-F., Allcock, J.B. and Bruner, E. (eds) *International Tourism: Identity and Change*. Sage, London, pp. 224–241.

Castells, M. (2004) *The Power of Identity*, 2nd edn. Blackwell, Oxford, UK.

Cattell, M.G. and Climo, J.J. (2002) Introduction: meaning in social memory and history. In: Climo, J.J. and Cattell, M.G. (eds) *Social Memory and History: Anthropological Perspectives*. Alta Mira Press, Walnut Creek, California.

Cavarero, A. (2000) *Relating Narratives: Storytelling and Selfhood*. Routledge, London, pp. 1–38.

Chamberlayne, P., Bornat, J. and Wengraf, T. (eds) (2000) *The Turn to Biographical Methods in Social Science: Comparative Issues and Examples*. Routledge, London.

Clifford, J. (1992) Travelling cultures. In: Grossberg, L., Nelson, C. and Treichler, P. (eds) *Cultural Studies*. Routledge, London, pp. 96–116.

Clifford, J. (1997) *Routes: Travel and Translation in the Late Twentieth Century*. Harvard University Press, Cambridge, Massachusetts.

Cohen, R. (1997) *Global Diasporas: an Introduction*. Routledge, London.

Coleman, S. and Crang, M. (eds) (2002) *Tourism: Between Place and Performance*. Berghahn Books, New York.

Coleman, S. and Elsner, J. (1998) Performing pilgrimage: Walsingham and the ritual construction of irony. In: Hughes-Freeland, F. (ed.) *Ritual, Performance, Media*. Routledge, London, pp. 46–55.

Coles, T. and Timothy, D.J. (eds) (2004) *Tourism, Diasporas and Space*. Routledge, London.

Crang, M. (1997) Picturing practices: research through the tourist gaze. *Progress in Human Geography* 21, 359–373.

Crouch, D. (ed.) (1999) *Leisure/Tourism Geographies: Practices and Geographical Knowledge*. Routledge, London.

Crouch, D. (2002) Surrounded by place: embodied encounters. In: Coleman, S. and Crang, M. (eds) *Tourism: Between Place and Performance*. Berghahn Books, New York, pp. 207–218.

Crouch, D. (2004) Tourist practices and performances. In: Lew, A., Hall, C.M. and Williams, A. (eds) *A Companion to Tourism*. Blackwell, Oxford, UK. pp. 85–96.

Dann, G. (1996) The people of tourist brochures. In: Selwyn, T. (ed.) *The Tourist Image: Myths and Myth Making in Tourism*. Wiley, Chichester, UK, pp. 61–82.

Desforge, L. (2000) Travelling the world: identity and travel biography. *Annals of Tourism Research* 27, 926–945.

Edensor, T. (1998) *Tourists at the Taj: Performance and Meaning at a Symbolic Site*. Routledge, London

Edwards, T. (2000) *Contradictions of Consumption: Concepts, Practices and Politics in Consumer Society*. Open University Press, Buckingham, UK.

Elsrud, T. (2001) Risk creation in travelling: backpacker adventure narration. *Annals of Tourism Research* 28, 597–617.

Elsrud, T. (2004) *Taking Time and Making Journeys: Narratives on Self and the Other Among Backpackers*. Department of Sociology, Lund University, Lund, Sweden.

Evans, M. (1993) Reading lives: how the personal might be social. *Sociology* 27, 5–13.

Featherstone, M. and Lash, S. (eds) (1999) *Spaces of Culture: City, Nation, World*. Sage, London.

Friedman, J. (1994) *Cultural Identity and Global Process*. Sage, London.

Friedman, J. (1997) Simplifying complexity: assimilating the global in a small paradise. In: Olwig, K.F. and Hastrup, K. (eds) *Siting Culture: the Shifting Anthropological Object*. Routledge, London, pp. 268–291.

Frow, J. (1997) *Time and Commodity Culture: Essays in Cultural Theory and Postmodernity*. Clarendon Press, Oxford, UK.

Gable, E. and Handler, R. (2000) Public history, private memory: notes from the ethnography of Colonial Williamsburg, Virginia, USA. *Ethnos* 65, 237–252.

Galani-Moutafi, V. (2000) The self and the other: traveller, ethnographer, tourist. *Annals of Tourism Research* 27, 203–224.

Giddens, A. (1991) *Modernity and Self-identity: Self and Society in the Late Modern Age*. Polity Press, Cambridge, UK.

Gurnah, A. (1997) Elvis in Zanzibar. In: Scott, A. (ed.) *The Limits of Globalization*. Routledge, London, pp. 116–142.

Hall, S. (2000) Cultural identity and diaspora. In: Mirzoff, N. (ed.) *Diaspora and Visual Culture: Representing Africans and Jews*. Routledge, London, pp. 21–33.

Hanefors, M. and Selwyn, T. (2000) Dalecarian masks: one souvenir's many voices. In: Hitchcock, M. and Teague, K. (eds) *Souvenirs: the Material Culture of Tourism*. Ashgate, Aldershot, UK, pp. 253–283.

Harrison, J. (2003) *Being a Tourist: Finding Meaning in Pleasure Travel*. UBC Press, Vancouver, British Columbia.

Held, D., McGrew, A., Goldblatt, D. and Perraton, J. (1999) *Global Transformations: Politics, Economics and Culture*. Polity Press, Cambridge, UK.

Howes, D. (ed.) (1996) *Cross-cultural Consumption: Global Markets, Local Realities*. Routledge, London.

Kopytoff, I. (1986) The cultural biography of things: commoditization as process. In: Appadurai, A. (ed.) *The Social Life of Things: Commodities in Cultural Perspective*. Cambridge University Press, Cambridge, UK pp. 64–94.

Lefebvre, H. (1991) *The Production of Space*. Blackwell, Oxford, UK.

Li, Y. (2000) Geographical consciousness and tourism experience. *Annals of Tourism Research* 27, 863–883.

Linnekin, J. (1997) Consuming cultures: tourism and the commoditization of cultural identity in the island Pacific. In: Picard, M. and Wood, R.E. (eds) *Tourism, Ethnicity and the State in Asian and Pacific Societies*. University of Hawaii Press, Honolulu, Hawaii, pp. 215–250.

Löfgren, O. (1999) *On Holiday: a History of Vacationing*. University of California Press, Berkeley, California.

Lovell, N. (ed.) (1998) *Locality and Belonging*. Routledge, London.

MacCannell, D. (1976) *The Tourist: a New Theory of the Leisure Class*. Schocken Books, New York.

Maitland, R. and Newman, P. (2004) Developing metropolitan tourism on the fringe of central London. *International Journal of Tourism Research* 6, 339–348.

Mars, G. and Mars, V. (2000) 'Souvenir-gifts' as tokens of filial esteem: the meanings of Blackpool souvenirs. In: Hitchcock, M. and Teague, K. (eds) *Souvenirs: the Material Culture of Tourism*. Ashgate, Aldershot, UK, pp. 91–111.

Martinez, D.P. (ed.) (1998) *The Worlds of Japanese Popular Culture: Gender, Shifting Boundaries and Global Cultures*. Cambridge University Press, Cambridge, UK.

Mathews, G. (2000) *Global Culture/Individual Identity: Searching for Home in the Cultural Supermarket*. Routledge, London.

Meethan, K. (2001) *Tourism in Global Society: Place, Culture, Consumption*. Palgrave, Basingstoke, UK.

Meethan, K. (2003) Mobile cultures? Hybridity, tourism and cultural change. *Journal of Tourism and Cultural Change* 1, 11–28.

Meethan, K. (2004) 'To stand in the shoes of my ancestors': tourism and genealogy. In: Coles, T. and Timothy, D.J. (eds) *Tourism, Diasporas and Space*. Routledge, London, pp. 139–150.

Mellor, A. (1991) Enterprise and heritage in the dock. In: Corner, J. and Harvey, S. (eds) *Enterprise and Heritage: Crosscurrents of National Culture*. Routledge, London, pp. 93–115.

Miles, S., Anderson, A. and Meethan, K. (eds) (2002) *The Changing Consumer*. Routledge, London.

Miller, D. (1994) *Modernity: an Ethnographic Approach*. Berg, Oxford, UK.

Miller, R. (2000) *Researching Life Stories and Family Histories*. Sage, London.

Misztal, B. (2003) *Theories of Social Remembering*. Open University Press, Buckingham, UK.

Morley, D. (2000) *Home Territories: Media, Mobility and Identity*. Routledge, London.

O'Reilly, K. (2000) *The British on the Costa del Sol: International Identities and Local Communities*. Routledge, London.

Rapport, N. (1997) *Transcendent Individual: Towards a Literary and Liberal Anthropology*. Routledge, London.

Rapport, N. and Dawson, A. (eds) (1998) *Migrants of Identity: Perceptions of Home in a World of Movement*. Berg, Oxford, UK.

Raz, A.E. (1999) *Riding the Black Ship: Japan and Tokyo Disneyland*. Harvard University Press, Cambridge, Massachusetts.

Ritzer, G. (2000) *The Macdonaldization of Society: New Century Edition*. Pine Forge Press, Thousand Oaks, California.

Ritzer, G. and Liska, A. (1997) 'McDisneyization' and 'post-tourism': complementary perspectives on contemporary tourism. In: Rojek, C. and Urry, J. (eds) *Touring Cultures: Transformations of Travel and Theory*. Routledge, London, pp. 96–112.

Robertson, G., Mash, M., Tickner, L., Bird, J., Curtis, B. and Putnam, T. (eds) (1994) *Traveller's Tales: Narratives of Home and Displacement*. Routledge, London.

Rojek, C. and Urry, J. (eds) (1997) *Touring Cultures: Transformations of Travel and Theory*. Routledge, London.

Sarup, M. (1994) Home and identity. In: Robertson, G., Mash, M., Tickner, L., Bird, J., Curtis, B. and Putnam, T. (eds) *Traveller's Tales: Narratives of Home and Displacement*. Routledge, London, pp. 93–104.

Selwyn, T. (1993) Peter Pan in South East Asia: views from the brochures. In: Hitchcock, M., King, V.T. and Parnwell, M.J.G. (eds) *Tourism in South East Asia*. Routledge, London, pp. 117–137.

Skultans, V. (1998) *The Testimony of Lives: Narrative and Memory in Post-Soviet Latvia*. Routledge, London.

Smith, V.L. (ed.) (1989) *Hosts and Guests: the Anthropology of Tourism*, 2nd edn. University of Pennsylvania Press, Philadelphia.

Stephenson, M. (2002) Travelling to the ancestral homelands: the aspirations and experiences of a UK Caribbean Community. *Current Issues in Tourism* 5, 378–425.

Suvantola, J. (2002) *Tourist's Experience of Place*. Ashgate, Aldershot, UK.

Tomlinson, J. (1999) *Globalization and Culture*. Polity Press, Cambridge, UK.

Urry, J. (1992) The tourist gaze revisited. *American Behavioral Scientist* 36, 172–186.

Urry, J. (1999) Sensing the city. In: Judd, D.R. and Fainstein, S.S. (eds) *The Tourist City*. Yale University Press, New Haven, Connecticut, pp. 71–88.

Urry, J. (2000) *The Tourist Gaze*, revised edn. Sage, London.

Van der Duim, R. (2005) *Tourismscapes*. University of Wageningen, Wageningen, The Netherlands

Wang, N. (1999) Rethinking authenticity in tourism experience. *Annals of Tourism Research* 26, 349–370.

Wang, N. (2000) *Tourism and Modernity: a Sociological Analysis*. Pergamon, Oxford, UK.

Warren, S. (1999) Cultural contestation at Disneyland Paris. In: Crouch, D. (ed.) *Leisure/Tourism Geographies: Practices and Geographical Knowledge*. Routledge, London, pp. 109–125.

Welsch, W. (1999) Transculturality: the puzzling form of cultures today. In: Featherstone, M. and Lash, S. (eds) *Spaces of Culture: City, Nation, World*. Sage, London, pp. 194–213.

Disjunctures in Nationalist Rhetoric at Ireland's Brú na Bóinne Visitor Centre

2

Stacey Lynn Camp

Department of Cultural and Social Anthropology Archaeology Program, Stanford University, USA

Introduction: Understanding and Negotiating Ireland's Nationalistic Project

In the 19th century, Ireland established a nationalistic project intended to unify its disenfranchized citizens and bolster its post-famine image. This nationalist project stressed Catholic values and redefined what it meant to be 'Irish' (O'Mahony and Delanty, 1998). The industrialization and modernization of Ireland in the 1960s and 1970s challenged these definitions, allowing Irish citizens to live in a more democratic and liberal society. This new-found freedom, however, was not to last. When industrialization failed to create a wealthier Ireland and an economic recession occurred, Irish corporations and governmental bodies looked to the nation's earlier nationalist venture to once again generate support outside and create unity within the country (Gibbons, 1996). Ireland's return to its former nationalist narratives can be seen in its recent (1990s) tourism literature and tourism centres. These narratives contain disjunctures and inconsistencies which reveal and compromise the nation's underlying project. In this chapter, I will look at how an Irish heritage site was constructed and shaped by local, national and global politics, as well as consider how their contradictory messages are received and interpreted by visitors. As the following study of these responses will illustrate, narrative contradictions may be extremely obvious to those visiting tourist sites and reading tourist literature. Visitors and citizens of Ireland are therefore not victims of the state's propaganda, but rather active agents capable of negotiating and interpreting the data presented before them.

As Meethan (2001) has discussed, little attention has been devoted to understanding the complexities of how individuals consume and respond to tourism narratives. Recognizing this dearth of research, I spent the summer of 2001 as a Richter International Fellow conducting an ethnographic examination of how nationalist ideologies infiltrate and influence the presentation of history at Ireland's archaeological tourist sites, museums and visitor centres. During this 3 month fellowship, I interviewed those who worked at and/or lived around these sites, and spoke with governmental officials regarding Ireland's tourism policies. For the sake of brevity, this chapter focuses on one particular area, Newgrange, a contested archaeological site located in Ireland's Boyne Valley, approximately 20 miles (32 km) north-west of Dublin (see http://www.heritageireland.ie/).

Newgrange is home to numerous burial mounds dating back to the late 5th millennium BC (Stout, 2002). Brú na Bóinne Visitor Centre, a facility meant to manage and control the large amount of visitors interested in touring three of Newgrange's largest burial mounds located close to each other, Newgrange, Knowth and Dowth, opened in June 1997. This date, as I will later discuss, coincides with an important point in Ireland's historical memory. In the following sections, I will elucidate how the Irish Republic's ideologies of 'Irishness' became embedded into Brú na Bóinne Visitor Centre, and then demonstrate how these political stances are negotiated by the tourists and interest groups consuming them.

20th Century Controversies in Irish Tourism: an Annotated History

Since the Second World War, when commercial transatlantic travel increased and international travelling began on a mass scale, tourism has been a vital part of Ireland's economy (Deegan and Dineen, 1997). Ireland, one of the many European countries receiving Marshall aid (Marshall Plan, 1948–1952), was pressured by the US government to reform their tourism policies in order to improve their economic position. Since then, Ireland's government has come to depend upon the economic benefits that tourism provides. Duchas, the Heritage Service, was created in the early 1990s by the Irish government to generate a steady source of income for the nation. Duchas' primary responsibilities included managing Ireland's natural and built heritage. The Heritage Service's managing of Irish 'heritage' has continued to spark controversy throughout Ireland. The governmental body has been attacked by Irish citizens, Ireland's media outlets, journalists and even by tourists from the USA for their conservation practices and inaccurate historical depictions of archaeological sites. These numerous attacks led to the eventual disbandment of Duchas in 2003.

The construction of Duchas' 'interpretation/visitor centres' has likewise resulted in numerous law suits over the sustainability and suitability of their construction (Deegan and Dineen, 1997). Many question the long-term viability of the centres. Today, the remnants of Duchas' former control over Ireland's parks, gardens, wildlife, monuments and archaeological sites remain visible on almost every Irish landscape. In fact, while in Ireland, a tourist would find it almost impossible to escape seeing a Duchas-designated heritage trail, site or road. Their visitor centres, one of which will be the primary focus of this chapter, are particularly imposing; they are physical reminders of a past that continues to be controlled and manipulated for nationalistic and economic purposes.

The profitability of these centres has been the driving force behind their production. Kockel writes that a site's supposed heritage is 'what economists call an added value product' (1994, p. 79). The past therefore becomes an object for consumption rather than a way in which one can critically engage with historical, ethnographic and archaeological data. Though Ireland's early tourism policies were the product of economic necessity, the recent increased production of these hotly contested visitor centres and heritage sites including the UNESCO World Heritage Site Brú na Bóinne is a result of Ireland's current struggle to define its identity as a post-colonial nation.

Modern Identity Politics in Ireland

The presentation of history in any country can communicate its government's political and economic motivations. History defines and constructs a nation's cultural identity which is often evoked or recalled to validate a governmental or capitalistic agenda. Portrayed to foreigners as 'picturesque, simple, and unique in its absence of modern world conveniences', Ireland has also been continually subject to historical and cultural stereotyping by both interior (local/national) and exterior (global) powers (Johnson, 1996, p. 56).

Before examining nationalist narratives at Brú na Bóinne Visitor Centre, it is therefore important to identify the origins and themes of modern day Irish nationalism. As a post-colonial nation, Ireland has attempted to re-establish its identity through educational and political reforms. Ireland has been in search of an 'authentic' Irish identity to 're-establish authority' (Graham, 2000, p. 25). Although claims of authenticity can 'be read as movements against colonialism', the notion of a universal Irish identity locks Ireland's citizens into an immovable, stereotyped identity (Graham, 2000, p. 25). History and the archaeological past offer a substantial reality in which a post-colonial government can establish its claims.

Gibbons (1996) offers a historical account of Irish modernity and the shifting faces of Irish nationalism. He cites Ireland's 1973 acceptance into the EEC as having a major impact on the country, as it allowed the nation to embrace technological change. With the importance of technology at its forefront, Ireland:

> saw a shift from agriculture to industry as the mainstay of the Irish economy: in the period of 1961 to 1980, employment in the agricultural sector fell from one-third to one-fifth of the workforce, while those working in industry increased from 16 to 30 per cent.
>
> (Gibbons, 1996, p. 83)

During this period of industrialization, Ireland's once rigid religious and gender restrictions began to dissipate; for example, it was at this time in history when the 'denial of the right to contraception was interpreted as an infringement on privacy' by Irish courts (O'Mahony and Delanty, 1998, p. 171). The once dominating narratives of Irish nationalism and unity also fell by the wayside. By the mid to late 1980s, however, it became clear that modernization was not as effective in stimulating the economy as it first appeared. Despite Ireland's technological transformation, the country was once again experiencing severe unemployment. The search for a unified 'Irish' identity was reinstated, since the 'equation of urbanization and industrial development with enlightenment values of progress, secularization and cosmopolitanism proved no longer viable in the austere cultural climate of the 1980s (Gibbons, 1996, p. 84).

At this point in history, the industrialization of Ireland had produced two contrasting environments: the countryside and the city. For the government, the city, modern, urban and industrialized, represented the failed promises of modernity. The countryside, formally criticized as non-progressive, became the new future of Ireland; it also became representational of the neo-traditional, Catholic values that were lost in the process of modernization. These values, which included 'myths of community, the sanctity of the family, devotion to family and fatherland' (Gibbons, 1996, p. 85), politicians argued, were inherent in 'Irish' culture and must be revived in order to stimulate the country's economy. These so-called 'values' were actually of 'quite recent vintage, dating in fact from what Emmet Larkin has called "the devotional revolution" in post-Famine Ireland' (Gibbons, 1996, p. 85).

It is no mistake that it is during this particular moment in Ireland's history that Newgrange became formally recognized as a national symbol by Ireland's government. Ireland had quickly realized that the 'ancient pasts of peoples could be invoked to direct the future', since such pasts 'could be synthesized or even invented and then represented to the world as "traditions"' (Brett, 1996, p. 15). It was also during this time that the 'Celtic Tiger' was introduced, an invasive marketing strategy used to stimulate tourism in the country. This form of marketing often made claims that Irish citizens were the direct ancestors of the Celts in order to sell products such as sweaters, jewellery and even potato chips. Dietler claims that these narratives of Celticism were essentially a 'new form of cultural imperialism' meant to 'delegitimize' Irish citizens' 'own sense of distinctive local cultural identity' (2000, p. 8). These ideologies of statehood, citizenship and regional identity were infused into the presentation of pre-history at Brú na Bóinne Visitor Centre, the product of a historical moment.

The Nameless Town: the 'Local' Politics of Newgrange

Local politics, in addition to these national and global issues, played a large part in the construction of Brú na Bóinne Visitor Centre. As Ronayne (2001) has noted, the signposting of Newgrange, as well as the building and establishment of Brú na Bóinne Visitor Centre, has attracted great local and governmental controversy. When the construction of the visitor centre was initially proposed by Duchas, several local factions formed: most were fighting for the visitor centre to be placed on the north side of the Boyne Valley River, while others argued for it to be built on the south. The burial mounds (most notably Newgrange, Knowth and Dowth) are located on the north side of the river, where a 'small-scale tourist industry had developed over the previous decades' (Ronayne, 2001, pp. 153–154).

   The construction of a centre to control the number of visitors to the site was needed, as the thousands of tourists visiting the site daily were trampling upon the burial grounds. At the time, no official methods of reducing visitor traffic and littering were in place. An informant who lives on Newgrange's road emphasized the number of people coming through the farmlands, pointing out that 'Something had to be done … its own popularity was causing problems. You couldn't even get out of your own driveway' (personal communication, July 2001). Another informant voiced concern over the fact that 'people were looking' into his house while visiting the monuments, though this still remains a problem for locals living on the road Duchas constructed when the visitor centre was built (personal communication, July 2001). Despite local efforts and opinions to the contrary, the centre was built on the south side of the Boyne Valley River, an area known as 'Donore'. According to a Newgrange local, the construction of the centre in Donore caused a huge 'rift in the community' (personal communication, July 2001); the same informant similarly noted that to this day 'people still don't speak to each other' (personal communication, July 2001). As mentioned earlier, the largest and most visually impressive burial mounds are located on the north side of the river, which is where the area of Newgrange is also situated. Prior to the 1997 opening of Brú na Bóinne Visitor Centre, millions of tourists passed through the area once known as Newgrange in order to access the burial mounds. Newgrange farmers and locals took advantage of their location, opening up bed and breakfasts, small souvenir shops and cafes along the dirt road leading to Newgrange.

Once Brú na Bóinne Visitor Centre opened for business, however, these local establishments quickly went out of business. While Brú na Bóinne Visitor Centre's Manager, Clare Tuffy, claimed that 'locals didn't become poverty stricken when the centre opened', the archaeological remnants of a once prosperous community remain on Newgrange's landscape (C. Tuffy, personal communication, July 2001). In contrast, one informant noted that the 'passing trade' completely dropped; as a result, bed and breakfasts, for the most part, closed on the north side of the river. Those that survived had to do 'aggressive advertising' and join the Irish Tourist Board or Irish Family Houses (personal communication, July 2001). These associations are quite costly for some bed and breakfast owners to join.

The implementation of a transit system taking tourists to and from Brú na Bóinne Visitor Centre has significantly reduced the number of tourists wandering around the farmlands and roads lining the burial mounds, though visitors can still stare into locals' homes during their bus rides to the monuments. While some residents were relieved to have visitors removed from their lawns and roads, other locals expressed sadness over the reduction of visitor traffic. As a result of the opening of Brú na Bóinne Visitor Centre, signs on the north side of the river were altered to direct tourists towards Donore rather than to the area of 'Newgrange' (Ronayne, 2001). This was extremely upsetting and obviously disorienting for the residents of the area formerly known as 'Newgrange'. Many of the residents I interviewed voiced concern over the change, several wondering what would happen if an emergency vehicle such as a fire engine or ambulance could not find them in the event of a disaster, since all emergency vehicles come from neighbouring cities.

Prior to the construction of the centre, two resident-initiated groups formed in protest: the Boyne Valley Trust and Newgrange Resident's Association. These groups were based on the north side of the river's arguments and opinions. According to several residents, these groups formed in response to the 'lack of information from the OPW [Office of Public Works, which was eventually renamed Duchas]' (personal communication, July 2001). The informants I spoke to were all members of these groups, and all lived on the north side of the centre. They claimed that the OPW used the 'threat of compulsory purchase' to force some Newgrange residents to sell their land which was needed for the centre (personal communication, July 2001). This threat was not in jest; as one resident put it, 'back then, the OPW didn't need permission to do works' (personal communication, July 2001). In this informant's opinion, the OPW had the power to remove citizens from their land without compensating them. Citizens of Newgrange were not made aware of the decision to place the centre on the south side of the river until construction was in progress; as one informant put it, 'citizens were not informed very well' and 'were given information on a need to know basis' (personal communication, July 2001). The construction of a visitor centre in Newgrange was thus not only a response to the need for large-scale visitor control, but also a political move meant to control, possess and manipulate both the current and prior identity of Irish citizens. As the following section will demonstrate, identity politics are not specific to Brú na Bóinne Visitor Centre.

Newgrange and Nationalism: a Case Study

The notion that visitor centres and tourism literature are nationalist endeavours, portraying 'the Irish' as a relatively homogenous race, is not an academically new concept (O'Mahony and Delanty, 1998, p. 188). Museums and visitor centres serve as ideal mediums for instilling 'imagined' concepts of innate characteristics that define a unified, national identity (Anderson, 1991; Werstch, 2002). As Anderson writes, 'museums, and the museumizing imagination, are both profoundly political' (Anderson, 1983, p. 178). McCarthy identifies the specific way in which governmental bodies in Ireland have tried to create a unified 'Irish' identity. In her article on Ireland's tourism literature, she analyses how 'official publications of Regional Tourist Offices, Bord Fáilte (the Irish Tourist Board), the Heritage Service or the visitor attractions themselves' portray Ireland as 'emphatically rural, traditional and undeveloped' (2002, p. 35). Brett agrees with McCarthy, writing that Ireland has continually been depicted to tourists as a locale of the 'primitive, the unspoilt, the wild and the natural' (1996, p. 127). The image of Ireland as untamed and picturesque, however, does not reflect the country's rapidly developing urban areas and technological-centred economy.

The aforementioned academic work on tourism disregards the incongruencies and disjunctures inherent in the mediums of visitor centres and tourism literature, as do those employed in Ireland's tourism industry. Brett, for instance, assumes that the 'cultural tourist looks for the cultural experience' of the sublime (1996, p. 127). For Brett, Celticism is part of this experience. The manager of Brú na Bóinne Visitor Centre likewise believes that certain ideologies sell: 'Celtic seems to sell ... call it Celtic and it sells. Perhaps it is tied in with

Riverdance' (personal communication, July 2001). This is the reasoning behind Brú na Bóinne Visitor Centre's bookshop's unparalleled amount of 'Celtic' ephemera. The Irish Tourist Board holds similar assumptions, arguing that:

> the tourist attraction of Ireland is firmly based on the heritage of the country. Tourists are attracted here to discover our distinctiveness – all those facets of the natural, human-made and cultural heritage which give us a unique identity. These features, reflecting character, authenticity and sense of place, all combine to create a distinctively Irish image.
>
> (Bord Fáilte, 1994, p. 5)

A closer look at the physical structure of Brú na Bóinne Visitor Centre, however, reveals the inconsistencies that underpin the nationalist narratives of Duchas. My analysis of Brú na Bóinne Visitor Centre hinges on the assumption that visitors acknowledge these narrative discrepancies, and have the ability to dispute these nationalistic claims.

'Rich in Tradition, Full of Excitement': Newgrange Tourism Literature

The tourism literature sold at Brú na Bóinne Visitor Centre as well as handed out free by regional tourism centres run by the Irish Tourist Board (Bord Fáilte) expose how tourism bureaux and government agencies wish to present Ireland as possessing a distinctive Irish character. This literature also seeks to demonstrate a natural continuity between Ireland's ancient and current inhabitants. Visitors to the Irish National Heritage Park are, for example, told that the 'Celts, Vikings and Normans came together, intermarried and developed into the rich tapestry which forms Irish society today', although archaeological evidence for such an occurrence is speculative (McCarthy, 2002, p. 40).

One of the most popular brochures handed out at the Meath Tourism booth in Brú na Bóinne Visitor Centre is entitled 'Meath: Rich in Tradition, Full of Excitement' (1999a). Circles derived from the decorative symbols carved into the stones of Newgrange's passage chambers are on each page of the brochure, although these spheres are not explained by the pamphlet. The brochure naively links the circles to the place name of 'Meath' rather than to the Neolithic peoples who created the symbols, an act which McCarthy (2002) describes as characteristic of global tourism marketing. This form of marketing is 'characterized by the identification and promotion of "unique selling propositions" (USPs), by which the tourism destination seeks to differentiate its "product" from that of its competitors' (McCarthy,

2002, p. 35). In the case of Meath, the brochure attempts to distinguish the county from surrounding counties by identifying its specific, 'unique' qualities while maintaining its connection with Ireland as a nation.

'Brú na Bóinne: Newgrange, Knowth, Dowth and the River Boyne', a special edition of the magazine, *Archaeology Ireland*, also alludes to a solidified 'Irish' identity; this identity, according to the author, extends all the way back into the Neolithic: 'Whereas the art in the Bend of the Boyne is an eclectic blend of Irish and overseas influences, transformed by an innovative spirit, the art found in the hinterland is relatively homogeneous and probably indigenous. The earliest megalithic art in the Boyne Valley belongs to this native Irish tradition' (O'Sullivan, 1997, p. 19). Like other authors, O'Sullivan attempts to establish a progressive narrative about Ireland's landscape, technologies and people. This process of rewriting Ireland's history is an attempt to exclude non-native residents of Ireland. Archaeological sites that do not assist in promoting the Irish government's current ideologies are ignored in tourism literature. This is partially due to the fact that Ireland's National Monuments Act does not recognize archaeological sites that post-date 1600. Such sites, Woodman asserts, do not legitimate Duchas' neat 'concept of Irishness' and are, as a result, left to disintegrate (1995, p. 294). Crooke (2000) came to similar conclusions with her research on museums in Ireland; she discovered that early archaeological sites are of more interest to museums and government officials as they lack historical documents. As a result, these sites are more open to interpretation than many historical sites. Crooke also found that a 'Gaelic and Catholic character was being nurtured for the state' and imposed upon archaeological data in an effort to create an authentic Irish identity (2000, p. 145). It hence comes as no surprise to find that the tourism literature surveyed on Newgrange has also ignored the Boyne Valley's modern-day history.

Brú na Bóinne Visitor Centre's Interpretive Exhibit

The nationalist ideologies that pervade the aforementioned promotional literature are infused into the physical and narrative structures of Brú na Bóinne Visitor Centre. Following in the footsteps of many cultural and space geographers, I will attempt to show how national and local politics have been weaved and inscribed into this site's very construction. Visitors begin their visit by parking in Brú na Bóinne Visitor Centre's car park, the one and only entrance to the site and to the centre. Several bridges lead visitors away from the car park (Fig. 2.1). Bridges are an important part of Brú na Bóinne Visitor Centre, as they are constructed over the Boyne Valley River in order for visitors to

Fig. 2.1. One of the many bridges installed at Brú na Bóinne Visitor Centre. From this side of the bridge, the centre looks as if it were part of the landscape (Camp, 2001).

get to shuttle buses leading to the burial sites. Bridges are also constructed to prevent visitors from disturbing the ecological and archaeological materials of the Boyne Valley. More importantly, bridges ensure that people do not have to walk on the 'natural' landscape. Those who were involved in the design of Brú na Bóinne Visitor Centre's footpaths, viewing stations and bridges did not intend to recreate the original pathways of the ancient peoples who inhabited Newgrange (personal communication, July 2001). Instead, they created a vision which objectifies those who inhabit the landscape as well as one which recalls the Irish government's obsession with images that exist in direct contradiction to industrialization (i.e. picturesque, sprawling farm-scapes). Brú na Bóinne Visitor Centre's 'viewing tower' (Fig. 2.2), a panoptical space inside the centre where tourists can obtain a better view of the Boyne Valley's monuments, residents and landscapes, similarly reframes the visitor's experience.

The designers were interested in introducing what I would term a politically motivated view of the Boyne Valley, a view that makes those living in and around Newgrange part of the tourist attraction. Those inhabiting the landscape of Newgrange become part of the overall tourist attraction of 'Meath'; one brochure from Meath even promises tourists, 'Your tour through Meath is an experience in living history' (Meath Tourism, 1999a). In fact, a bus driver employed by Duchas mentioned that many tourists naively think that the locals are 'part of the attraction'. For instance, one of my informants living on the road

Fig. 2.2. A circular 'viewing tower' inside Brú na Bóinne Visitor Centre.

leading to Newgrange was asked by a tourist if he 'really did live' in the house next to the site while he was watering his lawn (personal communication, July 2001). These objectifying views created by Duchas through the centre and tour buses' windows can be linked to how the government sidelined and ignored the citizens of Newgrange during the centre's initial planning process.

As the visitor approaches the centre, he or she encounters stone tiling as well as a waterfall. This design is intentional, as the architects of the centre wanted it to appear as though it is 'part of the landscape' (Keane, 1997, p. 36). Even a quick glance of the visitor centre yields an obvious vision: burial mounds. Like the burial mounds, the centre is made up of a series of circular structures with upwardly concave ceilings topped with exterior grass roofs. The centre's use of 'natural' stone and natural colours (green, brown, white and tan) as well as its repetitive use of concentric patterns also makes the building appear as though it is simply a part of the natural landscape. Such visual tropes may lead visitors to believe that the centre is an authority on the monuments, as it seems to become almost another 'monument' within nature. The centre's glass ceilings and windows add to its 'naturalness' by allowing natural light to filter throughout the exhibits and eating and resting areas.

The centre is physically embedded in a bank below the highway leading to Donore, an effect that likewise contributes to the naturalization of the centre. This placement makes the centre appear as though it is originally part of the embankment. This arrangement temporarily removes visitors from the modern and technological disturbances of the present, as it hides the noisiness and existence of a modern road. The car park also becomes 'invisible' from the centre and burial mounds (Keane, 1997, p. 36). The naturalization of the centre appears deliberate and intentional, as it is meant to assert continuity between the past and present inhabitants of Newgrange. The visitor is immediately greeted by one of the reception desk's several attendants upon stepping through the glass doors of Brú na Bóinne Visitor Centre. It is here that visitors must make a decision as to which tour they will take; there are numerous options which include a visit to the centre only (usually the only option available if it is near the end of the day), Newgrange and the centre, Newgrange, Knowth and the centre, or Knowth and the centre. Price ranges are dependent on the different tours; a tour of Newgrange and the centre, for instance, is more expensive than a tour of Knowth and the centre. If the visitor has arrived early enough in the morning (9.30 a.m. to 10.00 a.m.), it is likely that they will be able to visit Newgrange. Only 600 individuals can visit Newgrange every day, in contrast to the 800 visitors permitted to take tours of Knowth. The valuing of Newgrange over Knowth, Dowth and the other burial mounds is not only reflected in the tours' prices and traffic control; numerous burial mounds located alongside Knowth, Dowth and Newgrange are not mentioned in the directed tours.

This valuing can be attributed to a number of factors. Since many of the smaller burial mounds remain on private residential land, they are outside the government's economic and interpretive control. They are left out of the centre's interpretative material primarily for this reason. These burial mounds also contest the place name of 'Newgrange', a name given to the area by the government and which associates the site with only one mound, the largest. In some ways, this situation can be perceived as a way in which locals have maintained power over the landscape. The burial mounds, for the most part completely ignored by the centre, can be seen from its viewing tower. A visitor may question the integrity and validity of the centre's presentation if he or she catches a glimpse of these surrounding mounds.

Upon selecting and paying for a tour, visitors are handed a ticket indicating their time of departure from the visitor centre's bus depot. Depending on a number of factors, this time of departure can equal a wait of several hours. One of the main reasons the centre was opened was to extend the amount of time visitors spent at Brú na Bóinne (Keane, 1997, p. 36). Ironically, Keane insists that the centre was opened to foster growth in the local economy. As I have previously illustrated, Newgrange's local economy, for the most part, disintegrated upon the opening of Brú na Bóinne Visitor Centre. Once-successful bed and breakfast, restaurant and gift shop owners became seasonal and/or part-time bus-drivers, food servers and/or tour guides at the centre.

While waiting for a tour, a visitor has a number of options; he or she can go 'through the full interpretative display sequence or just a portion, to the orientation/viewing area, to the toilets/tea room/tourism information outlet downstairs, or directly out towards the sites' (Keane, 1997, pp. 36–37). The two most populated spaces in Brú na Bóinne Visitor Centre are the 'full-scale replica of the Newgrange passage and chamber' that includes a movie presentation, and an interpretive exhibition (Keane, 1997, p. 37). The interpretive exhibit, while supposedly designed to absorb a visitor's time, reduce visitor congestion and 'raise the level of awareness of conservation issues in a mass audience' (Keane, 1997, p. 37), is limited to a specific set of conflicting themes that reflect Ireland's projection of nationalist ideologies on to the past.

The exhibition begins with a huge, upright rock (Fig. 2.3) at its entrance that looks like many of the stones surrounding the burial mounds. A placard does not accompany the rock, which suggests that its placement is meant to emphasize the strength it took to haul such a large object to Newgrange. This creates what Sørensen describes as a 'hierarchy of importance', where panels, dioramas and other 'smaller', less attention-grabbing objects are diminished by 'large, male associated

Fig. 2.3. The upright rock that marks the beginning of the interpretive exhibit.

items of impressive dimensions and bulk that are untamed by the cases' (1999, p. 145). Next, a visitor encounters 'The Boyne Valley through Time', a panel that compares the progress of Ireland's Boyne Valley with other worldwide events. Like the tourism literature regarding Meath, this panel highlights the idea that the Egyptian pyramids were built after the burial mounds at Newgrange by using bold font for the wording. Other major worldwide events are left unemphasized.

As mentioned earlier, Gibbons argues that Ireland's economic recession led to a return to 'traditional' family values and gender roles (1996). Such roles are played out in the interpretive exhibit entitled 'Neolithic People – 3000 B.C.'. In this exhibit, a painted diorama depicting 'Neolithic People' details men and women in traditional, 'Irish-Catholic', male and female roles (Fig. 2.4). In it, women sit on the left side of a hut whereas men sit on the right. More men are featured in the painted diorama than women. It is important to note that in this painted diorama, women are turned away from the viewer. In contrast, the men confidently face the tourist's gaze. The women in the painting, adorned in dresses and braids, are associated with what are considered traditional Catholic female activities: one tends to a child's hair, while others work on pottery. Food, hides and pottery are all neatly arranged on the women's

Fig. 2.4. 'Neolithic People – 3000 B.C.' mural in Brú na Bóinne Visitor Centre.

side of the hut, while the men have hunting supplies and furs on their side of the household. The women and children appear emaciated and in bad health, whereas the men look strong and hardy. The women and men all have red or brown hair and light eyes, again paralleling what tourism literature has depicted as the typical 'Irish' citizen.

Along the circular outer walls of this room are several other placards. On a panel entitled 'Evidence from Bones', the writers claim that the physical characteristics of Newgrange's Neolithic inhabitants can be seen in the faces of modern day Irish ancestors: 'Neolithic people were in many ways quite similar to us. They were not as tall, but were strong and used to hard work; skin, hair, and eye colour was probably the same as today.' This placard also glorifies Ireland's supposed ancestors, describing them as 'strong' and hard working. Directly across from the mural is a panel on 'Food from the Wild'. The painting that accompanies this panel shows four men hunting deer with one man smiling as he chases a deer fleeing in terror. Women are not pictured. Though the painting focuses on men and hunting, the text on the placard reads: 'Though farming was the main source of nutrition, food from the wild varied the diet and supplemented stocks at times of shortage.' Despite this statement, the case next to the panel focuses on hunting, showing 'smoothing stones for arrow shafts', 'crow feathers for arrows', 'hazel arrow shafts with crow feather fletching', 'flint arrowheads', an 'Antler pick' and a 'deer skin quiver'. Artefacts associated with fishing and farming, the main methods by which Neolithic peoples at Newgrange obtained their food (Stout, 2002), are not shown or discussed. If a visitor reads the placard and then examines the display, he or she may notice the major discrepancy between narrative and image. Hunting and 'male' activities are emphasized because they are shown as involving strategy, stamina and physical strength, three qualities which are crucial to the final portion of the interpretive exhibit: 'Tomb Construction.'

An entire circular room is dedicated to this theme. Here, the work and ingenuity of Ireland's predecessors is once again highlighted: 'Tomb Construction: Finding the Stones' asserts this: 'Stones up to about 2 tons could be lifted by men with rope slings over shoulder posts.' There are >80 men and no women depicted (Fig. 2.5). The panel 'Tomb Construction: The Passage and Chamber' claims that the construction '*must* have been overseen by a social or religious leader' (emphasis added), and that its construction 'shows great skill in working and building with stone and knowledge of architecture, megalithic art and astronomy'. The latter quotation once again stresses the physical and mental abilities of Ireland's 'ancestors', while the former briefly alludes to modern Ireland's nationalist claim to a strong religious heritage.

The nationalist ideologies at Brú na Bóinne Visitor Centre are conveyed not only through the exhibit's texts and images, but also through its ordering of space. The way in which one proceeds through the exhibit has a 'narrative topology' of its own (Brett, 1996, p. 88). As the reader will recall, the first thing the visitor encounters in the exhibit is the male-associated rock. Meath Tourism's literature emphasized the strength and resourcefulness it took to move and build with these rocks

Fig. 2.5. Tomb construction: finding the stones.

(Meath Tourism 1999a, b). Furthermore, the symbols that are displayed on Meath Tourism's brochures are on a flag that hangs behind the rock; this intermingling of symbols is an attempt to reinforce nationalist ideologies of Ireland's superiority further in past and present creative, mathematical and astronomical endeavours. Like the 'burial mound' architecture of the building, the emphasis on men's work (hunting, building, etc.) as well as the placement of another gigantic stone in the last room of the exhibit demonstrates Duchas' interest in highlighting the 'achievements' of Ireland's ancestors. In effect, panels on cooking, pottery, and what Duchas would consider female-associated activities, are de-emphasized. The placement of panels on such activities on the outer walls of the exhibit illustrates this point.

Alternative Interpretations of Newgrange

So how do visitors interpret and consume Brú na Bóinne Visitor Centre? Do they become indoctrinated Irish subjects upon exiting the centre's doors? Is the presentation of history so persuasive that a visitor cannot avoid adopting the centre's point of view? Wertsch's (2002) study of how those living in the former Soviet Union responded to nationalist media and literature implies that these processes are not as strong as the nation would like to believe. He found that his respondents did not always become indoctrinated by such influences; individuals could repeat the media's messages (such as 'socialism is good') when questioned by authorities, but in private conversations and interviews, subjects would dispute the propaganda's validity. Wertsch concluded that:

> just because someone is exposed to a cultural tool – and just because she has mastered it – does not guarantee that she has appropriated it as an identity resource. Indeed, there are cases in which someone has clearly mastered a cultural tool, yet resists it.
>
> (Wertsch, 2002, p. 120)

Schudson also contends that while hegemonic processes commonly influence the construction of tourist sites and photographs, these forces do not necessarily work as planned:

> Dominant groups (like other groups) do try, intentionally or intuitively, to make their own ideas common property and common sense, as a variety of studies of ideological 'hegemony' have shown. What is significant here is the incompleteness of this hegemonic process and the social mechanisms that keep it incomplete.
>
> (Schndson, 1992, p. 209)

Moreover, Rosenzweig's study of how Americans integrate the 'past' and history into their daily lives also led him to the conclusion that 'people appropriate artefacts from popular culture in a selective way, possess and reshape them in an active and participatory manner' (Kammen, 2000, p. 230). Appadurai agrees, seeing the power of the nation-state dwindling in the face of a modernized and highly networked world by stating that nation-states often fail fully or partially to 'contain and define the lives of their citizens' (1996, pp. 189–190).

There are numerous alternative interpretations of Newgrange held by differing interest groups that attest to the claims of Schudson, Wertsch and Rosenzweig. These groups include individuals interested in Druidism, Celticism, Catholicism and goddess worshipping. It is important to note that these groups do not represent a cohesive whole; a quick Google search of each interest group and the term 'Newgrange' demonstrates the infinite number of individually and group-owned websites interested in the burial chambers of the Boyne Valley. These competing versions of the meaning of Newgrange demonstrate the way in which individuals appropriate and devise their own understandings of the exhibit. For example, at the website entitled 'Mythical Ireland', MacBain, an Irish citizen, criticizes the way in which Ireland's archaeological heritage is removed from the public:

> What I am calling for is the rescue of the passage mounds from the archaeologists' operating table, and their restoration as sites of spiritual significance. Here in Tipperary, the Rock of Cashel is abandoned to tourism, and it is part of the O.P.W. (Office of Public Works) lease that it is not to be used for religious purposes.
>
> (MacBain, 2000)

MacBain believes that Newgrange is purposely aligned with the 'star of Bethlehem' and argues that this alignment proves that the tomb is what we would today term a 'cathedral' (2000). As a result, the author feels that the tomb is an example of the origins of Catholicism in Ireland; Newgrange, for MacBain, is therefore a landscape where those of Irish descent can 'reclaim the roots' of their 'religion' (2000).

Anderson's 'The Body of the Earth Goddess: Ireland and the Passage Tombs' conversely insists upon a goddess-oriented reading of Newgrange. In Anderson's opinion, Newgrange's burial mounds were built by women as 'metaphors for the body of the Earth Goddess' (2001). Anderson also praises the technological abilities of 'Mesolithic women' for their construction of burial mounds in Ireland (2001). In contrast, McColman, an American web author of 'A Spiritual Pilgrimage to Ireland', believes that the Druids and Celts built Newgrange. He claims his journey to the burial mounds brought about a spiritual awakening within him which he describes as part of a biologically inherited 'Irish spirituality' (McColman, 2002).

The above descriptions are just a few of the alternative readings of Newgrange. While it is likely that the above writers visited Brú na

Bóinne Visitor Centre's interpretive exhibit, it is clear that all of the individuals interjected their own personal interpretations upon the burial mounds. It is also important to remember that the majority of individuals do not come to Brú na Bóinne Visitor Centre with pre-formulated interpretations relating to goddess cults, the Druids or the Celts. An in-depth analysis of the visitor population of the centre, however, is needed to solidify this assumption. Further studies should not only address visitors' pre-conceptions of the burial mounds, but also question how visitors react to the centre's interpretive exhibit and overall structural layout.

Steps, none the less, can be taken to address these varying versions of Newgrange's past. For starters, the management of Brú na Bóinne Visitor Centre should give tour guides the freedom openly to communicate varying interpretations of the past. While researching Newgrange, I obtained a copy of the script read by Newgrange's tour guides ('An Introduction for Guides at Newgrange'). Due to the uncertainty of the archaeological data, much of the script is self-admittedly speculative. Tour guides are, for example, given five interpretations of the megalithic art work at Newgrange, but on the same page are told: 'When explaining the artwork please do not give irrelevant or trivial interpretations.' It appears as though alternative ideologies are categorized by Duchas as 'irrelevant' or 'trivial', and are hence left out of the tour guide manuals.

I believe it is safe to assume that the alternative ideologies of McColman, MacBain and D. Anderson fall under this rubric. Neglecting to discuss these forbidden topics can sometimes provoke a visitor's curiosity: 'That which is apparently not articulated can be still more obvious and have more impact upon the visitor than something which is articulated' (Sørensen, 1999, p. 143). The centre's gift shop, for instance, sells Celtic memorabilia while the tour guides are told to stick to discussions of the functionality of the tombs. With the shop selling so many books on 'Celtic' spirituality and history, why would a visitor not contemplate or imagine certain 'alternative' ideologies?

Conclusions: the Future of Ireland's Heritage?

This chapter has attempted to articulate and reveal the disjunctures present in Brú na Bóinne Visitor Centre's architectural and interpretive narratives. It likewise has examined how these inconsistencies reveal underlying present-day assumptions about the identity of Ireland as a nation. In effect, these inconsistencies are often so obvious that visitors are likely to question the validity of the data before them. Brú na Bóinne Visitor Centre's blatant nationalist narratives may thus inadvertently provoke visitors to challenge the centre's interpretive exhibit. The aforementioned alternative readings of Newgrange are perfect examples of this.

I have also argued that this particular rhetoric, one that glorifies and claims an innate connection with the land and its ancient peoples, is a recycled narrative that originated in 19th century Ireland. During this post-famine era, Ireland sought 'an identity that would provide both a legitimating framework for resource distribution and a moral and emotional world-relation in a period of intense dislocation' (O'Mahony and Delanty, 1998, p. 183). In today's modernized Ireland, however, this nationalistic language does not have the same effect as it once did on Ireland's 19th century citizens.

This historical narrative tries to create an imaginary cultural bond between Ireland's native citizens. As a result, it excludes a number of populations. This may cause ignored populations to construct their own interpretations of Newgrange's burial mounds. Moreover, to exclude certain populations is to erase or ignore certain historical moments in Ireland's history. The fact that Brú na Bóinne's entire exhibit focuses on the Neolithic people of Newgrange, although the site contains strong archaeological evidence of activity throughout the late 19th century (Stout, 2002), demonstrates this erasing of history. Ireland's Strokestown Park House is an excellent example of a visitor centre which 'challenges and reconciles popular views of Ireland's past by restoring the historical narrative to its geographical context' (Johnson, 1996, p. 551), but it is likewise removed from Ireland's historical memory for nationalistic reasons. Strokestown Park House tells the story of the Irish Potato Famine, a tale that does not portray the Irish as heroic. It is one of the few Heritage Sites not designed by Duchas and is therefore ignored in much of Duchas' and Bord Fáilte's tourism literature.

Results from previous research on how visitors interact with other exhibitions can offer helpful suggestions for altering Brú na Bóinne's exhibition. Bender's reformulation of Stonehenge's interpretive exhibit is an example of an effective, multi-vocal presentation of history. In her exhibit entitled 'Stonehenge Belongs to You and Me', Bender allowed varying and often competing interest groups, including archaeologists, 'travelers, pilgrims', 'druids' and 'free festivalers' to create their own storyboards to be put on display at Stonehenge (1998, pp. 159–161). Other storyboards featured information on 'legal sanctions', 'police action' and 'media coverage' at Stonehenge (Bender, 1998, pp. 162–163). Another board allowed visitors to respond to the opinions voiced on the storyboards or simply to jot down their feelings regarding the archaeological site (Bender, 1998, p. 167). Here, visitors were encouraged to engage critically with the materials presented before them, an interpretive schema Owen (1996) similarly endorses.

Though Brú na Bóinne Visitor Centre's exhibit and tourism literature on Newgrange emphasize the 'experience' of the visitor, neither forum asks visitors to analyse the origins of these experiences critically. Merriman proposes a remedy to this problem by suggesting the use of theatre, juxtaposing interpretations on exhibit panels and digital audio guides to make sites multi-vocal (2002). Brú na Bóinne Visitor Centre has utilized none of the aforementioned technologies, and all, I believe, would serve to benefit a tourist's experience of Newgrange.

Before any alterations can be made to the centre, however, changes must occur within Irish society. O'Mahony and Delanty agree, stating that 'breaking with historical silences in late twentieth and early twenty first century Ireland involves the acceptance of differentiated perspectives arising from differentiated situations' (1998, p. 188). If Ireland's corporate and governmental powers are capable of generating a 'post-national' identity, a collective identity no longer focused on the fiction of an 'homogenous people' and their alleged common, cultural attributes but rather concerned with accepting people's differing views, positions and opinions (O'Mahony and Delanty, 1998, p. 188), only then can a multi-vocal, open-ended exhibit be established in Brú na Bóinne Visitor Centre.

References

Anderson, B. (1991) *Imagined Communities: Reflections on the Origin and Spread of Nationalism*. Verso, London.

Anderson, D. (2001) The body of the earth goddess: Ireland and the passage tombs. *Awakened Woman e-Magazine*. Available from: http://www.awakened-woman.com/body_goddess.htm (accessed 22 April 2004).

Appadurai, A. (1996) *Modernity at Large: Cultural Dimensions of Globalization*. *Public Worlds*, Vol. 1. University of Minneapolis, Minneapolis.

Archaeology Ireland (1998) Brú na Bóinne. Special edn. Wordwell, Bray, County Wicklow, Ireland.

Bender, B. (1998) *Stonehenge: Making Space*. Berg, Oxford, UK.

Bord Fáilte (1994) *Annual Report*.

Brett, D. (1996) *The Construction of Heritage*. Cork University Press, Cork, Ireland.

Crooke, E. (2000) *Politics, Archaeology and the Creation of a National Museum of Ireland: an Expression of National Life*. Irish Academic Press, Dublin.

Deegan, J. and Dineen, D. (1997) *Tourism Policy and Performance: the Irish Experience*. International Thomson Business Press, Cambridge, UK.

Dietler, M. (2000) *Cyber-Celts, Web-Druids, and Celt Fests: Constructing Global Ethnoscapes of Celticity and Consuming the Past in the Postmodern Era*. Paper given at the 98th Annual Meeting of the Society for American Archaeology, New Orleans.

Gibbons, L. (1996) *Transformations in Irish Culture*. Cork University Press, Cork, Ireland.

Graham, C. (2000) *Deconstructing Ireland: Identity, Theory, Culture*. Edinburgh University Press, Edinburgh, UK.

Johnson, N.C. (1996) Where geography and history meet: heritage tourism and the big house in Ireland. *Annals of the Association of American Geographers* 86, 551–566.

Kammen, M. (2000) Carl Becker Redivivus: or, is everyone really a historian? *History and Theory* 39, 230–242.

Keane, E. (1997) The visitor centre – gateway to Brú na Bóinne. *Archaeology Ireland* 11, 36–37.

Knowth.com (2005) Newgrange Excavation Report Critique by Alan Marshall. Available from: http://www.knowth.com/excavation.htm (accessed 1 February 2005).

Kockel, U. (1994) *Culture, Tourism, and Development: the Case of Ireland*. Liverpool University Press, Liverpool, UK.

MacBain, G. (2000) Newgrange, Knowth, and Dowth: calendars for the sun, moon and stars. In: *Mythical Ireland*. Available from: http://www.mythicalireland.com/astronomy/boynecalendars.html (accessed 22 April 2004).

McCarthy, S. (2002) Once upon a megalithic time: the representation of archaeology in Irish tourism literature. *Papers from the Institute of Archaeology* 13, 34–50.

McColman, C. (2002) *A Spiritual Pilgrimage to Ireland*. Available from: http://www.carlmccolman.com/eire.htm (accessed 22 April 2004).

Meath Tourism (1999a) *Meath: Rich in Tradition, Full of Excitement*.

Meath Tourism (1999b) *Meath Heritage Trails*.

Meethan, K. (2001) *Tourism in Global Society: Place, Culture, Consumption*. Palgrave, New York.

Merriman, N. (2002) Archaeology, Heritage and Interpretation. In: Cunliffe, B., Davies, W. and Renfrew, C. (eds) *Archaeology: the Widening Debate*. Oxford University Press, Oxford, UK, pp. 541–566.

O'Mahony, P. and Delanty, G. (1998) *Rethinking Irish History*. St Martin's Press, New York.

O'Sullivan, M. (1997) Megalithic art in the Boyne Valley. *Archaeology Ireland* 11, 19–21.

Owen, J. (1996) Making histories from archaeology. In: Kavanagh, G. (ed.) *Making Histories in Museums*. Leicester University Press, London.

Ronayne, M. (2001) The political economy of landscape: conflict and value in a prehistoric landscape in the Republic of Ireland. Bringing contemporary baggage to neolithic landscapes. In: Bender, B. and Winter, M. (eds) *Contested Landscapes: Movement, Exile and Place*. Berg, Oxford, UK, pp. 149–164.

Schudson, M. (1992) *Watergate in American Memory*. Basic Books, New York.

Sørensen, M.L.S. (1999) Archaeology, gender and the museum. In: Merriman, N. (ed.) *Making Early Histories in Museums*. Leicester University Press, London, pp. 136–150.

Stout, G. (2002) *Newgrange and the Bend of the Boyne*. Cork University Press, Cork, Ireland.

Wertsch, J.V. (2002) *Voices of Collective Remembering*. Cambridge University Press, Cambridge, UK.

Woodman, P.C. (1995) Who possesses Tara? Politics in archaeology in Ireland. In: Ucko, P. (ed.) *Theory in Archaeology: a World Perspective*. Routledge, London, pp. 278–297.

3

Ruining the Dream?
The Challenge of Tourism at
Angkor, Cambodia

Tim Winter

Asia Research Institute, Singapore

Introduction

For centuries, ruins have held an enduring fascination for artists,
writers, poets and scholars. Equally, cinematic history is replete with
images of ruins as metaphors of the mysterious or exotic, and the
lament come romance, over the demise of past grandeur.
Unsurprisingly, ruins have also played a significant role in luring
travellers to far-flung and remote locations. Numerous sites today such
as Machu Picchu, Tikal, Pagan or the Acropolis have become well
established 'must sees' within the global circuit of tourist spectacles.

The inherent complexities of these places as landscapes of tourism
have provided fertile ground for discussions concerning land rights, the
representation of place, the politics of the past, as well as the virtues and
ills of cultural commodification. This study furthers such debates by
exploring the tensions between paradigms of site presentation and
processes of touristic consumption at the World Heritage Site of Angkor,
Cambodia.

Although heritage tourism studies have continued to shift towards
ideas of multi-vocality and the social actualization of place in recent
years, the subtle and complex ways in which tourist landscapes are
made meaningful through intersecting representations, narratives and
embodied practices remains underdeveloped. The analysis presented
here of one of Angkor's most prominent ruins, Preah Khan, sets out
directly to address this gap.

More specifically, the chapter explores the strong correlations
between the ways in which tourists narrate and practice Preah Khan,

and the prevailing images and representations circulated within the tourism industry. It will be seen that this relationship creates a form of consumption which lies in tension with the model of 'cultural tourism' proposed by the site's administrative body, the World Monument Fund. Without doubt, questions of Preah Khan's management and presentation require an understanding of the values and landscape constructions held by Cambodian visitors today. However, rather than discussing policy conundrums based on now familiar debates of local versus global 'rights', this chapter steers in a different direction; examining the tensions created by conflicting visions of culture and landscape arising from intersecting, transnational tourism and heritage industries. For this reason, an analysis of domestic tourism is not included here.

Towards Metaphors and Praxis; Landscapes in and of Tourism

The area of landscape studies today reflects the fusion of two quite different forms of scholarly inquiry. In the hands of early physical geographers, landscapes were there to be observed, surveyed, mapped and disciplined. Whereas for poets, writers and artists, the concept of landscape was bound up in aesthetics and ideas of romanticism, the sublime or the picturesque. In many ways, early depictions of ruins were instrumental to the evolution of this latter category (Woodward, 2001).

Over recent decades, however, cultural geography has endeavoured to resolve this divide. Inspired by the work of John Berger and Raymond Williams, amongst others, cultural geographers have departed from discussing landscape in purely physical, material and absolute terms, in favour of an analysis of the socio-cultural, symbolic and relative nature of space (Rose, 1993). A central concern of this project has been the rupturing of polarized ideas of 'natural' versus 'cultural', and 'real' versus 'imagined' landscapes. The rise of more humanist geographies has also led to greater attention being given to the meanings and values ascribed to landscapes, and the complex ways in which they become intersubjectively actualized. Writers such as Cosgrove and Daniels, and Duncan and Duncan, for example, were highly influential in bringing such concerns to the forefront of scholarly writing on landscape. As Duncan and Duncan argued in the late 1980s:

> The web like character of places and landscapes means that they are capable of sustaining multiple meanings, and that multiple narratives criss-cross and thread through them.
>
> (Duncan and Duncan, 1988, p. 123)

Unsurprisingly, this evolution in landscape studies has also shaped, and been shaped by, literatures on tourism. John Urry's now seminal text on *The Tourist Gaze* represented a consolidation of previous accounts which explored how places, people and cultures were becoming encapsulated within the economic and cultural logics of tourism. In exploring ideas of representation, semiotics and commodification, Urry argued that the tourist gaze is characterized by 'things of significance in history/culture/nature/experience ... [being] ... identified, signified, and totalized' (1992, p. 172). The permeation of Urry's ideas led to a stream of studies on heritage sites, tourist brochures, guidebooks and theme parks, all seeking to illustrate the ways in which landscapes have become commodified within a web of signification and offered up for symbolic exchange (Hughes-Freeland, 1993; Selwyn, 1993; Andrew, 1994; Dann, 1996; Edwards, 1996; Picard, 1996; McGregor, 2000).

Critics of Urry's portrayal of *The Tourist Gaze* and these subsequent studies have invariably pointed to their ocular-centrism and neglect of materiality (Hollinshead, 1999). Interestingly, Urry's own response to this criticism has been influential in moulding a trend towards examining tourism landscapes in terms of multi-sensory consumption and embodiment (1995). For Edensor (1998, 2001), Goffman's dramaturgical metaphor provided a valuable theoretical vantage point for discussing the Taj Mahal in terms of tourist performances. Yalouri (2001) drew upon Bourdieu's notion of *habitus* to examine consumption at the Acropolis as a spatialized cultural form; where landscape was known and enacted through the body. David Crouch, on the other hand, approached tourism geographies as forms of everyday spatial praxis, emphazising that tourists 'figure and refigure [their] knowledge of material and metaphorical spaces ... [by] ... trying out, coping, negotiating, and contesting' (1999, p. 3). These studies reflected a departure from viewing consumption as a mere passive process, towards a greater appreciation of the ways in which tourist landscapes are subjectively produced, valued and appropriated (see also Hutnyk, 1996; Bender, 1999; Lewis, 2000).

However, although authors like Crouch call for an examination of tourist landscapes as an interweaving of material and metaphorical spaces, the connections between everyday knowledge and practices, and the broader representations and discourses familiar to tourism often remain underdeveloped. Indeed, Franklin and Crang (2001) suggest that tourism studies generally have yet to address this issue fully. While the two authors acknowledge the insights provided by the plethora of studies focused on the presence of institutionalized 'ways of seeing' which selectively identify and construct places of tourism, they maintain that little acknowledgement has been given to their role in informing practices of spatial consumption. Meethan (2001) also suggests that more detailed accounts are still required concerning the dialectic complexities of subject/discourse or symbolic/material relationships within tourism.

Finally, in the case of ruins, the focus of this study, there has yet to be a detailed examination of the ways in which they are discursively constructed and actually encountered within a context of international tourism. This short study sets out to fill that void, and to offer a small contribution to our understanding of ruins by examining how they become repackaged and reinscribed within a socio-cultural landscape of contemporary international tourism.

Vibrant City to Ruined Temple: a Brief History of Preah Khan

Situated towards the north-east quarter of the Angkor World Heritage Site – just beyond the boundaries of the large Angkor Thom complex – Preah Khan was one of several sites conceived and built by Jayavarman VII (1181–*c*.1219). Following decades of instability, Jayavarman seized the vacant throne at Angkor and embarked upon the construction of roads, reservoirs, hospitals, rest houses and numerous temple complexes. The immense scale of Jayavarman VII's building programme essentially secured his position as Cambodia's most revered monarch, with his reign now widely regarded as the apogee of Khmer history.

Increasingly inspired by a Mahayana Buddhist concern for egalitarianism, Jayavarman conceived Preah Khan as a poly-functional site. The town was surrounded by a moat and outer laterite wall measuring 640 × 820 m. Inscriptions found within the site claim Preah Khan's population reached 97,000 at its peak, and produced approximately 10 t of rice a day (Jacques and Freeman, 1997, p. 218). At the heart of the enclosure was a central temple complex, which according to Briggs covered an area of 175 × 200 m (1951, p. 218). French archaeologists working in the early decades of the 20th century suggested that Preah Khan functioned principally as a monastery. More recently, however, Claude Jacques has argued that the site needs to be seen more as a university rather than the residence for a monastic community (Jacques and Freeman, 1997, p. 218). Consecrated in 1191, the complex housed a veritable pantheon of deities. According to George Coedès (1963), a total of 282 shrines were dedicated to the worship of Buddha, Siva, Vishnu and numerous ancestral spirits. Coedès also maintained that an understanding of Preah Khan's spiritual and symbolic significance required a reading of its connections to two further temple complexes constructed by Jayavarman VII: Ta Prohm and Bayon.

Along with numerous other temple sites in the region, Preah Khan steadily deteriorated after the fall of the Angkorean kingdom in the mid 15th century. By the time the French research and conservation school, École Française d'Éxtrême Orient (EFEO), began restoring Angkor at the beginning of the 20th century, Preah Khan was in an advanced state of disrepair. In the late 1920s, Henri Marchal set about freeing the temple from a forest of trees and vegetation. However, unlike other sites in the Angkor region, most notably Angkor Wat and Banteay Srei, the level of reconstruction remained limited. In fact, by the 1930s it was decided to maintain both Preah Khan and Ta Prohm as partial ruins. This strategy was partly driven by the idea of providing the growing numbers of tourists visiting the region at that time with a sense of what Angkor was like when it was supposedly 'discovered' by the French botanist Henri Mouhot in 1860. Preserving these sites as partial ruins formed an important stage in the establishment of a mythology around the idea that Angkor was abandoned and buried in the jungle awaiting discovery by European explorers; a myth which, as we shall see shortly, endures to this day.

As Cambodia descended into war and civil unrest in the early 1970s, EFEO were forced to abandon their efforts at Angkor. In addition to suffering two decades of neglect, Preah Khan was sporadically occupied and mined by Khmer Rouge troops until the early 1990s (Thibault, 1998). In November 1992, however, Preah Khan's fortunes reversed once again with the arrival of the World Monument Fund (WMF). Under the management of the WMF – and within the overall jurisdiction of the local APSARA[1] authority since 1995 – Preah Khan has benefited from a three-pronged strategy. Essentially funded by private donations, the WMF have set about ensuring architectural stability across the site, trained a number of young Cambodians in the skills of conservation and temple maintenance, and placed a strong emphasis on 'enhancing' the site for tourists. In approaching both the conservation and presentation of the site, the organization has had to reflect continually upon the relationship between the temple architecture and the surrounding forest. As Figs 3.1 and 3.2 illustrate, this forest also dominates the inner regions of the complex. Over the course of hundreds of years, several trees have become intricately enmeshed with the temple itself.

The visually spectacular nature of Preah Khan, along with Angkor's other 'partial ruin' Ta Prohm, means it retains an extremely high profile within the imagery of international tourism. As we shall see shortly, these two sites have become iconic landscapes for a tourism industry selling the romance of 'ruins' buried in the jungle. Indeed, with its accessible location along the popular *Grand Circuit*, Preah Khan is typically regarded as a 'highlight' for many tourists visiting Angkor today.

Knotty Problems and Thorny Issues

Across the Angkor complex, the major temple sites such as Angkor Wat, Bayon, Ta Prohm, Baphuon and Preah Khan vary considerably in their state of disrepair. Conservation agencies from around the world have

Fig. 3.1. A tree located near the east entrance of the temple.

therefore adopted a range of philosophies for preserving and restoring Angkor's landscape; tailoring approaches in accordance with the demands of a specific site. Since taking on Preah Khan's management in the early 1990s, the WMF have maintained a policy of minimal intervention. Conservation projects have been oriented towards structural preservation and consolidation rather than large-scale restoration.[2] The explicit philosophy underpinning this strategy has been to maintain the site as a 'partial ruin'.

However, within this philosophical framework, the organization's proclivity towards monumental conservation means the site remains principally conceived, valued and managed in architectural terms. Overwhelming priority is given to structural protection, and this has led to a strict control being maintained over the surrounding forest. As a consequence, recent years have seen the removal of a number of large trees deemed to be dangerous to the temple structures. The logic underpinning this strategy is demonstrated in their contribution to the 1996 UNESCO report outlining conservation activities conducted at Angkor during that year:

> On 8th June two fromager trees fell down onto the south-west courtyard of the Buddhist complex and caused damage to four individual shrines. The trees were removed and the damage repaired. This caused the WMF to wonder about the advisability of cutting down all trees in the vicinity of the temples.

(ICC, 1997, pp. 36–37)

Fig. 3.2. A tree located near the 'Hall of Dancers'.

This excerpt vividly indicates how a concern for architectural preservation invokes a strong distinction between the 'cultural' and 'natural' elements of the landscape. More specifically, within a framework of landscape management, nature is continually regarded as a threat to the site's 'cultural heritage', requiring constant monitoring and control. To cite once again their contribution to UNESCO's annual report on Angkor:

Preah Khan is one of the few monumental complexes at Angkor that is still surrounded by an almost intact jungle, and this has led the WMF to draw up a short and long term plan to manage the immediate natural environment of the site and control the growth of vegetation.

(ICC, 1995, p. 22)

Decisions regarding the retention or removal of individual trees have been principally driven by a concern for the preservation of an architectural heritage and the technical challenges of meeting that objective. The high density of Preah Khan's architecture and lack of accessibility to central areas means that removing trees inevitably involves a degree of risk. For this reason, certain high profile trees, including one threatening to collapse on to the central 'Hall of Dancers' (Fig. 3.2), have yet to be removed. It can thus be suggested that the decision to preserve Preah Khan as a 'partial ruin' is driven more by technical and financial constraints rather than the adoption of a particular aesthetic sensibility.[3]

For an organization dependent upon private donor support, the WMF have understandably looked towards tourism as a vital mechanism for maintaining their public profile and generating the funds necessary for a long-term commitment to Angkor. In response to the steadily increasing levels of international tourists visiting Cambodia towards the end of the 1990s, the WMF paid greater attention to issues of site presentation. As their mission director John Sanday stated:

Yes we saw that as crucial. We see it as our responsibility to look after the maintenance, but we want to be 'visitor friendly', it is an important part of our project here.[4]

Unsurprisingly, the organization's orientation towards architectural conservation also underpins their approach to being 'visitor friendly'. Once again, we can see from their 1999 report of activities that there is a strong sense of the surrounding forest and vegetation being kept under careful observation:

Preah Khan has become a very attractive site for visitors. It is therefore essential to maintain the site in an orderly fashion, to keep it tidy and free of rubbish and keep the vegetation trained.

(ICC, 1999, p. 53)

In addition to site maintenance, the organization have also installed a number of notice boards, signs and a visitor centre as a way of disseminating information concerning their activities. Located just inside the walled enclosure, and adjacent to the popular west entrance, the visitor centre was designed to blend in harmoniously with its surroundings. Although significantly upgraded in 1997, the centre remained a simple, single-storey, timber structure designed to have minimal visual impact.

In addition to these structural interventions, the WMF also recently produced an 'Official Souvenir Brochure' for visitors. Available in several languages, the brochure provides an overview of the temple complex, a visitor map and detailed descriptions of the site's 'highlights'. Analysis of the brochure reveals the overwhelming priority given to the surviving stone structures and the religious iconography contained therein. Lengthy accounts are given of areas such as the *Vishnu and Siva complexes*, the *Central Sanctuary*, *The Cruciform Shrine* and various Garuda carvings. The descriptions offered for these areas essentially attend to the religious motifs in terms of their Indian origin with little or no attention given to how these were reappropriated at the local level. The lack of references to other forms of spirituality, including animistic and ancestral belief systems, reproduces a construction of Angkorean culture advanced by French scholars in the early 20th century which prioritized a 'greater' classical Indian civilization over the 'lesser' cultural indigene.

This categorization of the site according to a number of 'highlights' is also intended to create a form of informal routing for visitors; drawing them from the points of interest in the east through to the west. In this respect, the brochure forms part of a broader organizational concern for moulding how the site is encountered by tourists. In recent years, the WMF have undertaken a number of feasibility studies into the viability of reversing the tourist flow away from the current point of entry in the west in favour of the east. As Sanday (2001) states:

> We think the temple should be experienced as it was meant to be
> experienced, i.e. from the east entrance, as Jayavarman VII intended it to
> be experienced. ... I want visitors to enter the compound from the East and
> we create a one-way system through the temple.

Plans for this routing scheme are largely driven by the idea of presenting the visitor with the series of 'highlights' documented in the brochure. It can thus be seen that the spatial narrative being promoted is essentially underpinned by a conception of a 'high' culture. In many respects, this situation stems from the current ambiguities of knowledge concerning Preah Khan's importance as a scholarly institution or as a residential space. Although the WMF have recently stabilized and fully uncovered a dharmasala, or rest house, the site's current state of dilapidation has greatly inhibited further archaeology and research. In the absence of such information, the official brochure relies upon the body of knowledge previously cultivated from the interpretation of inscriptions and stone sculptures. The stories told therefore reflect the organization's concern for working within the strict boundaries of rigorous, scholarly and scientific research. Their reluctance to present alternative histories based on inadequate tangible evidence is illustrated in the following statement by their director:

> As an organization, we wouldn't want to speculate, we need to be ethical
> and professional.

By implication, this approach means little attention is given to those features of the landscape associated with its ruinous state. The brochure map, for example, makes no visual or textual references to either the trees within the temple complex or the surrounding forest itself. Within the strict, scholarly framework of religious and architectural historiographies, there is little scope for presenting romanticized ideas of 'ruins lost in the jungle'. The absence of such imagery within the brochure once again reaffirms how the site is primarily conceived, managed and presented as an architectural heritage.

Keeping up with the Jones'

If, however, we turn to the ways in which the tourism industry presents Preah Khan, we see a series of very different representations. Since re-emerging as a major site of national and international tourism in the mid 1990s, Angkor has become synonymous with two particular visions of history. In addition to being regarded as one of the world's great 'ancient' civilizations, Angkor has also become an icon of loss, decay, rediscovery and restitution. The following description presented in the travel section of the *New York Times*, 21 July 2002, illustrates some of these themes:

> Some people are suckers for lost cities. I am. I've sought out, among others, Machu Picchu, Pompeii, Petra, Ephesus, Karnak and Uxmal. But Angkor, the jungle-covered capital of the ancient Khmer civilization in Cambodia, has always seemed to me the Mother of All Lost Cities. … The romance of its 'discovery' and exploration by the French in the mid-19th Century was part of Angkor's glamour. … Sometimes I just sat trying to contemplate cosmology and civilization, or trying to pretend I was Henri Mouhot, who came upon the ruins in 1861.
>
> (Rose, 2002)

Unsurprisingly, within a cultural economy of international tourism, these themes are continually embellished, romanticized and commodified for touristic consumption. Indeed, in many instances, the travel industry constructs a narrative of Angkor using cultural references which have absolutely no connection to the site itself. For example, as an internationally familiar icon of danger and archaeological intrigue, Indiana Jones has become an indicator of what a trip to Angkor today might entail:

> Henri Mahout's 'discovery' of the Angkor temples in 1860 opened up this lost city to the outside world. At its zenith, Angkor Wat spread over 256 sq km. … While you don't need Indiana Jones' whip, pistol and fedora to visit Angkor, the swashbuckling archaeologist's spirit of adventure will come in handy. With more than 1000 archaeological sites scattered across 200 sq km of lush Cambodian jungle, Angkor is a beacon to global explorers.
>
> (Anonymous, 2001, pp. 82–83)

Similarly:

> The unreconstructed temple of Ta Prohm makes the visitor feel like
> Indiana Jones. For deep in the jungle a short distance beyond Angkor
> Thom, Ta Prohm lies more or less as the French naturalists found it 130
> years ago. Trees, some of them more than 300 years old, grow right over
> the collapsing structure of the temples themselves … it is spooky, overgrown
> and crude … when you walk along the narrow path that takes you to Ta
> Prohm, your heart jumps into your mouth just as it might have for those
> 19th century Frenchmen who, stumbling through the jungle, came upon it
> for the very first time.
>
> (*Washington Post Sunday*, 24 January, 1999)

These statements also illustrate how the idea that Angkor remained
buried in the jungle awaiting 'rediscovery' by French explorers has
resolidified through the imagery circulating within the travel and
tourism industry. Themed hotels, airline magazines and countless guide
books continually portray Angkor as a lost, ruined civilization through
lengthy descriptions, paintings and reproductions of late 19th century
French engravings. Invariably evoking romanticized visions of mystical
temples buried in the jungle, these accounts also construct a nostalgia
for a bygone era of European travel and exploration (see Fig. 3.3).

Fig. 3.3. Colonial themed hotel, Siem Reap.

A recent popular guide by Dawn Rooney (2001), for example, focuses purely on recounting the 'numerous firsthand accounts written by explorers to Angkor in the last half of the nineteenth century and early western travellers from the beginning of the twentieth century onwards'.[5] Entitled *Angkor Observed*, the book utilizes numerous quotes from the diaries of travellers, along with sketches of Angkor, to present a narrative of exploration, discovery and awe. Eschewing lengthy descriptions of architecture or temple sculpture, the author frames the site as a series of labyrinthine ruins, engulfed by thick tropical forest. With its focus upon centuries of dormancy and a 19th century moment of awakening, the book conceives Angkor as a landscape 'heavy with time' (Urry, 1995). Further layers of temporality are added by connecting today's landscape with this historical narrative. Unsurprisingly, the 'partial ruins' of Preah Khan and Ta Prohm represent powerful mechanisms for drawing the reader back in time. The following description of Preah Khan illustrates how this is done:

> When the jungle invades a temple you see nature and stone cohabitating, in both positive and negative ways. ... So we see nature and man feeding on one another. In a strange way they have become friends, supporting, protecting each other and simply growing old together. Today, as the trees and stones are in their golden years of life ... the jungle continues its relentless crush on the stones and provides a timeless changing mélange of nature and man.
>
> (Rooney, 2001, pp. 93–94)

Throughout the book, depictions of architectural structures held in the 'stranglehold' of nature are inscribed as metaphors of 'lost time', 'organic time' or 'times of exploration'. In this respect, a 'patina of age' (Macnaghten and Urry, 1998, p. 160) is invoked through an aesthetic sensibility which nostalgically constructs the past and romanticizes decay.

When considered together, we can see that the cultural artefacts of the international tourism industry today constitute a very different representation of Angkor and Preah Khan from that promoted by the WMF. The following two sections suggest that this divergence creates a number of tensions between prescribed policies of site presentation and the values and aesthetic sensibilities underpinning processes of consumption.

Ghostly Narratives

Unsurprisingly, the representations highlighted above closely correspond to the ways in which Angkor is imagined by many tourists prior to their arrival in Cambodia. The following excerpts from interviews conducted with tourists from a number of countries illustrate how a vision of Angkor as lost ruin remains a prevalent intersubjective 'imagined geography' (Edensor, 1998):[6]

I am expecting a lot of damage, beheaded torsos for example. Lots of vegetation, jungle, things like that, because of the books I was reading, you know the famous 'fromagie' on the temples. ... the iconic image of Angkor for me is very much the large Buddha heads imprisoned by the roots, well it has been depicted so many times in the books like that, that is what I am expecting.

(Jean Luc; 45, French, living in Singapore, in Siem Reap for 3 days)

For me Angkor is all ruins and the world's largest monastery, but I hope we can see them, are they not all covered up in vines? I hope you can see something and that it's not all covered in vines. I hope we can see the buildings.

(Jennifer; 64, American, on 7 day tour of Thailand and Cambodia)

Well it was those temples lost in the jungle feeling. I once saw a documentary about Hue in Vietnam and how the city was lost in the jungle, but there was this other city lost in the jungle too. I don't remember a lot else, just these roots growing through things. First time I was in Thailand I went to Ayutthia and sort of thought I was going to Angkor, but I was really disappointed as it wasn't lost in the jungle.

(Rad; 37, Australian, living in Singapore, in Cambodia for 3 days)

I knew Angkor was buried by the jungle, and that it was discovered by explorers. I saw a video of how it was lost to the jungle .... I am expecting we will have to travel through the thick jungle on the bus.

(Akiko; 40s, Japanese, in Thailand and Cambodia for 3 days)

For many tourists, visits to the two partial ruins of Preah Khan and Ta Prohm also emerge as instrumental moments in the creation of a sense of continuity between their pre-conceived imaginings of Angkor and an actual encounter. In fact, these two sites often prove to be the 'highlights' of a trip. Natalie, a school teacher from Italy, explained why Ta Prohm and Preah Khan made the biggest impression on her:

Oh because of the jungle, it is just eating the stone, the force of nature, to see that nature is stronger than anything man can create. I have been to India many times and Angkor Wat reminded me so much of India, it is beautiful, but the emotion is at Ta Prohm and Preah Khan. It was so unusual to see them being eaten by the jungle, it is beautiful there, I love the jungle. I felt something direct the nature it was little to do with the architecture.

(Natalie; 55, Italian, travelling in Thailand, Laos and Cambodia for 2 months)

Patently, Natalie's 'emotion' draws upon a deep-seated romanticism associated with ruined landscapes, where the 'dialogue with the forces of nature is visibly alive and dynamic' (Woodward, 2001, p. 73). For many visitors, this very dialogue between nature and culture is central to their aesthetic sensibility:

Having trees there are part of it, it's overgrown, and these trees enhance that. You can't pull the trees down, they have as much right to be there as the ruins, you can't chop a tree down that is 250 years old. It should stay as it has become part of the ruin. A ruin's a ruin.

> (Dani; 28, Belgian, in Thailand and Cambodia for 1 week)

I would prefer to see the large trees left there. When I saw that it helped me understand more what a 1000 years is, because of the roots. The trees on the temples make us feel the history. If they were not there we would not be able to feel the history any more.

> (Masa; 24, Japanese, backpacking round South-East Asia for 3 months, 1 week in Cambodia)

Masa's concern for preserving the trees, as markers of time, begins to illustrate the subtle ways in which ruins portray history through an interweaving of their 'cultural' and 'natural' elements. Ruins tell stories of the glory and decline of past civilizations through their overgrown vegetation, and simultaneously remind us of nature's eternal power through their decaying architecture. For example, in the case of Preah Khan, we can see how the presence of engulfing trees, vines and surrounding wildlife all act as signifiers of 19th century European exploration and the romance of rediscovering lost civilizations. Together, these natural elements constitute a cultural landscape haunted by the ghosts of previous dwellings, previous encounters:

> I first learnt of Angkor at school, about colonial history, but we learnt nothing about Khmer history. I just remember being taught about temples in the jungle, and about the adventures of French travellers, including Henri Malraux of course, in these exotic, far off lands.
>
> (Pauline; 22, French, 'doing Asia' for around 3 months)

> These monuments have a natural life, and therefore if it decays that is okay. They remind me of John Ruskin and of course the writing of Victor Hugo.
>
> (Antonio; 26, Spanish, in Burma, Thailand and Cambodia for 1 month)

> The fact that these temples were hidden for many centuries, and rediscovered in recent times by the French, that's very exciting.
>
> (Gérard; 30s, French, living in Indonesia, in Cambodia for 3 days)

Somewhat unsurprisingly, tourists appropriate the narratives of these previous visitors to frame their own encounters with the site. The following responses indicate how tourists deliberately invoke ghosts of former 'explorers' as a way of haunting their own visit to Preah Khan:

> It was the sheer romantic nature of it, the organic nature and power of the trees ... those manmade structures being devoured by the trees ... it was sheer self-indulgence, 'I want to be an explorer, the one who discovered it', to come across something and you really get that here.
>
> (Pearce; 38, Canadian, travelling in Thailand and Cambodia for 3 weeks)

> I loved the ones with the trees. It was more romantic actually as I felt like we were some explorers who had discovered a temple. It gave you the idea of that.
>
> (Jacqueline; 60, French, 14 day group tour of Vietnam and Cambodia)

We saw a programme on Angkor just before we went away and the image
was predominantly of you as the explorer, the archaeologist going through
these completely unexplored temples, these magical mystical temples, of
you exploring something that hasn't been discovered before ... you have
this idea that it was not 'touristy' at all. You arrive at this temple, you're
Indiana Jones exploring this place.

> (Michael; 40, British, travelling across Asia for 6 months)

Accepting Schama's assertion that landscape 'is built up as much
from strata of memory as from layers of rock' (Schama, 1995, p. 7), the
reappearance of Indiana Jones here as a metaphor for exploration and
discovery indicates how fluid and playful that process can be.

Over the course of the previous two sections, it has been suggested
that Preah Khan needs to be conceived as a text of interweaving human
and natural histories. The arguments offered so far have been based on
an analysis of various discursive and symbolic representations. The
following section pursues these threads further by considering tourism
as a form of embodied spatial practice.

The Path Less Travelled

In previous sections, we have seen how Preah Khan's tree roots, vines
and fallen stones emerge as metaphorical representations for
constructing narratives of the mysterious, the exotic, the strange and the
ghosts of previous travellers. This final section illuminates how these
narratives are also performed spatially. In an attempt to offer an
understanding of Preah Khan which moves beyond accounts of mere
textual and image-based constructions, De Certeau's notion of
'kinaesthetic appropriation' is instructive here. De Certeau's major
contribution to spatial theory is his concern for highlighting how place is
rendered meaningful through forms of 'artful practice' (De Certeau,
1984). The following responses indicate the value of examining the
tourist encounter in such terms:

> My favourites were Preah Khan and Ta Prohm, you find yourself going in
> caverns and passageways which you need a flashlight for and clambering
> over rocks, the idea that there are these carvings just lying on the ground.
> It looks as though nature has run its course with this temple, it is
> weathered, decrepit, you do get that feeling you are exploring, I love that.
> The trees just add to the atmosphere, it's old and they add to that.
>
> > (Barry; 33, Australian, visiting South-East Asia for 1 month)

> It was nice to climb, to feel the heat of the steps and squeeze in tight spaces,
> you feel as though the temple has a life.
>
> > (Pauline; 22, French, 'doing Asia' for around 3 months)

> Yes it was magical to touch the walls, just to feel the rock.
>
> > (Val; 50s, American, in Thailand and Cambodia for 3 week holiday)

But I understand that the acid in your skin, as millions of people touch it, makes the stone wash away. So I didn't do a lot of that. But when I was climbing, walking around, just wandering, I was able to feel what it was like to have been there.

(VJ; 50s, American, travelling with Val)

Yes by crawling inside we could see how things were constructed and how they decayed. Walking in small rooms, climbing steps, that's important to me. It helps you work out how in the world they managed to create it, and what happened to it over the centuries.

(John; 40s, American, on a trip to Thailand and Angkor, in Cambodia for 2 days)

These responses indicate how the activities of climbing and feeling create a sense of simultaneous proximity and distance, where other times are imagined and brought close through the body. Within these portrayals of wandering and contemplative reflection, there is an implicit concern for an organic, fluid and uninhibited form of spatial consumption. Indeed, closer examination of this desire for 'freedom' indicates its centrality within the feelings and emotions articulated by tourists visiting Preah Khan today:

Yes one of the great things about Preah Khan is that you can walk through, wander through on your own and be left alone. The freedom in the temples is enormous and it is wonderful and they need to keep that. For those of us who want to pretend we are ancient people living in the temple we could do that.

(Val; 50s, American, in Thailand and Cambodia for 3 week holiday)

Yes I wanted to be on my own there, to feel the calm and just sit. I just thought it would be lovely to just sit down and exist for a couple of hours, to appreciate the beauty. You can't do that in Singapore.

(Polly; 34, English, living in Singapore, in Cambodia for 3 days)

If I was in a group or on my own, to be able to just hang around and walk wherever you want. ... It just wouldn't be the same visit if I was told where and when to go, how can I explain it? I had some really strong feelings, which surprised me. I spent hours and hours just watching the carvings, the beauty of them, it was just a feeling, I can't explain it. I spent hours looking at the carvings and the trees, and that would be so different if you are told to move through the temple.

(Emilie; 27, French, travelling South-east Asia for 3 months)

Emilie's preference for maintaining control over her own speed and direction was central to her decision to tour the site independently. Clearly, she perceived that such autonomy would be lost in a group and that her experience would have been fundamentally different. However, if we turn to consider those who do travel as part of a group with a guide, we see the same tactics in place. Even for those visitors directed along orderly, linear routes, this desire for an individualistic, creative, self-exploratory experience triggers a process of negotiation with the discipline imposed by the presence of the guide:

> Yes our guide walked off for a few minutes and that allowed us to sit, wander, even do our exploring a little bit, really feel the place. They were the most enjoyable moments for me.
>
> (George; 75, American, trip to Thailand and Cambodia for 7 days)

> Yes our guide was too fast. I wanted to stop and really look at the carvings and the nature, and I did sometimes. There were so many things to see and learn about and so I ignored our guide sometimes to do that.
>
> (Ming; 44, Chinese, in Cambodia for 3 days)

Today Preah Khan suffers from a profusion of 'copycat' itineraries where travel agents continually reproduce similar itineraries for their groups. With the site located on the mid point of the *Grand Circuit* – a road layout constructed during the former French colonial period – the vast majority of guided groups arrive at Preah Khan during either the mid-morning or mid-afternoon. At these times, the site can become somewhat crowded. For both Lee and Jonathan below, these other visitors are regarded as 'aliens' in the landscape compromising their ability to capture a 'solitary gaze' (Urry, 1990). In what de Certeau (1984) refers to as 'artful practices', they describe how they avoided such intrusions:

> Tourists are a distraction, I can't help tuning in on them which is annoying. When there is just me and the temple there is no other distraction, which is why if I see a big group I deliberately walk the other way. Like today, I went through small corridors when I saw a big group in front of me, but by doing that I fell in love with the place.
>
> (Lee; 27, English, travelling for 1 year on 'world' ticket, travelled from Bangkok by bus)

> For me the quiet is very important. If it's noisy with other tourists then it makes my experience less than it could have been, they distract you from concentrating and absorbing the surroundings. For instance in Preah Khan there were big groups of Germans and Japanese there and they were so loud. I realize I am very hypocritical because I want the temple to myself and I am just another tourist. But if I knew there were few people going early in the morning then I would go then. I know it's very egotistical but it makes the experience more rewarding, more satisfying if I have it for myself.
>
> (Jonathan; 20s, Dutch, travelling Asia for 1 year)

Finally, we can see in this second statement by Jonathan a regret for not having more information at hand concerning the local patterns of tourism. For a number of tourists travelling independently, seeking out such information plays an important role in the construction of their own, personal itineraries. One popular strategy is attempting to work against the prevailing flows created by guide books such as *Lonely Planet*.

The wisdom of subverting these texts is demonstrated in the final response below:

> We deliberately went first thing in the morning to get that special light, to get those sounds of the birds, the whole atmosphere of it. But to experience that, it was important to avoid all the other tourists who would visit later in the day.
>
> (Stuart; 20s, English, 2 month trip to Thailand and Cambodia)

> If there are no other people there, you really do feel like you are the explorer. We were deliberately there very early, there was nobody else there, and in that case you do get that feeling that you are the first person to go there, you can really lose yourself there.
>
> (Sandy; 26, Australian, travelling Thailand, Laos and Cambodia for 6 weeks)

> Yep we read the *Lonely Planet* and it advised that you get there in the late afternoon. So we knew that most people reading this would follow that. Our idea was to do just the opposite of what was recommended and get there around lunchtime. Yeah it was hot, but quiet.
>
> (David; 40s, British, 'travelling' Cambodia and Thailand for 10 days)

Throughout these various depictions, it is apparent that freedom of movement, the ability to spend time independently, away from other tourists, and create personalized, reflexive and fluid forms of spatial consumption are recurring themes. Strong continuities can therefore be seen between these accounts and the tourism industry representations and touristic narratives of Preah Khan outlined earlier. The tri-focal approach to consumption adopted here reveals a process whereby certain symbolic and discursive constructions of Angkor are re-articulated through enunciatory acts of embodied spatial praxis. Crucially, it is this very combination of the material and symbolic, the real and imagined, which makes Preah Khan meaningful as a landscape for visitors today.

Conclusion

The chapter has examined tourism as a series of intersecting representations, narratives and embodied practices in order to reveal significant disparities between the approach adopted for managing and presenting one of Angkor's most prominent landscapes and the values ascribed to the site by tourists visiting today. It has been suggested that the idea of the ruin, as a deep-seated landscape construction, has been embraced by a tourism industry promoting Angkor as a destination. This has led to a touristic encounter with sites such as Preah Khan overwhelmingly oriented around romanticized notions of lost antiquities, exploration and wilderness. Crucially, these framings have come to over-ride the narratives of history and culture which the site's administrators and guardians are attempting to convey to their international audience.

As the number of tourists arriving at Angkor continues to increase, the WMF are looking to impose a greater degree of surveillance and policing within the Preah Khan complex. Given the organization's proclivity towards architectural conservation premised on a strong culture, nature binary, the analysis offered here poses a number of pertinent questions concerning such policies. The organization's desire to present Preah Khan 'the way it should be experienced' is challenged by an increasingly prominent international tourism industry heavily oriented around notions of romance and nostalgia. Any further installation of routing schemes, signage and barriers will clearly represent a move towards the 'museumification' of the site. The resultant reduction in the freedom of movement, an inability to wander, linger or sit will make the tourist encounter with Preah Khan a more collective, disciplined and visual experience.

It is therefore suggested that a policy of preservation not only conserves, but also transforms as well. Although the WMF's concern for architectural protection is understandable, and not the issue in question here, the analysis offered above highlights how it also transforms processes of consumption. It is highly likely that their approach to developing a model of 'quality tourism' will lead to ruptures emerging between how the site is imagined prior to arrival and the ways it is actually encountered by visitors.

In this respect, the appearance of Angkor as a set of ruins frozen in time belies their state of flux today. Within the cultural and structural logics of tourism and heritage, a number of different framings of landscape are converging, opposing and realigning to create increasingly discordant forms of production and consumption. It remains to be seen how future visitors to Angkor will render its ruins meaningful as landscapes of the past, imbued with multiple histories and memories.

Notes

1 Authority for the Protection and Safeguarding of the Angkor Region (French original: Autorité pour la sauvegarde et l'aménagement de la region d'Angkor).
2 For further details concerning conservation activities, see Sanday (2001).
3 Early in 2001, the WMF director John Sanday outlined plans to remove two large trees 'of no particular value' in Preah Khan and nearby Ta Som complex which threatened further structural damage.
4 This and the following quotes are from a personal interview with John Sanday, Programme Director of World Monument Fund Cambodia, Siem Reap, 6 February 2001.

5   See also Dagens (1995) and Dieulefils (2001).
6   While the responses offered throughout this chapter intentionally
    incorporate tourists from a broad geographical base, the accounts offered
    should in no way be regarded as representative of any universal,
    transnational or national aesthetics.

References

Andrew, C. (1994) Visual complexity: are we cleaning up our heritage to death?
    In: Fladmark, J. (ed.) *Cultural Tourism*. Donhead, London, pp. 23–32.
Anonymous (2001) *Time Traveller: Access Asia, Spring*. Time Warner Publishing,
    London, pp. 82–83.
Bender, B. (1999) *Stonehenge: Making Space*. Berg, Oxford, UK.
Briggs, L. (1951) *The Ancient Khmer Empire*. Philadelphia Philosophical Association,
    Philadelphia.
Coedès, G. (1963) *Angkor: an introduction*. Oxford University Press, London.
Crouch, D. (1999) Introduction: encounters in leisure/tourism. In: Crouch, D.
    (ed.) *Leisure/Tourism Geographies: Practices and Geographical Knowledge*.
    Routledge, London, pp. 1–16.
Dagens, B. (1995) *Angkor: Heart of an Asian Empire*. Thames and Hudson, London.
Dann, G. (1996) *The Language of Tourism: a Sociolinguistic Approach*. CAB
    International, Wallingford, UK.
de Certeau, M. (1984) *The Practice of Everyday Life*. University of California Press,
    London.
Dieulefils, P. (2001) *Ruins of Angkor, Cambodia in 1909*, Facsimile edn. River Books,
    Bangkok.
Duncan, J. and Duncan, N. (1988) (Re)reading the landscape. *Environment and
    Planning D: Society and Space* 6, 117–126.
Edensor, T. (1998) *Tourists at the Taj: Performance and Meaning at a Symbolic Site*.
    Routledge, London.
Edensor, T. (2001) Performing tourism, staging tourism: (re)producing tourist
    space and practice. *Tourist Studies* 1, 59–77.
Edwards, E. (1996) Postcards – greetings from another world. In: Selwyn, T. (ed.)
    The Tourist Image: Myths and Myth Making in Tourism. Wiley, Chichester, UK,
    pp. 197–221.
Franklin, A. and Crang, M. (2001) The trouble with tourism and travel theory?
    Tourist Studies 1, 5–22.
Hollinshead, K. (1999) Surveillance of the worlds of tourism: Foucault and the
    eye-of-power. *Tourism Management* 20, 7–23.
Hughes-Freeland, F. (1993) Packaging dreams: Javanese perceptions of tourism
    and performance. In: Hitchcock, M., King, V. and Parnwell, M. (eds) *Tourism
    in South-east Asia*. Routledge, London, pp. 138–154.
Hutnyk, J. (1996) *The Rumour of Calcutta: Tourism, Charity and the Poverty of
    Representation*. Zed Books, London.
ICC (1995) *International Co-ordinating Committee for the Safeguarding and Development
    of the Historic Site of Angkor; Report of Activities 1994*. ICC, Phnom Penh.
ICC (1997) *International Co-ordinating Committee for the Safeguarding and Development
    of the Historic Site of Angkor; Report of Activities 1996*. ICC, Phnom Penh.

ICC (1999) *International Co-ordinating Committee for the Safeguarding and Development of the Historic Site of Angkor; Report of Activities 1998*. ICC, Phnom Penh.

Jacques, C. and Freeman, M. (1997) *Angkor: Cities and Temples*. Thames and Hudson, London.

Lewis, N. (2000) The climbing body, nature and the experience of modernity. *Body and Society* 6, 58–80.

Macnaghten, P. and Urry, J. (1998) *Contested Natures*. Sage, London.

McGregor, A. (2000) Dynamic texts and tourist gaze: death, bones and buffalo. *Annals of Tourism Research* 27, 27–50.

Meethan, K. (2001) *Tourism in Global Society*. Palgrave, Basingstoke, UK.

Picard, M. (1996) *Bali: Cultural Tourism and Touristic Culture*. Archipelago Press, Singapore.

Rival, L. (1998) *The Social Life of Trees: Anthropological Perspectives on Tree Symbolism*. Berg, Oxford, UK.

Rooney, D. (2001) *Angkor Observed*. Orchid Press, Thailand.

Rose, G. (1993) *Feminism and Geography*. Polity, London.

Rose, P. (2002) *New York Times* 21 July.

Sanday, J. (2001) *A Summary Report on the Activities at the World Monuments Fund Conservation Program in Angkor, December 2001*. WMF, New York.

Schama, S. (1995) *Landscape and Memory*. HarperCollins Publishers, London.

Selwyn, T. (1993) Peter Pan in South East Asia. In: Hitchcock, M., King, V. and Parnwell, M. (eds) *Tourism in South-east Asia*. Routledge, London, pp. 117–137.

Thibault, C. (1998) *Siem Reap-Angkor: Une Région du Nord-Cambodge en Voie de Mutation*. Prodig, Paris.

Urry, J. (1990) *The Tourist Gaze: Leisure and Travel in Contemporary Societies*. Routledge, London.

Urry, J. (1992) The tourist gaze 'revisited'. *American Behavioural Scientist* 36, 172–186.

Urry, J. (1995) *Consuming Places*. Routledge, London.

Woodward, C. (2001) *In Ruins*. Chatto and Windus, London.

Yalouri, E. (2001) *The Acropolis*. Berg, Oxford, UK.

Archaeology Under the Canopy: Imagining the Maya of El Pilar

4

Anabel Ford[1] and Megan Havrda[2]

[1] *ISBER/MesoAmerican Research Center, University of California, Santa Barbara, USA*
[2] *Independent Consultant, Northern New Mexico, USA*

Introduction

For thousands of years, countless locations on earth have been inhabited by productive societies and then 'discovered' by one or several heroic, mostly Western, adventurers. These adventurers, whether they be diplomats, writers, surveyors or of another profession, eventually contract their artists or photographers to document their findings and advertise the knowledge to be gained, the experiences to be had and the cultures to be witnessed at their newly discovered destination (see Osborne, 2000; Castleberry, 2003). Ancient America was exposed to these adventurers at a time when it was presumed that the New World was occupied by nothing but 'savages', denying the existence of great civilizations (Von Hagen, 1973). Though sometimes misinterpreted, these adventurers revealed evidence of civilizations past and present, challenging the previous assumptions. Such truths, and sometimes tales, generally initiate preliminary and then rigorous scientific investigation, as with the Maya (Adams, 1969). The development strategy for such a destination can then take many forms depending on a variety of geographic, socio-economic and environmental factors (Honey, 1999). For the Maya region of Mesoamerica, the scientific exploration and study evolved an archaeology-focused tourism model which is still dominating the region today (Fig. 4.1).

Starting at the beginning of the 20th century, Mexico's Yucatan developed Chichén Itzá with a focus on the monumental pyramids (see, for example, Castaneda, 1996). By the end of the century, each of the five countries (Mexico, Guatemala, Belize, El Salvador and Honduras)

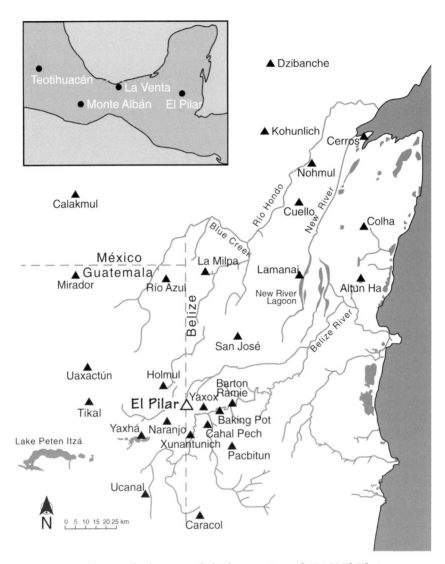

Fig. 4.1. Map showing the location of El Pilar (courtesy of BRASS/El Pilar).

that had an ancient Maya presence were all pyramid destinations
(Brown, 1999; Bawaya, 2003–2004). What worked at the start of the
20th century is still the vogue at the start of the 21st century. This focus
on the elite paints a glamorous picture of the Maya, over-riding the
strong foundation of their agricultural base that fuelled the
magnificence of the Maya. Why is this foundation invisible to the tourist
visitor, even though it surrounds them? This may not have been a
pressing question in the 20th century but, as we experience the scarcity
and limitations of our current natural resources, understanding

alternative strategies is vital to the management and cooperation of humanity and the natural world, let alone our coveted tourism destinations.

In this chapter, we will look at the standard tourism model for the Maya world, and alternative components to it, on a micro and macro level. On a micro level, we will consider how the model has shaped regional tourism consumption within the Maya context and impacted the sense of place for visitors and community members alike. On a macro level, we will entertain how this example of tourism's impact can help us better steward tourism's effect on global issues that cut across disciplinary boundaries. On both the micro and macro level, we will reveal that interconnectedness is key for human and nature relationships in the context of development in general, and tourism in particular. The World Tourism Organization (WTO) states that:

> At the start of the new millennium, tourism is firmly established as the number one industry in many countries and the fastest-growing economic sector in terms of foreign exchange earnings and job creation. International tourism is the world's largest export earner and an important factor in the balance of payments of most nations. Tourism has become one of the world's most important sources of employment ... Intercultural awareness and personal friendships fostered through tourism are a powerful force for improving international understanding and contributing to peace among all the nations of the world.
>
> (World Tourism Organization, 2005)

In the Americas specifically, tourism today has a unique opportunity to acknowledge lost societies and civilizations, such as those of the Maya. We also have the opportunity in this specific case to celebrate the gifts of the present day communities, of which varying proportions are of Maya descent, and the various landscapes of the region from coastal to forested ecosystems. Yet we argue that for this to be achieved, an alternative is required to the dominant tourism model that inspires much of the Maya tourism today. Our example is that of El Pilar, a major centre from 800 BC to AD 1000, located in the lowlands of what is today Belize and Guatemala (Fig. 4.2). El Pilar will aid us in addressing the following questions: first, what kind of values for conservation can be inspired by a place? Secondly, what kind of preservation of both nature and culture can exist hand in hand with flourishing tourism and what pattern of tourism consumption does this entail? Finally, what alternatives for tourism development are available for the Maya region?

Present Day Tourism in Central America

Although the natural environment of the Maya region withstood millennia of occupation, today its forest is at risk (Mittermier *et al.*,

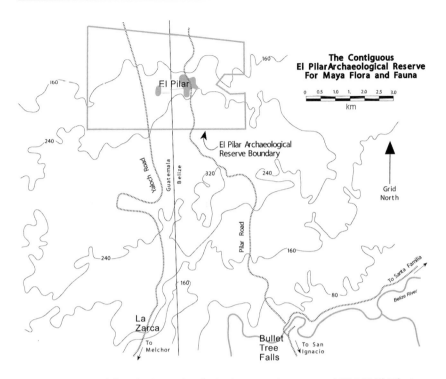

Fig. 4.2. Extent of the El Pilar archaelogical reserve (courtesy of BRASS/El Pilar).

2000). Contemporary agricultural strategies, population growth and movement, and human development programmes that lack environmental consideration now threaten the rich, biodiverse forest that the Maya cultivated four millennia ago. Today, the International Union for the Conservation of Nature and Natural Resources (IUCN) reports that only one-fifth of the Maya forest remains intact and 1300 species of plants are threatened. In addition, it is ranked among the tropical resources most at risk by IUCN (2004). Alternative management strategies are needed to ensure that the culture and nature of the Maya have a chance to coexist for many millennia to come (see Daltabuit Godás *et al.*, 2000).

Over the course of the last three decades, the Maya forest has undergone a profound change. Concomitant with the population growth and expansive agricultural practices in the Maya region is the burgeoning tourism industry. Capitalized by tourism professionals, the Maya forests that encompass the countries from Mexico south into Central America are sought-after targets. Tourism is a means by which these targeted areas can enter into the global economy, in particular by featuring their historical, cultural and environmental heritage. The ecological bounty that provided the Maya and other prehistoric cultures with their wealth is now a potential for an inviting adventure (Garrett, 1989).

The most recent statistics demonstrate that tourism accounts for the growing proportion of income in the Central American region, where per capita income averages US$4100 per annum and the gross domestic product (GDP) ranges from under a billion dollars for Belize to over 23 billion for Guatemala (CIA, 2005). This is also a region where approximately 50% of the population is rural and 50% are under 15 years of age. As the second world region in terms of international tourism receipts, the Americas earned US$114 billion in 2002, US$8 billion less than in the previous year (World Tourism Organization, 2005). While tourism is growing worldwide, the Americas have been suffering a decline of 4%. In the context of this downturn, Central America, with little more than 4% of inbound tourism, was the only subregion in the Americas to record an increase in tourism of >6% (World Tourism Organization, 2005) (see Tables 4.1 and 4.2).

Belize takes only an overall 3% share of Central America's tourism, yet posted the best result of the subregion by increasing at an astonishing rate of +14%. This is a rapidly growing market that is largely based on the expansion of cultural and nature-based tourism.

Tourism is the only product where the consumer must go to the source to consume it (LeLaulu, 2003; see also Meethan, Chapter 1, this volume), and this is ever apparent in the Maya world where major archaeological destinations, such as Chichén Itzá and Tulum in Mexico,

Table 4.1. America and subregions: inbound tourism. International tourism arrivals 2002.

	%
North America	71.4
Caribbean	14.0
South America	10.9
Central America	4.1

Source: World Tourism Organization.

Table 4.2. America and subregions: inbound tourism. International tourism arrivals, change from 2001 to 2002.

	%
Americas	−4.4
North America	−3.3
Caribbean	−4.0
South America	−13.4
Central America	+6.4

Source: World Tourism Organization.

anticipate in the order of a million visitors a year. As a result of their proximity to the cruise ship ports at Cancun, these cultural heritage sites are at risk of becoming overwhelmed (ICOMOS, 1964; see Gurucharri, 1996). Now within an hour's travel time from the comforts of a cruise ship's cabin, one can experience the rush of seeing the Castillo of Chichén – the temple-gaze takes hold of many a visitor before their attention span wanes. Prepared by the tourism industry's grandiose advertisements, many inquiring minds are put to rest and offered a spoon-fed version of Maya history and a 'classic' photo opportunity. These destinations exist now and will continue to attract visitors, but newly targeted archaeological sites do not need to follow a similar destiny. For the continuum of visitors from the one-time trip to the inveterate traveller, there is a call for variety. The division of markets into niche specialties creates opportunities for new forms of tourism that are not dominated by a monocultural gaze. As globalization brings humanity together specifically through communications and commerce, there is an increasing responsibility to remember and represent our diverse pasts and cultural uniqueness. The 1964 ICOMOS Venice Charter further supports this need:

> People are becoming more and more conscious of the unity of human values and regard ancient monuments as a common heritage. The common responsibility to safeguard them for future generations is recognized.
>
> (The Venice Charter, Preamble)

It is with these aims in mind that we see that the El Pilar project provides an opportunity to explore alternative possibilities. At El Pilar, there are two sister community groups called Amigos de El Pilar, one based in Melchor, in the Petén of Guatemala, and the second in Bullet Tree Falls in Cayo, Belize (Awe, 2000b; Ford, 2006). Together they have sponsored joint activities largely centred around the Fiesta El Pilar, an annual celebration of nature and culture typically held in Belize. The steady participation of local non-governmental organizations (NGOs), Help for Progress in Belize and recently Naturaleza para la Vida in Guatemala, lend their expertise to the implementation and ongoing promotion of the El Pilar Forest Garden Network, an encompassing programme developed by El Pilar's core team. Equally, the protected-areas managers in both countries are involved and work to develop El Pilar within the context of their governmental agenda. Orchestrating the process and linking its many parts is the Belize River Archaeological Settlement Survey (BRASS)/El Pilar research programme at the University of California Santa Barbara (http://maec.ucsb.edu/elpilar/) and the US-based non-profit organization of Exploring Solutions Past: the Maya Forest Alliance (espmaya.org). Yet in order to appreciate the current tourism situation fully, we first have to consider the evolving history of narratives concerning the Maya.

The Invention of Maya Tourism

In the middle of the 19th century, a pair of intrepid travellers by the names of John Lloyd Stephens and Fredrick Catherwood were among the first Westerners to see the monumental architectural feats of the Maya and, in many ways, set the tone for future travellers. Their tremendous coverage of the ancient Maya monuments in Central America featured many of the now famous destinations: Palenque, Chichén Itzá, Tulum and Copan. Their travels were initiated on an errand of diplomacy, but Stephens' appetite was already whetted for the ancient monuments and they made it a point to cover the difficult terrain of the Maya world by mule, carts, horse, carriage and even sedan chair. Catherwood, an architect, provided drawings with faithful detail (Bourbon, 1999), for Stephens' picturesque prose (Stephens, 1841, 1843). His lithographs provide a benchmark for appreciating the majesty and mystery the Maya architecture evoked. He depicted vine-wrapped structures covered by the forest canopy, protecting the remains of the ancient Maya civilization (Fig. 4.3). Catherwood's perception of structural details, temples *en toto* and the delicate hieroglyphs on monolithic stela were rendered in such clarity that the glyphs are able to be interpreted by scholars today. If Catherwood had an ability to capture the elements of the glyphs accurately, might we expect that the

Fig. 4.3. Catherwood's vine-covered ruins (courtesy of BRASS/El Pilar).

overall treatment of the temples and buildings was equally specific? If so, we must ask, what is the relationship between Catherwood's iconic views from the 19th century and the same structures today?

As the 20th century began, inquisitive visitors from foreign lands went out to find the fabled temples that had by then been published in traveller's tomes and new academic treatises that included views through artists' sketches and photographers' lenses (Catherwood in Stephens 1841, 1843; Maler, 1928; see also Winter, Chapter 3, this volume). One of these visitors was scholar, archaeologist and adventurer Sylvanus Morley who visited the Yucatan before 1910 and set his sights on the investigation of the Maya. The creation of the Maya world was under way.

Scientific inquiry was the logical next step of exploration in the Maya region, and Sylvanus Morley, newly signed on with the Carnegie Institute of Washington, facilitated this initiation process (School of American Research, 1950; Harris and Sadler, 2003). In the context of Morley's research agenda, a framework of Maya tourism was established. At that time, what lay beneath the crumbling surfaces of the monuments was unknown and the questions demanded excavations, exposing the collapsed and buried temples. Then, what followed were the analyses of the artefacts, investigations of the contemporary Maya and their languages, and descriptions of the epigraphy and iconography, not to mention studies of the region's botanical riches published consistently by the Carnegie Institute of Washington (e.g. Lundell, 1937; Thompson, 1960; Shepard, 1964; Roys, 1976). The Carnegie investigations canvassed the greater Yucatan of Mexico and the Petén of Guatemala, generating the foundation of Maya studies still used today. Their extraordinary contribution to understanding the Maya world began at a time when the population of the earth was only 25% of today's, when the tropical forests gave the impression of an uninterrupted canopy, and when water resources were still plentiful around the world. It was in this pioneering context that the Maya region was transformed from the unknown to one of the great mysteries of the world.

Morley saw Chichén Itzá in Mexico before the First World War, but was only able to bring his research to fruition afterwards. Touted today as the most complete restoration of an archaeological site in the Maya region, Morley spent 20 years of his life on Chichén. One of the main goals for the restored site was to attract visitors from all over the world. Morley and his benefactors accomplished this goal and catalysed the awe-struck travellers' gaze upon Maya monuments. However, the indigenous American narrative was imbued from the European perspective, laced with fanciful tales destined to become guidebook facts.

Compare Catherwood's drawing of Chichén's Castillo, Chichén Itzá's main temple-pyramid, with the one you see today (Fig. 4.4) and you will find only a superficial resemblance. How were the present day details of the Castillo evoked and what determined their inclusion? What then, was the evidence for the reconstruction of the temples and pyramids? The ICOMOS Venice Charter states that the integrity of the ancient architecture must be upheld and that one should not use imagination when consolidating monuments. Yet, in the case of Maya monuments and their mystique as a culture, many professionals have influenced the vision and the end results. The first impulse has been fuelled by the international tourism industry and by the impression that this, and only this, is what tourists want to see on a visit to the Maya world. What we have therefore seen is the creation of a narrative of 'lost' civilizations and their 'discovery' by intrepid explorers (see also Winter, Chapter 3, this volume). While this narrative does indeed capture an essential quality of the ancient Maya encounter, the exposed result raises the issue of authenticity (Fedick, 2003). Is the moment of archaeological interpretation static or dynamic? Of course, this begs the questions of what is an authentic representation of time past (Orphal, 2000), and how any given generation can place a value on a historical site and dictate its importance. The conservation of the authentic is an essential contribution to the clarification and illumination of the collective memory of humanity (National Archives and Records Administration (NARA), 1994; Jokilehto, 1995). Yet arguments concerning what is and what is not authenticity are far from being cut and dry. Wang (1999) suggests that authenticity can not only be defined in terms of absolute or 'museum' definitions, such as the narrative portrayed by Morley and others, but also at an existential level by each individual through their own intuition. This is exactly what the El Pilar Archaeological Reserve for Maya Flora and Fauna inspires, and yet it has been called a mundane experience by critics because of its diversion from the classically accepted Maya 'norm' set out by Morley and others and epitomized by examples such as Chichén.

Fig. 4.4. Catherwood's view (left; courtesy of BRASS/El Pilar) and a contemporary view (right; courtesy of Hollie Moyes) of the Castillo.

Let us look at this more closely and consider its impact on the authentic treatment of ancient Maya sites today and the potential expansion of current and future translations. Can the narrative created for Chichén Itzá, so long ago, be effectively challenged and supported by today's academic and tourism circles? The NARA Conference on Authenticity proclaimed that it is 'not possible to base judgments of values and authenticity with fixed criteria' (NARA, 1994). We understand this dynamic and yet this is what has happened at many destinations in the modern Maya world to date.

While celebrating the beauty of such sites and without casting any blame on their interpreters, let us consider that this cycle of representation can continue to evolve and perhaps better reflect the essence of Maya monuments, the past and present people of the region, and the exquisite yet threatened natural environmental context of the present day. If the established narrative is perpetuated, do we not threaten, discredit and devalue the very thing we are trying to preserve and learn from? Our foundation of knowledge has greatly expanded over the past century. Isolated sites are now known and 'packaged' as stylistic clusters, such as the Puuc Hills route (Yucatan Today, 2005), while stubborn temples protruding from the jungle canopy are recognized as the core of cities, and unknown origins have been transformed into detailed chronologies (e.g. Smith, 1955 for Uaxactún; Willey and Sabloff, 1975 for Seibal; Gifford, 1976 for Barton Ramie). Would not a diverse treatment of Maya sites increase tourism destination value, steady scientific inquiry and general fascination?

El Pilar of the Maya World

Let us reflect on the example at El Pilar that has evolved beyond the 'fixed criteria' revered and still maintained today. Rediscovered in the 1980s, El Pilar is among the grand public monuments of the Maya region, covering >50 ha of public monumental temples, palaces and plazas, surrounded by a densely settled residential area that stretches across the border of Belize and Guatemala (Fig. 4.5). Its history is not linked to the great explorers of the 19th century and emerged for development at the threshold of the 21st century at a time when we recognize that not only are our earth's resources limited but also that those same scarce resources are the increasing focus of a growing tourism industry.

In 1989, the Maya region was promoted in the impressive October *National Geographic* debut of the La Ruta Maya, 'an all weather route that encircles the area' (Garrett, 1989). This sweeping initiative was designed to link the five countries with ancient Maya presence – Mexico, Guatemala, Belize, Honduras and El Salvador – to fortify their assets and

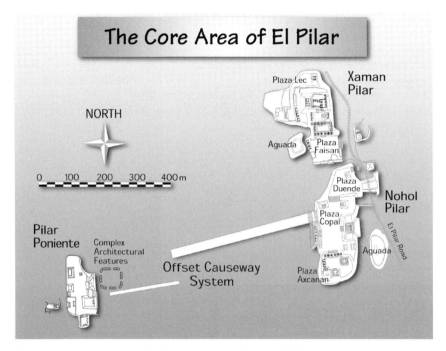

Fig. 4.5. Detailed plan of El Pilar (courtesy of BRASS/El Pilar).

complement their development activities with an adventure circuit that featured the culture and nature of the region. The article extolled that La Ruta Maya included more cities than ancient Egypt, traditions and crafts that have survived three millennia, endangered plants and animals living in the wild, the longest barrier reef in the Americas, and underscores the economic and population pressures poised to threaten all of these treasures (Fedick, 2003). With first-hand knowledge, Wilbur Garrett (1989, p. 435) reversed the perception of the fearsome jungle to 'ecological cornucopias that provided the ancient Maya with " 'a good living" '. In recognition of the legacy of the ancient Maya, Garrett (1989, p. 438) envisaged La Ruta Maya as a regional collaboration across modern political borders presaging the potential foundation for the Peace Park concept. While this aspiration has yet to transpire, La Ruta Maya has morphed into Mundo Maya, a theme branded and adopted symbolically by all five nations with Maya sites. The Mundo Maya is a very large undertaking and yet its committed partners have the unprecedented opportunity to reveal a five nation tourism strategy and development process (Inter-American Development Bank, 2003). The impacts of this bank-driven initiative will take years to unfurl; however, it is an effort worth tracking as we all seek new, fresh, mutually validating models for improved Maya site representation and tourism consumption.

The Maya ancient monuments of El Pilar cover >50 ha and now straddle the present political boundaries of two countries, incorporating three main architectural complexes, two in the eastern section (Belize) and one in the western section (Guatemala). There is an offset limestone causeway, a stone promenade, connecting the monuments in Belize with the monuments in Guatemala, which symbolically reminds us that the Maya forest is a regional asset managed by multiple interests.

El Pilar's physical location across an international boundary has been both good and bad news. Initially, as the vision for one El Pilar took shape from 1993 to 1995, its geography was perceived as an obstacle that would be difficult to surmount. Guatemala's territorial claim on Belize was a long-standing divide between the countries (Inter-American Development Bank, 2003). It was only in 1991 that Guatemala formally recognized the right of the Belizean people to self-determination, and in so doing established diplomatic relations between the two countries (Gobierno de Guatemala, 2004; Government of Belize, 2005). In 1996, with the support of regional treaties, such as the CCAD (Comisión Centroamericana de Ambiente y Desarrollo, www.ccad.ws), the two countries came together to examine the potential of col-laboration at El Pilar. This began a continuing sequence of meetings and encounters we refer to as the Mesa Redonda El Pilar (BRASS/El Pilar, 2002, 2005). Through this process, the governmental stakeholders were involved and willing to protect El Pilar as one resource. In 1998, the protected areas were declared with statutory instruments in both countries, and the contiguous boundaries were established and have been maintained since that date (Ford and Montes, 1999). Today, the Institute of Archaeology in Belize supports caretakers at the site that serve as the entry point for visitors to El Pilar. In parallel, the Guatemala government, under the governmental wing of CONAP (Consejo Nacional de Areas Protegidas), has endorsed the management plan for El Pilar (CONAP, 2004).

Integrated park management for The El Pilar Archaeological Reserve for Maya Flora and Fauna as one cultural and natural resource in two nations is fundamental to the long-term dynamic research and development design as well as to the reserve's future. The success of the El Pilar model is dependent upon the results of integrated, collaborative and multi-disciplinary programmes and adaptive management activities with full participation of the officials, the community and the experts that are involved directly or indirectly in maintaining the reserve on a lasting basis (see Taylor-Ide and Taylor, 2002).

When full archaeological investigations were launched at El Pilar in the early 1990s, vegetation of the tropical forest had taken over the site's temples, plazas, palaces, residential areas and causeways. The feeling was startling. It was such a peaceful, unmanipulated space that it gave visitors a personal sense of discovery. Though the ancient site of El Pilar has since had extensive mapping and excavation, much of the archaeological excavations have been covered and backfilled. Visitors today can, therefore, experience a similar setting and feeling to those of the first archaeologists when the site was rediscovered. This poses a challenge to the present day visitors however, a challenge to explore for themselves. This experience is daunting for some and exhilarating for others, and yet everyone appreciates their time at El Pilar once they are made aware of what might rest beneath the looming 'mounds' of stone, humus and vegetation. They are of course covered temples and palaces. This style of tourism destination model may be found in and among various international tourism sites; however, it is unique to the treatment of Maya archaeology sites. To consider the validity of this model in the context of the Maya region opens the door for variations to the 'Chichén' model, giving way to the fresh treatment and holistic stewarding of future Maya sites, preservation of their natural surroundings and recognition of the neighbouring communities which maintain and surround them.

When the Maya mystery is left to be divined by the visitor, whether international researcher or national tourist, it need not be carved out and handed over in a limited amount of time like many of the cruise-crowd experiences. This is, therefore, a very different model of tourist consumption requiring active engagement and interpretation rather than a passive acceptance of presentations. Three important aspects help to maintain the Maya mystery and experience at El Pilar (Orphal, 2000). First, access to the site is best navigated by tourist agents and local guides, therefore management of tourism flow to the site can be monitored so as to maintain a reasonable carrying capacity at all times and in each season, wet and dry. The rainy season, June to December, for example, may have less traffic on the 7 mile dirt road up to the site. Secondly, once tourists reach the site, an established trail system helps guide their way and prevents them from diverting at will and damaging the monuments or flora. Thirdly, the visitor is provided with an excavated, conserved and partially reconstructed residential area, Tzunu'un – Hummingbird in Mayan – that represents a Maya household and serves as a tangible example of 'visible or uncovered ruins' within a natural setting (Fig. 4.6). How do tourists and visitors of El Pilar value these aspects?

Let us consider the topic of 'value'. The values of a site can be 'aesthetic, historic, scientific, social or spiritual for past, present or future generations' (Australia ICOMOS, 1999; Marquis-Kile and Walker, 1992). The vision statement and management style at El Pilar reflect these sentiments (Ford and Miller, 1994, 1997; Ford, 1998; Rolex, 2000). It is also founded on archaeological research regarding the evolution of the landscape, in this case the ancient Maya landscape, that acknowledges that the clues to sustaining the complex habitats of today's

The Maya House and Forest Garden
Tzunu'un ~ El Pilar

Emergent Production
Palms and Trees

Managed Foliage
and Nitrogen
Fixing Legumes

Ornamental
Shade and
Fruit Trees

House Garden
Domestics and
Cover Crops

Edible and
Regenerative
Root Crops

12–15 m

9–12 m

6–9 m

3–6 m

Paul Bailly Architect   31 January 2000

Fig. 4.6. The Maya house and garden (courtesy of BRASS/El Pilar).

Maya forest environment are embedded in Maya prehistory (Fedick and Ford, 1990; Ford, 1990, 1991, 1992, 1993, 2004; Ford and Fedick, 1992). Ancient Maya settlement and local community patterns provide material evidence for the evolution of sustainable economies in one of the planet's last frontiers: the tropics. This plays out in the El Pilar Vision:

> El Pilar Archaeological Reserve represents an innovative example of cultural resource conservation in relationship to the natural environment and to contemporary peoples. As the largest Maya archaeological site in the Belize River area, El Pilar is unique in its presentation of ancient daily life through household structures and forest gardens, located in the shadows of monumental Maya architecture. This shared resource serves as a symbol of cooperation between Belize and Guatemala, and as a model of collaboration between the reserve and local communities and between the cultural and natural resource researchers and conservators. Involvement in reserve planning and management links the communities to their cultural heritage

and encourages their social and economic development. Documentation and evaluation of this holistic approach to resource conservation will allow El Pilar to serve as a model for other important sites of world heritage.

(www.marc.ucsb.edu/elpilar)

Professionals and visitors have recognized El Pilar for its unique aesthetic, scientific, social and spiritual value. The site's scientific value has been developed over the past several decades, given the various themes that the site encompasses, including archaeology, ecology, plant and animal biology, land use management and tourism planning (Ford, 1999, 2006; Ford and Clarke, 2000; Ford and Wernecke, 2002). The site's location straddling the border between two nations (Gaunt and Estrada, 1995; Matadamas, 1995; Topsey, 1995; Golden, 1996; Gomez, 1997; Ford and Montes, 1999), as well as its current and potential economic and educational opportunities, add tremendous social value to the site and its surrounding area (Hartke, 1995; Ford, 1996; Seelhoff, 1996; Dye, 1999; Ageton, 2000; Awe, 2000a, b, 2001a, b; Shaw, 2000; Mancilla and Pereira, 2001; Tzul, 2001; Help for Progress, 2004; Wilhelm, 2004).

The spiritual value of El Pilar cannot necessarily be seen by the naked eye in terms of sacred artefacts or ritual sites; however, one can sense the richness of the cultural activities that occurred at El Pilar and its evolving place in the contemporary landscape. It is also reflected in the visitor's comments in the caretaker's book. Often, it is in the simple residential areas that visitors are struck by the Maya's close connection to nature and animals, and their sense of the sacred (Ford, 2001; Ford and Wernecke, 2002). Overgrown gardens, once managed by local villagers, grow in scattered locations and can be appreciated from the trails (Friends for Conservation and Development, 2000). Even with this support, El Pilar's inclusive 5000 acres of monuments, flora and fauna remain threatened by social and environmental impacts and suffer from a lack of economic support. Different forms of authenticity are not then mutually exclusive and can coexist for different purposes and different audiences (see Nigh and Ochoa, 1996). El Pilar offers a new narrative that embraces the entwined context of nature and culture in the Maya forest, providing a glimpse into the everyday aspects of ancient Maya life and its link to the contemporary peoples of the region.

Archaeology Under the Canopy

Archaeology Under the Canopy at El Pilar involves four main components: (i) the tiered feral forest canopy (Campbell *et al.*, 2006); (ii) the current practice of forest gardening; (iii) the rich decomposing leaf litter on the forest floor; and (iv) the ancient monuments themselves. In fact, the shade of the forest canopy serves to maintain the stability of the ancient monuments, where exposure subjects them to accelerated deterioration (Larios and Ford, 1999; Larios Villalta, 2000a, b; Perry *et al.*, 2004). Forest gardening, at El Pilar and in the surrounding communities of the Maya forest, is simply an act of people treating the diverse forest as a useful and maintained garden. This old practice incorporates the management of the organic leaf litter as a chief soil enhancer. The effect that the tall canopy and the rich forest floor have on preserving the fertile landscape and monuments is augmented when forest gardening is integrated as a land management practice. This has been instituted at El Pilar slowly but surely, though its value has been questioned by those unfamiliar with the practice. Forest gardening existed with the Maya and is still present in the cultural fabric and ecological practices in the surrounding communities of El Pilar today, as well as worldwide in forest communities (Senanayake and Jack, 1998; Fundacion Rescate del Bosque Tropical, 2001). The concept, however, is so interwoven into the lives of present day farmers of the Maya region who practise this method that they do not completely realize its tremendous value outside of their communities, for both humanity and the natural environment. The macro impacts are innumerable yet easily imagined. Forest gardening alone could catalyse healthier populations worldwide simply by the diverse uses it provides from its plant matter.

The rich archaeological heritage at El Pilar, and many other undeveloped Maya sites, is matched by remarkable biodiversity. Together, these two facets offer a new way of perceiving the relationship between people, place and history. Interviews with 18 forest gardeners living adjacent to El Pilar, in 2004, revealed their dynamic, interactive relationship with nature by collectively identifying >350 useful plants in their gardens. The plants in their gardens are nurtured for medicine, ornaments, food, spices, dyes, poisons, construction, household products, toys, beverages, fodder and more (Ford and Gerardo, 2001). While many of the gardens reflect the global influence of the last 500 years, more than half of the plants are native and nearly all the dominant species of the forest are found in the gardens (see Campbell *et al.*, 2006). They identified 175 tree species, 140 shrubs and 135 herbs alone, not to mention the various vines, epiphytes, palms, ferns and grasses. These forest gardeners show an astounding appreciation for ecological practice in their gardens and understand the need for conscientiously managing the landscape at El Pilar. They are equally aware of the complexities of the insects, birds and bats when it comes to pollination as well as seed viability and dispersal (Atran, 1993). These forest gardeners are the ultimate conservationists who recognize the importance of their role in the future of El Pilar.

Archaeology Under the Canopy at El Pilar creates a rich natural environment in balance with the memory of humanity's fragility and interdependence on natural resources. Further, it brings the traditional forest gardener back into focus as the manager of the canopy and rich understorey. Archaeology Under the Canopy supports the nature/culture balance of Maya sites, but what do visitors think of this concept?

Presently, The El Pilar Archaeological Reserve's entrance gate is through Belize. The average visitor we speak of below is, therefore, a tourist who entered the Maya world via Belize. They may have experienced other Maya sites locally or in Guatemala and Mexico, or they may have just come from the coastal cayes and chanced on an inland expedition. Data from a survey conducted in the 1990s can provide a standard.

For decades, the archaeological destination in Belize was Xunantunich. The site is visible from the main western highway and has been a well-toured destination in Belize for decades. From a survey of foreign visitors to Xunantunich conducted by the Getty Conservation in 1993 (Belize Ministry of Tourism and Environment, 1993), we know some basics about the travellers to the Maya world of Belize. Generally it was found that:

- the majority are from the USA;
- average income is US$70,000–US$90,000 (adjusted to 2004 US$);
- 80% achieved university/graduate degree;
- 54% did not know about Xunantunich and the Maya before arriving;
- nearly half had been to Belize before;
- would spend 2–3 days in Cayo, Belize;
- spent an average US$28–US$167 a day in Belize (adjusted to 2004 US$);
- wished to know more about Xunantunich;
- will visit Tikal, Guatemala.

El Pilar emerged as a potential tour destination in the 1990s. In 1993, a caretaker was appointed at El Pilar, the reserve boundaries in Belize were established in 1995, and the statutory instruments of Belize and Guatemala were signed in 1998, formally creating the El Pilar reserve. Reviewing a selection of the comments in the El Pilar guest book from 1994 to 2001 shows that they are representative of the initial years at El Pilar and visitor's reactions to the diverse treatment of the site. Meanwhile the site was beginning to be discovered by intrepid travellers:

> It was amazing to see a site in its natural state. We'll come back in 20 years and see what's happened.
>
> (Vicki and Jack Weisman, USA)

> A major site and a major step forward in bi-national cooperation.
>
> (John and Iona Howell, Forestry Department/Natural History Museum of London)

> The five days I spent at this amazing site was the best way I could imagine to get in touch with the ancient spirit of the Maya.
>
> (Patricia Watson, USA)

Pilar is a great place for lessons in herbs, temples, life.

(Heleen Diks, Holland)

Magical – I felt like a 19th century explorer deciphering temples from jungle hills.

(Tim McGirk, Mexico)

A unique and pleasing aesthetic that is both challenging and stimulating for the imagination.

(Joseph Mowers, USA)

These candid comments of visitors who encountered El Pilar reveal the struggle and the engagement of the experience. They also demonstrate that there is room for something different, and a difference can be appreciated and admired.

A decade later, in 2004, the El Pilar Program team comprising local and international stakeholders conducted a survey as part of our 2 week Think Tank expedition through Guatemala and Belize. The Think Tank travelled with 17 members including development professionals, donors, students, volunteers, local NGO partners and archaeologists. Immersed in the El Pilar mission, the core El Pilar team members worked to reveal together the whole picture of El Pilar, expose the programme's strengths and weaknesses, and open up new ideas and resources for moving the vision forward. Once at the site, a survey was conducted, completed by 13 Think Tank members and 13 local community members, and unearthed perceptions about El Pilar, its inherent value, and reactions to its Archaeology Under the Canopy concept. A few facts are listed here:

- 100% of all respondents said that forest gardening could be successfully used as a trail and forest management tool at El Pilar;
- 100% of local community members and 85% of Think Tank participants said that revealing sections of the monuments would enhance their experience;
- 93% of local community members and 77% of Think Tank participants said that revealing the causeway would indeed improve bi-national collaboration at El Pilar;
- 100% concurred that they would like to see El Pilar developed using the Archaeology Under the Canopy concept.

Clearly, the reception of 'Archaeology Under the Canopy' was positive. Both the first-time visitors and the community members embraced the concept of the forest as a garden and would like to see this developed. At Tzunu'un, the Maya house and forest garden, survey respondents were enthusiastic about the views of Maya household life. Foreign visitors, unfamiliar with seeing residential settings, were engaged and interested in understanding the concept of forest gardening. Still many, when confronted with the plazas under the shady canopy, would appreciate more architectural revelation while universally agreeing that the canopy should be maintained overhead. This is our vision (Fig. 4.7). Curiously, the foreign visitors rated the Tzunu'un house and garden and main Plaza Copal as the highest priorities for attention, while the community participants saw the ranger's station and causeway as most important. This points out the issue of perspective and value when seeking common goals among diverse stakeholders.

Communication and Engagement with Stakeholders

As evident with regional resources, the creation of El Pilar relies on bilateral agreements between the two national governments. Yet, at a more localized level, there is also the consideration for the needs and interests of the community, which we can define as any group that has something in common and the potential to act together (Taylor-Ide and Taylor, 2002, p. 19). At El Pilar, this definition includes governmental leadership in both Belize and Guatemala, as well as people with vested interest in El Pilar, from career agriculturists and farmers to village school teachers to tourism professionals and archaeological investigators. Due to the breadth of self-identifying stakeholders involved in the El Pilar model, it has been increasingly significant to acknowledge all parties, whether their involvement has been peripheral or central to the on-the-ground action. The most important aspect of acknowledgement should ideally come from within the community, not from outside influences and partner NGOs. Though this is still very

Fig. 4.7. El Pilar today (courtesy of BRASS/El Pilar).

much a habit in the making, our core team has seen the benefits of local stakeholders acknowledging one another's contributions to the vision. This intimate level of acknowledgement, however, needs reinforcement annually to lead to the defining and redefining of each stakeholder's role and responsibility – from the small to the grand. Clear roles encourage accountability and inspire new stakeholders to become involved and bring their gifts towards a more inclusive shared goal and vision.

The Mesa Redonda El Pilar process created a basis for such dynamic collaboration; however, this process was initiated by international interests with foreign monies. Although local stakeholders were invited to the meetings, and many attended and participated enthusiastically, there was still an underlying tone of the outside-in approach set into place which gave perceived power to the purse strings and/or political wills present instead of to in-the-field motivations and assets. Despite the successes of the Mesa Redonda process through the mid 1990s, the bottom-up community participation has waned and waxed as a reaction to funding or lack thereof over the past decade of development. This has created fear and separation among El Pilar's stakeholders, resulting in miscommunication and systems breakdown. The breakdown, however, has created an opportunity, allowing a new wave of leaders to step forward and ask the grounding question, 'what wants to happen here?'. This question is being asked among the various El Pilar stakeholders, and the responses are coming from all corners – towards a shared vision.

As the barriers and challenges to stakeholder alignment are peeling away from the process, this is allowing steady and renewed motivation to set the course for El Pilar's development. With a small amount of funding from Guatemala's USAID office coupled with a large amount of local skill and motivation, the El Pilar Forest Garden Network project is gaining footing in the border area of Belize and Guatemala – forming organically through right timing, right relationships and affinity groups interested in forest gardening, technology, tourism and environmental education. Doing what has always been done, the forest gardeners are the inspired heroes of this project and the hope of El Pilar's future, catalysing the project's impact on local and regional conservation.

Could this project and the model evolving at El Pilar train and inspire a new kinship of tourism providers and visitors? With the research and garden circuits coming out of the El Pilar Forest Garden Network, there is a lot of material that can be authentically shared with visitors in the intimate setting of people's homes and gardens. Imagine visiting an orchard on horseback, one with rich plants from grasses to herbs to vegetables to fruit trees, being told of each plant's uses and enjoying a meal from the garden's rich bounty. In such a context, each forest gardener can aspire to create their own presentation and divulge the very uniqueness of each garden. The knowledge and experiences within them will touch visitor's hearts and minds in a way that slows down time, creates thoughtful space and entices cultural and natural connection. As El Pilar continues to be developed utilizing the forest gardening techniques, as well as revealing portions of its existing monuments in partnership with governmental authorities, can you imagine the visitor's experience? We can, and we plan to provide the space for this unfolding.

Though this method may take time to evolve, given its organic nature, it does stand to keep dominator models at bay and allow local leadership to rise and define the process more and more. Tourism professionals and visitors alike may begin to see value in this 'process' orientation versus 'outcome' orientation. Shaded monuments, and archaeology under the canopy, is our envisaged outcome for El Pilar. This vision is compatible with and complementary to existing sites – offering a different experience for the visitors of the Maya region. El Pilar may inspire the explorer in each visitor, the piece in every person which craves to connect their interests and values to a place and its people; this is when tourism consumption shifts from being an experience of passive consumption to a reflexive experience. The old and new aspects of the site then have an opportunity to mirror their qualities for each other; the old is observed and admired, and the new is provoked and inspired. By providing ample peace and quiet for new thoughts to emerge, El Pilar stands to encourage visitors to accept greater self-responsibility at home and on tour; the connections between nature and culture can be experienced and applied elsewhere, from forests to cities, humanity just needs to remember how to take time to observe.

A Vision Forward

Natural and cultural heritage sites are an expanding theme in tourism, and the narratives of sites within these contexts emphasize discovery, novelty and adventure. Most often, however, such sites have been developed to spoon-feed the visitor without challenge. Where is the interaction with the site? As these resources are becoming more scarce and increasingly at risk (Nations, 1999; Mittermeier *et al.*, 2000), the alternative is to encourage an engagement with our surroundings. Understanding El Pilar and other such sites worldwide, one can see the application of a very basic principle: instead of wishing for what you do not have, work with what you do have, and its value and assets will expand. This is our answer, a destination where the focus is less on the drama of the elite temples and more on the holistic value of the site and its people, past and present. In our current era of excess, we are, paradoxically, experiencing that resources of the earth are increasingly scarce (Wilson, 1998, 2002; Pimm, 2001); it is our responsibility to work with and appreciate what we have: our skills, our resources, our energy, our environment. Applying this idea to El Pilar, we have come to appreciate the natural phenomenon of archaeology under the canopy where the live forest ground cover of fallen leaves, tannins and humus encases the monuments.

A century of development of the ancient Maya as worshippers at enormous temples at the expense of the whole society exaggerates the mystery and propels the distinctions that separate the rise and fall of the Maya from us. People constructed the temples and the people were thriving in the Maya forest as the civilization developed. Their mastery of the nature of the Maya forest and emergence as a civilization has been made something other than explicable. However, if we are to learn from our collective human history so as to improve life as we know it and safeguard our planet for future generations, we need to engage with the Maya myth and collapse and not continue to separate from them and merely maintain our tourist's gaze. Consider this: it has taken humanity 100 years to transform the verdant Maya forest of the early 20th century into a fraction of its coverage, putting at risk flora and fauna that abounded in ancient Maya art. Yet, when the ancient Maya thrived, they supported no less than three times and, if archaeological assertions are believable, more than nine times the population found in the region today. We are in the 21st century and need to engage with our surroundings, for it is all we have. It is time to ask the question, is there another way to depict the Maya and further appreciate their story? Our answer is resoundingly *yes*.

Ultimately, responsibility can lead a new kinship of tourism professionals and visitors to connect to their own personal narrative, their myth within the context of a strange land and other people across both space and time. A healthy future for humans, animals and plants alike depends on our awareness of lessons learned from the past and practical applications of new solutions in the present – not tomorrow. Our future depends on this self and group level of responsibility. So what threatens our newly coined term of 'Archaeology Under the Canopy' recognizing an age-old principle? Our reply – development activity wrapped in a promise of progress yet based on immediate returns. With global, regional and local recognition and support, El Pilar's inclusive model can be realized in our lifetime. Building this model into the regional Maya archaeological framework, the treatment of Maya sites can evolve and support greater diversity of visitors, educating humanity on behalf of the great Maya civilization for generations to come.

References

Adams, R.E.W. (1969) Maya archaeology 1958–1968 a review. *Latin American Research Review* 4, 3–45.

Ageton, C. (2000) *Breaking New Ground: Community Development at El Pilar, Belize.* MesoAmerican Research Center, University of Calidornia, Santa Barbara, California.

Atran, S. (1993) Itza Maya tropical agro-forestry. *Current Anthropology* 34, 633–700.

Australia ICOMOS (1976) *The Australia ICOMOS Charter for the Conservation of Places of Cultural Significance (Burra Charter).* Vol. 1999. Australia ICOMOS.

Awe, E.A. (2000a) *Regional Community Action and the El Pilar Archaeological Reserve for Maya Flora and Fauna.* Help for Progress, Belmopan, Belize.

Awe, E.A. (2000b) *Trans-boundary Initiative for Cooperative (Joint) Management of El Pilar Archaeological Reserve for Maya Flora and Fauna and the Promotion of Community Based Ecotourism and the Development of Sustainable Agricultural and Forestry Practice in Belize.* Help for Progress, Belmopan, Belize.

Awe, E.A. (2001a) *Progress Report: Creating a Livelihood at the Nexus of Culture and Nature.* Help for Progress, Belmopan, Belize.

Awe, E.A. (2001b) *The Establishment of the Consultative Council and Initial Implementation of the Strategic Plan for El Pilar.* Help for Progress, Belmopan, Belize.

Bawaya, M. (2003–2004) Archaeotourism: increasing tourism and knowledge of the Maya are the goals of a major project at a site in Belize. *American Archaeology* 7, 12–19.

Belize Ministry of Tourism and Environment (1993) *Visitor Profile Xunantunich.* Ministry of Tourism and the Environment, Belize.

Bourbon, F. (1999) *The Lost Cities of the Mayas: the Life, Art and Discoveries of Frederick Catherwood.* Abbeville Press, New York.

BRASS/El Pilar Program (2002) *Adaptive Management in the Maya Forest: the Contiguous Parks at El Pilar.* Exploring Solutions Past: the Maya Forest Alliance.

BRASS/El Pilar (2005) *Mesa Redonda Process.* BRASS/El Pilar Program http://marc.ucsb.edu/elpilar/archives/archives.html.

Brown, D.F. (1999) Mayas and tourists in the Maya world. *Human Organizations* 58, 295–303.

Campbell, D.G., Ford, A., Lowell, K.S., Walker, J., Lake, J.K., Ocampo-Raeder, C., Townesmith, A. and Balick, M.J. (2006) The feral forests of the eastern Petén. In: Erickson, C. and Baleé, W. (eds) *Time and Complexity in the Neotropical Lowlands.* Columbia University Press, New York, pp. 1–51.

Castaneda, Q.E. (1996) *In the Museum of Maya Culture: Touring Chichen Itza.* University of Minnesota Press, Minneapolis.

Castleberry, M. (ed.) (2003) *The New World's Old World: Photographic Views of Ancient America.* University of New Mexico Press, Albuquerque, New Mexico.

CIA (Central Intelligence Agency) (2005) The World Factbook Central Intelligence Agency. http://www.cia.gov/cia/publications/factbook/

CONAP (Consejo Nacional de Areas Protegidas) (2004) *Plan Maestro Monumento Cultural El Pilar En La Reserva De La Biósfera Maya.* Consejo Nacional de Areas Protegidas.

Daltabuit Godás, M., Cisneros Reyes, H., Vazquez Garcia, L.M. and Santillan Hernandez, E. (2000) *Ecoturismo y Desarrollo Sustentable: Impacto en Comunidades Rurales de la Selva Maya*. Universidad Nacional Autónoma de México Centro Regional de Investigaciones Multidisciplinarias, Cuernavaca, Morelos, Mexico.

Dye, L. (1999) Understanding the Maya: Their Rise, Their Fall, Their Way of Life. ABCNEWS.com. www.marc.ucsb.edu/clpilar/index.html

Fedick, S. (2003) In search of the Maya forest. In: Slater, C. (ed.) *In Search of the Rain Forest*. Duke University Press, Durham, North Carolina.

Fedick, S.L. and Ford, A. (1990) The prehistoric agricultural landscape of the central Maya lowlands: an examination of local variability in a regional context. *World Archaeology* 22, 18–33.

Ford, A. (1990) Population growth and development of complex societies: theoretical considerations for the evolution of the classic period Maya. In: Cameron, C. (ed.) *Agriculture: Origins and Impacts of a Technological Revolution*. Occasional Papers of the Archaeological Research Facility (5), California State University, Fullerton, California.

Ford, A. (1991) Economic variation of ancient Maya residential settlement in the upper Belize river area. *Ancient Mesoamerica* 2, 35–45.

Ford, A. (1992) The Ancient Maya Domestic Economy: an Examination of Settlement in the Upper Belize River Area. Paper presented at the Primer Congreso Internacional de Mayistas.

Ford, A. (1993) Variaciones regionales de antiguos asentamientos Maya e implicaciones económicas para el area superior del río Belice. *Mesoamérica* 25, 39–61.

Ford, A. (1996) Hidden boundaries: the El Pilar archaeological reserve for Maya flora and fauna. *Belize Magazine Belmopan* 14–19.

Ford, A. (ed.) (1998) *The Future of El Pilar: the Integrated Research & Development Plan for the El Pilar Archaeological Reserve for Maya Flora and Fauna, Belize–Guatemala*. Bureau of Oceans and International Environmental and Scientific Affairs, Washington DC.

Ford, A. (1999) Using the past to preserve the future. *Discovering Archaeology* 1, 3, 98–101.

Ford, A. (2001) El Pilar: gateway between Belize and Guatemala. *Washington Report on the Hemisphere* 21, 4–5.

Ford, A. (2004) Integration among communities, centers and regions: the case from El Pilar. In: Garber, J. (ed.) *The Ancient Maya of the Belize Valley: Half a Century of Archaeological Research*. University of Florida Press, Gainesville, Florida.

Ford, A. (2006) Adaptive management and the community at El Pilar: a philosophy of resilience for the Maya forest. In: Agnew, N. (ed.) *Out of the Past, for the Future: Integrating Archaeology and Conservation*. Getty Conservation Institute, Los Angeles, pp. 105–113.

Ford, A. and Clarke, K. (2000) UCSB Maya Forest GIS 2000. Alexandria Digital Library www.alexandria.ucsb.edu/adl/

Ford, A. and Fedick, S. (1992) Prehistoric Maya settlement – patterns in the upper Belize River area – initial results of the Belize River archaeological settlement survey. *Journal of Field Archaeology* 19, 35–49.

Ford, A. and Gerardo, N. (2001) *The Tzunu'un Forest-Garden Trail Guide*. BRASS/El Pilar Program, Cayo, Belize.

Ford, A. and Miller, C. (1994) Arqueología de acción en la selva: creación de la reserva arqueológica de El Pilar, Guatemala–Belice. *Utzib* 1, 19–21.

Ford, A. and Miller, C. (1997) *Creación de la Reserve Arqueológica El Pilar en Guatemala y Belice*. Museo Nacional de Arqueología e Ethnología, Guatemala.

Ford, A. and Montes, J.A. (1999) Medio ambiente, uso de la tierra y desarrollo sostenible: la reserva arqueológica El Pilar para flora y fauna Mayas de Belice y Guatemala. *Mesoamérica* 37, 31–50.

Ford, A. and Wernecke, D.C. (2002) *Trails of El Pilar: a Comprehensive Guide to the El Pilar Archaeological Reserve for Maya Flora and Fauna*. Exploring Solutions Past: The Maya Forest Alliance, Santa Barbara, California.

Friends for Conservation and Development (2000) *El Pilar Community Creek Trail: Life Returns to the Forest: an Interpretive Historical Trail*. Friends for Conservation and Development, Cayo, Belize

Fundacion Rescate del Bosque Tropical (2001) *Manual Práctico de Forestería Análoga*. Rimana, Quito, Ecuador.

Garrett, W. (1989) La Ruta Maya. *National Geographic* 176, 442–479.

Gaunt, F. and Estrada, A. (1995) Frontiers of ecotourism. *Santa Barbara Magazine* 21, 47–52.

Gifford, J.C. (1976) *Prehistoric Pottery Analysis and the Ceramics of Barton Ramie in the Belize Valley*. Memoirs of the Peabody Museum of Archaeology and Ethnology, Harvard University, Vol. 18. Cambridge, Massachusetts.

Gobierno de Guatemala (2004) Discurso del Señor Presidente de la República, Licenciado Oscar Berger ante la 59ª Asamblea General de Naciones Unidas. vol. 2005. Government of Guatemala http://www.guatemala.gob.gt/index.php/cms/content/view/full/415.

Golden, F. (1996) Archaeologist brings Guatemala, Belize together over Maya site. *Coastlines* 24.

Gomez, E. (1997) La zona Maya, un patrimonio conjunto. *El Nacional*, p. 42.

Government of Belize (2005) Belize–Guatemala Relations. Vol. 2005. Government of Belize http://www.belize-guatemala.gov.bz/

Gurucharri, M.C. (1996) Fragile forests and trampled temples: nature, culture and tourism in the Maya world. Paper presented at the Tourism Development and Lanscape Changes, Bangkok, Thailand.

Harris, C.H. and Sadler, L.R. (2003) *The Archaeologist Was a Spy: Sylvanus G. Morley and the Office of Naval Intelligence*. University of New Mexico Press, Albuquerque, New Mexico.

Hartke, J.A. (1995) Saving what we visit. *HSUS News* (Fall), 38–40.

Help for Progress (2004) *Forest Garden Network Workshop*. Help for Progress, Belmopan, Belize.

Honey, M. (1999) *Ecotourism and Sustainable Development: Who Owns Paradise?* Island Press, Washington DC.

ICOMOS (1964) The Venice Charter. www.international.icomos.org/e_venice.htm

Inter-American Development Bank (2003) Initiative launched to promote sustainable tourism in Mayan region of Central America. Inter-American Development Bank http://www.iadb.org/NEWS/Display/PRView.cfm?PR_Num=10/03&Language=English.

IUCN (2004) Red List: Threatened Species. http://www.redlist.org

Jokilehto, J. (1995) Authenticity: a General Framework for the Concept. Paper presented at the Nara Conference on Authenticity, Japan.

Larios Villalta, C.R. (2000a) Criterios de Restauración Arquitectónica en el Área Maya. vol. 2005. FAMSI www.famsi.org/reports/99026es/index.html.

Larios Villalta, R. (2000b) *Lineamientos Para la Conservación y Restauración Aplicables al Sitio Arqueológico el Pilar*.

LcLaulu, L. (2003) Address to the Mundo Maya Development Presentation. Paper presented on 16 February 2003.

Lundell, C.L. (1937) *The Vegetation of Petén. With an Appendix: Studies of Mexican and Central American Plants – I*. Carnegie Institution of Washington Publication no. 478. Carnegie Institution of Washington, Washington DC.

Maler, T. (1928) Bosquejo histórico del Petén-Itzá. Sociedad de Geografía e Historia e Guatemala. *Anthropological Literature* V, pp. 204–210.

Mancilla, M. and Pereiva, M. (2001) *Estudio de Capacidad de Carga de la Reserva Arquelogica El Pilar para la Flora y Fauna Maya y Estimacion de la Capacidad de Atencion Turista en la Comunidad de Bullet Tree Falls*. Help for Progress, Belmopan, Belize.

Marquis-Kile, P. and Walker, M. (1992) *The Illustrated Burra Charter*. Australian ICOMOS Inc. with the Assistance of the Australian Heritage Commission.

Matadamas, E. (1995) Patrimonio natural y cultural – El Pilar podria ser un model de conservacion en centroamerica: aunque no esta extento de riesgos. *El Universal*, pp. 1, 4.

Mittermeier, R.A., Myers, N. and Mittermeier, C.G. (2000) *Hotspots: Earth's Biologically Richest and Most Endagered Terrestrial Ecoregions*. CEMEX, Mexico.

NARA (1994) The Nara Document of Authenticity. www.international. icomos.org/naradoc_eng.htm

Nations, J.D. (ed.) (1999) *Thirteen Ways of Looking at a Tropical Forest: Guatemala's Maya Biosphere Reserve*. Conservation International, Washington DC.

Nigh, R. and Ochoa, F. (1996) Community ecotourism and organic agriculture sustainable development for Maya communities at Lake Miramar, Chiapas. Paper presented at the Workshop for the Evaluation of the Conservation of the Maya Forrest, San Cristobal de Las Casas, Chiapas.

Orphal, F. (2000) Authenticity: how can we balance the need for conserving the authenticity and the significance of the site with other potentially conflicting values? University College London Institute of Archaeology. Submitted Essay.

Osborne, M. (2000) *The Mekong: Turbulent Past, Uncertain Future*. Allen & Unwin, New York.

Perry, T.D., Breuker, M., Hernadez Duque, G. and Mitchell, R. (2004) Interaction of microorganisms with Maya archaeological materials. In: Gomez-Pompa, A., Allen, M.F., Fedick, S.L. and Jimenez-Osornio, J.J. (eds) *The Lowland Maya Area: Three Millennia at the Human Wildland Interface*. Food Products Press, New York.

Pimm, S.L. (2001) *The World According to Pimm: a Scientist Audits the Earth*. McGraw Hill, New York.

Rolex Award for Enterprise (2000) Cultural Heritage: Anabel Ford. Rolex Award. www.rolexawards.com/laureates/home_assoc.html

Roys, R. (1976) *The Ethno-botany of the Maya*. Institute for the Study of Human Issues, Philadelphia, Pennsylvania.

School of American Research (1950) *Morleyana: a Collection of Writings in Memoriam Sylvanus Griswold Morley, 1883–1948*. School of American Research and the Museum of New Mexico, Santa Fe, New Mexico.

Seelhoff, I. (1996) Maya-Steinwerkzeuge made in El Pilar. *DAMALS: Vereinigt Mit Dem Magazin Geschichte*.

Senanayake, F.R. and Jack, J. (1998) *Analogue Forestry: an Introduction 49*. Monash Publications in Geography and Environmental Science, Victoria, Australia.

Shaw, R. (2000) Maya Forest Gardens touted as conservation tool. National Geographic.com News. Available at: www.marc.ucsb.edu/elpilar/news/copied_news_items/nat-geo_forest.html

Shepard, A.O. (1964) *Ceramics for the Archaeologist*, 5th edn. Carnegie Institution of Washington, Washington DC.

Smith, R.E. (1955) *Ceramic Sequence at Uaxactun, Guatemala*, Vol. I. Middle American Research Institute Tulane University, New Orleans, Lousiana, p. 2.

Stephens, J.L. (1841) *Incidents of Travel in Central America, Chiapas and the Yucatan*. 2 Volumes. Harper & Brothers, New York.

Stephens, J.L. (1843) *Incidents of Travel in Yucatan*, 2 Volumes. Harper & Brothers, New York.

Taylor-Ide, D. and Taylor, C.E. (2002) *Just and Lasting Change: When Communites Own Their Futures*. The Johns Hopkins University Press in association with Future Generations, Baltimore, Maryland.

Thompson, J.E.S. (1960) *Maya Hieroglyphic Writing*, 3rd edn. University of Oklahoma Press, Norman, Oklahoma.

Topsey, H.W. (1995) Collaboration and cooperation in archaeology in border areas of Belize. *Public Archaeology Review* 3, 12–14.

Tzul, A. (2001) *First meeting of farming communities in the Maya Forest for the Design of an Agroforestry Model – El Pilar: Retrieving Old Traditions*. Help for Progress, Belmopan, Belize.

Von Hagen, V.W. (1973) *Search for the Maya: the Story of Stephens & Catherwood*. Gordon & Cremonesi, London.

Wang, N. (1999) Rethinking authenticity in tourism experience. *Annals of Tourism Research* 26, 349–370.

Wilhelm, K. (2004) Die Schonheit des Wildwuchses. *Frankfurter Allgemeine Zeitung*, Frankfurt, p. R5.

Willey, G.R. and Sabloff, J.A. (1975) *Excavations at Seibal, Department of Peten, Guatemala*. Peabody Museum of Archaeology and Ethnology Harvard University, Cambridge, Massachusetts.

Wilson, E.O. (1998) *Consilience: the Unity of Knowledge*. Vintage Books, New York.

Wilson, E.O. (2002) *The Future of Life*. Alfred A. Knopf, New York.

World Tourism Organization (2005) Facts and figures. www.world-tourism.org/facts/tmt.html

Yucatan Today (2005) Puuc Route. http://www.yucatantoday.com/destinations/eng-puuc-route.htm

Sensing Place, Consuming Space: Changing Visitor Experiences of the Great Barrier Reef

5

Celmara Pocock

University of Tasmania, Australia

Introduction

Almost 2 million visitors are drawn to the Great Barrier Reef each year by iconic images of pristine island beaches shaded by coconut palms, dazzling marine life and spectacular aerial vistas of deep blue seas and coral cays. The Reef is set apart from other tropical island destinations by the sheer scale of the region which stretches more than 2000 km along the north-east coast of Australia. This unique quality is recognized, encapsulated and confirmed by the listing of more than 348,000 km² as World Heritage. The Reef is thus inscribed as a single place or destination, and regarded as such by many visitors.

This understanding contrasts strongly with how the Reef was first perceived in the late 18th century. The earliest European navigators to encounter the region struggled to extricate themselves from the myriad of shoals, islands, lagoons and cays of these waters. It was through their efforts to navigate a way through this labyrinth successfully that the first cartographic images were created. Charting the Reef remained a preoccupation through most of the 19th century as the fledgling British colony sought to secure its trading and transport routes.

The navigational expeditions also provided opportunities for the earliest observations of the now famous underwater life of the Reef (Bowen and Bowen, 2002). However, it was only at the end of the 19th century that the first systematic attempts to investigate the region were undertaken with the work of William Saville-Kent (Harrison, 1997; Love, 2000, pp. 99–103; Bowen and Bowen, 2002, pp. 156–160). In the decades following the publication of his book *The Great Barrier Reef of*

©CAB International 2006. *Tourism Consumption and Representation: Narratives of Place and Self* (eds K. Meethan, A. Anderson and S. Miles)

Australia: Its Products and Potentialities (Saville-Kent, 1893), a host of naturalists, including those from the British and Australian Museums, undertook a number of large-scale expeditions to investigate marine and island flora and fauna.

The escalation in scientific activity at the Reef led to unprecedented public exposure of the region through popular magazine, journal and newspaper articles. The scientific expeditions also offered amateur naturalists and holidaymakers an opportunity to visit the Reef for themselves. Tourism thus emerged alongside scientific discovery, and these experiences are narrated through diaries, journals, letters, photographs, albums, scrap books, home movies, newsreels, advertisements, shell collections and coral displays. This wealth of material makes it possible to reconstruct visitor experiences of place and space throughout the 20th century (Pocock, 2002a).

Place and Space

Place is understood in everyday language to be nothing other than a particular locality. It is used in this way in relation to tourism destinations, and hence the Reef is often referred to as a 'place'. However, place is more than mere locality or geographic reference. This long-standing philosophical debate is increasingly considered within anthropology, geography and other disciplines concerned with human relationships to place and space (Augé, 1995; Casey, 1996; Kahn, 1996). It is also timely to consider this in relation to tourism which is assumed to be 'place' based (Urry, 1995; Bærenholdt *et al.*, 2004, pp. 4–5).

Philosophy has traditionally created a dualism between place and space, and defined space as the abstract, prior concept in which particular places are inscribed. Within this division, most would agree that space is the general and absolute category while place is that which is imbued with social meaning. Thus Augé (1995) defines 'anthropological place' to emphasize the human association of the term. The inter-relationship between place and human knowledge is also the basis of an extended review and argument by Casey (1996). In contrast to the commonly held position that space is prior and abstract, he makes a convincing argument that in human experience it is in fact place that precedes space, and that human beings are always emplaced. These ideas parallel those of Ingold (2000, pp. 198–201) who maintains that people are inscribed in the landscape, and do not merely ascribe meanings to it.

The integration of people in landscapes and places highlights the physicality of place and the importance of orientation and location. It is impossible to know or sense a place except by being *in* it, and the primary means of emplacement is through orientation of the body. Orientation stems from bilateral awareness; of left and right, and other relative positions such as up/down and front/behind. Each of these is a specific referent of the conscious human body, and as such orientation is the first aspect of a sensuous knowledge of place (Tuan, 1977; Rodaway, 1994, pp. 31–34; Casey, 1996, p. 18). Geometric or Cartesian location is complementary to the configuration of spatial elements in place. Spatial forms include lines, intersections of lines and points of intersections. These are the paths, crossroads and open spaces in everyday life and are neither static nor mutually exclusive. Fixed points are part of routes, journeys take people through multiple centres, and centres themselves form and collapse in response to particular events and circumstances (Augé, 1995, pp. 56–57). This mobility is especially important in tourism, which is dependent on the differences between places and the travel between them (Ingold, 2000; Bærenholdt *et al.*, 2004).

Mobility also highlights place as both spatial and temporal (Augé, 1995; Ingold, 2000; Bender, 2002; Bærenholdt *et al.*, 2004, p. 7). All places have the capacity to contain animate and inanimate entities which include a variety of objects or physical elements without which place ceases to exist (Casey, 1996, pp. 24–26; Ingold, 2000, p. 200). Significantly, however, they also include experiences, memories, histories, language and thoughts. The temporal sequences through which these are ordered in human experience allows the (re)presentation of places to be controlled and understood, and for different people to build their own particular sense of place from the same location (Casey, 1996). Place is thus derived from the particular way that localities are described and narrated in time and space.

As places are constituted though social interpretations of physical elements and time, the prerequisite to knowledge of place is to be *in* place. Thus it is through the lived body that time and space are encapsulated in place (Casey, 1996). The body is intelligent about the specifics of place and hence the knowing subject is central to particular and personal places (Taussig, 1993; Casey, 1996, Grace, 1996). Local knowledge of place is appropriate to the particular qualities of place and is consistent with the sensuous properties and cultural characteristics of that place. This knowledge derives from a range of senses including sight, sound, touch, taste, smell and the interaction of these through the sensate moving body. In other words, through the lived body, the knowing subject perceives the particularities of any given place (Casey, 1996, p. 44).

Hence all places are simultaneously spatial, temporal and cultural. A tourist destination cannot be understood as a place without people being oriented in a particular location and engaging sensuously with its particular physical attributes to build personal and temporal narratives. It is this configuration of place that is used to understand changing visitor experiences of the Great Barrier Reef.

Reef Tourism Now and Then

In spite of the enormity of the Great Barrier Reef World Heritage Area and the large numbers of tourists that visit the region each year, nearly all tourist activity is confined to a very small geographic area (Great Barrier Reef Marine Park Authority, 2005). Most tourists visit one of two major tourism regions; the islands and reefs in the vicinity of Cairns and Port Douglas in the far north and the Whitsunday island group towards the southern end, near Proserpine (Fig. 5.1). The less frequented areas of the Reef are either those locations where camping is permitted or the high end luxury resorts. The former are rarely promoted, are controlled by government agencies and are largely unprofitable. The latter are the preserve of the truly rich and famous including high profile Hollywood stars and political leaders.

The vast majority of tourists to the Reef use facilities based on islands or in mainland centres such as Airlie Beach adjacent to the Whitsundays, and Cairns and Port Douglas in the north. Those who visit the islands inevitably stay in holiday resorts of an international standard where rooms include air-conditioning, private bathrooms, comfortable beds, televisions, mini-bars and other hotel conveniences. Communal areas feature swimming pools, restaurants, bars, spas and souvenir shops. Resorts also offer a range of activities either as part of their own service or in association with other tourism operators in the region. Resort-based activities include motorized and non-motorized water sports, golf, tennis, beach volley-ball, and bird and fish feeding. More wide-ranging activities tend to be associated with trips to the Outer Reef, and include snorkelling and scuba diving, helicopter and seaplane rides, and skydiving. It is through these facilities and locations that we can best understand how the majority of contemporary tourists experience the Great Barrier Reef.

These same regions, the islands and reefs off Cairns and the Whitsundays, have been tourist destinations since the beginning of the 20th century (Barr, 1990; Blackwood, 1997; King, 1998; Bowen and Bowen, 2002; Pocock, 2003). Despite this continuity, past visitor experiences of these locations stand in stark contrast to those of today.

Early Reef tourists comprised locals from the adjacent mainland who used the Whitsunday islands for holidays. By the late 1920s and early 1930s, visitors accompanying scientific expeditions travelled from southern states of Victoria and New South Wales, as well as from other parts of Queensland. These early visitors included professional and amateur scientists, journalists, photographers, film-makers, writers and artists, as well as amateur enthusiasts from medical, legal and teaching professions. While some were expressly holidaymakers, almost all accompanied voyages as a leisure activity. This early development in tourism was fostered by a number of family-operated businesses in the

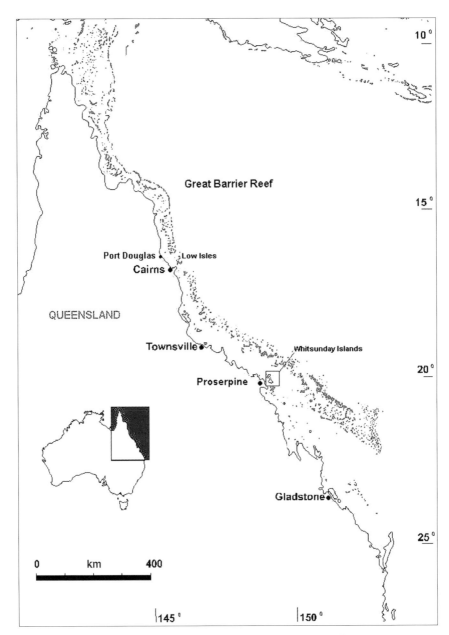

Fig. 5.1. Representational location map of the Great Barrier Reef.

Whitsundays. Island families were primarily pastoralists, and they provided access to the islands as an additional source of income. Initially visitors were self-sufficient, but as tourist numbers increased some basic purpose-built accommodation was constructed.

A school teacher from New South Wales, Mont Embury, was one of the first to organize large-scale group visits to the Great Barrier Reef islands. He first ran a number of campsites on coral cays, and was later successful in gaining a lease on Hayman Island where he established the first island resort in the region in 1932. All his ventures were undertaken in association with scientists from the Australian Museum and a number of amateur naturalists. His expeditions were particularly popular with women school teachers who enjoyed the group activities, including the educational component that stemmed from their participation in scientific investigations. Like other island expeditions and holidays, the Embury expeditions provided very basic facilities. Holidaymakers slept in tents, bathed in the sea and ate fish they caught. Like fishing, fossicking on exposed reefs for shell and coral specimens was a very popular activity. Evening amusements included lectures and lantern slide presentations about scientific enquiry and discovery, as well as singing and storytelling around camp fires.

Records from these early times are surprisingly rich. There are many letters, diaries and notebooks from scientists and holidaymakers, as well as published accounts in books, journal and magazine articles, and newspaper stories. The enquiring and experimental nature of scientific activities created an environment in which recording techniques were also used extensively. Still and motion photography were both applied, tested and extended in these contexts (Pocock 2004). Consequently, the Reef is well represented in photographic images from the earliest times. These images record not only the diversity of marine life, but also the environments, activities and people involved in early tourism. They were reproduced in many magazines and journals, and also formed an important component of many private collections. Personal photograph albums are carefully composed. They include hand-drawn maps of localities visited, detailed captions, and carefully selected and chronologically arranged images. As such, they provide strong narratives that complement the written records. These are used to reconstruct past experiences that can be compared with contemporary tourism to provide an understanding of changing perceptions of place and space at the Great Barrier Reef during the 20th century (Pocock, 2002a).

Narratives of Reef Places

The early visitors who accompanied scientific expeditions, and even those who travelled aboard cruise ships or stayed in early holiday accommodation at the Reef, inevitably encountered the physicality of the local environments. Journeys to the Reef were as much a part of the visitor experience as being at the Reef itself. These journeys were long and slow, usually taking several days to travel from a southern city by rail or ship. Holidaymakers were then transferred to the islands by way of launch, often enduring rough weather, cold and seasickness. The temporal and spatial duration of these journeys ensured that even the most impervious travellers were aware of their distance from home. Visitors also developed an awareness of the spatial relationship between different locations or destinations within the region. They were usually based at a particular island camp from which they made shorter journeys to other islands and, weather and tides permitting, the Outer Reef. Early visitors thus came to know particular localities and their relative geographic positions. Narratives of these journeys recorded in diaries, maps and photographs suggest that visitors had a strong sense of orientation. Photograph albums include maps that show routes travelled, and captioned photographs detail compass directions, landmarks and other geographical features that indicate a clear consciousness of locality. The narratives of these journeys also reflect on earlier navigations, particularly the voyage of Captain James Cook, so that visitor experiences were complemented by a sense of history. Temporality also formed an integral element of the trips through the nature of tourist mobility; the slow speed of transport; the long distances travelled; and the duration of the holidays which were often weeks rather than days long.

The length and duration of the journeys and visits meant that many excursions were scheduled for the December to January holiday period, the longest in Australia. At this time of year, the region is at its warmest and most humid. A newspaper reported that the expeditioners at Low Isles 'sank slowly into a sort of melting decay under the savage heat of a humid summer' (*Sydney Morning Herald*, 1928). Visitors lived outdoors so they were frequently stung and bitten by insects and 'sandflies and mosquitoes left a trail of woe and drove many from shorts into long trousers' (Wigmore, 1933). These were not always comfortable trips, but the cost was worth the reward of the experience, so that the story of the Low Isles expedition concluded that 'there are such a lot of delightful things to be collected in the place that they put up with the inconveniences' (*Sydney Morning Herald*, 1928).

Many pleasurable holiday impressions also derived from a range of physical experiences encountered in everyday activities. Holidaymakers slept outdoors – on sandy beaches, in tents or on the purpose-built verandahs of the Embury headquarters. The darkness and dwindling human activity at night heightened these visitors' awareness of non-visual sensations. The smells and sounds of the island environments became acutely conspicuous. Casuarinas were especially valued for their gentle sighing in the evening breezes and became a strongly evocative sound for many Reef visitors (Pocock, 2002b). Holidaymakers also wrote of 'the leafy smell of luxuriant vegetation' (Stainton, 1933), and of flocks of birds 'heard wailing and shrieking at night' (Gilbert, 1926).

Visitors' waking hours were equally sensuously informed. They washed and swam in the sea, enjoying the novelty of warm tropical waters. Fishing was enjoyed for its own sake, but without refrigeration fish catches contributed to many breakfasts, lunches and dinners. Turtle also constituted an unusual and characteristic food source of particular voyages. As part of capturing their food and in a range of other activities, visitors interacted with objects and life forms of the islands and reefs. They spent most of the daylight hours in pursuit of naturalist activities such as bird watching, counting and tagging, and egg collecting. However, it was the spectacle of coral reefs and fishes that was recounted with greatest awe and excitement. '[T]he incredible, blazing beauty of coral hues of every conceivable shade and color [*sic*], and of infinitely varied structure such as no human mind could conceive, leaps to the eyes. It is a shock that electrifies the imagination' (Wigmore, 1932). As brilliant as the Reef appeared, underwater life could only be glimpsed in the still pools left on the exposed reefs at high tide. Consequently, the living reef was also experienced through pursuits other than gazing. Holidaymakers assisted and mimicked scientific investigations to collect many specimens of corals and shells. The tactile interactions of turtle riding, catching slithering slippery reef slugs and fishes, breaking off hard and spiky corals, and cautiously handling venomous cone shells were all part of the experience of being at the Reef.

> [O]ne could easily fill pages with untechnical ravings about the loveliness of the marvellous burrowing clams, the queer thrill of holding a little cat shark up by his tail, and the collecting mania which seems to descend on everyone paddling among the pools and coral boulders.
>
> (Stainton, 1933)

Access to the reef was generally restricted to times of low tide. So fossicking and collecting took place when the corals were exposed to the air and gave off a 'faint odour of things of the sea', which was regarded as part of its 'very special character' (Council for Scientific and Industrial Research, 1936). The smells of shells and corals also became potent through the process of preserving them. Coral and shell collections were boiled in tins on the shore, while other specimens were left to dry in the sun.

> Branches of various corals were taken ashore, boiled and bleached, while to camp were brought shells of many kinds, in varying stages of decomposition, causing at least some variety to the disagreeable odour of the guano from the seabirds.
>
> (Pollock, 1926)

As early visitors developed their knowledge of the life forms of the Reef, they also came to know the habitats of species and the individual reefs that were home to their most prized prey. Consequently, they knew not only the islands as localities, but also particular reefs and lagoons.

They were thus aware of the Reef as a complex of individual reefs. This knowledge of location and orientation was also enhanced by their knowledge of the Australian colonial past. Their awareness of navigational histories is testified by many accounts that make reference to landmarks, and passages named and encountered by the earlier navigators. Visitors were acutely aware of the relative dangers of the Outer Reef as positioned in narratives about the courage and skill of Captain James Cook. Hence the routes he navigated among the islands and shoals, and the opening in the outer barrier through which he eventually sailed, are particularly significant and duly noted.

The collections of corals and shells played an important role in the construction of Reef places that extended beyond these immediate sensory encounters. Extensive collections of shells and corals, together with smaller collections of photographs, were an important means of constructing holiday narratives. By taking these collections home from the Reef, visitors were able to relate their experiences to those who had not shared the journey. However, they were also used to reinforce the group relationships of the holidaymakers. The living conditions and modes of travel enforced a strong sense of cohesion among the members of parties who visited the Reef at any particular time. There were certainly some annoyances and disagreements, but the friendships formed were most often related as a positive and central part of the experience. Newspaper advertisements of the time indicate that 'reefers' held reunions in cities such as Sydney as a means to maintain friendships and to share their knowledge of the Reef. These occasions provided an opportunity to reinforce narratives through repetition, refinement and embellishment of stories, and through sharing photographs. Some visitors, especially the amateur naturalists, returned to the same Reef locations each year, thus reinforcing the highly social and temporal nature of these visits.

These accounts and their transmission through time indicate that visitors gained a fully embodied experience of the particular locations they visited. They were consciously embodied and oriented, with their own sense of history and time and space. Their encounters produced sensory knowledge that was particular to the locations they visited and shared and narrated with fellow travellers. As such, their experiences can be understood as contributing to a knowledge of place. This kind of knowledge was significantly diminished as the 20th century progressed.

Agents of Change

The impetus for change at the Reef came from a combination of forces, including the emergence of a formal tourism industry in Australia, a colonial desire to realize paradise on earth, the rise of environmental ideologies, and advances in technology (Pocock 2003, 2005).

The economic potential of Australian tourism was recognized in the first decades of the 20th century and resulted in coordinated efforts to attract tourists and promote Australia overseas (Davidson and Spearritt, 2000). The American market was regarded as particularly lucrative, and there was a push by organizations such as the Australian National Travel Association to match promotion with the provision of suitable accommodation and other facilities. The informal arrangements in areas such as the Whitsundays were seen as inadequate for these lucrative overseas markets. Tourism all but ceased in the region during the Second World War but, following its resumption, there was a slow, but persistent trend towards more organized and uniform tourism amenities on Reef islands (Barr, 1990). In this period, a commissioned report made a number of recommendations for change (Queensland Tourist Development Board, 1947). Improvements included transport infrastructure and the provision of comfortable accommodation, meals and entertainment. The structures became more substantial and fully enclosed, screening out heat and insects. Swimming pools were constructed on islands from the 1950s onwards. By the end of the 20th century, every resort offered freshwater showers, restaurants and air-conditioning. Such amenities have even become common on pontoons anchored in lagoons on the Outer Reef. The beaches adjacent to the resorts are swept clean of seaweed and other debris to avoid any unpleasant odours.

While some of these improvements were introduced to minimize the extreme discomforts and inconveniences of an earlier era, their particular physical manifestation was shaped by an imaginary ideal. The idea of paradise on earth had become synonymous with tropical islands since the European discovery of the Pacific islands (Smith, 1992; Grove, 1995; Sheller, 2001). Although a distortion of Pacific culture and environment, selected and stereotyped elements such as hula skirts and coconut palms came to signify paradise on earth. In spite of the Australian bush character of the Reef islands, early visitors imagined themselves to be travelling to a tropical location. They were excited when they encountered a coconut palm, and were disappointed if they did not (Pocock, 2005). The power of this imaginary was such that as facilities were upgraded on Reef islands, accommodation, activities and gardens were designed to meet this Pacific ideal. Thus, the coconut palm, which is thought to have been introduced to Australia after European colonization, became widely represented in those areas frequented by visitors. Coconut palms and other introduced species thus gradually replaced the native bush in the vicinity of tourist facilities, to provide a visual symbol of both tropical location and tourist status (Pocock, 2005).

The changes on Reef islands were matched by equally significant changes in access to the underwater reefs. The earliest visitors were only able to peer into coral pools at low tide, or see glimpses of corals and fishes through the restricted lens of a water telescope or glass-bottomed boats. These were voyeuristic views, restricted by tides and weather. However, technological and engineering innovation in the second half of the century changed this perpendicular view to one that was more participatory. In the 1950s, underwater viewing chambers were constructed on Hook Island in the Whitsundays and Green Island near Cairns. These submerged chambers allowed visitors to climb down below the surface to view the surrounding corals and fishes through small glass portholes in the sides of the structure. While this was a view from below the surface, visitors remained separated from the underwater world. The chambers relied on marine life to accumulate around and swim past the fixed glass panels. This was a static view in which the human audience was passive and physically distant. More kinaesthetic experiences of the underwater world were not readily available until the advent of diving and snorkelling as tourist activities.

Some early scientists had experimented with diving goggles from the early 1920s, but the use of facemasks and snorkels to view the Reef only became popular in the late 1960s and 1970s. With this simple technology, swimmers are able to view the living reefs while immersed in the water. By making short duck dives underwater, it is possible to move as one with the underwater world. Such short forays have been extended and enhanced through modern aqualung equipment. Diving in this way, visitors take their own air supply with them and are able to remain underwater for longer and swim to greater depths. A stream of inventions continues to increase visitor participation. Technology has also increased the spatial access to the Reef. A range of rapid transport ferries passengers to various islands and a number of locations on the Outer Reef. The Outer Reef is historically the most dangerous part of the Reef and was rarely accessible to visitors for a large part of the 20th century. However, the installation of semi-permanent pontoons in lagoons of outlying reefs makes it possible to visit the Outer Reef in all but the very worst of weather conditions. These pontoons act as small artificial islands and so make it possible to dive or snorkel in the reef wall of the surrounding lagoon.

While contemporary tourists enjoy easy access to the Reef and have a greater sense of participation and immersion underwater, other forms of access have been diminished. Embodied access has been heavily affected by a conservation ideology that gained sway towards the end of the 20th century. As early as the 1920s, the negative impact of collecting on shell and coral populations had been noted as a problem. The diminished populations of particular species posed a threat to continuing scientific collecting, and it was this rather than the protection of species for their own sake that was raised as a problem. Environmental concerns as we now understand them only emerged as a strong political issue in Australia during the 1960s and 1970s. One of the most significant environmental campaigns of this time was the 'battle' to protect the Great Barrier Reef (Wright, 1977). The push to ban developments and extractive activities such as mining and oil exploration culminated in the creation of the Great Barrier Reef Marine Park in 1975, and the listing of the region as World Heritage in 1981. The management of the region is now oriented towards the conservation of the region's natural attributes. This has brought numerous restrictions on various human activities including not only development and mining, but also existing practices of tourists and scientists. In particular, there has been a radical shift from touching, tasting, collecting and watching reef life to a focus on singularly visual experiences and photographic collecting.

The emphasis on visual rather than sensory encounters is not simply a response to a conservation agenda. It has also been made possible and desirable through advances in visual reproductive technologies (Pocock, in press). There were numerous and considerable developments in photography during the 20th century. Underwater cameras, colour emulsion, motion film, microscopic and time-lapse photography, aerial and satellite imagery have all been employed in the representation of the Reef. As these technologies became more affordable, they also became available to many more individuals. Tourists therefore use photography to capture, collect and order their own memories and narratives of the Reef. Furthermore, photography is a particularly effective medium because of the perception of contact between the subject and the photograph (Sontag, 1973; Taussig, 1993). This perception of a continuing association with the original makes photography analogous to collecting and, to some extent, photographs have been able to fulfil some of the functions of the shell and coral collections (Pocock, in press). However, unlike collecting and fossicking, photography is more clearly focused on exclusively visual qualities, and it is this that characterizes contemporary Reef experiences.

Reef Space

Changes to facilities, transport, technology, access and ideology significantly altered the way in which tourists engaged with environments of the Great Barrier Reef region during the 20th century. Transport to, from and within the region is high speed, and it is no longer necessary to spend a long time at the Reef. Many visitors only stay for a day or two. The journeys, although shorter, are now regarded as something to be endured rather than constituting an integral part of the experiences. This is suggested by the kinds of entertainment provided on board the catamarans that ferry passengers between island locations and Outer Reef pontoons. Like many commercial flights, voyages to the islands or Outer Reef region are accompanied by the screening of television programmes and documentaries. Tourists subsequently pay little attention to any specific route travelled or the particular geographic location that they visit.

Like the transport, accommodation, dining and entertainment facilities at Reef resorts are largely air-conditioned. Contemporary tourists now spend considerable periods indoors where air-conditioning screens out not only heat and humidity, but also the sounds and smells of the environment. On the beachfronts close to the resorts, seaweed and other debris are swept from the sand each day, eliminating some of the characteristic odours of the sea and Reef. The predominant smells around the resorts come from sunscreen lotion, fried foods and chlorinated water. While amplified music eclipses many sounds particular to the locality, the resort landscaping further excludes many sounds native to the locality. The areas most commonly used by tourists are those in the immediate vicinity of the resorts. The landscapes in these areas have been dramatically transformed to create lush tropical gardens that exclude much of the local vegetation. Consequently, many of the associated sensations are also lost. For instance, the sound of casuarinas that was once integral to holidaymakers' experiences has largely been displaced (Pocock, 2002b). Even where the trees still grow, their gentle whispering is rarely perceptible above noises of the resort. As one long time tour operator noted, the sigh of the casuarinas is 'infinitely more subtle than the rustle of palm fronds' (McLean, 1986, p. 2) which now dominate the resorts.

Some of the most elemental experiences of island holidays have also been diminished. Almost all contemporary resorts offer at least one swimming pool, and sunbathing tourists line the edges of these chlorinated lagoons only metres from the warm tropical sea and white sand beaches. Very few resort guests swim in the salt water or feel the sand beneath their feet. Rather than experiencing the particular physical characteristics of the place, the location is predominantly a visual backdrop to the resort gardens and pool areas. This displacement of the particular by the generic in accommodation, environment, gardens and pools renders contemporary island experiences displaced rather than emplaced.

Tourists are buffered from sounds, smells, tastes and even the visual qualities particular to the landscapes of the Reef, and this is also true of tourist knowledge of the living Reef. In spite of the greater access afforded by various diving technologies, contemporary tourists engage with the underwater world in a form of disoriented embodiment. A number of operators offer voyages to fringing reefs or even the Outer Reef. The destination is usually a semi-permanent pontoon or a particular reef where the operator is permitted to take tourists.

However, the rapidity of transport and its focus away from the surrounding environment ensures that visitors barely identify the route travelled, the particular location visited or its relationship to points of origin or departure.

On arrival at an Outer Reef destination, it is notionally possible for visitors to swim wherever they like. However, the very deep water and strong currents in these areas make it unsafe to do so, and visitors are guided by ropes and floatation devices while lifeguards watch over them. Diving is similarly guided and structured by trained staff. These necessary safety measures ensure that tourists' experiences are confined to very particular areas. There is a loss of location and orientation at the Outer Reef, and the artificial pontoons become the sole reference point. So although tourists have readier and more frequent access to the Outer Reef than in the past, they continue to engage with only small parts of the whole. Unlike tourists in the past, however, contemporary visitors have much less awareness of the spatial relationships within or between these particular localities. Even the broad distinction between fringing reefs and the Outer Reef is sometimes deliberately blurred in a competitive tourism market.

The sensory experiences of floating and free-diving are now shared by many more visitors than in the past. However, humans only have limited ability to acquire a full range of sensory data underwater. It is particularly difficult to smell or taste anything within the confines of a silicone-rimmed face mask. The exception is the concentration of salt water which eventually numbs the lips and tongue. The experiences of the underwater are thus disoriented and of limited sensory capacity. Together with the prohibition on touching Reef life, these experiences are inevitably dominated by visual experience.

In contemporary Reef tourism, there is also a loss of sociality. While holidays are largely social activities, most contemporary tourists travel in couples, family groups or small groups of friends. While individuals may come to know one another on these voyages, for the most part the experience remains contained within existing social relationships. There is certainly no group cohesion of the kind noted in earlier times. While there are exceptions to these patterns, particularly for young backpackers and people who might sail in the area for instance, the vast majority of Reef tourists are now much more fragmented even when they are part of large groups. Entertainment, meals and activities can all be undertaken alone or in the company of particular friends and partners. Tourists come and go at different times, and few stay for very long so that there is little common time among disparate groups of travellers. Even on day trips to the Outer Reef, the time spent together is short and the provision of videos makes conversation unnecessary. It is even difficult to share underwater discoveries with anyone unfamiliar because snorkelling and diving gear limits communication. On return to the resort, individuals and groups return to their self-contained accommodation and eat their own meals at a time convenient to them.

In this way, it is possible to see that contemporary tourist experiences of travel, islands and underwater life at the Great Barrier Reef do not contribute to a sense of place. In spite of a range of technologies that increase access and participation, and the role of conservation in preserving aspects of the physical environment, visitor knowledge and experience of place have been diminished. Tourists now have little sense of orientation, location, time, history, social cohesion, or local sensory knowledge that is particular to being at the Reef. This constitutes a loss of place and a reversion to space in contemporary knowledge of the Reef. Furthermore, tourist experiences focus on forms of visual consumption that allow the Reef to be misconceived.

Visual Consumption

Photography has changed how the Reef is perceived, understood and experienced by visitors. While conservation favours visual engagement in preference to other forms of sensuous encounter, visual experiences of the Reef are themselves increasingly removed from personal engagement. Many of the Reef images most commonly pedalled through advertisements, documentaries and postcards are beyond the physical capacity of human experience. However, photography is a particularly potent conveyer of 'reality', and hence these images are regarded as equivalent to human experience.

The complex of islands, cays, shoals and lagoons that comprises the region is only understood as a single 'place' or destination through visual representation. This is not the way in which the Reef is experienced as a place or series of places constructed through direct embodied engagement. The first means through which the complexity of geographical features was envisaged as a single entity was through the imagined bird's eye view of early cartography. It was through these constructions that Matthew Flinders first coined the term 'the great barrier reefs'. Even this suggests a plurality that is not present in the contemporary appellation: the imagined conceptual whole that makes the Great Barrier Reef a unique phenomenon and has gained greater credence through advances in photography. Satellite images show the Reef as an enormous, endless geographic feature as though this is a view or experience that is available to the human eye.

Similarly, other visual images that purport to represent the experience of being at the Reef are not possible through personal experience. For instance, brightly coloured underwater corals are more vivid when filmed at night than during the day when most people view the Reef. Images of microscopic life, including the spawning of coral polyps, is only truly understood through the intimate and close-up footage of sophisticated microphotography. Nevertheless, the magical quality of photography that is underscored by a sense of connection or contact between the original and that which has been copied (Sontag, 1973; Taussig, 1993) gives these images strong currency in tourists' own visits. Photography now provides experiences of the Reef that are not possible in person, but which nevertheless are as meaningful for those who have visited it and those who have not. Tourists make reference to secondary representations of the Reef rather than their own experience. This is further inverted in that the fulfilment of tourist expectations is made analogous with secondary forms of representation such as motion films and aquaria. In commenting on her first dive at the Great Barrier Reef, Karen Miller recalled 'many mixtures of parrotfish and butterfly fish, which always remind me of aquarium fish' (Miller, 2001). The visual images are the same whether you have been *there* or not.

While such analogies are not uncommon in relating contemporary experiences more generally, it is the disoriented nature of many contemporary Reef experiences that facilitates the effectiveness of visual consumption. Without the particularities of location and place, selected elements of Reef life can act as symbols of *the* Great Barrier Reef. In the way that coconut palms have come to represent the tropics and paradise on earth (Pocock, 2005), any singular coral pool or a part of a particular reef has come to represent the Great Barrier Reef as a whole. Whereas people once understood their particular location within the geographic region of the Great Barrier Reef, the way in which coral vignettes act as synecdoches of the Reef allows any part of the Reef to represent the whole which is only constructed through visual representation. The underwater gardens mimic the idealized tropical island in this construction in that the colourful butterfly fish and coral gardens reflect the colourful butterflies and gardens of a tropical paradise. Together, these produce a single commodity which is neither emplaced nor embodied, but is a fusion of visual symbols.

The way in which the Reef is experienced by tourists through particular visual imagery is not simply the result of an aggressive tourism industry. It has arisen through a complex mix of colonial imagination, technological invention, changing ideology and scientific specialization. Photographic imagery has been particularly effective in realizing different aspects of these diverse agendas. However, this imagery remains outside the construction of place. Photographs play an integral role in the anticipation and realization of contemporary Reef experiences. While Bærenholdt *et al.* (2004) suggest that such anticipation is part of the experience of place, the anticipation and experiences arising from Reef imagery do not constitute local knowledge of place, but constitute a highly symbolized space. Some early Reef visitors were disappointed when they first encountered Reef islands that did not fulfil their imagined destination, and almost all suffered some form of discomfort or another. However, they often discovered new paths to knowledge of their particular holiday places that surpassed their own imagining. For instance, the journalist Wigmore, who observed the initial trail of woe among early visitors to the Reef, also recounted the joys of the same holidaymakers as they came to know their particular location and what it had to offer during the ensuing days. Such transformations and constructions of particular places through tourists' own embodied experiences are seldom encountered by contemporary Reef tourists. Contemporary tourists enjoy facilities that are luxurious and comfortable, and are provided with visual imagery symbolic of the Reef as a single unique destination, but not a place understood in time and space.

Acknowledgements

The research for this project was made possible through the financial support of the Cooperative Research Centre for the Great Barrier Reef World Heritage Area. I would like to thank colleagues at James Cook University and the University of Tasmania for discussions in the development of the research. Particular thanks to Dr Marion. Stell and Dr David Collett.

References

Augé, M. (1995) *Non-Places: Introduction to an Anthropology of Supermodernity.* Verso, London.
Bærenholdt, J.O., Haldrup, M., Larsen, J. and Urry, J. (2004) *Performing Tourist Places: New Directions in Tourism Analysis.* Ashgate, Aldershot, UK
Barr, T. (1990) *No Swank Here? The Development of the Whitsundays as a Tourist Destination to the Early 1970s: Studies in North Queensland History.* James Cook University, Townsville, Australia.
Bender, B. (2002) Time and landscape. *Current Anthropology* 43 (Supplement), S103–S112.
Blackwood, R. (1997) *Whitsunday Islands: an Historical Dictionary,* Central Queensland University Press, Rockhampton, Australia.
Bowen, J. and Bowen, M.J. (2002) *The Great Barrier Reef: History, Science, Heritage.* Cambridge University Press, Cambridge, UK.
Casey, E.S. (1996) How to get from Space to Place in a fairly short stretch of time: phenomenological prolegomena. In: Feld, S. and Basso, K. (eds) *Senses of Place.* School of American Research Press, Santa Fe, New Mexico, pp. 13–52.
Council for Scientific and Industrial Research (1926) Note for paper on the Great Barrier Reef of Australia, to be read before the Manchester Geographical Society on 7 December 1926 Commonwealth Government

Records). *National Archives of Australia* A8510 (A8510/1), 201/8 (Canberra), pp. 1–25.

Davidson, J. and Spearritt, P. (2000) *Holiday Business: Tourism in Australia Since 1870*. Melbourne University Press, Melbourne, Australia.

Gilbert, P.A. (1926) Women naturalists on North-West Island. *The Australian Woman's Mirror*. 5 January, p. 9. (Australia Museum AMS 139, Box 32).

Grace, H. (1996) Introduction: aesthesia and the economy of the senses. In: Grace, H. (ed.) *Aesthesia and the Economy of the Senses*. University of Western Sydney, Kingswood, Australia, pp. 1–15.

Great Barrier Reef Marine Park Authority (2005) Tourism on the Great Barrier Reef (cited 7 January 2005). Available from http://www.gbrmpa.gov.au/corp_site/key_issues/tourism/tourism_on_gbr.html

Grove, R. (1995) *Green Imperialism: Colonial Expansion, Tropical Island Edens and the Orgins of Environmentalism, 1600–1860*. Cambridge University Press, Cambridge, UK.

Harrison, A.J. (1997) *Savant of the Australian Seas: William Saville-Kent (1845–1908) and Australian Fisheries*. Tasmanian Historical Research Association, Hobart, Tasmania.

Ingold, T. (2000) *The Perception of the Environment: Essays on Livelihood, Dwelling and Skill*. Routledge, London.

Kahn, M. (1996) Your place and mine: sharing emotional landscapes in Wamira, Papua New Guinea. In: Feld, S. and Basso, K.H. (eds) *Senses of Place*. School of American Research Press, Santa Fe, New Mexico, pp. 167–196.

King, B. (1998) *Creating Island Resorts*. Routledge, London.

Love, R. (2000) *Reefscape: Reflections on the Great Barrier Reef*. Allen & Unwin, St Leonards, Australia.

McLean, G. (1986) *Captain Tom*. Boolarong Publications, Mackay, Australia.

Miller, K. (2001) The Great Barrier Reef, a Dive Come True (on-line document). Naples Daily News, Wednesday, 12 September (cited 5 February 2002). Available from http://www.marcodailynews.com/01/09/marco/a1419a.htm.

Pocock, C. (2002a) Identifying social values in archival sources: change, continuity and invention in tourist experiences of the Great Barrier Reef. In: Gomes, V., Pinto, T. and das Neves, L. (eds) *The Changing Coast*. Eurocoast/EUCC Porto, Portugal, pp. 281–290.

Pocock, C. (2002b) Sense matters: aesthetic values of the Great Barrier Reef. *International Journal of Heritage Studies* 8, 365–381.

Pocock, C. (2003) Romancing the Reef: History, Heritage and the Hyper-Real. Unpublished PhD Thesis, James Cook University, Townsville, Australia.

Pocock, C. (2004) Real to reel reef: space, place and film at the Great Barrier Reef. In: Ferrero-Regis, T. and Moran A. (eds), *Placing the Moving Image*. Griffith University, Brisbane, pp. 53–68.

Pocock, C. (2005) Blue lagoons and coconut palms: the creation of a tropical idyll in Australia. *Australian Journal of Anthropology* 16, 335–349.

Pocock, C. (in press) Photography and tourism on the Great Barrier Reef. In: Picard, D. and Robinson, M. (eds) *Tourism and Photography: Aesthetics. Performance, Memoryalisation of Peoples and Places*.

Pollock, E.F. (1926) The naturalist: expedition to the Capricorns: birds and turtles. No. 2. *The Australasian*. 23 January, p. 227. (Australia Museum AMS 139, Box 32).

Queensland Tourist Development Board (1947) *Report on the Tourist Resources of Queensland and the Requirements for Their Development*. Ferguson, E.A., Harvey, J.P., Byrne, F.P. and Rogers, W.A. (eds). Government Printers, Brisbane, Australia.

Rodaway, P. (1994) *Sensuous Geographies: Body, Sense, and Place*. Routledge, London.

Saville-Kent, W. (1893) *The Great Barrier Reef of Australia: its Products and Potentialities*. W.H. Allen, London.

Sheller, M. (2001) Natural hedonism: the invention of Caribbean islands as tropical playgrounds. In: Courtman, S. (ed.) The Society for Caribbean Studies Annual Conference. http://www.scsonline.freeserve.co.uk/olvol2.html

Smith, B. (1992) *Imagining the Pacific, in the Wake of the Cook Voyages*. Melbourne University Press, Melbourne, Australia.

Sontag, S. (1973) *On Photography*. Farrar, Straus and Giroux, New York.

Stainton, D. (1933) Holiday impressions of a tropic isle. *Bank Notes* (Australia Museum AN 90/72 Book 3).

Sydney Morning Herald (1928) On a coral isle – not all romance – British scientists' discomforts. 29 November (Australia Museum AN 90/72/Book 1).

Taussig, M. (1993) *Mimesis and Alterity: a Particular History of the Senses*. Routledge, London.

Tuan, Y. (1977) *Space and Place: the Perspective of Experience*. Edward Arnold, London.

Urry, J. (1995) *Consuming Places. International Library of Sociology*. Routledge, London.

Wigmore, L. (1932) Blazing beauty – new world of coral reef – Man Friday – will be world's playground (No. 1). *Sun* 9 January. (Australia Museum AN 90/72/Book 1).

Wigmore, L.G. (1933) Call of the coral. *Daily Mail* 14 January.

Wright, J. (1977). *The Coral Battleground*. 20th anniversary commemorative edn 1996 edn. Angus & Robertson, Sydney.

Production and Consumption of Wildlife Icons: Dolphin Tourism at Monkey Mia, Western Australia

6

Amanda J. Smith[1], Diane Lee[2], David Newsome[1] and Natalie Stoeckl[3]

[1]School of Environmental Science, Murdoch University, Perth, Western Australia; [2]Murdoch University, Perth, Western Australia; [3]James Cook University Townsville, Australia

Introduction: Wildlife Icon Tourism

This chapter reports on a study supported by Sustainable Tourism Cooperative Research Centre, Australia (STCRC) concerning dolphin tourism at Monkey Mia in Western Australia (Smith *et al.*, 2006). Production and consumption of wildlife in terms of tourist space can be discussed through a spectrum of approaches from the anthropocentric form of narrative, where wildlife are viewed only in terms of their value to human kind, through to an ecocentric narrative where wildlife are seen to have their own right to existence. In essence, this represents the range of arguments from those who view wildlife as existing to be packaged and produced for consumption, to those who argue that wildlife should be simply that, and not be made available as a product. Dolphins have been the focus of tourism production and consumption at Monkey Mia since the 1970s, and this chapter endeavours to explore management of the conflict between preservation and use, and examine conservation management, in this case undertaken by the Midwest Region of Conservation and Land Management (CALM), as a means to provide optimum outcomes for both wildlife and human life. Conservation seeks to balance the potential conflict and tensions between the anthropocentric and ecocentric approaches.

Natural resources are an important basis for the development of a tourism industry (Gunn, 1993). A number of studies have indicated that one of the major motivational factors influencing a visitor's decision to travel to Australia is the desire to experience aspects of the natural and cultural heritage (Allcock *et al.*, 1994; Kim, 1994; Burns and Murphy, 1998, see also Pocock, Chapter 5, this volume).

In Australia, there are well-established tourism industries of international significance that are focused on charismatic or endangered species of animals, often referred to as iconic wildlife settings. For the purposes of this chapter, a brief exploration for a definition of a 'tourism icon' is necessary. The term is commonly referred to in tourism literature (Tremblay, 2002; Corkeron, 2004), but a singular definition is elusive. It may be suggested that the term has moved into the tourism lexicon with a general understanding of the notion but without a clear definitive meaning. In order to provide a working rationale for the term 'wildlife icon', it may be suggested that 'iconic' tourism sites and experiences have evolved around the notion of the sacred experience, enhanced by MacCannell's (1976) thesis of the modern tourist as being on a pilgrimage, moving from the 'profane' everyday routine to the 'sacred' experience of being a tourist (Graburn, 1989). It may be argued that postmodern tourists have incorporated the sacred pilgrimage into 'a must see' focus for the purpose of their travels. Tourism Western Australia, the government arm of tourism marketing in Western Australia, have defined their notion of a tourist icon as follows '... the iconic significance of an attraction came from its ability to create a sense of awe in tourists, draw large numbers of visitors and be readily identifiable as West Australian' (Lam, 2005). Tremblay (2002), in his discussion of wildlife icons, notes the long spiritual relationship between resident human populations and animal species. He supports the notion that some species are representative (and therefore key images) of scarce natural environments. He suggests that wildlife icons are further enhanced by anthropomorphism, where tourists are able to empathize with attributed 'human-like' qualities. The red back spider may be endemic and therefore unique in terms of Australian fauna but is not considered a wildlife icon; similarly, the box jellyfish of northern Australia is not considered as iconic marine wildlife. Dolphins, with their long history of spirituality and associated anthropomorphism, have become a prime focus for wildlife icon research (O'Neill *et al.*, 2004, p. 848). Corkeron (2004) noted the emergence of whales as developing 'iconic value for the conservation movement in the 1970s and discussed the ecocentric and anthropomorphic approaches to the value of whales in a wider economic sense. Whilst not advocating whale watching, Corkeron (2004) suggested that, 'perhaps whales can have their iconic value refashioned. Perhaps the whale watching industry can use whales to help spread new messages about marine conservation' (p. 848).

Wildlife Tourism

The viewing and visiting of wild animals for recreational purposes or as a tourist attraction is a relatively recent phenomenon that is growing at a rapid rate (Orams, 1996; Roe *et al.*, 1997; Hoyt, 2001; Wilson and Tisdell, 2001; Newsome *et al.*, 2005). Wildlife tourism in Australia consists of a wide range of different types of activities, involving a wide range of species (Higginbottom *et al.*, 2001). Wildlife tourism globally attracts very large numbers of tourists. Whale watching alone, which includes dolphins, in 2000 was a US$1 billion industry attracting >9 million participants in 87 countries and territories around the world (Hoyt, 2001).

In recreation ecology, wildlife tourism is discussed in terms of consumptive or non-consumptive activities. The consumptive form of wildlife tourism, as defined by ecologists and wildlife managers, includes the hunting, capture, death or removal of a wildlife species from its natural habitat (Mathieson and Wall, 1982; Sinha, 2001). This may include recreational hunting and fishing or trophy hunting and fishing. Non-consumptive wildlife tourism is the human recreational interaction with wildlife wherein the focal organism is not purposefully removed or permanently affected by the interaction (Duffus and Dearden, 1990). Such interactions may include viewing, observing and photographing. Dolphin interaction experiences can include shore-based viewing, boat-based viewing, swim-with-dolphins and feeding dolphins. Non-consumptive wildlife tourism, where animals are viewed from the shore and provisioned, is the focus of this chapter in terms of the product (dolphin interaction) offered.

Wildlife viewing (tourism product) is consumed in terms of tourist space in various passive forms. Wilson and Tisdell (2001) categorized wildlife viewing activities into two situations. The first was where tourists visit a national park or protected area to watch wildlife in their natural environment without a focal species in mind, while the second category involved visiting a designated area with the intention of watching a focal species in its natural habitat. In such situations, the wildlife viewing product is characterized by minimal or incidental human-made structures, and animals that are not restrained in any way (Orams, 1996). Orams (1996) identified interaction opportunities that involve greater effort on the part of the tourist to view the animal (product) that may be located on breeding sites (e.g. albatross viewing in the breeding grounds at the Northern Royal Albatross Colony, Taiaroa Head, New Zealand (Higham, 1998)), along migratory routes (e.g. Hervey Bay whale watching in southern Queensland (Corkeron, 1995)), or at feeding and drinking sites. Additionally, there are situations where animals are manipulated in some way in order to allow tourists an opportunity for regular or closer interaction (e.g. feeding dolphins at Monkey Mia, Western Australia (CALM, 1993)).

A third interaction category could be added to this, that of the incidental tourist. Grossberg *et al.* (2003) described this as the situation where tourists with multiple interests encounter wildlife or fragile ecosystems inadvertently. Additionally, incidental contact may also occur when visitors, whilst engaging with one species, incidentally come in contact with other species (Wilson and Tisdell, 2001), for example the presence of Australian pelicans at Monkey Mia, Western Australia. This chapter focuses on the intentional viewing of a focal wildlife species in its natural habitat where the species is manipulated through feeding to allow closer interaction (Grossberg *et al.*, 2003).

Wildlife Attributes as a Tourism Product

Wildlife possess various attributes that make them attractive as a tourism product for the wildlife user. Duffus and Dearden (1990) described the wildlife user as individuals who are induced to undertake a particular activity by a set of antecedent conditions that form an image of the subject and drive the desire to encounter wildlife under natural conditions. Certain physical and behavioural characteristics such as mental ability, phylogenic similarity, body shape and size, aesthetic appeal, means of locomotion and ability to form attachments tend to make certain wildlife species more attractive to humans (Eddy *et al.*, 1993; Tremblay, 2002; Bentrupperbaumer, 2005).

Animals that have a physical similarity to humans, for example apes, or which display similar emotions and cognitive processing abilities to humans, tend to create more interest for wildlife viewing (Bentrupperbaumer, 2005). Additionally, animal species which have aesthetic appeal such as colour, shape, movement and visibility also tend to hold greater attraction to wildlife tourists (Tremblay, 2002; Bentrupperbaumer, 2005). For example, larger animals are generally preferred to smaller animals due to the ease of viewing (Hammitt and Cole, 1998; Tremblay, 2002; Bentrupperbaumer, 2005).

Spectacular and charismatic species are often the focus of wildlife tourism, e.g. species such as gorillas in Africa; swimming with dolphins in Western Australia; and whale watching in Australia, New Zealand, South Africa and North America. Charisma can entail such things as cuteness, approachability of the animal, playfulness and the animal's tendency to relate to humans (Tremblay, 2002). Bentrupperbaumer (2005) suggested that for some wildlife tourists, just being in the presence of other animal species is sufficient to satisfy their need at the time. The presence of animals can instigate higher levels of relaxation and offer companionship by reducing human isolation (Brodie and Biley, 1999; Bentrupperbaumer, 2005). Additionally, humans form emotional attachment to wildlife, which is associated with pro-environmental behaviour (Bentrupperbaumer, 2005).

A strong focus in wildlife tourism is also placed on rare or endangered species (Shackley, 1996; Reynolds and Braithwaite, 2001). It may be that rare or endangered animals offer the wildlife tourist an encounter which is considered as exceptional, extraordinary or a unique opportunity (Bentrupperbaumer, 2005). Additionally, certain species have been afforded recognition as a result of being used as symbols of conservation effort, such as the Bengal tiger, giant panda and humpback whale (Duffus and Dearden, 1990). Animals are used as visual images in promotional brochures and as marketing symbols for businesses, and therefore may increase the tourist's desire to view such animals. Higginbottom *et al.* (2001) examined tourism business brochures that included wildlife as part of the itinerary for tourists visiting Australia. They found that the most frequently used symbols promoting free-range activities were kangaroos followed by dolphins/whales.

The sustainability of wildlife tourism has in recent times been questioned in relation to various influencing factors such as coral bleaching events, hunting in international waters, lobbying by animal rights groups and the impacts of tourism. Moreover, there is growing visitor dissatisfaction with management styles, overcrowding and public concerns regarding proposed tourism developments (Smith *et al.*, 2005). Managers are often faced with a lack of baseline data including biological data, and visitor wants and needs associated with the problem of potential negative environmental impacts, and increasing tourism pressures (Smith *et al.*, 2005). These factors at wildlife icon sites such as Monkey Mia call for an investigation into stakeholder attitudes and perceptions of such attractions, an exploration of new ways of managing tourism focused on icon species and an examination of alternatives should impacts, in terms of both wildlife and visitor, become unacceptable (Smith *et al.*, 2005).

Issues for the Development of Dolphin Tourism

Indirect impacts on wildlife as a result of tourism may be in the form of creating unintentional, stressful situations from coincidental disturbance. Wild animals may respond to humans according to various behavioural responses including avoidance, attraction and habituation (Kuss *et al.*, 1990; Cole and Landres, 1995; Hammitt and Cole, 1998;

Green and Higginbottom, 2001; Newsome *et al.*, 2002). These influences may result in changes to wildlife physiology, behaviour, reproduction, population levels and species composition and diversity (Cole and Landres, 1995).

Concern for provisioned dolphins has been emerging as a result of developing research findings (Bejder and Samuels, 2003; Mann and Kemps, 2003; O'Neill *et al.*, 2004). A number of deleterious effects of feeding have been documented for both dolphins and humans. These include: alteration of natural foraging, resting and social behaviour; disruption to breeding behaviour and possible deleterious effects on reproductive success; loss of wariness of humans leading to injuries from boats or from people who may regard them as pests; indiscriminate acceptance of food possibly leading to ingestion of harmful or contaminated substances; deleterious effects on health and increased exposure to health risks; alteration to distribution and ranging patterns, or access to preferred habitat; and can result in aggressive behaviour (including biting patrons, sexual aggression towards patrons, rough behaviour with patrons, pushing swimmers away from shore and butting swimmers in the chest) causing injury to humans (Wilson, 1994; Orams *et al.*, 1996; Orams, 1997a, b; Neil and Brieze, 1998; Constantine, 1999; Orams, 2002; Bejder and Samuels, 2003; Mann and Kemps, 2003; Samuels *et al.*, 2003).

While the above notes possible negative impacts associated with human–dolphin interactions, there are some potential positive benefits for dolphins. Orams (1997b) reports on the important part that play has in dolphins' behavioural routine. Consequently, many dolphins find unusual objects and activities, such as interacting with humans, stimulating and an opportunity for play. Orams (1997b) also suggested that dolphins that are exposed to regular interaction with humans might learn to avoid risks, such as fast-moving vessels, engine propellers and hooks. Samuels *et al.* (2003) reported a study that contradicted the statement by Orams (1997b) of dolphins avoiding risks with boats. Samuels *et al.* (2003) reported a situation where a spotted dolphin calf that was habituated to tour vessels suffered life-threatening wounds presumably from a boat propeller. Additionally, behavioural studies of dolphins interacting with boat-based tours show that dolphins are often disturbed by the presence of tour vessels, resulting in avoidance behaviour, and disruption to resting and socializing behaviours (Constantine, 1999; Nichols and Stone, 2001; Constantine *et al.*, 2003, 2004; Lusseau, 2003; Lusseau and Higham, 2004).

Interacting with dolphins can also have many positive benefits for humans. These can be psychological, educational and economic benefits. Dolphins interacting with humans results in extremely positive feelings of enjoyment and connection with nature for humans, and these experiences may result in humans adopting more environmentally responsible attitudes and practises that may have indirect long-term conservation benefits for dolphins (Orams, 1997b). Education programmes associated with dolphin–human interactions can result in significant learning. For example, Orams (1997b) reported a study conducted at Tangalooma, Moreton Island, Queensland, Australia where dolphins are provisioned and a commentary is given, which revealed that tourists who received educational material as part of their experience with the dolphins improved their knowledge about dolphins and marine environmental issues.

Economic benefits were highlighted in a report by Hoyt (2001) where it was stated that whale watching in Australia, which also includes dolphin watching and other wild dolphin-based tourism, contributes close to AU$S300 million to the economy, attracting almost 1.5 million participants. This represents a 15% per annum increase in a 5 year period. In many places, whale watching provides valuable, sometimes crucial income to a community, with the creation of new jobs and businesses. It helps foster an appreciation of the importance of marine conservation and offers communities a sense of identity and considerable pride. In addition, the political importance of recreation and tourism in natural areas is discussed by a number of authors (Davis, 1984; Hough, 1987; McNeely and Thorsell, 1988; Butler and Butler, 1992). When tourists visit natural areas, they feel a part of nature and so will encourage the government to look after the natural environment, thereby providing the conservation lobby with stronger support.

Monkey Mia, Western Australia

There are a number of sites within Australia that may be regarded as iconic wildlife tourism destinations such as the Northern Territory and crocodiles (Ryan, 1998; Tremblay, 2002); Phillip Island, Victoria and fairy penguins (Head, 2000; Phillip Island Nature Park, 2005); Fraser Island, Queensland and dingoes (Lawrance and Higginbottom, 2002); Monkey Mia, Western Australia and dolphins (CALM, 1993); and Hervey Bay and humpback whales (Corkeron *et al.*, 1994; Corkeron, 1995); (see also Pocock, Chapter 5, this volume).

Monkey Mia, is geographically isolated, located on the eastern shore of the Peron Peninsula, 25 km east of Denham and 856 km north of the capital city of Perth in the Shark Bay World Heritage Area, Western Australia. It consists of the terrestrial reserve, an area of 477 ha adjoining Shark Bay Marine Park which is approximately 13,000 km^2 in area (CALM, 1996) (see Fig. 6.1). The site is one example of a multi-million dollar tourism industry that has developed surrounding the viewing and feeding of wild dolphins. Local authorities report that dolphin tourism is the prime attraction for some 100,000 visitors to Shark Bay

Fig. 6.1. Location of Monkey Mia, Western Australia. Source: Smith *et al.* (2005).

region each year (CALM, 1993). As many as 700 people can be in attendance at the Monkey Mia Dolphin Interaction Area each day, and it is estimated that the population of the current food-provisioned dolphins is worth approximately AU$S30 million (CALM, 1993; IFAW, 2004). The problem is that the habituated dolphins are now mature adults, and research has shown that careful management and supervision by researchers is necessary if new dolphins are to be introduced to the food-provisioned scheme (Mann and Kemps, 2003). Furthermore, animal rights groups are opposed to the manipulation of wild dolphins for tourism purposes. In recent years, visitor experience has also been clouded by overcrowding, regimentation of feeding, loss of naturalness and a perception that the site is becoming overdeveloped (Smith *et al.*, 2006). These are issues that are faced by other species promoted as 'icons' both in Western Australia and at the national level. The apparent reliance on just a few species or sites makes the Shark Bay and Exmouth regions in Western Australia of particular significance as tourist destinations (Smith *et al.*, 2006).

Monkey Mia is located near, and accessed by, a sealed road (Figs 6.2 and 6.3) (CALM, 1993). Renowned for the bottlenose dolphins (*Tursiops truncates*) that have been entering the shallows of the bay since the 1960s to interact with people on the beach and also to take fish from humans (CALM, 1993), the site has high conservation and economic values for the region and is one of the major attractions for visitors to Shark Bay (CALM, 1993). While the dolphins provide a focus for tourism in Shark Bay, they remain only a small part of the total spectrum of recreational opportunities in the region. Recreational fishing is also a popular pursuit and includes boat-, net- and shore-based fishing (CALM, 1996). The waters of Shark Bay also contain a diverse array of marine wildlife that are a mix of both tropical and temperate species (CALM, 1996).

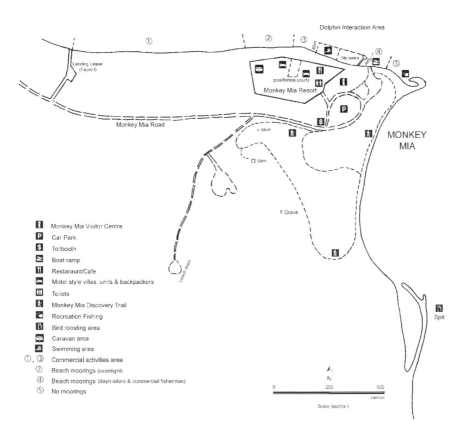

Fig. 6.2. Monkey Mia showing location of Monkey Mia Resort, Monkey Mia Visitor Centre, facilities and Dolphin Interaction Area. Adapted from CALM (1993).

Fig. 6.3. Monkey Mia including dolphin interaction area, visitor centre, Monkey Mia Resort and caravan park. Source: Raffaele (2003).

The Development of Dolphin Tourism

For many years, fishing was the mainstay of the local economy, and in the 1960s local fishers began feeding bottlenose dolphins at Monkey Mia in the shallows of the bay when they returned with their catch. This attraction led to a caravan park being established in 1975 (CALM, 1993). Visitation at this time was still relatively low, approximately 10,000 people, due to difficult access (unsealed roads), lack of facilities and a lack of public awareness of its attractions (CALM, 1993). In 1985, the Denham–Hamelin Road was sealed, bringing more visitors to the Shark Bay region (CALM, 1993), and, at the same time, an information centre was constructed at Monkey Mia, and in 1986 a boat ramp, entrance tollbooth and barbecues were established (CALM, 1993).

In 1988, a State Government grant provided monies for the Denham–Monkey Mia Road to be sealed, car parks and toilets to be developed and for landscaping (CALM, 1993). At this time, an influx of visitors came to Monkey Mia over a short period of time as a result of improved access and an increased public awareness of dolphins interacting with people at Monkey Mia. In response, the caravan park was redeveloped and upgraded in 1989/90 (CALM, 1993). This redevelopment included the construction of the Monkey Mia Resort. In June 2001, the Monkey Mia Visitor Centre was completed to provide a focal point for visitors so that more could be learnt about the dolphins and other marine wildlife. The highest visitation at Monkey Mia was in 1989, which coincides with the sealing of the Denham–Monkey Mia Road and the opening of the Monkey Mia Resort and facilities. Since 1998, visitor numbers have stabilized, with the mean visitor numbers being 101,170 per annum (Smith *et al.*, 2006).

At the time of writing, four adult females, Nicky (29 years), Surprise (24 years), Puck (28 years) and Piccolo (12 years), are provisioned. Their calves Yadgalah (2 years), Burda (2 years), India (1 year) and Eden (1 year), respectively, also come inshore but are not provisioned (Smith *et al.*, 2006). Kiya (7 years) and Shock (10 years) are also non-provisioned adult females that regularly come in to shore (Smith *et al.*, 2006). A range of measures and management strategies have been put in place by managers (CALM) to ensure the sustainability of the dolphin–human interaction. These measures were implemented in 1995 and are described in Table 6.1.

From this overview, we can see how the tourism product has evolved from the early spontaneous dolphin feeding by the fishermen through to what is now carefully orchestrated and stage managed; it is not just nature on show, but a very specific and carefully controlled performance that attracts the visitors, yet the question remains as to how these visitors actually perceive it.

Consuming the Tourism Product at Monkey Mia

The study conducted by Smith *et al.* (2006), on which this chapter is based, aimed to evaluate iconic wildlife in terms of intrinsic values in

Table 6.1. Feeding dolphins at Monkey Mia, Western Australia – the tourism product.

- Only adult female dolphins are provisioned. They are fed a maximum of 2 kg of fish per day, restricted to no more than three feeds a day. Feeding times vary between 8 a.m. and 1 p.m. and times are variable and dependent on when the dolphins come in-shore.

- No touching of dolphins is permitted and unregulated feeding is strongly discouraged.

- Rangers impart information over a PA system broadcast at the beach during the dolphin interaction.

- In preparation for feeding, rangers ask visitors to move out of the water; buckets are then bought down to the water and each ranger takes a bucket to a specific female (Fig. 6.4). The feeding begins with rangers selecting one person at a time and asking them to approach each bucket. The ranger hands each person a fish and they feed it to the dolphin head-first. After they have given the fish to the dolphin, they are asked to leave the water immediately so the next person can be called. The last fish is offered to each dolphin simultaneously to avoid competition over buckets. After the final fish is offered, the buckets are tipped over and dipped in the water to show the dolphins that the feed is over. The entire feeding regime usually takes three to five minutes. The dolphins almost always leave the dolphin interaction area within five minutes after the feed.

- Pelicans are fed on the beach at the same time as the dolphins to reduce the incidence of pelicans competing with dolphins for provisioned fish.

Sources: Wilson (1994); CALM (1996); Mann and Kemps (2003).

Fig. 6.4. CALM Rangers preparing for a dolphin feed (July 2004). Source: Smith *et al.* (2005).

terms of visitor perceptions and experiences, and extrinsic values in terms of the economic contribution of visitors to the destination. Ecocentric approaches to the value of wildlife were not addressed in the study, but it can be argued that by taking an anthropocentric view of the value of wildlife to the tourism industry, the study aimed to add to the ecocentric view rather than detract from it (Smith *et al.*, 2006). Wildlife has a right to a healthy environment. History has shown that wildlife does not need 'management'; it is the interaction between humans and wildlife that needs to be managed. The mass movement of people through travel requires management. Tourist sites dependent on single icons require management, and those sites dependent on wildlife icons require very careful management.

A visitor survey was used to establish how, and to what extent, existing recreational opportunities within Monkey Mia were being used and conducted (Smith *et al.*, 2006). A sample of the population of visitors were surveyed on-site during the peak period (Western Australian July school holidays) for visits (for further details, see Smith *et al.*, 2006). In addition, a number of tour operators who offered a variety of tours were interviewed as well as a number of stakeholders involved in the management of the area, including staff from CALM, Yadgalah Aboriginal Corporation and Monkey Mia Resort itself.

The Tourism Experience

For this case study, the definition for an 'overall destination product' is 'a bundle of tangible and intangible components, based on activity at a destination. The package is perceived by the tourist as an experience, available at a price' (Richardson and Fluker, 2004, p. 50). Tourism products undergo continuous development, graphically displayed by Butler and Waldbrook's Tourism Destination Life Cycle as an evolutionary process (see Fig. 6.5).

In global terms, the 1960s saw a growth in concern for the environment in industrialized nations, but it was not until 1972 and the establishment of United Nations Environment Program that developing countries began to realize that environmental policies should not be considered as 'unaffordable luxuries' (Pearce and Turner, 1990, p. 23). The issues for iconic sites focus on managing the integrity of the icon and the visitor experience under increasing numbers of visitors who are increasingly interested in conservation. Scott and Willits (1994) undertook to examine the link between environmental attitudes and behaviour with the hypothesis that whilst attitudes do not always reflect behaviour, 'it nevertheless seems likely that those who hold the most supportive attitudes would be more inclined than those with less supportive attitudes to act in ways that protect the environment' (p. 241).

In terms of total visitation, Monkey Mia could be positioned at the stagnation level of Butler and Waldbrook's (1991) model (Fig. 6.5) with mass tourism. Figure 6.6 graphically reflects visitor numbers over a 28 year period. The peaks of 1987 and 1989 coincide with improved access to and further development at the destination. Surveys of operators and interviews of managers showed that while visitor levels are stagnating, there is concern that the overall destination product needs to be rejuvenated through the marketing of a wider diversity of attractions in the region, with a focus on the World Heritage status of the region. Currently there is a proposal for an expansion of the existing resort at Monkey Mia that will accommodate a total of 1200 people (double the existing capacity) (Bowman Bishaw Gorham, 2004). The increase in visitor numbers would entail that it is necessary to diversify the overall destination product in order to relieve pressure on dolphins as an attraction.

In the 2004 survey, Smith *et al.* (2006) found that visitors were generally first-time visitors, with Monkey Mia being part of a multi-destination trip. If dolphin viewing did not exist at Monkey Mia, a majority of visitors indicated that they still would have taken the trip to the Shark Bay region. Visitors were most likely to visit Monkey Mia with family or as part of a couple in a group of 2–4 persons aged in the 25–39 year age bracket. Visitors were mostly 'white-collar' workers (managers, professionals or para-professionals), implying they were of a

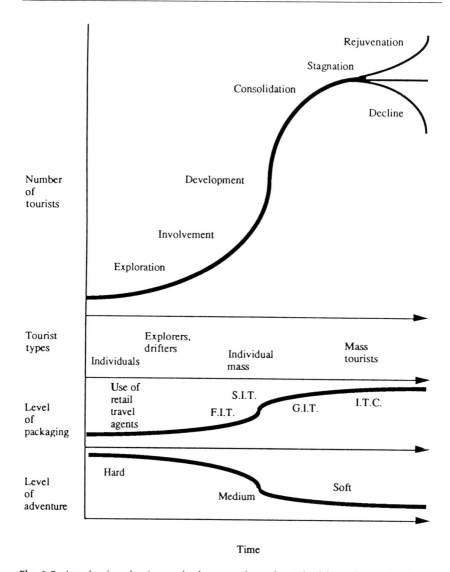

Fig. 6.5. Levels of packaging and adventure throughout the life cycle of a tourist destination. Source: Butler and Waldbrook (1991).

relatively high socio-economic status. There was a high proportion of females to males and a majority of visitors were from Western Australia and overseas, with the lowest proportion of visitors coming from interstate. These visitors mainly travelled to the region by passenger vehicle and four-wheel drive and stayed in caravan park or hotel/motel accommodation. Visitors generally stayed in the Shark Bay region for 1–2 nights and spent half a day at Monkey Mia (Smith *et al.*, 2006).

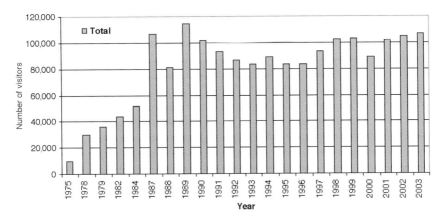

Fig. 6.6. Annual visits to Monkey Mia Reserve 1975–2003. Source: CALM VISTAT (unpublished).

In terms of the overall destination product of Shark Bay, visitors visited other destinations in the region, with Shell Beach, Denham Township and Hamelin Pool (stromatolites) being the most frequently visited (Smith *et al.*, 2006). While visiting Monkey Mia, visitors generally participated in a wide variety of activities, with seeing dolphins in their natural environment being the most important reason for visiting Shark Bay (Smith *et al.*, 2006). The absence of dolphins from Monkey Mia would greatly detract from the visitor experience, while the dolphin interaction and experience and seeing dolphins so close was the best part of visitors' wildlife experience. A majority of visitors indicated that the visit to Monkey Mia was better than expected (Smith *et al.*, 2005).

As indicated in Fig. 6.7, when asked 'if dolphin viewing at Monkey Mia did not exist would you still have taken this trip?', the majority of visitors (36%) responded that they would have still taken the trip and would have spent the same amount of time visiting the Shark Bay Region (Fig. 6.7). A further 24% replied that they still would have taken the trip but would have spent less time/fewer days in Shark Bay (Fig. 6.7). This suggests that 60% of the visitors surveyed would still have visited Shark Bay in the absence of dolphins.

The survey of tour operators and interviews of managers showed similar findings to those of visitors in relation to the absence of dolphins. Operators generally thought that if there were no dolphins at Monkey Mia then tourists would still come to Shark Bay but there would be a reduction in the number of visitors. Most of those operators surveyed also commented that if dolphin viewing was not available, other wildlife experiences and attractions in the region would need to be promoted (Smith *et al.*, 2006). Managers also felt that visitors would still come but there would be a reduction in numbers and that other attractions would need to be marketed.

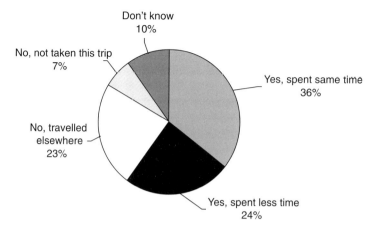

Fig. 6.7. 'If dolphin viewing at Monkey Mia did not exist, would you still have taken this trip?' (*n* = 355). Source: Smith *et al.* (2005).

There was, however, a differing opinion when tour operators and managers were asked how their operations would be affected and how industry would react if dolphins at Monkey Mia did not turn up for a month or a season, or if the dolphins died (Smith *et al.*, 2006). Operators expressed concern if dolphins were absent for long periods of time. Operators commented that they would probably change their itinerary and would consider no longer coming to Monkey Mia, with only a single operator commenting that there would be no change (Smith *et al.*, 2006). Operators gave similar responses if the dolphins were to die, with the additional comment that there would be a large decrease in visitor numbers (Smith *et al.*, 2006).

Managers commented that, while it was common for individual dolphins to go missing from beach visits for up to 4–5 weeks, particularly during the breeding season (November to April), if the dolphins went missing for longer periods there would be an economic impact on local businesses and the tourism industry (Smith *et al.*, 2006). There would be an enquiry into the reasons why the dolphins were missing and surveys would be conducted to try and locate the dolphins. Additionally, in the event of dolphin absence for long periods of time, staffing levels would be reduced both at CALM and at the Resort (Smith *et al.*, 2006). If the dolphins died, CALM commented that new dolphins would not be recruited into the feeding programme, even though there would be community and political pressure to do so, without a full enquiry as to the reasons why the initial beach-feeding dolphins died, and recruitment would not be considered until this was fully understood (Smith *et al.*, 2006). Managers felt that Monkey Mia would suffer a loss of identity if the dolphins no longer visited the beach; there would be a reduction in visitor numbers and the site and visitor centre would change focus to promoting other marine wildlife, with dolphin viewing occurring from boats (Smith *et al.*, 2006).

Smith *et al.* (2006) asked visitors to determine if a range of 12 items added to or detracted from the quality of their experience at Monkey Mia. Most of the items detracted from the visitor experience or had no influence. When the results for detract and greatly detract were combined, visitors indicated that 'absence of dolphins' (93%), '>200 people in the dolphin interaction area' (88%), 'degraded condition of natural environment' (86%), 'no staff present' (80%), 'advanced booking to view dolphins' (74%), '>100 people in dolphin interaction area' (68%) and 'very few sightings of other wildlife' (68%) were the attributes that would most detract from the quality of the visitor experience (Smith *et al.*, 2006).

The results in Fig. 6.7 showed that if dolphin viewing did not exist at Monkey Mia, then visitors would still have taken the trip to Shark Bay. In contrast, 93% of respondents commented that if dolphins were absent from Monkey Mia, then this would detract from the quality of their visit. This shows a conflict in visitor responses.

In order to manage visitor numbers at the dolphin feed, a fixed viewing platform, where visitors are able to sit and view the rangers feeding the dolphins, has been suggested. When visitors were asked to comment on this proposal, over half (59%) indicated that such infrastructure would detract from their experience of the dolphins (Smith *et al.*, 2006). Smith and Newsome (2004) surveyed visitors to Monkey Mia about a wide range of available facilities and asked visitors to respond about the use of facilities, importance of facilities in relation to reason for visiting, and whether facilities added to or detracted from the quality of the visit. Surveyed visitors used a wide range of the available facilities and rated the presence of these facilities as being of minor importance in relation to the reasons for visiting Monkey Mia. Most of the facilities, e.g. toilets, beach shelters, lawns and the Monkey Mia Visitor Centre, were seen to enhance the visitor experience. This may be because of the convenience such facilities offer the visitor. Important reasons for respondents visiting Monkey Mia were natural attributes and not built facilities (Smith and Newsome, 2006).

The current facilities do not affect the way in which visitors interact with the dolphins. The lack of support for a viewing stadium may be because the dolphin experience would be changed. When asked about the best part of the wildlife experience, 85% of respondents made comments that were dolphin related. Key reasons for the enjoyment of their experience were noted as: the dolphin interaction (41%), seeing dolphins so close (17%), feeding dolphins (12%) and seeing dolphins in their natural environment (6%) (Smith *et al.*, 2006). These attributes are closely linked with the reasons visitors considered most important in visiting Shark Bay. The most important reasons were: seeing dolphins in their natural environment, the opportunity to see dolphins, to be in and enjoy a natural environment, and being able to get close to dolphins (Smith *et al.*, 2006). This emphasizes that the experience currently offered is part of what attracts visitors to Monkey Mia, and development that would alter this interaction may change the experience.

Interviewees from CALM also commented that people come to Monkey Mia to interact with dolphins in a natural setting (Smith *et al.*, 2006). The interviewee from the Monkey Mia Resort also commented that the current feeding situation is already crowded. Perhaps people do not want further development because it not only changes the setting, but also would mean more people at the feeds. Also, more development and a change in the feeding regime, such as only rangers feeding the dolphins, may create a situation that is too regimented and detracts from the natural experience (Smith *et al.*, 2006). Additionally, a viewing stadium would alter the close contact visitors currently experience, a situation that is used in marketing the unique experience offered at Monkey Mia.

Encounters with other visitors are important in affecting the quality of the visitor experience. Visitors surveyed at the site participated in the dolphin interaction with between 100 and 300 other visitors, yet over two-thirds (68%) indicated that sharing the experience with >100 people would detract from their experience (Table 6.2). Interestingly, of those visitors, 59% rated their experience as better than, or much better than expected (Table 6.2).

The high level of satisfaction indicates that even though visitors felt that >100 people would detract from their experience, during the dolphin interaction visitors were fairly tolerant of other visitors they encountered considering visitor numbers were higher than 100 at each feed. In reviewing comments about best and worst experiences, negative comments were made about visitor behaviour, for example, 'children were overwhelmed by "pushy" adults', 'poor behaviour of other visitors' and 'people ignoring the ranger during the feed'. This implies that visitors were more greatly affected by the behaviour of the visitors rather than the number of other visitors during their interaction.

Respondents in another survey held at the site (Smith and Newsome, 2006) also commented on inappropriate behaviour during the dolphin interaction that was related to unacceptable visitor

Table 6.2. Rating of visit to Monkey Mia visit overall (% of respondents, $n = 343$).

Much worse than expected	Worse than expected	About the same as expected	Better than expected	Much better than expected
1	2	38	45	14

behaviour. Encounters with other visitors are important in affecting the quality of the visitor experience, so that negative perceptions of the presence, behaviour and characteristics of other people depending on the normative behaviour and conditions accepted for the situation and setting can potentially result in visitor conflict (Lucas, 1990; Cessford, 2000). Smith and Newsome (2006) found that visitors to Monkey Mia generally preferred a natural area experience where meeting others is fairly likely to highly unlikely. This further implies that behaviour is an important aspect of social conditions and that respondents are fairly tolerant of meeting other visitors providing the numbers are not beyond an individual's social norms.

Visitors were asked to describe the best and worst part of their wildlife experience. A list of 67 reasons was given for the best and 51 reasons were given for the worst part of the wildlife experience. These reasons were categorized for ease of analysis. A majority of visitors commented that the best part of the wildlife experience was dolphin related (85%) (Table 6.3) (Smith *et al.*, 2006). A variety of reasons were given, but a majority related to the dolphin interaction and experience, and seeing dolphins so close (Smith *et al.*, 2006). Responses with regard to the worst part of the wildlife experience were none (34%), about the site (25%), followed by visitor behaviour (23%). In relation to site-based comments, a majority of visitors commented on cooler weather and cold water, while visitor behaviour related to too many people or poor behaviour (Smith *et al.*, 2006).

Richardson and Fluker (2004) noted that the tourism experience can be summarized through a four quadrant model, with 'physical' and 'interpersonal' contact experienced in 'tangible' and 'intangible' forms. They noted that physical/tangible contact is more significant to the experience than physical/intangible forms and that interpersonal/ intangible contact is more significant than interpersonal/tangible, and it is this interpersonal/intangible experience that is most difficult to manage. Image and construction of image are key issues in the development of a tourism destination product (Table 6.3) (Richardson and Fluker, 2004, p. 212).

Monkey Mia visitors indicated that their best and worst experiences were primarily of the physical/tangible nature (Fig. 6.8). Physical/ tangible elements (e.g. interacting with dolphins) contributed more to the enjoyment of the overall experience than physical/intangible contact (e.g. seeing dolphins willingly interact); they also contributed to the worst experience in a similar manner (e.g. physical/tangible, micro-phone too low/couldn't hear talk; physical/intangible, cooler weather/ cold water), as indicated in Fig. 6.8.

Interpersonal/intangible (e.g. best, interaction between rangers and dolphins; worst, being a tourist) contact was felt more strongly in best and worst experiences than interpersonal/tangible (e.g. best, ranger and

Table 6.3. Characteristics of the dolphin interaction experience at Monkey Mia, Western Australia.

Nature of the contact	Tangible	Intangible
Physical	Product: dolphin interaction at Monkey Mia, Western Australia	Atmosphere: viewing dolphins in a natural environment, seeing dolphins willingly interact
	Facilitating goods: Monkey Mia Resort and facilities, hotel situation	Aesthetics: condition of the environment, blue sky, blue sea and clear water, clean/fresh environment
	Information processes: interpretation offered on-site and during dolphin interaction experience including Visitor Centre. Availability of staff at visitor centre	Feelings: crowding, too many children, worrying about sharks
		Comfort: weather, cold water
Interpersonal	Actions: management of dolphin interaction experience by CALM	Warmth: behaviour of other visitors, e.g. meeting other people
	Process: how people were selected to feed dolphin and the way dolphins were fed	Friendliness: informative and friendly rangers and staff
	Speed: length of the dolphin interaction	Care: e.g. dolphins being respected, interaction between rangers and dolphins
	Script: interpretation offered by staff during dolphin interaction, ranger and researcher talks	
	Corrective action: method in way that CALM controlled the crowd	

Adapted from Richardson and Fluker (2004).

researcher talks; worst, not enough time here). For management purposes, physical/tangible is the most manageable aspect of the total product, whilst interpersonal/intangible focuses on the behaviour of other visitors to the site and is the most difficult to manage. Therefore, managers should focus on physical/tangible aspects such as providing quality interpretation both during dolphin interaction and in the visitor

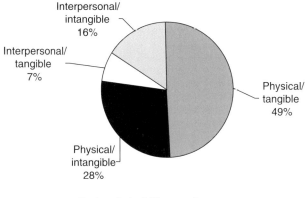

Best part of wildlife experience

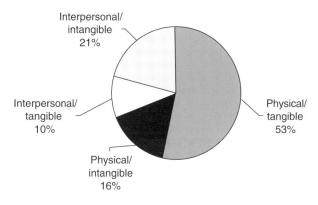

Worst part of wildlife experience

Fig. 6.8. Characteristics of dolphin viewing/interaction – best and worst part of wildlife experience at Monkey Mia.

centre, and interpersonal/intangible aspects such as friendliness and approachability of the rangers and staff.

Conclusion

By its nature, wildlife tourism contains a high element of unpredictability (Smith *et al.*, 2005), and this central dilemma raises a number of questions addressing the dependence of a site on a singular icon, and the extrinsic and intrinsic value of the icon to tourism in the region based on the postmodern tourist's experience of the destination (Smith *et al.*, 2005). The tourism experience at Monkey Mia is primarily related to the unique experience of close viewing and the structured feeding of dolphins that takes place on a daily basis because landscape, vegetation and other forms of wildlife, although important at Monkey Mia, can also be found elsewhere, and arguably perhaps, in a more pristine form.

There is a limit to the extent of control in situations such as this, for by its nature wildlife tourism contains an element of unpredictability, so there is an inherent tension within a narrative of place that emphasizes a form of anthropocentrism which requires the presence of dolphins. This tension is clearly seen in the perceptions of visitors that large numbers of 'other' visitors whose behaviour is 'inappropriate' are viewed, at best, as a form of distraction, and at worst as an intrusion.

Although respondents indicated they would still visit the area if dolphin viewing did not exist, further questionnaire data suggest otherwise. Visitors, managers and tour operators alike all agree that the dolphin experience is significant and forms the best part of the experience. Moreover, 93% of surveyed visitors indicated that the absence of dolphins would detract from the quality of their visit. This in turn has implications for tourism operations and the need to manage an icon-dependent tourist site. As we noted, it is not nature that needs to be managed, but the relationship between people and nature. Unlike other forms of tourism, those based on natural attractions and resources require very careful stewardship, as they are arguably more susceptible to problems caused by overcrowding. Whether or not these are anthropocentric or ecocentric is perhaps beside the point (see also Ford and Havdra, Chapter 4, this volume). Under current global conditions and particularly in tourism settings, each exist together and, where symbiotic relationships can be developed (in the sense that one helps the other to exist), there is potential for positive outcomes in terms of both anthropocentric and ecocentric outlooks.

References

Allcock, A., Jones, B., Lane, S. and Grant, J. (1994) *National Ecotourism Strategy.* Commonwealth Department of Tourism, Australian Government Publishing Service, Canberra, Australia.

Bejder, L. and Samuels, A. (2003) Evaluating the effects of nature-based tourism on cetaceans. In: Gales, N., Hindell, M. and Kirkwood, R. (eds) *Marine Mammals: Fisheries, Tourism and Management Issues.* CSIRO Publishing, Collingwood, Victoria, Australia.

Bentrupperbaumer, J.M. (2005) Human dimension of wildlife interactions. In: Newsome, D., Dowling, R.K. and Moore, S.A. (eds) *Wildlife Tourism.* Channel View Publications, Clevedon, UK.

Bowdler, S. (1995) The excavation of two small rockshelters at Monkey Mia, Shark Bay, Western Australia. *Australian Archaeology* 40, 1–13.

Bowman Bishaw Gorham (2004) *Expansion of Monkey Mia Dolphin Resort Environmental Scoping Document – Public Environmental Review.* Assessment Number 1455. Bowman Bishaw Gorham, Subiaco, WA, Australia.

Brodie, S.J. and Biley, F.C. (1999) An exploration of the potential benefits of pet-facilitated therapy. *Journal of Clinical Nursing* 8, 329–337.

Burns, D.L. and Murphy, L. (1998) An analysis of the promotion of marine tourism in far North Queensland. In: Laws, E., Faulkner, B. and Moscardo, G. (eds) *Embracing and Managing Change in Tourism: International Case Studies.* Routledge, London, pp. 415–430.

Butler, J.R. and Butler, E. (1992) Fostering the spiritual and affective (emotional) values of protected areas. In: 4th World Congress on National Parks and Protected Areas. 10–21 February 1992. Caracus, Venezuela.

Butler, R.W. and Waldbrook, L.A. (1991) A new planning tool: the tourism opportunity spectrum. *Journal of Tourism Studies* 2, 2–14.

CALM (1993) *Monkey Mia Reserve: Draft Management Plan.* Department of Conservation and Land Management, Perth, WA, Australia.

CALM (1996) *Shark Bay Marine Reserves Management Plan 1996–2006.* Department of Conservation and Land Management, Perth, WA, Australia.

CALM (2000) *Shark Bay Terrestrial Reserves Management Plan 2000–2009.* Department of Conservation and Land Management, Perth, WA, Australia.

Cessford, G.R. (2000) Identifying research needs for improved management of social impacts in wilderness recreation. In: Cole, D.N., McCool, S.F., Freimund, W.A., Borrie, W.T. and O'Loughlin, J. (eds) Wilderness Science in a Time of Change Conference. Missoula, Montana. 23–27 May 1999, Proceedings RMRS-P-15-VOL-4, Vol. 4: Wilderness visitors, experiences, and visitor management. USDA Forest Service, Rocky Mountain Research Station, Ogden, Utah.

Cole, D.N. and Landres, P.B. (1995). Indirect effects of recreation on wildlife. In: Knight, R.L. and Gutzwiller, K.J. (eds) *Wildlife and Recreationists: Coexistence Through Management and Research.* Island Press, Washington DC, pp. 183–202.

Constantine, R. (1999) *Effects of Tourism on Marine Mammals in New Zealand.* Science for Conservation no. 106. Department of Conservation, New Zealand.

Constantine, R., Brunton, D.H. and Baker, C.S. (2003) *Effects of Tourism on Behavioural Ecology of Bottlenose Dolphins of Northeastern New Zealand.* DOC Science Internal Series no. 153. Department of Conservation, New Zealand.

Constantine, R., Brunton, D.H. and Dennis, T. (2004) Dolphin-watching tour boats change bottlenose dolphin (*Tursiops truncatus*) behaviour. *Biological Conservation* 117, 299–307.

Corkeron, P.J. (1995) Humpback whales (*Megaptera novaeangliae*) in Hervey Bay, Queensland: behaviour and responses to whale-watching vessels. *Canadian Journal of Zoology* 73, 1290–1299.

Corkeron, P.J. (2004) Whale watching, iconography, and marine conservation. *Conservation Biology* 18, 847–849.

Corkeron, P.J., Brown, M., Slade, R.W. and Bryden, M.M. (1994) Humpback whales, *Megaptera novaeangliae* (Cetacea, Balaenopteridae), in Hervey Bay, Queensland. *Wildlife Research* 21, 293–305.

Davis, B.W. (1984). Management of non-wood values in state forests: should the user pay. *Australian Forestry* 47, 143–147.

Duffus, D.A. and Dearden, P. (1990) Non-consumptive wildlife oriented recreation: a conceptual framework. *Biological Conservation* 53, 213–231.

Eddy, T.J., Gallup, G.G. Jr, and Povinelli, D.J. (1993) Attribution of cognitive states to animals: Anthropomorphism in comparative perspective. *Journal of Social Issues* 49, 87–101.

Government Gazette (2003) *Wildlife Conservation (Specially Protected Fauna) Notice 2003*. Government Gazette, Perth, WA, Australia, 11 April 2003, pp. 1158–1167.

Graburn, N.H.H. (1989) Tourism: the sacred journey. In: Smith, V.L. (ed.) *Hosts and Guests*. University of Pennsylvania Press, Philadelphia.

Green, R. and Higginbottom, K. (2001) *Negative Effects of Wildlife Tourism on Wildlife*. Wildlife Tourism Research Report Series: No. 5. Status Assessment of Wildlife Tourism in Australia Series. CRC for Sustainable Tourism, Queensland, Australia.

Grossberg, R., Treves, A. and Naughton-Treves, L. (2003) The incidental ecotourist: measuring visitor impacts on endangered howler monkeys at a Belizean archaeological site. *Environmental Conservation* 30, 40–51.

Gunn, C.A. (1993) *Tourism Planning: Basics, Concepts, Cases*. Taylor & Francis, London.

Hammitt, W.E. and Cole, D.N. (1998) *Wildland Recreation: Ecology and Management*. 2nd edn. John Wiley & Sons, Inc., New York.

Head, L.M. (2000) Renovating the landscape and packaging the penguin: culture and nature on Summerland Peninsula, Phillip Island, Victoria, Australia. *Australian Geographic Studies* 38, 36–53.

Higginbottom, K., Rann, K., Moscardo, G., Davis, D. and Muloin, S. (2001) *Status Assessment of Wildlife in Australia: An Overview*. Part I: Descriptive Overview of Wildlife Tourism. Wildlife Tourism Research Report Series: No. 1. CRC for Sustainable Tourism, Queensland, Australia.

Higham, J.E.S. (1998) Tourists and albatrosses: the dynamics of tourism at the Northern Royal Albatross Colony, Taiaroa Head, New Zealand. *Tourism Management* 19, 521–531.

Hough, J. (1987) New directions for parks? Issues from the 20th International Parks Seminar. *Parks Parques Parcs* 12(2), 9–11.

Hoyt, E. (2001) *Whale Watching 2001: Worldwide Tourism Numbers, Expenditures, and Expanding Socioeconomic Benefits*. International Fund for Animal Welfare, Crowborough, UK.

IFAW (2004) *From Whalers to Whale Watchers: The Growth of Whale Watching Tourism in Australia*. International Fund for Animal Welfare, Surry Hills, NSW, Australia.

International Hotel Search.com (2005) *World Map*. (Homepage of International Hotel Search.com) (Online). Available: internationalhotelsearch.com/html/map.html. (26-1-05).

Kim, E.Y.L. (1994) Pre expectation of Korean tourists to Australia. In: *Australian National Tourism Education and Research Conference*. February, 1994. Gold Coast, Queensland, Australia.

Kuss, F.R., Graefe, A.R. and Vaske, J.J. (1990) *Visitor Impact Management: a Review of Research*. 1. National Parks and Conservation Association, Washington DC.

Lam, M. (2005) Tourist icons lose their lustre. *The West Australian* 11 January 2005, p. 13.

Lawrance, K. and Higginbottom, K. (2002) *Behavioural Responses of Dingoes to Tourists on Fraser Island.* Wildlife Tourism Research Report Series: No. 27. CRC for Sustainable Tourism, Queensland, Australia.

Lucas, R.C. (1990) Wilderness recreation management: a general overview. In: Hendee, J.C., Stankey, G.H. and Lucas, R.C. (eds) *Wilderness Management.* North American Press, Colorado, pp. 401–422.

Lusseau, D. (2003) Effects of tour boats on the behavior of bottlenose dolphins: using Markov chains to model anthropogenic impacts. *Conservation Biology* 17, 1785–1793.

Lusseau, D. and Higham, J.E.S. (2004) Managing the impacts of dolphin-based tourism through the definition of critical habitats: the case of bottlenose dolphins (*Tursiops* spp.) in Doubtful Sound, New Zealand. *Tourism Management* 25, 657–667.

MacCannell, D. (1976) *The Tourist: a New Theory of the Leisure Class.* Schoken Books, New York.

Mann, J. and Kemps, C. (2003) The effects of provisioning on maternal care in wild bottlenose dolphins, Shark Bay, Australia. In: Gales, N., Hindell, M. and Kirkwood, R. (eds) *Marine Mammals: Fisheries, Tourism and Management Issues.* CSIRO Publishing, Collingwood, Victoria, Australia, pp. 305–317.

Marsh, H. (1994) The distribution and abundance of the dugong in Shark Bay, Western Australia. *Wildlife Research* 21, 149–161.

Mathieson, A. and Wall, G. (1982) Environmental impacts of tourism. In: Mathieson, A. and Wall, G. (eds) *Tourism: Economic, Physical and Social Impacts.* Longman, London, pp. 105–112.

McNeely, J.A. and Thorsell, J.W. (1988) Jungles, mountains and islands: how tourism can help conserve the national heritage. In: D'Amore, L.J. (ed.) Tourism – A Vital Force for Peace. First Global Conference. L.J. D'Amore & Associates, Canada.

Neil, D.T. and Brieze, I. (1998) Wild dolphin provisioning at Tangalooma, Moreton Island: an evaluation. In: Tibbetts, I.R., Hall, N.J. and Dennison, W.D. (eds) Proceedings of Moreton Bay and Catchment Conference. School of Marine Science, The University of Queensland, St Lucia, Queensland, Australia.

Newsome, D., Moore, S. and Dowling, R. (2002) *Natural Area Tourism: Ecology, Impacts and Management.* Channel View Publications, Clevedon, UK.

Newsome, D., Dowling, R.K. and Moore, S.A. (2005) *Wildlife Tourism.* Channel View Publications, Clevedon, UK.

Nichols, C. and Stone, G.S. (2001) *Observations of Interactions Between Hector's Dolphins* (Cephalorhynchus hectori)*, Boats and People at Akaroa Harbour, New Zealand.* Science for Conservation no. 178. Department of Conservation, New Zealand.

O'Neill, F., Barnard, S. and Lee, D. (2004) *Best Practice and Interpretation in Tourist/Wildlife Encounters: a Wild Dolphin Swim Tour Example.* CRC for Sustainable Tourism, Queensland, Australia.

Orams, M.B. (1996) A conceptual model of tourist-wildlife interaction: the case for education as a management strategy. *Australian Geographer* 27, 39–51.

Orams, M.B. (1997a) Historical accounts of human-dolphin interaction and recent developments in wild dolphin based tourism in Australasia. *Tourism Management* 18, 317–326.

Orams, M.B. (1997b) Wild dolphin based tourism: minimising the risks and maximising the benefits. In: Saxena, N.K. (ed.) *Recent Advances in Marine Science and Technology, 96.* Pacific Congress on Marine Science and Technology, Honolulu, Hawaii.

Orams, M.B. (2002) Feeding wildlife as a tourism attraction: a review of issues and impacts. *Tourism Management* 23, 281–293.

Orams, M.B., Hill, G.J.E. and Baglioni, A.J. (1996) 'Pushy' behavior in a wild dolphin feeding program at Tangalooma, Australia. *Marine Mammal Science* 12, 107–117.

Pearce, D.W. and Turner, R.K. (1990) *Economics of Natural Resources and the Environment.* Harvester Wheatsheaf, Sydney, Australia.

Phillip Island Nature Park (2005) Discover Phillip Island Naturally. (Homepage of Phillip Island Nature Park) (Online). Available: http://www.penguins. org.au/welcome_whatnew/index02.asp#top. (19 January 2005).

Preen, A.R., Marsh, H., Lawler, I.R., Prince, R.I.T. and Shepherd, R. (1997) Distribution and abundance of dugongs, turtles, dolphins and other megafauna in Shark Bay, Ningaloo Reef and Exmouth Gulf, Western Australia. *Wildlife Research* 24, 185–208.

Raffaele, P. (2003) Return to Shark Bay. *Australian Geographic* 72, 101–115.

Reynolds, P.C. and Braithwaite, D. (2001) Towards a conceptual framework for wildlife tourism. *Tourism Management* 22, 31–42.

Richardson, J.I. and Fluker, M. (2004) *Understanding and Managing Tourism.* Pearson Education Australia, Frenchs Forest, NSW, Australia.

Roe, D., Leader Williams, N. and Dalal Clayton, B. (1997) *Take Only Photographs, Leave Only Footprints: the Environmental Impacts of Wildlife Tourism.* Wildlife and Development Series No. 10. International Institute for Environment and Development, London.

Ryan, C. (1998) Saltwater crocodiles as tourist attractions. *Journal of Sustainable Tourism* 6, 314–326.

Samuels, A., Bejder, L., Constantine, R. and Heinrich, S. (2003) Swimming with wild cetaceans, with a special focus on the southern hemisphere. In: Gales, N., Hindell, M. and Kirkwood, R. (eds) *Marine Mammals: Fisheries, Tourism and Management Issues.* CSIRO Publishing, Collingwood, Victoria, Australia, pp. 305–317.

Scott, D. and Willits, F.K. (1994) Environmental attitudes and behavior: a Pennsylvania survey. *Environment and Behaviour* 26, 239–260.

Shackley, M. (1996) *Wildlife Tourism.* International Thomson Business Press, London.

Shire of Shark Bay (1998) *Shark Bay Regional Strategy: A review of the 1988 Shark Bay Region Plan.* Shire of Shark Bay, Denham, WA, Australia.

Sinha, C. (2001). Wildlife tourism: a geographical perspective. In: Geography Curriculum Inservice Conference. Tourism Geography: Issues, Challenges and the Changing Nature of Contemporary Tourism. July 27, 2001. University of Western Sydney, Hawkesbury Campus, Sydney, NSW, Australia.

Smith, A.J. and Newsome, D. (2006) *An Investigation into the Concept of and Factors Leading to Impact Creep, and its Management.* CRC for Sustainable Tourism, Queensland, Australia.

Smith, A.J., Newsome, D., Lee, D., Stoeckl, N. (2006) *The Role of Wildlife Icons as Major Tourist Attractions*. Case Studies: Monkey Mia Dolphins and Hervey Bay Whale Watching and CRC for Sustainable Tourism, Queensland, Australia.

Tremblay, P. (2002) Tourism wildlife icons: attractions or marketing symbols? *Journal of Hospitality and Tourism Management* 9, 164–181.

Wilson, B.F. (1994) *Review of Dolphin Management at Monkey Mia*. Murex Consultants, Perth, WA, Australia.

Wilson, C. and Tisdell, C. (2001). Sea turtles as a non-consumptive tourism resource especially in Australia. *Tourism Management* 22, 279–288.

7

Teppich-Swingers and Skibums: Differential Experiences of Ski Tourism in the Tirolean Alps

Jacqueline McGibbon

Independent Consultant

Introduction

International ski resorts have become sites set aside within the global cultural economy for the intense, mass consumption (and production) of tourism, sport and leisure. They are complex, transnational spaces that draw together a diverse range of people to participate in winter sports and in the nightlife and other forms of entertainment that surround them. In Western Europe, where today the differences in wealth between tourists and hosts are often less extreme than in other regions and eras, these people include not only tourists from various backgrounds, but also many local residents and seasonal workers. Local residents are often consumers, as well as producers, of the facilities and products of the ski tourism industry, although they may employ distinctive modes of consumption to distinguish themselves from outsiders, while seasonal workers are often attracted to working in ski resorts because of the sports and leisure facilities these places provide them with. The interaction of this diverse mix of peoples in the transnational space of the ski resort generates new social forms and patterns of consumption. This consumption revolves around just a few products – winter sports equipment, clothing and services, food, alcohol, accommodation, and the image or idea of the ski resort itself.

The images and discourses of advertising, along with images and discourses drawn from other sources, play an important role in converting places into products for tourist consumption and in motivating tourists (and often seasonal workers) to visit them. It is for this reason that they have received considerable attention in the tourism literature. Far less attention has been given to the actual practices of consumption that tourists engage in – both as individuals and in groups – once they arrive in tourist destinations. Yet, as a growing body of literature indicates, tourism is not simply about the passive consumption of visual images and the discourses associated with them. Rather, tourism is also an interactive experience involving the entire body and all its senses, and never more so than in the case of an active sport holiday, such as a ski holiday. Ideally, for a balanced understanding of tourism as a process of consumption, both these aspects must be addressed, i.e. the broader symbolic field shaping tourist destinations as sites of consumption and people's differential experiences and practices of consumption within this symbolic field.

What follows is an analysis of one particular ski resort, the village of St Anton am Arlberg in the Tirolean Alps, as a site for the mass consumption of tourism, sport and leisure. This analysis examines both the complex symbolic field surrounding ski tourism in Tirol and the different patterns of consumption that individuals and groups engage in once in the village. It begins with a brief discussion about the significance of both these dimensions for understanding tourist consumption. Then it examines some of the images and discourses associated with ski tourism and the various sources from which they are drawn. The diverse ways in which people participate in snow sports is the subject of the next section. Finally, two quite different patterns of tourist consumption in the village are described – that of the '*Teppich-Swingers*', or a group of well-off regular guests who have formed their own ski club, and that of the 'skibums', or young travellers who work the winter season to fund their extended ski holidays. The practices of both these groups of visitors have, over time, played a role in shaping the ski resort itself and in stimulating further consumption within it.

The Role of Images and the Discourses of Advertising

Advertising plays an important role in stimulating the consumption of tourism, sport and leisure, and millions of dollars are spent on it annually. Images of tourist destinations are generated by tourism bodies at local, regional and national levels, as well as by individual businesses selling products within destinations. Advertising does not simply transfer images of tourist destinations to potential customers. In today's media-driven world, advertising actively creates images of tourist sites and helps turn places into products for tourist consumption. Further, it provides coherent ideologies for consuming entire 'systems of objects', which are systems of signs (Thurot and Thurot, 1983; Baudrillard, 1988, pp. 10–25).

Touristic advertising images are created in a complex process involving many influences and participants (Morgan and Pritchard,

1998, pp. 43–62). Nevertheless, these images tend to reflect and reinforce the dominant ideologies of the societies within which they are formed (Morgan and Pritchard, 1998, pp. 46–51). They also typically simplify, sanitize, stereotype and commodify tourist sites and local life. In different contexts, however, they do so in different ways, drawing on existing themes and images in regional and national socio-cultural complexes. These images not only speak to and generate the desires of tourists, but also influence the self-perceptions and national identities of hosts (Ivy, 1988; Morris, 1991; Rowe, 1993; Morgan and Pritchard, 1998). Further, they create a type of imagined community for tourists and hosts, the context in which interactions between them take place (Anderson, 1983).

The ways in which tourists perceive destinations and their inhabitants are not influenced by touristic advertising images alone. Tourist sites are surrounded by entire symbolic complexes of images originating from diverse sources, including art, photography, literature, film, music, television and other forms of advertising. Game's analyses of the images and discourses surrounding English heritage sites and Bondi Beach in Australia clearly illustrate the intertextuality of touristic narratives with other cultural productions (Game, 1991; see also Morgan and Pritchard, 1998). Tourism officials wishing to project a particular view of a destination cannot always control the nature of the images drawn from these other sources.

A Range of Subjective, Embodied Experiences

Despite the important role of advertising and other images in shaping tourist locations, it is important to recognize the gap between touristic discourses about a place and the variety of people's lived experiences of that place. In her thought-provoking work, *Undoing the Social*, Ann Game argues that there are 'always different ways of being in a place', which are different ways of meaning inscribed through the body and its senses (1991, p. 148). So, for example, she challenges the oft-repeated assertion that the traditional in tourism predominantly helps to satisfy the nostalgia of urban dwellers for a less alienating rural past (e.g. Enzensberger, 1962; McCannell, 1976). Instead, she argues that besides nostalgia, which is based on a lack, there may also be a 'positive desire to feel, touch, smell, and move', a desire for the mastery of a place (1991, p. 166).

Further, although the images used to market tourist sites do inform both tourist experiences and local self-perceptions, the precise effects of advertising are hard to gauge, particularly given that the symbols and texts employed are open to interpretation. As Game notes, while touristic discourses, particularly advertising, tend to reduce the diversity of ways of being in a place into homogenized codes of meaning, 'practices transform texts [and] "open up space to something different"' (1991, pp. 153, 184 quoting de Certeau, 1984, pp. 106–107).

In line with much of Western culture and social theory, tourism studies tend to have a visual and intellectual bias (Turner, 1984; Game, 1991; Veijola and Jokinen, 1994; Rojek, 1995, pp. 61–64; Wearing and Wearing, 1996;). Studies tend to focus on the passive gaze of sightseeing and the visual consumption of cultures, landscapes, events and displays. This has led several commentators to remark that studies of tourism are insufficiently embodied. Yet tourism is always an active and interactive phenomenon involving the entire body and all its senses, and not just visual processes (Game, 1991; Meethan, 1996). Far from being a passive activity, tourism is a dynamic and creative process (Wearing and Wearing, 1996, p. 229). Even if tourists are protected by the tour group or Western-style hotel, they still encounter different physical spaces, environments, weathers, temperatures, foodstuffs, sounds, smells and sensations – different ways of 'being in place' and 'moving in space' (Game, 1991, pp. 145, 151). Similarly, even if interactions with people in destinations (hosts, local residents, seasonal workers and other tourists) are brief and transitory, and in many cases commodified, tourists still encounter different people and ways of behaving.

The embodied nature of tourism particularly comes to the fore in active, sport-oriented, ski holidays. Sightseeing is not the primary focus of a ski holiday, although aspects of the romantic and historical gaze may certainly be involved. Instead, in any one holiday, people repeatedly ski down the same mountain slopes, and over the years they often repeatedly return to the same resort and even hotel. Ski holidays do, however, involve intense, active bodily participation: motion (skiing, falling over), physical sensations (tiredness, coldness, muscle pain) and altered states of being (intoxication, injury).

In an attempt to capture the subjective and experiential aspects of tourism, Wearing and Wearing (1996), drawing on the work of de Certeau (1984), conceptualize the tourist destination as a type of interactive space. Within this space, tourists interact with the various inhabitants, symbols and environments they encounter, to generate their own subjective meanings of the destination. The sorts of subjective meanings they generate depend on such things as the tourist's socio-cultural background, his or her experiences in the destination, and the images used to market the destination (Wearing and Wearing, 1996, p. 237). Tourists then 'creatively incorporate' these subjective experiences of the tourist space into their own sense of self, historical narratives and identities (Wearing and Wearing, 1996, p. 235). Meanings are not only generated by individual tourists, but also by groups of tourists. A destination can become a collective material resource, when groups of people attach specific meanings to it and it takes on a particular social significance for them (Wearing and Wearing, 1996, pp. 235–236). Further, gradually these interactions and collective meanings can become incorporated into the destination's image.

In sum, analyses of tourism consumption gain from a two-pronged approach, assessing, first, the images and discourses shaping tourist sites and, secondly, the subjective, embodied experiences and interactions of both individuals and members of social groups within these sites. It is this approach that will be employed in the following analysis of the Austrian ski resort of St Anton.

Snow Sports in St Anton: a Complex, Shifting, Symbolic Field

Although only a small rural community of some 2400 permanent residents, St Anton is also a thriving international tourist resort. Tourism in the village dates back to the mid-1800s when wealthy travellers and Alpinists began to visit the region in the summer months to enjoy the spectacular landscapes and mountain air. Winter tourism began later, around the turn of the century, with the development of modern alpine skiing, but quickly became the most significant form of tourism in the village. Currently, St Anton caters to >160,000 tourists and to almost a million overnight stays annually, with >80% of these guests visiting in the winter months. Thus the village is now dependent on the wealth generated by ski tourism. Ski tourism has also become a central aspect of local culture, with local identity often forged around the industry. This discussion focuses on winter tourism and the experiences of visitors in the region; however, for information about summer tourism and local consumption of the products and facilities of the ski tourism industry, see McGibbon (2000a).

When ski tourism began, it was an elite domain attracting mainly wealthy, urban professionals and industrialists, and the early discourses and practices associated with the new and fashionable sport of skiing were intertwined with discourses of Alpinism and athleticism (see Hargreaves, 1987; Robbins, 1987; Tschofen, 1993; McGibbon 2000a). At this time, there were no devices for transporting skiers uphill, and skiing involved challenging climbs, day-long tours and the exploration of previously inaccessible, pristine mountain environments.

Today, in contrast, skiing is a mass sport in which many are able to participate. In the course of the 20th century, skiing was modernized, industrialized, commercialized and firmly incorporated into the realm of consumer culture. A major factor in these developments has been the introduction of devices to transport skiers uphill. A network of some 84 chair-lifts and cable-cars now transports thousands of people around the mountains each hour, and purchasing a ski pass provides access to

>260 km of clearly marked, artificially prepared ski runs, known as 'pistes'. Each day, the lift company uses heavy machinery to remove excess snow and bumps from pistes and, at times, it also removes trees and rocky outcrops to create suitable ski runs. Large restaurant complexes have been constructed in the mountains, and numerous shops, products, bars and other facilities have emerged in the village to cater for the needs of ski consumers. A mass of images from various sources circulates within the resort and beyond, promoting and glamorizing skiing.

Despite the mass nature of contemporary ski tourism, people participate in skiing and other snow sports in a myriad of different ways. Since its inception, alpine skiing has constantly changed in form and style, a result of the complex interplay of new technologies and equipment, skiing techniques and fashions. Modern skiing, with its high technology, fibreglass skis and high fashion, functional, protective clothing, has come a long way from the heavy wooden skis, leather boots, plus-fours, ankle-length skirts and elegant hats of the early 20th century. Further, in recent decades, skiing has diversified into an array of different winter sports, including snowboarding, telemarking and mono-skiing, each with its own specialized equipment, clothing styles, ideologies and practices. Snow sports not only change over time, but also involve various dimensions (such as speed and style) and various terrains and conditions (such as prepared slopes, bumps, deep-snow), each of which demand different techniques, with people often preferring to specialize in one or another. Other people prefer to focus on the social life and vibrant nightlife that surrounds skiing.

This diversity renders it impossible to offer a single coherent description of the meanings of snow sports. Rather, it is useful to conceptualize snow sports as part of a complex, transnational, continually shifting symbolic field, which includes a range of discourses, practices and institutions, from which people draw various, even contradictory, cultural meanings and satisfactions. While a detailed description of this symbolic field is impossible in the space allowed, what follows is a brief discussion of some of the advertising and other images glamorizing snow sports and of some of the diverse modes of participation in these sports that people engage in.

Images and Discourses Surrounding Snow Sports

In addition to the marketing images they encounter in holiday brochures and advertisements when considering or planning a ski holiday, tourists are bombarded by an array of images promoting ski tourism and its associated businesses and products, once they arrive in a resort. These images are found in brochures, placards, billboards, window displays, diverse media (television, newspapers, magazines), postcards, souvenir books and local museums, and are based on a range of quite distinct, sometimes even contradictory, themes.

Contemporary advertising for ski tourism is dominated by the themes and icons of consumer culture, which Hargreaves describes as follows:

> the main orchestrating themes are youth, beauty, sexual liberation, movement/variety/change, excitement, luxury, fun and entertainment, individual choice, fulfilment and freedom. Its dominant icons are the young attractive healthy person and the happy family.
>
> (1987, p. 150)

Snow sports are marketed as active, adventurous and challenging, and Tirol as an exciting 'adventure play park with a surface area of 12,648 square kilometres' (*Tirol, Herz der Alpen – Schnee*, 1987, p. 15). Typical images are action shots of proficient skiers and snowboarders in energetic poses. Simultaneously, a ski holiday is presented as a time for recuperation and relaxation, a time to escape the pressures of everyday life and to pay extra attention to the body (through exercise, the fresh mountain air, saunas and massage). It is also a time to socialize, to meet new people and spend time with family and friends. Sexuality is another important theme: models are young and beautiful and advertisements suggest endless parties and romance. Photographs are colourful: bright outfits and tanned skins against the backdrop of pure white snow and a perpetually blue sky. The common denominator is an 'ambience' of pleasure: individuals, couples and families are laughing, smiling, happy and satisfied.

From its inception at the turn of the century, skiing was considered a most modern activity, associated with new technologies and progress, and these associations continue today. Advertisements emphasize that St Anton has the most modern of comforts in its cable cars, hotels and other facilities, while ski shops sell the latest ski equipment such as 'dynamic, high-tensile, vacuum skis'. At the same time, other advertisements hark back to an earlier era, playing on notions of Alpinism. Images of lone skiers appear against the backdrop of pristine, alpine environments devoid of the crowds and infrastructure associated with mass tourism. Other images picture adventurous individuals in extreme contexts – atop rugged mountain peaks or skiing extraordinarily steep slopes.

Some advertisements involve historic images of early mountaineers, ski pioneers and the equipment they used. St Anton has a particularly rich history to draw on in this respect (see Hopplicher, 1989; Thöni, 1990; McGibbon, 2000b). An important ski pioneer, Hannes Schneider, emerged from the region, developing the world-renowned Arlberg Ski Technique in the early 1900s and establishing the world's first ski school with graded classes and a specific teaching plan in 1922. Between 1920 and 1931, the German director Arnold Fanck made no less than nine films starring Schneider and featuring other locals. These films, which were designed to promote the new sport of skiing and convey the newly discovered beauty of the mountains in the winter, were immensely popular and had an international impact.

Images associated with Alpinism are not confined to direct marketing. Alpinism is celebrated in the region in numerous exhibitions, film festivals, books, magazine articles, documentaries, museums and alpine clubs. Interest in these cultural productions spans local residents, seasonal workers and tourists, and the images they draw on originate from mountain environments around the world, not just the Alps. Often these cultural productions are intertwined with marketing in complex ways. The annual Banff Mountain Film Festival that tours ski resorts such as St Anton is sponsored by the mountain clothing company Peak Performance, and most of the films in the festival are sponsored by various ski equipment companies. Some equipment companies sponsor teams of extreme skiers and snowboarders, and use the images these teams generate in their marketing campaigns. Their glossy brochures are more like magazines complete with long articles and photographic spreads of alpine adventures. Videos of extreme skiing that play through the night in bars and shop windows are also sponsored by ski clothing and equipment companies.

Other images glamorizing and popularizing ski tourism come from the realm of competitive sport. Ski racers advertise products for ski tourism and set equipment fashions and goals in skiing ability, while ski races and snowboard competitions are major media events, promoting the resorts that stage them and the numerous companies from the winter sports and tourism industries that sponsor them. Over the years, numerous famous ski racers and Olympic medallists have emerged from the region, and the village has often hosted World Cup ski races, including the World Skiing Championships in 2001.

Diverse Modes of Participation in Snow Sports

Just as a diverse range of images serve to market ski tourism, so too there are diverse modes of participating in snow sports. This section introduces a few of these modes, including two skiing techniques (*Wedeln* and carving), snowboarding, touring and extreme skiing, illustrating the complex interplay of factors involved in their ongoing development and the various ideologies and practices with which each is associated. It also outlines some of the liminal or *carnivalesque* aspects of a ski holiday.

In the 1950s and 1960s, a new skiing technique was developed in Austria that was to revolutionize the sport and contribute to the massive post-war explosion in its popularity. This technique, called 'Wedeln', which literally means to wag or wave (as in to wag a tail), involved skiing in short, precise, rhythmic and measured turns, moving only the legs, with the knees held firmly together and the upper body held still and upright. A ski pole was held in each hand and used to help maintain balance. The new technique was made possible by the development of stiff plastic shoes and shorter, lighter skis with steel edges, which together made it easier to turn and enabled more control. Compared with earlier techniques, which required the use of the entire body to turn the long, heavy, wooden skis clumsily, Wedeln looked neat and elegant: skiers appeared to glide effortlessly over the snow. In addition, the new technique made skiing easier to learn, rendering it more accessible to the public. It was at this time that skiing became a mass movement in Austria and the most important factor in the country's rapidly expanding tourism industry. With its increased precision and control, the new technique also enabled people to ski together in synchronized patterns. Footage from the time shows large groups of people skiing in perfect symmetry to a background of light-hearted, optimistic songs about the pleasures of skiing, mountain environments and pretty girls (see Maurer *et al.*, 2001).

The technique of Wedeln dominated leisure skiing for some 40 years. Recently, however, another new technique known as 'carving' has been rapidly gaining popularity and is set to revolutionize the sport once more. Influenced by techniques used in ski racing, carving involves long, rapid, sweeping turns, and employs a strikingly different bodily posture from that of Wedeln. In carving, the knees are set aggressively apart and the upper body is bent forward. Ski poles are discarded and instead during each turn the skier's arms dip towards the ground, hands scraping over the snow (rather like the dipping movement of a motorcycle when turning). Carving is a faster, more dynamic technique than Wedeln. Skiers no longer glide over the snow, but rather use the ski's razor sharp edges to cut through it – hence the name 'carving' (from the English 'to carve', meaning 'to cut up'). Whereas in Wedeln turns slowed the skis, giving the skier the sensation of precision and control, carving uses the body's mass and gravity to accelerate in turns, giving the skier the sensation of 'flying' down the mountain. Carving has been made possible by the development of even shorter, specially shaped skis, which render turning easier still. Thus, carving skis, which were first developed in Austria, have the added benefit of further speeding up the learning process for the novice skier. The images associated with carving usually picture individuals, rather than groups, sweeping down the mountains, and video images are set to powerful techno beats.

To some extent, carving is the ski industry's answer to snow-boarding. Snowboarding originated in the late 1970s when surfboards were adapted to winter conditions. Since the early 1990s, snowboarding has rapidly increased in popularity, particularly amongst the young, and has been perceived by some as a major threat to skiing. Some sources estimate that around 80% of the under-14-year-old market in Austria prefer to snowboard than ski, raising the question of who will be the skiers of the future. There are several reasons why snowboarding is so popular. For one thing, it is easier to master than skiing, allowing the practitioner to progress more rapidly than the skier to difficult conditions, such as steep slopes and deep-snow (see Hudson, 2000, pp. 14–16). For another, like carving, snowboarding offers a more rapid and dynamic way to descend the mountain than traditional skiing. Further, snowboarding culture, which is influenced by surfing and skateboarding cultures, shares a rebel image with these sports that particularly appeals to the young.

These cultural influences and the rebel image are evident in the design and decoration of snowboarding equipment, the organization of competitive events and the advertising images used to promote the sport. Snowboarding fashions are influenced by an aesthetized US 'street culture', as presented in popular music videos and sports/fashion advertisements alike: headscarfs, oversized trousers and sweatshirts. An Americanized jargon has emerged around the sport in German-speaking lands, and snowboarding competitions blast out contemporary 'grunge' rock bands (Pearl Jam, Nirvana, Sonic Youth) instead of the usual Tirolean style *Volksmusik* played at all other local events. Snowboarding's rebel image was strengthened by the initial reaction of older generations and ski officials to the sport. In the media, snowboarders were stereotyped as long-haired, drug-using, antisocial youths most likely to cause avalanches, and in some places snowboards were or still are banned from the ski slopes altogether. Recently, however, residents of St Anton have realized that snowboarding is an important commercial market and have attempted to incorporate the sport into the village's tourist-leisure offer: for example, opening up snowboard shops and offering snowboard instructors in the ski school.

In response to the industrialization and commercialization of skiing, many skiers prefer to ski 'off-piste', away from crowds and prepared tracks, particularly in 'deep' or 'powder' snow. To do so requires advanced skiing skills and substantial knowledge of alpine conditions. For many proficient skiers, the only way to 'really' ski is to go touring. Touring involves challenging climbs, day-long trips and sometimes overnight stays in isolated mountain huts, without the use of ski lifts or prepared pistes. Tourers attach skins to the base of their skis allowing them to walk uphill on the snow. Skins are then removed for downhill runs. The attractions of touring include pride in the self-reliance and competence it demands, spectacular views devoid of human habitation, wide expanses of powder snow, and the sense of being alone and at one with nature. Some also take pleasure in being different from the majority of skiers who are constrained to the pistes. In the words of one alpine documentary: 'Luckily touring is not for everyone, but only for experienced individuals. If the masses were to rush off-piste, it would damage the environment' (Maurer *et al.*, 2001).

Another group of skiers who like to differentiate themselves from the mainstream are extreme skiers. Extreme skiing, also known as freeriding, involves negotiating dangerously steep slopes, often narrow gullies flanked by rocks on either side. Expert practitioners risk life and limb jumping metres down cliff faces and skiing over small avalanches that they themselves set off. The attractions of extreme skiing include the adrenalin rushes it induces, since even the smallest error could lead to serious injury or death, and the sense of achievement at having survived its challenges and tested one's physical and mental limits. In addition, extreme skiers are often held in awe by other skiers.

Regardless of the mode of participation that people prefer, a ski holiday can have distinct liminal or *carnivalesque* aspects, in the sense of play, excesses and reversals (see Graburn, 1983; Lett, 1983; Featherstone, 1991, p. 22). A ski holiday involves a spatial change, a physical change of context, and marks a break from usual routines. The ski slope, like the beach, is a 'complex space, anomalously located between land and sea [or in this case between mountain and valley], nature and culture' (Urry, 1990, p. 38). Just as there 'might be a way of being in the beach – a drifting of the body, qualitative differences of the senses, involuntary memory – which refuses the quantification of commodification', there might be similar ways of being in the mountains or on the ski slope (Game, 1991, p. 179). Writing in 1924, Thomas Mann describes how the central character of *Der Zauberberg* finds the beach in more ways than one 'a relative' of the snow-covered mountains.

Whether one is an extreme skier or not, through skiing and other snow sports it is possible to play with and challenge the body's usual constraints, such as gravity. One can move rapidly, turn upside down and obtain a sense of bodily freedom: 'be weightless, flying over the powder snow' (*Tirol, Herz der Alpen – Schnee*, 1987, p. 7). For skiers of all levels of skill, ski holidays often involve excesses, taking risks and altered states of mind, such as skiing dangerously (taking a spectacular fall), staying out all night and excessive consumption of alcohol.

Further, a ski holiday can involve reversals or inversions of the normal order of things and transgressions of social boundaries. Strikingly brightly coloured and multi-patterned ski clothes and equipment turn the sombre routines of industrial and office life on their head. Businessmen, usually dressed in the black or grey suits of the business world, don pink, polka-dotted one-piece suits, or lime green and purple fluorescent combinations. The intense consumption of alcohol, crowded village environments and the existence of a common interest (skiing) promote conviviality in public spaces, and social barriers are often relaxed. German speakers often say that over 1000 m, one should always use the 'Du' informal form of address. Typical status differentials of centre and periphery are also partly reversed. The modestly educated and generally 'poorer' village residents have superior skiing skills and knowledge of the mountains than their often wealthy guests from the urban elite, frequently making them objects of admiration and envy.

Despite these reversals, ski holidays are still associated with wealth, class and status. Skiing remains an expensive sport, requiring a costly investment of time and money to master it, and a symbol of wealth, luxury and glamour. For certain class fractions in European societies, a ski holiday is considered an essential part of the annual routine. The ski resort is also a site for conspicuous consumption and to display distinctions of class and status. Facilities such as hotels are graded (three-star, four-star), and people can display their wealth and/or cultural capital in their choice of the most expensive or latest clothing and equipment. At the same time, different groups (class fractions, generations, etc.) are likely to practise the same sport in quite different ways, as the next section illustrates.

Consumption Among Different Social Groups: the *Teppich-Swinger*

In St Anton, many tourists use the ski school as the basis of their socializing activities. By joining a ski group, tourists meet other skiers of a similar level with whom they can ski and participate in the rituals of après-ski. In particular, over the years, regular guests often ski with the same group and instructor, forming long-lasting friendships. Regular guests or *Stammgäste* are an important category of tourist in St Anton. Frequently they have been coming to the same pension or hotel for >20 years, and many return several times a year. The Tourist Association estimates that about 30% of the village's guests are *Stammgäste*. While these guests come from various places, such as England, the USA and Sweden, the majority come from Germany and other parts of Austria. Many are wealthy businessmen and women or urban professionals. *Stammgäste* often form long-standing relationships with local families that cross the boundaries of a strictly economic relationship between hotel owner and paying guest. These relationships can involve socializing, gift exchange and even mutual visits.

In 1981, one group of *Stammgäste* who skied with a particularly flamboyant instructor decided to form a club, which they called the *Teppich-Swinger Verein* (literally the Carpet-Swinger Association). They dedicated the club to the 'promotion and spread of alpine *Teppich-*

swingen' and to the holding of various events promoting *Bergkameradschaft* (Teppich-Swinger Verein, 1981). *Teppich-swingen* refers to the practice of several people skiing in formation alongside each other in deep-snow using the technique of *Wedeln*, leaving behind distinct, symmetrical patterns (*Teppichs* or carpets) on the slope that can be admired and analysed. *Bergkameradschaft* (mountain friendship) refers to the increased social intimacy generated by peoples' shared presence in and love of the mountains.

The club is well organized with its own rulebook, official positions (e.g. president, cashier), membership fees, printed T-shirts and other paraphernalia. Those wishing to join the club must undergo a test, whereby they must help create three *Teppichs* in the presence of the instructor and other group members. Thus novices must be accomplished in the difficult art of deep-snow skiing since, in order to create the symmetrical patterns, skiers must be fully in control of their skis and coordinate their movements to make turns of equal length. The club has other rituals too. Each afternoon members meet in a particular village café, at a table set aside for them, where they drink together, converse and re-live the events of the ski day. The walls surrounding the table are decorated with framed photographs of the group.

Although a social club, there are competitive elements and considerable social pressures associated with the *Teppich-Swingers*. Not only must people be skilled skiers to join, but once members, if they spoil a *Teppich* by falling over, they are subject to a fine in the form of paying for the group's wine that afternoon at the café. They are also subject to substantial ridicule from other members and the instructor. It is striking to observe members, most of whom are in their 50s, well off and well established in their chosen professions, being castigated for their poor skiing abilities by the local instructor.

Members attach considerable prestige to being a part of the group and able to keep up with its skiing rituals. Some *Teppichs* can be observed in the valley, and participants proudly point them out to others. Since there are some 80 members of the club, but only 15 places in a ski group on any one day, at busy times of the year members must compete to be included. Prestige also comes from the fact that members must be well off enough to participate in the club. They must be able to afford regular holidays in St Anton, the cost of the ski school, tips for the instructor and the club's daily drinking rituals.

Most members have been in the club for years, and it plays an important part in their lives. It brings not only a sense of prestige and achievement, but also an international network of friendships and a deeper involvement with St Anton. Members frequently spend several weeks a year skiing in the village and also meet there and elsewhere for special events in summer, such as the ski instructor's annual birthday celebration. Like other regular guests, they often take an interest in the local community, joining village associations, such as the Ski Club Arlberg, and participating in fundraising and other village events. Over the years, some members have rented out or purchased their own apartments in the village. For economic reasons, the tourist association and local businesses are keen to encourage well-off regular guests such as the *Teppich-Swingers* and, in winter, members of the group are treated like honorary villagers, with club activities regularly reported in the local newspaper.

Consumption Among Different Social Groups: Skibums

A quite different group consuming ski tourism products in the village are the so-called 'skibums'. Skibums are generally young people from Western nations such as Australia, the UK, New Zealand, Sweden and South Africa, who primarily come to St Anton to ski and socialize, but who also work to cover the costs of their ski holidays. Many skibums are employed in jobs that no-one else wants: jobs that offer only 2 h of work a day or that need someone only when it is snowing. They often work for low wages and poor quality accommodation. Some return repeatedly, however, gradually obtaining better paid positions and forming patronage relationships with a local employer and a range of friendships with locals and other seasonal workers. It is difficult to estimate the number of skibums in the village, since some are employed illegally; however, official sources estimate as many as 800 find work each season, with many more unsuccessfully looking for work. Most hear about St Anton from friends or the travellers' grapevine while working their way through Europe. St Anton is considered a good place to spend a winter season, since it offers seasonal jobs, a chance to ski and a well-developed travellers' scene.

The term 'skibum' is a convenient label that covers a range of people in quite different circumstances. For many locals, the term is infused with negative connotations, and skibums are accused of everything from being lazy and undisciplined workers to leading irresponsible and hedonistic lifestyles. Many younger locals, however, keenly await their arrival each year and enjoy the excitement and ambience they bring to the village. Some businesses are renowned for employing primarily skibums, partly because they are less costly workers with useful language skills, and partly because they bring a relaxed and fun attitude to work that suits the atmosphere of an international ski resort.

Although not recognized as such, skibums lie somewhere between tourists and seasonal workers and, although, unlike regular guests, they are not encouraged by the tourist office, they make extensive use of local sport and leisure facilities, investing a substantial amount of their earnings back into the village. Indeed, often they need to subsidize their winter working holidays with money earned in summer. Most purchase a ski pass for the season and spend much of their free time skiing or, more commonly these days, snowboarding, while at night they congregate in bars with cheaper prices.

Unlike regular guests, most skibums are on a budget and therefore rarely make use of the facilities of the ski school. Rather, they generally learn to ski from each other or by trial and error, and many of their conversations involve the transfer of knowledge about the mountains (where to ski, how to ski, which equipment to purchase, etc.). At first, they often make do with old equipment either borrowed or left behind by former skibums, but as they become more established they often invest substantial sums in high quality and fashionable equipment.

Like the *Teppich-Swingers*, the goal of many skibums is to ski off-piste and if proficient enough many prefer to go touring. However, unlike the *Teppich-Swingers*, they do not ski in organized groups or clubs. Rather, they tend to ski in small groups of 2–5 people. Although they may plan their skiing activities with particular companions in advance, the dominant ethos among skibums is 'taking it as it comes'. Thus their ski days usually depend on how late the party went on the night before, what the weather is like and who they happen to meet on their way to the slopes. They are not to be found creating *Teppichs*, but tend to take a more individualistic approach to getting down the mountain. One skibum described the pleasure he and his friends had 'skiing like madmen around the haunts of the rich and famous'. Since they stay for the entire season, they get to know less used areas of the mountain and exploit alternative, less crowded spaces than the majority of skiers. They also avoid commercialized spaces on the mountain such as expensive restaurants and bars. Instead they often take a packed lunch and eat somewhere picturesque on the mountain. After skiing, they often gather in the village pedestrian zone or around the supermarket.

Skibums have developed their own subculture and traditions, although the forms these traditions have taken change over time. There is the annual production of a skibum video and sweatshirt that can be purchased as souvenirs of the season, as well as a series of regular events. In the 1980s, one tradition was a nude ski race, held at Easter, but after a number of arrests this practice came to an end. In the early 1990s, musicians in the skibum community put on several large concerts each year, while currently a couple of bars popular with skibums hold regular parties and an annual ski race. Although skibums stem from many backgrounds, the dominant language of this subculture is English. There is a strong sense of community between skibums, and like the *Teppich-Swingers* they form long-lasting relationships with each other and also with locals (including marriage and business relations). They often work for several seasons in the village, and many return in later years to visit friends or as tourists.

Conclusion: Shaping the Tourist Space

The consumption of tourism and leisure is used not only to shape individual personas, but also to mark people belonging to particular social groups, and struggles between different groups (such as generations and social classes) are often mediated by different strategies of consumption (Bourdieu, 1984; Featherstone, 1987). Further, as Wearing and Wearing (1996, p. 236) suggest, the social interactions occurring within a tourist site and the subjective meanings groups of tourists ascribe to it can gradually become a part of the destination and its image.

In St Anton, this has happened with both the *Teppich-Swingers* and the skibums. In part, participants of both groups keep returning to the village because of the communities of regular guests and skibums, with whom they can socialize during their stays. In addition, participants of both groups act as embodied advertisements for St Anton, stimulating further consumption, when they tell others of the attractions of the resort. Young backpackers, for example, often come to the village after hearing about it from other travellers who have experienced it first hand.

Both groups shape the destination in other ways too. The *Teppich-Swingers* have colonized part of the public space of a central local café and have helped popularize the practice of skiing in formations in the village. They are also featured regularly in the village newspaper and in local magazines aimed at tourists. The skibums promote the international feel of the village, almost exclusively staffing well-known village bars with foreign themes, such as the 'Krazy Kangaruh' and 'The Underground'. They also bring a distinctive life and colour to the streets when they gather in the pedestrian zone. For several years, a sunny ski area has officially been named 'Rendl Beach', a term drawn directly from skibum terminology. Skibums also form friendships with local youths, helping the latter to build up international travel networks and to learn English. Articles about skibums appear in local newspapers, although these are often critical in nature, and the skibums form one chapter of a recently published coffee table picture book about the village (Schmidt, 2000, pp. 70–71).

In the context of mass tourism, as many have pointed out, tourist–local interactions are often brief, transitory and commodified, and local life is often stereotyped and homogenized by the tourism industry's advertising codes. Despite this, however, the various, embodied and interactive touristic experiences that individual tourists have cannot be reduced into a neat theory of tourism. In other words, through the agency of the body – of engaging with new sensations and of being in, moving through and interacting with different environments – individual subjects convert the experience of 'mass tourism' into a personal experience.

This is particularly evident in contexts such as St Anton where there is a high level of repeat visits, giving visitors the chance to form networks of relationships with other guests, hosts, local residents and seasonal workers, and where, over time, the practices of guests can become incorporated into and shape the tourist space itself.

References

Anderson, B. (1983) *Imagined Communities: Reflections on the Origins and Spread of Nationalism*. Verso, London.

Baudrillard, J. (1988) Poster, M. (ed.) *Selected Writings*. Stanford University Press, Stanford, California.

Bourdieu, P. (1984) *Distinction: a Social Critique of the Judgement of Taste*. Nice, R. (Transl.), Harvard University Press, Cambridge, Massachusetts.

de Certeau, M. (1984) *The Practice of Everyday Life*. University of California Press, Berkeley, California.

Enzensberger, H.M. (1962) Eine Theorie des Tourismus. In: Enzensberger, H.M. (ed.) *Einzelheiten 1. Bewusstseins-Industrie*. Suhrkamp Verlag, Frankfurt am Main, Germany, pp. 147–168.

Featherstone, M. (1987) Leisure, symbolic power and the life course. In: Horne, J., Jary, D. and Tomlinson, A. (eds) *Sport, Leisure and Social Relations*. Routledge and Kegan Paul, London, pp. 113–138.

Featherstone, M. (1991) Theories of consumer culture. In: Featherstone, M. (ed.) *Consumer Culture and Post-modernism*. Sage, London, pp. 13–29.

Game, A. (1991) *Undoing the Social: Towards a Deconstructive Sociology*. Open University Press, Milton Keynes, UK.

Graburn, N. (1983) The anthropology of tourism. *Annals of Tourism Research* 10, 9–33.

Hargreaves, J. (1987) The body, sport and power relations. In: Horne, J., Jary, D. and Tomlinson, A. (eds) *Sport, Leisure and Social Relations*. Routledge and Kegan Paul, London, pp. 139–159.

Hopplichler, F. (1989) *Ski With Us: The Teaching Method of the Austrian Ski School*. Pelham Books, London.

Hudson, S. (2000) *Snow Business: a Study of the International Ski Industry*. Cassell, London.

Ivy, M. (1988) Tradition and difference in the Japanese mass media. *Public Culture* 1, 21–29.

Lett, J.W. (1983) Ludic and liminoid aspects of charter yacht tourism in the Caribbean. *Annals of Tourism Research* 10, 35–36.

Mann, T. (1994) *Der Zauberberg*. Fischer Taschenbuch Verlag, Frankfurt am Main, Germany (first published 1924).

Maurer, L., Seidel, B., Gabrielli, M. and Stauber, H. (2001) *Land der Berge*. ORF Television, 29 January.

McCannell, D. (1976) *The Tourist: a New Theory of the Leisure Class*. Shocken Books, New York.

McGibbon, J. (2000a) *The Business of Alpine Tourism in a Globalising World: an Anthropological Study of International Ski Tourism in the Village of St. Anton am Arlberg in the Tirolean Alps*. Vetterlingdruck, Rosenheim.

McGibbon, J. (2000b) Tourism pioneers and racing heroes: the influence of ski tourism and consumer culture on local life in the Tirolean Alps. In: Robinson, M., Long, P., Evans, N., Sharpley, R. and Swarbrooke, J. (eds) *Reflections on International Tourism: Expressions of Culture, Identity and Meaning in Tourism*. Business Education Publishers, Sunderland, UK, pp. 151–166.

Meethan, K. (1996) Consuming (in) the civilised city. *Annals of Tourism Research* 23, 322–340.

Morgan, N. and Pritchard, A. (1998) *Tourism Promotion and Power: Creating Images, Creating Identities*. Wiley & Sons, Chichester, UK.

Morris, M. (1991) Metamorphoses at Sydney Tower. *Australian Cultural History* 10, 19–31.

Robbins, D. (1987) Sport, hegemony and the middle class: the Victorian mountaineers. *Theory, Culture and Society* 4, 579–601.

Rojek, C. (1995) *Decentring Leisure: Rethinking Leisure Theory*. Sage, London.

Rowe, D. (1993) Leisure, tourism and Australianness. *Media, Culture and Society* 15, 253–269.

Schmidt, F. (2001) *St. Anton am Arlberg: Kultur – Sport – Natur*. Tyrolia-Verlag, Innsbruck, Austria.

Teppich-Swinger Verein (1981) *Statuten*.

Thöni, H. (1990) *Hannes Schneider: zum 100. Geburtstag des Skipioniers und Begründers der Arlberg-Technik*. Verlaganstalt Tyrolia, Innsbruck, Austria.

Thurot, J.M. and Thurot, G. (1983) The ideology of class and tourism: confronting the discourse of advertising. *Annals of Tourism Research* 10, 173–189.

Tirol, Herz der Alpen – Schnee (1987) Tirol Werbung Brochure, Innsbruck, Austria.

Tschofen, B. (1993) Aufstiege – Auswege. Skizzen zu einer Symbolgeschichte des Berges im 20. Jahrhundert. *Zeitschrift für Volkskunde* 89, 213–231.

Turner, B. (1984) *The Body and Society. Explorations in Social Theory*. Basil Blackwell, Oxford, UK.

Urry, J. (1990) *The Tourist Gaze. Leisure and Travel in Contemporary Societies*. Sage, London.

Veijola, S. and Jokinen, E. (1994) The body in tourism. *Theory, Culture and Society* 2, 125–151.

Wearing, B. and Wearing, S. (1996) Refocussing the tourist experience: the Flâneur and the Choraster. *Leisure Studies* 15, 229–243.

8

Consuming Images: Young Female Japanese Tourists in Bali, Indonesia

Mika Toyota

Asia Research Institute, National University of Singapore

Tourism as a Form of Consumption

Tourist settings provide an interesting venue of consumption. They are not just about the purchase of commodities or consuming the symbolic significance of material objects, they are also about consuming services, time and images. Seen thus, tourism is not just an economic activity but a social experience which involves the whole process by which images of places are socio-culturally produced and consumed both by local people and by tourists. Consumption today, argues Strinati (1995), cannot simply be understood as a process of subordination. Like Miller (1987), he sees it as a means of asserting and reforming identity. When this is applied in the context of tourist settings, I argue that tourist images and experiences are not shaped just by the producer but also by tourists who as active agents interpret and negotiate with producers. What I intend to examine in this chapter is this arena of negotiation. In particular, I will look at the ways in which Bali images are reproduced in Japanese tourist literature and the ways in which these images are consumed by young female Japanese tourists in their actual tourist experiences.

As many recent studies note, identities today can no longer be reduced simply to a number of identifiable characters based on things such as roles in the family, educational background or occupational position, but increasingly they become wrapped up in consuming activities, including the consumption of places, images and pastimes. In this context, travel becomes an important way of expressing pursuit of a particular taste, lifestyle and/or identity. Tourism for the Japanese has now shifted from being a mass (Fordist) phenomenon, where one product fits all, to being post-Fordist, where individualism and standing out from the crowd take precedence.

The Role of Tourism in Identity Formation for Both Hosts and Guests

Many analyses of tourism focus on the effects of tourism on host societies and the response of host societies to the impact of tourism in reconstructing local identity (Smith, 1989). Using the term 'tourist gaze', Urry (1990) suggests that host societies are compelled to become part of the 'tourist gaze'. Lanfant *et al.* (1995), on the other hand, challenges the existing framework based on host subordination to the guest by pointing out that social causality is not unidirectional, North–South, centre–periphery, but a circular process. By calling this 'reciprocal interpenetration', she notes that 'tourism is fundamentally at the heart of the exchange'. This is a useful way of thinking about the complex interconnections of global and local processes.

Emphasis in the analysis of tourism then shifts from the impact of tourism on the host society to the agency of the local people, regarding them not as passive targets but as active agents (Toyota, 1996a, b; Wood, 1998), and Balinese tourism is no exception. The focus of more recent studies has been on the dynamic relocalization process in association with identity expressions of the host society (Picard, 1993, 1997). Picard (1995) argues that 'interaction with tourists and the tourist industry has become a central component in the definition of ethnic identity in Bali'.

While tourism today is regarded as an integral part of the construction of ethnic identity for the host, and the significance of the tourist experience in the expression and consumption of identity is acknowledged, few studies look at the impact of tourism on the guest's identity formation. In my study, I intend to take Lanfant *et al.*'s understanding of the circular process a step further. I will argue that identity becomes an object of exchange in the international tourism contact zone and it is necessary to consider the possibility of not just hosts, but of tourists transcending and transforming their self-images and identities, in order to understand Lanfant *et al.*'s circular process better.

Consumption and Group Identity

With regard to the role of consumption in shaping identity, some previous works have looked at the implications on the formation of 'class'. For example, Young (1999) examines the ways in which department stores have transformed modernity into a consumer-oriented identity targeted at middle-class Japanese. Young points out that the consumption of products functions as a marker of a new middle-class identity. Anderson and Wadkins (1992), on the other hand, analyse this emerging new middle class using the term, 'The New Breed' (*Shinjinrui* in Japanese) who are characterized by an emphasis on individuality, instant gratification and the desire for more leisure time activities. The implications of these phenomena have been analysed in relation to the development of a consumer culture. My intention here is to analyse the role of tourist media in producing the Balinese images which reflect the diversity of Japanese usages and meanings of the group identity formation process, by focusing on a specific social group of Japanese tourists – young, unmarried females, in their 20s and 30s.

Young Japanese Females as New Consumers

Since the mid-1970s, the overall rate of female participation in the Japanese labour force has increased, and by the mid-1980s young females working on a full-time basis had become one of the most powerful and influential consumer groups within Japan. These females often live with their parents, and so have considerable disposable income to spend on luxury and leisure. From the 1980s onwards, Japan has seen a sharp increase in the number of young unmarried women in their 20s and 30s going abroad. This of course coincides with the rapid increase in the number of Japanese tourists generally (see Table 8.1).

What strikes one, however, is not just the dramatic increase in the overall number of Japanese international tourists, but the heavy concentration of young females in their number. According to official statistics, 32% of Japanese female tourists are in their 20s and 18% in their 30s. Taken together, there are 4.15 million young female Japanese tourists a year travelling round the world (see Table 8.2).

In turn, this indicates that gender relations in contemporary Japan have undergone a profound change, at least among the younger generations, due to a complex set of factors. A full analysis of these is beyond the scope of this particular chapter, but nevertheless the main factors can be outlined as follows.

West Versus East?

As a result of studying the role of modernity in the formation of identity among Japanese career women, aged 23–40, working in Tokyo, Kelsky (1999) argues that they have embraced Western ideology as an escape from traditional Japanese gender restrictions. She also sees the women's sexual/romantic unions with white Western men as an expression of cultural liberation. Kelsky concludes that the West

Table 8.1. The total number of Japanese international tourists from 1964 to 2000 (units of 1000).

Year	1964	1968	1972	1976	1980	1984	1988	1990	1992	1994	1996	1998	2000
Number	128	344	1,392	2,853	3,909	4,659	8,427	10,997	11,791	13,579	16,695	15,806	17,819

Source: Kanko Hakusho (2001), p. 28.

Table 8.2. The total number of Japanese tourists in top ten destinations (units of 1000).

	1	2	3	4	5	6	7	8	9	10		
	USA	Korea	China	Thailand	Taiwan	Hong Kong	Australia	Singapore	Italy	Indonesia	Total	
Male	2,486	1,388	983	530	595	447	327	294	184	209 (47%)	7,443	54.5%
Female	2,588	999	486	356	250	364	373	292	267	235 (53 %)	6,210	45.5%
Total	5,074	2,387	1,468	886	845	811	700	585	452	444	13,652	100%

Kanko Hakusho (2001), p. 36.

provides an arena for female agency, freedom and achievement, a place where they search for 'an alliance with the "universal" ideals of Western modernity in Japan' (Kelsky, 1999, p. 230). What we are witnessing, she says, is a defection, under the influence of Western feminism, not to the West but to an idea of the West, which is synonymous with the international (Kelsky, 1999). Such a search for liberation is in part due to changes in employment legislation, such as the 1986 Equal Employment Opportunity Law, the creation of the Council for Gender Equality (_Danjo Kyodo Sankakusingikai_) in 1994 and the Basic Law for a Gender-Equal Society of 1999.

Despite these changes, and the narrowing of the female/male wage gap among young age groups, fundamental gender asymmetries of the labour system remained unchanged, and women's continuous full-time employment also did not rise. For some women then, equal opportunity was sought not within Japanese corporate establishments, but abroad. As loyalty and a sense of security within the workplace decrease, we see a corresponding turn from group commitment to self-development. The tendency to look abroad for personal fulfilment, self-development, self-discovery and self-satisfaction grows, not only in terms of employment, but also in terms of leisure.

However, becoming 'non-traditional' for Japanese women does not necessarily coincide with becoming 'westernized'. Reducing the phenomenon to westernization fails to capture the complexities that are emerging. Increasing numbers of Japanese young women are heading not only to the West, but also to the East – Thailand, Hong Kong, China, Indonesia, Taiwan and Singapore, not only as tourists but for jobs. As time passes, the foreign sojourns of these young Japanese females abroad tend to be ever more extended and repeated. Some will get married and settle overseas. A similar tendency is also found among young Japanese females studying abroad. Matsui (1994) suggests that the ratio of Japanese female students studying in the USA who do not return to Japan is as high as half. With regard to Bali, the official statistics of the Japanese Consulate on that island show that the number of Japanese resident in Bali has increased from 43 (1987), to 595 (1995) and to 921 (1999), and the majority of these are young females (Toyota, 1999).

Overall, the findings of a number of other studies (Katsurada and Sugihara, 1999; Kanbayashi, 2000; Muramatsu, 2000) also indicate that today young Japanese women no longer hold that clear, fixed gender attitude held by their mothers. The emergence of global migration resulting from travel, studying and working abroad has contributed to changing Japanese gender roles, and is becoming one of the key factors shaping identities. Influential in this change too are the popular media through the way they shape the lifestyles and aspirations of Japanese youth.

The Role of Popular Media in Constructing Identity

It has been argued that Japanese society shows an extraordinary cultural homogeneity for which the mass media and education are responsible. Martinez (1992, 1998) challenges the notion of a single Japanese culture by exploring the arena of popular culture and consumption. She points out the importance of understanding the narration of the mass media as myth-making, 'not as false history, but rather as a series of continually re-worked narrations which reflect and reinforce the values of constantly changing societies'. For her, popular culture is not only mass culture, but is also consumed in various ways, by different people. Skov and Moeran (1995) further articulate the argument against the homogeneity of Japanese culture by stressing the ways in which magazines have played a crucial role in developing market segmentation, albeit in a didactic kind of way. While the mass media can be a tool for creating a sense of unified national identity (Anderson, 1991; Yoshino, 1992), they can also reflect age, gender, class and rural–urban differences. Moeran (1983) notes that 'different consumers get different things from the mass media and are targeted as specific groups by manufacturers and advertisers'.

It was in the 1970s, a time of high economic growth, when the number of women going to work increased dramatically and women's disposable income grew, that consumer culture in Japan began (Koide, 1992). In the 1980s, with the emergence of market segmentation according to the age and taste of the target audience, the popular media began to think about catering for the various niches in the market. As Tanaka notes, 'as many as 1,300 new magazines were launched or re-launched between 1980 and 1985' (Tanaka, 1998, p. 113). Reflecting the changes in Japanese society, in terms of the higher proportion of women in employment and the increasing number of unmarried, career-minded women with their disposable income, these magazines specifically targeted the new generation of young Japanese women between 16 and 35 years old as the key audience for the promotion of new leisure activities. The popular media did not simply introduce new fashions, foods and travel, but they laid down a catalogue of what is desirable, cool, modern, fashionable and sophisticated, just like an alternative lifestyle textbook for young people. The instruction covered not only skirt length, hairstyles and make-up, but lifestyle, goals, aspirations, and ways to relax, enjoy, rediscover and shape one's personality.

Passive Consumers?

Tanaka (1998) argues that Japanese female magazines treat their readers as pupils who have to learn to achieve standards defined by the editors.

'Japanese magazines know what is right for their audiences and tell them so in no uncertain terms' (Tanaka, 1998, p. 119). She found that the prescriptive expressions in women's magazines are strikingly similar to the language of cramming schools (Tanaka, 1998, p. 121). While Tanaka was aware of the strength of young Japanese women as consumers, she found little evidence of their role as active agents. She concluded that these young women are passive consumers with high insecurity, who respond to prescriptive instructions with a tone of authority from the editors.

While I agree with Tanaka's view of the directive and patronizing tone of the popular media, particularly female magazines, with their heavy emphasis on what to do and what not to do, where to go, what to buy, what to expect and so on, I believe that their young readers are not just passive consumers. The ideas and images constructed by the editors are interpreted and absorbed in different ways by the different readers. Tanaka's study was made on the basis of the material as it was presented, and little consideration was given to the ways it might be interpreted by the readers. Analysis of the product is just one dimension of an analysis of the whole consumption process. My study will investigate both production and consumption sides and *the interaction* between them. In order to demonstrate the multiple and intersecting dimensions of individual identity formation in the contact zone of tourist settings, the following empirical case studies explore the interplay between the two dimensions. First, I will look at the ways in which the images of Bali are represented in Japanese tourist literature. Secondly, I will analyse the personalized narratives at the contact zone on the basis of fieldwork interview data.[1]

Images of Bali in Japanese Tourist Literature

Urry (1990) suggests that we conceptualize tourism as the collection of signs; he sees tourism as a modern system of representation. These signs (images) are not simply given but have to be worked at and continually negotiated and contested. Tourism creates the image production mechanism which reflects the different concerns of consumers and producers. This section intends to examine the mechanism of 'place myths', seeing how it develops and comes to organize packaged forms of collective signs. Bali images become the object of the 'tourist gaze' which is constructed within a complex interaction of demands and needs of both tourists and hosts, which are self-consciously produced and consumed. It is critical to understand various layers of this process. First, I will look at the strategies of the state and other agencies in both host and guest societies. Secondly, I will examine to what extent these collective images have significant effects on the ways in which consumers actually experience foreign travel.

The State Strategies of Attracting Japanese Female Tourists

Thailand set out to exploit the economic and political potential of tourism in its 1987 campaign 'Visit Thailand', tying this in with the special occasion of King Bhumipol's 60th birthday. While this was successful in increasing the number of visitors and foreign currency earnings, the sex entertainment industry which had already been established during the Vietnam War as the rest and recreation destination of US military, expanded at the same time, as implied in the Tourism Authority of Thailand (TAT) figures which show that 89% of the visitors to Bangkok were male (Richter, 1989, p. 86).

Learning from this experience, when the Association of South-East Asian Nations (ASEAN) set out to promote tourism as part of their regional economic development policy, the emphasis of the 'Visit ASEAN year' strategy was very much on increasing the number of female tourists. Hence they put the accent on cultural (ethnic) and eco-tourism attractions. The TAT and a leading anti-AIDS campaigner, Minister Mechai Viravaidya, also launched the 'Women's Visit Thailand Year' in 1992 to eradicate Thailand's reputation as 'the brothel of the world'. One obvious target was to attract Japanese female tourists (Leheny, 1995) as Japanese are the largest grouping among international tourists to ASEAN countries (see Table 8.2) At the same time, Japan was seeking to increase outbound international tourism by launching the 'Ten Million Programme' (1987). This was an attempt to meet trade and cultural policy goals, in particular with the Asia-Pacific Economic Cooperation (APEC) countries, and reflects the development of the APEC Tourism Charter. The programme reached its target a year ahead of schedule when the number of Japanese holidaying abroad reached 11 million in 1990 (see Table 8.1).

In 1999, of the 444,000 Japanese tourists to Indonesia, a majority, or 290,000 (65%), went to Bali. Bali became conscious of its distinct attractions and, when attacks against ethnic Chinese during the protest against the Suharto regime in Indonesia received adverse media coverage in Japan in 1997, the Bali tourism industry took immediate steps to distinguish between Bali and the rest of Indonesia. Bali tourism was promoted as Bali *per se* not as a part of anything else. This seems to have worked, for it was observed in interviews (1997) with young Japanese females heading for Bali that the majority were not worried about political instability for, as far as they were concerned, Bali was different from the rest of Indonesia. Some did not even recognize that Bali was a part of Indonesia. In the course of the interviews, it was interesting to find that female magazines and the experience of friends were considered more reliable sources of information than an authority, such as the NHK news, or major newspapers. This illustrates the complex influences on the tourist's perception of their destination. It is not just state actors who control the images of destination, but other things also have significant influence. In this sense, representation is not necessarily a form of power and dominance, but rather a field of negotiation. Personal narratives do not necessarily mirror other forms of literary discourse or public narratives. The images created by official and/or professionals' gaze are interpreted and even challenged by consumers.

Reflecting this negative feeling towards authoritative information sources among young Japanese females, recent popular tourism literature uses personalized narratives, couched as if one of your friends is talking about their experience to you. To give it the look of authenticity, instead of using print font, they tend to use manuscript fonts, and include lots of hand-written illustrations, to provide that personal feel. Hayashi (1997) analysed the language used in four Japanese women's magazines and finds this is common to all of them. As she observes, 'the interaction through which they overcome their anxiety and loneliness, to which they escape and against which they protest'. Their reading is, in this sense, subjective and they are 'actively involved in processes of interpretation' (Talbot, 1995, p. 145 cited by Hayashi, 1997, p. 360). Conversational styles are strategically employed by tourism literature in order to help the readers personalize the messages and to invite readers to form a solidarity. Because of the consumers' preference for non-professional, non-authoritative narratives, some tourism articles actively invite readers to participate in producing items. In this way, the boundary between the producer and the consumer becomes blurred.

Home Village Imaginary: Nostalgia for the Rural Past

Another characteristic of these Japanese female tourists is that their home lives are mostly urban based. Some have grown up in cities, but many others have moved in from the countryside, either for further education or to find employment. The tourist literature of Bali conjures up nostalgic images of a happy rural past, and so appeals to feelings of 'homelessness' that many urban Japanese have. Here MacCannell's classic notion of the tourist's quest for authenticity is useful in understanding the mentality of Japanese tourists going to Bali. He points out that 'touristic consciousness is motivated by a desire for authentic experiences' (MacCannell, 1976, p. 101) because as he notes 'Modern Man [Women] is losing his [her] attachments to the work bench, the neighbourhood, the town, the family, which he [she] once called "his [her] own" but, at the same time he [she] is developing an interest in the "real life" of others' (MacCannell, 1976, p. 91). According to the intervewees, the life of a female office worker in a Japanese company is often seen as 'shallow' and 'inauthentic'. The office is a place where individuals are absorbed into the system of bureaucracy and incorporated. This disengagement from real life stimulates the 'simultaneous emergence of a fascination for the "real life" of others' (MacCannell, 1976, p. 91). Bali for the young Japanese female is a quest for an authentic experience that cannot be had at home, a means of gaining entry to a less synthetic life. Needless to say, what I mean by 'authenticity' here is not something primordially attributed to the objects but is always defined within the present both by tourists and local hosts.

Creighton (1997) noted that Japanese women who find it difficult to travel just for pleasure seeking can do so under the cloak of 'cultural legitimacy'. According to my interviewees, one of the elements of this legitimacy in Bali tourism is 'self-discovery' and/or 'healing'. Self-discovery through travelling is hardly a new phenomenon. Graburn's classic article (1989) analysed tourism as a sacred journey, just like a religious pilgrimage in traditional society.

While the modern process of self-discovery is more about being fashionable and sophisticated, and is associated more with images and style, than a religious act, there is no doubt that the issue of 'self-discovery' is an important element in the discourse, continually recurring in both advertising brochures to attract tourists and the tourists' own narratives. Destinations such as Hong Kong and Singapore have been viewed as places to do mass 'brand shopping', but Bali tourism is associated with the discovery of another possible 'true' self through the contact with aesthetic Bali culture. Bali is projected as a place where you can liberate yourself from the daily drudgery and rediscover a hidden identity which finds no place in humdrum daily existence back home. Bali's appeal is that it is associated with spiritual experience and healing pastimes for those who want more than just a standard 'brand shopping tour'. Bali is represented as where you can consume not just goods but tailor-made 'authentic experiences'.

At the beginning of the 1970s, the Bali beaches used to cater mainly to young backpackers and surfers from Europe, the USA, Australia and Japan. However, coinciding with the rapid development of luxury resorts in South-East Asia in the 1970s and 1980s, Bali has repackaged itself as a 'sophisticated' resort for the international tourism market. Ngurah Rai international airport in Bali has been extended twice with the support of Japanese aid to cater for the rapidly increasing number of tourists. An official figure indicates that the number of tourists in Bali has increased tenfold in 25 years, from about 10,000 (1969) to >1,000,000 (1994). A special effort has been made to attract Japanese tourists, and Garuda Indonesian Airlines provide frequent direct flights between Bali and the main Japanese cities (Tokyo, Osaka, Nagoya and Fukuoka). While the Indonesian government set new target areas in the sixth 5-year plan (1993–1998) with its 'Beyond Bali' campaigns, and the initial explorer-type of tourists moved elsewhere, the focus of the regional government has been fixed on attracting 'quality' tourists.

This shift in emphasis from 'explorer, traveller' mass tourism to appealing to 'quality' tourists is reflected in a change in Japanese tourist publicity – away from the Lonely Planet type and mass tourist guide books to a more 'personalized' kind of material full of detailed anecdotal accounts and experiences. The accent is on the differences between Bali and other Asian resorts. Bali is presented as a deeply aesthetic place, a rich cultural heritage where tourists can go to learn traditional music, take dance lessons, enjoy art and theatre – in other words, polish their aesthetic senses. Magazines aimed at young females project Bali as the place where 'adult women' who have style go to enjoy themselves. The adjective 'adult' is used to distinguish the taste of late 20 and 30 year olds from that of those in their early 20s. Stories are written about places in a way that suggests they are revealing exclusive, hidden spots which only sophisticated experts (*Tatsujin* in Japanese) would appreciate. Those identified as 'travel experts' in the tourist literature are usually internationally successful career women, often working as fashion designers, artists, etc., to demonstrate that these places are judged of high quality by those with 'cosmopolitan' taste. This stylish image is an important ingredient in the legitimacy of tourism for those aspiring to go beyond the ordinary and acquire something distinctive. For them it is often not work but leisure that is the central interest in terms of establishing a personal lifestyle and identity. Interestingly, and contrary to Graburn's model – work as a profane domain and leisure as a sacred domain – many young female Japanese office workers regard work as ritualistic (the sacred?) and selfless, whereas leisure is the domain of the profane in their lives, and the time when they can express their own identity.

Kelsky's study examined the eroticized narratives of new self-hood, provided by encounters with Westerners in Japanese female literature. She noted that 'in the distilled utopianism of some of the published autobiographical accounts, the Western man provides the seed in the birth of a new Japan and a *"new self"'* (Kelsky, 1999, p. 238). This understanding, however, needs to be extended beyond the dichotomy of West versus East. Rather, it is better understood within a framework of 'cosmopolitanism'. My interview data reveal that many Japanese female tourists heading to Bali have already visited Europe and the USA. Some have studied there or stayed there. They consider that they are able to position their lifestyle within the wider world and have been establishing their own judgement, taste and 'cosmopolitan' identity, in a way that goes beyond the simplistic contrast between West and East.

Gazing at the Familiar 'Others'

While the tourist harbours the desire to construct their experience as part of a 'back stage' and an affiliation for the rural past, Bali tourism for the Japanese additionally provides an experience of the familiar 'other'. The narratives of Japanese tourists emphasize 'sharing empathy', the commonality of Asian-ness, along with 'exotic otherness', thus combining both nostalgia for an idealized past with a sense of the new dynamic Asia. It is important to note that the tourism experience is not just about constructing a 'gaze' upon the host society, but also involves the experience of being 'gazed' at by the local people. While Urry's term 'tourist gaze' looks at things just one way, from tourists to host people, culture and society, I would like to stress the significance of tourists being gazed at by the host when we consider the way in which the tourists' identities and self-images are constructed in the contact zone. In other words, tourists can be the object as well as the subject of the tourist gaze.

When travelling in the USA or Europe, Japanese tourists are perceived as 'strangers' or 'exotic others' by the people among whom they travel. They also have to force themselves to speak the languages of these countries. When they fail to communicate, the Japanese tourist tends to feel inadequate. On the other hand, when travelling in Bali or South-East Asia, the same tourists, especially if they are female, will be warmly welcomed as 'familiar others' by their hosts. The negative historical relationship between Japan and South-East Asian countries does not normally extend to the perception of the Japanese female. Also, while Japanese males tend to be associated with the conservative businessman stereotype, Japanese females are seen more positively, though perhaps as the idealized wife who supports her husband. Moreover, the popularity of Japanese products in the host countries reflects the popularity of Japanese tourists, particularly among the young generation. English is normally used to communicate with people in the host society. Since English is a second language for both tourists and hosts, the expressions used tend to be simple and thus easy for Japanese to understand. Also, since neither side is a native speaker, the Japanese will feel less uncomfortable in cases of misunderstanding than they would do in native English countries. Indeed the Japanese tourist may find that some hosts even speak good Japanese and they will come across people in the host society keen to learn Japanese.

Most of the existing literature on gender relationships at the contact zone between tourists and local people has focused on male tourists from the richer nations interacting with 'native' females from developing countries. The dominant paradigm used in the analysis of this gender relationship is the dichotomy of power: male dominance versus female weakness, where the Asian female will be presented as exploited, 'submissive', with an 'oriental sexuality' made available to the Western male tourist. Accordingly, much existing literature has focused on the problem of 'sexual entertainment' associated with the expansion of tourism in South-East Asia and presents this as an institutionalized system of female exploitation, particularly in Thailand (Phongpaichit, 1982; Truong, 1983; Ong, 1985; Hall, 1994; Hodgson, 1995).

Pruitt and LaFont (1995), however, take a different tack. Their study deals with intrinsic structural inequality between host and guest relationships, but through reversing gender roles. Their study is on the relationship between economic power and domination in the context of the Western female tourists in Jamaica. They apply the term 'romance tourism' instead of sex tourism to distinguish between this and the more familiar type of encounter. In their words, 'Whereas sex tourism serves to perpetuate gender roles and reinforce power relations of male dominance and female subordination, romance tourism in Jamaica provides an arena for change' (p. 423). Tourism functions to fulfil desires of the Western female tourists. The Jamaican male in the host society has to manipulate his identity to meet the needs of the tourists, by parading himself as a 'natural' man. The authors' key conclusion is that it is the female tourist who controls and shapes the relationship. They suggest that female tourists are exploring new gender roles, identities and potential transformation through tourism, and that women can enjoy power and control over men in the host society.

Pruitt and LaFont noted that the people involved do not consider their interaction as prostitution, but rather as courtship. Nevertheless, their analytical framework of a power paradigm is based on an assumption that economic advantage is the key to the exercise of power. I argue instead that the relationship between the host and the guest involves more than just 'monetary exchange' and that the economic dimension does not fully explain the complex process of identity negotiation at the contact zone. As Oppermann (1999) and Schlehe (2001) also suggest, viewing this intimate gender relationship simply as a matter of politico-economic exchange is analytically inadequate. While much existing literature looks at the host–guest relationship in terms of political and economic dimensions, little attention has been paid to the socio-cultural interactions and their symbolic implications in the contact zone. Using host and guest narratives, I rather see this interaction as a negotiation process involving the production and consumption of 'authenticity'.

The 'authentic experience' of place in Bali is produced by local male small-scale entrepreneurs in the informal sector and consumed by the Japanese female tourists. In this context, romantic encounters are an important element, not so much because of the actual sexual dimension but because it creates a tailor-made personalized 'authentic' memory for those who no longer enjoy mass-market package holidays. The interviewees often use the term 'special' when they reflect on their travel experience in Bali. This 'special' memory also provides a base upon which to construct 'new' self-images, lifestyles and identities, not only on the part of the tourists but also on the part of the local host boys. Because of the threat of AIDS and other diseases, it should be said that it was a rather smaller proportion of female Japanese tourists who actually claimed that they had sexual contact with locals than it is pruriently presumed by some Japanese media. Besides, the interviewees noted that it is not the actual sexual experience that has primary value, rather value comes when symbolic meanings such as 'beyond standard', and 'different from others' are attached to it. Identity is not simply constituted in the binary relationship of host and guest. What they want by using the term 'special' is to differentiate themselves from other Japanese tourists and to see themselves as exceptional.

Romance Abroad

Most Japanese females in Bali find it difficult to escape the offer of 'passionate' services by locals. Self-employed male entrepreneurs hanging around the tourist areas, not only on the beaches, but in hotels, shops, cafes, restaurants, street corners, the post office, markets, stations, etc. – everywhere tourists go – vie to attract female tourists. Indonesia's tourist development has generated great numbers of self-employed, small-scale entrepreneurs in the informal economic sector. While the beach boys, Gigolos or the 'Kuta cowboys' tend to receive most attention from academics and the media, it is not only these 'beach boys' who proffer their services as 'personal' guides to Japanese females. Many others do too, in both the formal and informal tourism sectors. Female Japanese tourists are almost besieged by local youths offering their services. My interviewees reckon that 80–90% of the Bali males these women had come across had expressed sexual interest in them. Such a high figure indicates that it is not just a particular type of local male – the so-called 'Kuta cowboy' – who specializes in establishing 'intimate' relationships with female tourists. While 'beach boys' are not allowed to hustle tourists at the star-rated hotels or resorts, these non-beach boys find other ways and other places where they make their interest known. From the moment the young female Japanese tourists enter the aeroplane, starting with the Indonesian stewards, then the immigration officers, hotel receptionists, taxi drivers, in encounters with local businessmen, teachers, students and artists, everywhere they are subjected to the 'romantic gaze'. Because there is no clear boundary between the 'beach boy' and other young Bali males, like Dahles and Bras (1999) I would argue that their occupation should be understood as an extended field of the petty production of goods and services in the informal sector rather than prostitution as such. Most of them are in multi-occupations, for beyond being 'informal guides' they may be taxi drivers, waiters, receptionists, bellboys, shop assistants, formal city guides, and so on.

Their motives may be as much economic as sexual. One reason for the popularity of Japanese females is a generous purse and a strong

Yen. Also, as the female tourists tend to be young and unmarried, they often become 'repeaters', i.e. they return as tourists again and again. Things may proceed to a long-term relationship, and eventually there is a possibility that the couple may marry and the woman may settle in Bali to set up in the tourist trade.

One interesting point here is that most of these 'local' entrepreneurs are sometimes anything but local. Many are from less prosperous and less touristic parts of Indonesia, such as Java. This means that the 'authentic experience' of Bali is to an extent the product of the imagination of Japanese females and the salesmanship of non-Bali male entrepreneurs. Some are even temporary visitors from other parts of Indonesia. In fact, they are tourists themselves and simply accompany Japanese female tourists so that they can enjoy the 'authentic Bali experience' of eating, drinking and tourist tripping at someone else's expense. Being a 'personal' guide enables them to go to fashionable restaurants, discos and enjoy cultural performances such as a gamelan orchestra, Bali dance, etc. which otherwise they could not afford. In a sense, these informal tourist guides are socio-cultural brokers not simply because they provide the Japanese tourist with access to the local culture, but also because they are agents in constructing the 'authentic experience' of Bali for tourists and, indeed, for themselves. Bali is the place where the local young male can chat up international female tourists and present a 'cosmopolitan' self-image and lifestyle not only to the tourists but also to the 'local' host peer group. In this way, the guides are also consuming the 'glamour' of self and place.

Fierce and growing competition for customers requires informal guides to invest time, effort and skills to outperform other guides. Dahles and Bras (1999) identified the trade mark of 'Kuta cowboys' as 'cool deadly', wearing 'tight black jeans, loose shirts that are unbuttoned to the belly, long black hair and dark sunglasses' (p. 281). In contrast to these are the other types who target middle-aged and middle-class 'quality' tourists. These present a different image. With 'short and neatly cut hair, pin-stripe pants, white shirt, "pilot-style" sunglasses, ballpoint in breast pocket, and some papers in their hand, apparently on their way to some very important business or sipping coffee in an expensive cafe and only by coincidence bumping into some lost tourists. They do not visit the downtown pubs, but prefer to associate with the more stylish places of entertainment' (pp. 283–284). Evidently, at the contact zone it is not just tourists who are searching for a new self and style by separating themselves from the mass tourist. The guides too are doing something similar.

The 'Personalized' Tour and 'Authentic Experience'

Because they are catering for the ever-increasing demands of various types of tourists, it is no longer possible to speak of the typical informal guide.

However, they do have some shared characteristics, and ones that are attractive to Japanese females. First, these guides offer flexible and personalized arrangements. Unlike the standard tour guide who offers a set menu, the informal tour guide does not offer something pre-set, but tries to find out what the individual tourist wants. They take into account not only the when and where, but also the tastes and styles of the individual concerned. Whereas the standard tourist guide will cover a pre-planned route according to a schedule, the informal guide will be much more flexible and will tailor proceedings to individual needs. He will also seek to offer something more 'authentic', such as including meeting his friends and family or attending local events such as weddings and funerals.

Although the informal guide relies on tips and commission (which may include a percentage of the price paid by the tourist for purchases) and their income will be higher if the tourist buys many souvenirs, they do not normally ask for money straight away. The informal guide presents things as if he were doing a favour for a friend, and this is part of his attraction. Unlike the standard tour where contact between tourists and guides is limited to business hours, the informal tour has no time limit. No distinction is made between official and non-official hours. The aim of the guide is to build the fullest relationship possible with the tourist, for, who knows, the female tourist may be a future wife with whom he can establish a small business in the lucrative tourist industry. For this reason, the young unmarried Japanese female receives special attention. The time spent together will be intense and intimate.

Memory and the Narratives of Experiences

How is the memory of the tourist constructed, internalized and projected? How do tourists select the memories they bring back home with them? Here it is important to note the role of popular tourist literature in the anticipation, constructing and sustaining of these memories. The term 'truth marker' was introduced by MacCannell (1976). It is a useful concept in understanding the way in which tourists connect their own experience with the collective markers already constructed by others. Tourist literature provides the 'truth marker' by which one understands and interprets one's own experiences based on a pre-established collection of signs and recognizing certain elements as a meaningful Bali 'authentic' experience. MacCannell says the 'truth marker functions to cement the bond of tourist to the place and increases its attraction by elevating the information they've acquired to privileged status' (MacCannell, 1976, pp. 137–138). Arguably, the process of memory selection is to a degree shaped by the images/signs that have been pre-constructed by the popular tourism media, although it cannot be denied that self-image also features.

MacCannell's concept is based on the assumption that there is a distinctive contrast between work and leisure. However, the difference between 'here'/home and 'out there'/paradise becomes blurred. Initially, most Japanese tourists intend to return 'home' within a relatively short period of time. However, the young Japanese female, unlike her Western counterpart, tends to be a repeater. While young Western tourists take long breaks to travel round the world and Bali is just one item in the circuit, Japanese female tourists tend to take short breaks to a specific destination such as Bali and then come back regularly. This gives rise to the so-called 'Bali freak'. These people, even when back in Japan, listen to Indonesian music, learn the language, cook using Indonesian ingredients, take Bali dance lessons and decorate the interior of their houses in Bali style. Because of this and because the marriage ceremony in Japan is expensive and has the complexities of families, relatives and rituals, an increasing number of young couples prefer to get married abroad and spend the money on the honeymoon instead. A 'Bali cultural wedding' is now becoming popular with the Japanese 'Bali freaks'.

Even where marriage to a Balinese or marriage in Bali is not the issue, Japanese tourists often prolong the relationship with their local guide by exchanging letters, photos and gifts. In this way the boundary between the tourist experience and everyday life becomes indistinct. For this reason, it is not surprising, therefore, to find that an increasing number of Japanese females tourists end up marrying 'locals' and moving to Indonesia. However, since the Japanese government does not accept double passports, Japanese females tend to continue holding a Japanese passport even after the marriage and occasionally go back 'home' (to Japan).

Conclusion

This chapter has examined the interface between the production and consumption of tourist space in relation to young Japanese women's trips to Bali. What is clear is that tourism consumption, far from being a passive process of accepting dominant gazes, rather involves the consumer as agent, with the capacity to negotiate and construct their own particular interpretation of place, and to incorporate experiences of travel and otherness reflexively into their own narratives, even if such narratives are tentative, shifting and contingent. The exercise of such agency and reflexivity then needs to be seen as the result of a dynamic interaction between the public representation, the commodification of the tourist gaze, and consumption of images at a personalized level.

In the material presented here, this was apparent by readers' participation in the construction of tourism guidebooks, and the ways in which the nature of guidebooks has changed in the last 10 years or so. In this way, the commodification of the gazer and the creation of personalized narratives exist in a dialectical relationship. In addition, tourists themselves can be subject to the 'tourist gaze' by the local people. How the tourists are 'being gazed at' by the host society is a critical element in understanding the ways in which 'authentic experiences' are consumed in destination societies.

Note

1   The field work was conducted at two sites, Bali in Indonesia and Tokyo in Japan, in 1997 on the basis of interviews with 50 young Japanese female tourists. An earlier version of this chapter was presented at the ASEASUK (Association of South East Asian Studies in UK) conference at the Royal Pavilion in Brighton, UK, 1 June 2000, The Bali bombing of 12 October 2002, like the bombings in Sharam El Sheik in 2005, has had an impact on Bali tourism; however, the basic point of the analysis, which is as much about conceptualization and image making as the desirability of particular destinations, is not essentially affected by these unfortunate events.

References

Anderson, B. (1991) *Imagined Communities, Reflections on the Origin and Spread of Nationalism*. Verso, London.

Anderson, L. and Wadkins, M. (1992) The new breed in Japan: consumer culture. *Canadian Journal of Administrative Sciences* 9, 146–153.

Creighton, M. (1997) Consuming rural Japan: the marketing of tradition and nostalgia in the Japanese travel industry. *Ethnology* 36, 239–254.

Dahles, H. and Bras, K. (1999) Entrepreneurs in romance: tourism in Indonesia. *Annals of Tourism Research* 26, 267–293.

Graburn, N. (1989) Tourism, the sacred journey. In: Smith, V.H. (ed.) *Hosts and Guests: the Anthropology of Tourism*, 2nd edn. University of Pennsylvania Press, Philadelphia, pp. 171–186.

Hakusho, K. (2001) Ministry of Land Infrastructure and Transport. White Paper on tourism.

Hall, M. (1994) Gender and economic interests in tourism prostitution: the nature, development and implications of sex tourism in South-east Asia. In: Kinnaird, V. and Hall, D. (eds) *Tourism: a Gender Analysis*. Wiley, London, pp. 142–160.

Hayashi, R. (1997) Hierarchical interdependence expressed through conversational styles in Japanese women's magazine. *Discourse and Society* 8, 359–389.

Hodgson, D. (1995) Combating the organised sexual exploitation of Asian children: recent developments and prospects. *International Journal of Law and the Family* 9, 23–53.

Kanbayashi, H. (2000) Do gender role attitudes affect aspirations of female high-school students?: a quantitative study on determinants of aspirations of female high-school student. *Riron to Hoho (Sociological Theory and Methods)* 28, 359–374.

Katsurada, E. and Sugihara, Y. (1999) Gender differences in gender role perceptions among Japanese college students. *Sex Roles* 41, 775–786.

Kelsky, K. (1999) Gender, modernity and eroticized internationalism in Japan. *Cultural Anthropology* 14, 229–255.

Koide, T. (1992) *Gendai shuppan sangyô ron: Kyôsô to kyôchô no kôzô (Debate on Contemporary Publishing Industry: The Structure of Competition and Cooperation)*. Nihon Editor School Publications, Tokyo.

Lanfant, M.-F., Allcock, J. and Bruner, E. (1995) *International Tourism: Identity and Change*. Sage, London.

Leheny, D. (1995) A political economy of Asian sex tourism. *Annals of Tourism Research* 22, 367–384.

MacCannell, D. (1976) *The Tourist: a New Theory of the Leisure Class*. Schocken Books, New York.

Martinez, D.P. (1992) NHK comes to Kuzaki: ideology, mythology and documentary film-making. In: Goodman, R. and Refsing, K. (eds) *Ideology and Practice in Modern Japan*. Routledge, London, pp. 153–170.

Martinez, D. (ed.) (1998) *The World of Japanese Popular Culture: Gender, Shifting Boundaries and Global Cultures*. Cambridge University Press, Cambridge, UK.

Matsui, M. (1994) Nihonjosei no beikoku ryûgaku taiken: seibetsu yakuwari bunka kara no bômei. *Joseigaku Nenpo* 15, 128–139.

Miller, D. (1987) *Material Culture and Mass Consumption*. Blackwell, Oxford.

Moeran, B. (1983) The language of Japanese tourism. *Annals of Tourism Research* 10, 93–108.

Muramatsu, M. (2000) The life course expectation of women students in Japan. *Kyoiku-shakaigaku Kenkyu* 66, 137–155.

Ong, A. (1985) Industrialisation and prostitution in south-east Asia. *South-east Asia Chronicle* 96, 2–6.

Oppermann, M. (1999) Sex tourism. *Annals of Tourism Research* 26, 251–266.

Phongpaichit, P. (1982) *From Peasant Girls to Bangkok Masseuses*. International Labour Office, Geneva.

Picard, M. (1993) Cultural tourism in Bali: national integration and regional differentiation. In: Hitchcock, M., King, V. and Parnwell, M. (eds) *Tourism in South-east Asia*. Routledge, London, pp. 71–98.

Picard, M. (1995) Cultural heritage and tourist capital in Bali. In: Allcock, J.B., Bruner, E.M. and Lanfant, M.F. (eds) *International Tourism: Identity and Change*. Sage, London, pp. 44–66.

Picard, M. (1997) Cultural tourism, nation-building and regional culture: the making of a Balinese identity. In: Picard, M. and Wood, R. (eds) *Tourism, Ethnicity and the State in Asian and Pacific Societies*. University of Hawaii Press, Honolulu, Hawaii, pp. 181–214.

Pruitt, D. and LaFont, S. (1995) For love and money: romance tourism in Jamaica. *Annals of Tourism Research* 22, 422–440.

Richter, L. (1989) Thailand: where tourism and politics make strange bedfellows. In: *The Politics of Tourism*. University of Hawaii Press, Honolulu, Hawaii, pp. 82–101.

Rosenberger, N. (ed.) (1992) *Japanese Sense of Self*. Cambridge University Press, Cambridge, UK.

Schlehe, J. (2001) Income Opportunities in Tourist Contact Zones: Street Guides and Travellers. Paper presented at the 3rd EUROSEAS Conference, London 2001.

Skov, L. and Moeran, B. (eds) (1995) *Women, Media and Consumption*. Curzon Press, Richmond, UK.

Smith, V. (ed.) (1989) *Hosts and Guests: the Anthropology of Tourism*. University of Pennsylvania Press, Philadelphia.

Strinati, D. (1995) *An Introduction to Popular Culture*. Routledge, London.

Talbot, M. (1995) A synthetic sisterhood. In: Hall, K. and Bucholtz, M. (eds) *Gender Articulated*. Routledge, New York, pp. 144–165.

Tanaka, K. (1998) Japanese women's magazines: the language of aspiration. In: Martinez, D. (ed.) *The World of Japanese Popular Culture: Gender, Shifting Boundaries and Global Cultures*. Cambridge University Press, Cambridge, UK, pp. 110–132.

Toyota, M. (1996a) The effects of tourism development on an Akha community: a Chiang Rai village case study. In: Parnwell, M. (ed.) *Uneven Development in Thailand*. Avebury, Ashgate, UK, pp. 226–240.

Toyota, M. (1996b) Tourism and sexuality: an image of hill tribe women in north Thailand. In: Yamashita, S. (ed.) *Anthropology of Tourism*. Shinyosha, Tokyo, pp. 131–140.

Toyota, M. (1999) Tourism, development and gender. In: Institute of Asian Cultures, Sophia University (ed.) *Introduction to South-east Asian Studies*. Mekon Publishing, Tokyo, pp. 246–259.

Truong, T.-D. (1983) The dynamics of sex tourism: the case of South-east Asia. *Development and Change* 14, 533–553.

Urry, J. (1990) *The Tourist Gaze*. Sage, London,

Wood, R. (1998) Touristic ethnicity: a brief itinerary. *Ethnic and Racial Studies* 21, 218–241.

Yoshino, K. (1992) *Cultural Nationalism in Contemporary Japan, a Sociological Enquiry*. Routledge, London.

Young, L. (1999) Marketing the modern: department stores, consumer culture and the new middle class in interwar Japan. *International Labour and Working Class History* 55, 52–70.

Gender Creation in Travelling, or the Art of Transforming an Adventuress

9

Torun Elsrud

Department of Humanities and Social Sciences, Kalmar University, Sweden

> Adventure (…) *n.* a remarkable incident: an enterprise a commercial specu-
> lation: an exciting experience: the spirit of enterprise.—*n.* adven'turer one
> who engages in hazardous enterprises: a soldier of fortune, or speculator:
> one who pushes his fortune, esp. by unscrupulous means:—*fem.*
> Adven'turess (chiefly in bad sense).

The citation above, found in the *Wordsworth Reference Concise English Dictionary* (1994, p. 12), points to the essence of the gender-related problem that this chapter focuses on. According to the above definition, the female adventurer – the adventuress – is a hard case to handle. As a female 'soldier of fortune' she is transformed into an insult. The adventurous woman of today, appearing here as a negative representation of the adventurous man, seems to be caught between moments in time, and between different and opposing discourses. A single citation in a dictionary needs to be treated with caution, but this one is not alone in downgrading the female adventurer, as the same tendencies are also lurking behind more 'neutral' statements in travel magazines and interviews with independent long-term travellers concerned with the backpacker trail.

Women, as well as men, narrate adventurous identity stories and, although the matter remains statistically unexamined, Hillman (1999) finds that female solo backpackers seem to outnumber male solo backpackers in Australia, and my own research, including fieldwork in Thailand (Elsrud, 2004) suggests a fairly even distribution of solo women and men both on and off the beaten track. In interviews with travellers, most of whom were women, it also seems obvious that female travellers, just as much as male travellers, engage in what are often described as adventurous activities. It appears obvious that as narrators of adventure stories and as consumers of adventurous 'properties' and experiences – such as travelling off-the-beaten-track, interacting with residents, buying clothes symbolizing 'rough living', staying at guesthouses lacking everything but the most basic amenities, and so on – women are just as active as men. Meethan (2001) addresses how avoidance, as well as affirmation, of risk is intrinsic to different modes of tourism. While the adventurous journey requires and thrives on an element of risk, the package tour traveller hopes to eliminate as much risk as possible. Thus the consumption of risk (as action, expression or choice of destination) becomes a differentiating factor in tourism research. This has been noted, not least, by Adams (2001), who describes a growing interest in so-called 'danger-zone tourism' where some travellers actually seek out areas of conflict and danger.

Nevertheless, as mentioned above, behind the actual acts lurk uncertainty and problems of definition. This is caused by a cultural frame of understanding, a discourse in which women of adventure are violating a practice – previously but even now – protected as a playground for masculinity alone (see, for example, Mills, 1991, 2002; Blunt, 1994). Accordingly, what is usually not articulated in most texts about women adventurers, but still very much present, is the astonishment caused by the sex of the actor, rather than by the quality of the act. While acting men are 'capable', women capable of the same acts are 'exceptional', 'extraordinary' or even 'fakes'. That is of course if they are acknowledged at all. An inability to acknowledge adventurous women is present among researchers, who have tended to see them almost exclusively as acts of masculinity (see, for example, Goffman, 1967; Simmel, 1971; Scheibe, 1986). Although males outnumbered women to a greater extent as travellers in past times, there were still enough mobile women to make them as valid and interesting to study (Mills, 1991, 2002; Blunt, 1994; Swain, 1995). Unfortunately, and possibly due to the lack of research interest in the area of adventure and travel, this tendency to overlook female adventurous travelling is carried on into present day research. Potential sceptics should note that the women addressed in this chapter are 'capable' of engaging in adventurous acts and narratives. If at times, as when the telling of myths works to enhance a good story, they appear as 'fakes', they are in the good company of just as many men.

Thus, there are two over-riding purposes then to this chapter. First, I will show that the old historically burdened *masculine adventure discourse* is threatened but still alive. This cultural 'guide' encroaches upon women's possibilities to manifest a newer discourse claiming that people (i.e. in wealthy Western societies) are expected to form and manifest their own identities, creating their own life stories. The foundation to this discourse is described by Giddens (1991) in referring to identity as a *reflexive project* and by Ziehe's concept *makeability* (Ziehe, 1991; see also Fornäs, 1995). Makeability describes the possibility for individuals in contemporary society, as opposed to traditional societies, actively to create their own identities. Regardless of actual circumstances, reflexive and makeable women are often taught they have equal rights to movement and to the public arena. Clearly then, the travelling women narrating adventurous identities are situated in an intersection of two opposing discourses.

The second aim is to address the various routes, the paths, women travellers take in order to balance between these two, a balance that is often manifested in a challenging of masculine adventure stories. While the chapter will discuss some responses, which are quite according to expectations, it will continue into topics less investigated, one such being the use of irony. Irony is a practice of distancing, which in this case has a number of meaning-bearing levels with the potentiality to work as an effective tool of opposition to those with the power to define, as well as a last resort when one just does not feel at home within the discursive categories.

The analysis is based on interviews with 50 'long-term budget travellers' predominantly from northern Europe, but also some from Australia and the USA. The term budget travellers was coined by Riley (1988) to describe backpackers' common interest to keep spending at a minimum, and I consider 'budget' in this context as much a 'social construction' as a reality. Managing to budget your funds through eating, sleeping and travelling 'cheap' is an admirable skill in narratives on travel, both in travellers' testimonies and in written texts. The lack of money and little spending often increases the possibility of escalating from novice to experienced, or from tourist to traveller and then to adventurer. It should be remembered though that, despite a restrained and moderate spending each day, many travellers are quite well off in terms of economic security if something should go seriously wrong, as credit cards, money in the bank, supportive parents and possibly a job to return to make 'poverty' so much easier to cope with, for as Bourdieu (1984) points out, gaining symbolic capital through poverty and 'roughing it' is a prerogative of the rich.

Most of my interviewees were women, and the interviews themselves were carried out during fieldwork in Thailand, as well as in Sweden with prior travellers. They were conducted with an emphasis on *form* of travel rather than *type* of traveller (see Uriely *et al.*, 2002). This means I regard backpacking as a practice in which the structural arrangements such as length of journey, route, accommodation status and transport arrangements are more predictable than the values and expectations found among the travellers. Efforts have been made to interview people travelling for at least 6 months, using 'budget' transportation and accommodation, not travelling on a package holiday, and when possible travelling 'off-the-beaten-track'. In addition, empirical material has been gathered from observation notes in backpacker areas as well as from articles in travel books and magazines.

There are a number of reasons for focusing on women here. Tourism research has, since its early beginnings, focused on travel predominately as a male practice with a male bias (Riley, 1988; Mills, 1991, 2002; Clifford, 1992; Veijola and Jokinen, 1994; Swain, 1995; Elsrud, 1998). In feminist research, it is often stressed that arenas such as the one described, i.e. contexts traditionally controlled and 'normalized' by masculine values, are now being entered and challenged by a large number of women (see also Toyota, Chapter 8, this volume). The perspectives presented by women, in doing what traditionally has been withheld from them, offer researchers a number of possibilities to broaden enquiries about a phenomenon. At the very least, it can increase our understanding of knowledge as both positioned and situated and of our research production as representations which are informed by, among other things, gendered subjectivities (see also Keller, 1985; Haraway, 1991; Widerberg, 1995; Skeggs, 1997; Pritchard and Morgan, Chapter 12, this volume).

Adventure as an Identity Narrative

The backpackers themselves have defined the adventure as well as the adventurous act, and whether or not these are 'real' adventures is irrelevant to the arguments. Of much more importance instead is the fact that they are constructed narratives, acts transformed into such by the will and creativity of people. Independent travelling is in itself often equated with 'adventure' in interviews and in media texts, with its 'risky' elements, socially constructed or 'real', highlighted as important components in building both adventure tales and identity stories. Frederick and Hyde (1993, p. xxiii) note when investigating female travel experiences, and writing, that '[t]he journey is often presented not only as a risk but as a risk well worth taking, a means of self-transformation and self-discovery'.

The journey alone is not enough, however, to make a good adventure story, as it also takes specific action and appearance (Elsrud, 2001, 2004). In testimonies both in interviews and texts, an image appears of the adventurer as a person in torn and worn-out cotton clothes who travels 'off-the-beaten-track' to destinations that are often expressed as 'primitive', 'poor' and 'unexplored', at least by 'whites'. The aesthetic appearance is an important aspect of the adventure identity (Elsrud, 2001). Shorts with flowers on them, feet with socks on them or hairspray to keep the wisps of hair in place are not appropriate in this context. Tattoos, piercing, shaved head or dreadlocks do, however, fit well with the worn cotton clothes of the adventurer image.

The adventurer also travels for a long time, without travel companions, and mingles with the 'locals'. The adventurer takes 'risks' in encounters with nature, with local transport and in social interaction, and the adventurer does as the 'locals' regarding health and food matters. Most importantly, the adventurer in media texts and interviews does it all with some style; it is the handling of novelty and risk with routine which turns the actor into an adventurer (see also Simmel, 1971; Pocock, Chapter 5, this volume). Adventure is a construction, a shared narrative that is kept alive by those who believe in it and subscribe to it.

A constructed adventure has any number of discursive narratives attached to it which work to enhance the action. These stories, often describing the 'nature' of a people, a place, an event, do come across as 'truths' but are really social and cultural constructions. These may work as both magnifying glasses and filters in that they may be used to make an event larger and more powerful than it is or discard unwanted particles and make disturbing impressions disappear. While adding socially and culturally constructed 'truths' to an event making it larger and more powerful than it really is, these stories also filter off and discard unwanted elements. These discursive narratives structure expectations before as well as interpretations after the encounter with a particular image or event. In travelling, they are often exactly what is needed to make an ordinary event into a narrative of identity. Before moving on, it should nevertheless be noted that at times the constructions addressed above are accompanied by the 'real thing' as for those travellers seeking out 'danger zones', i.e. riot areas, war zones and areas of poverty and poor health conditions (see Adams, 2001).

Lightfoot (1997) and Scheibe (1986) have argued that adventures are particularly effective in the narration of identity stories as they are pregnant with events. At the same time, they place the 'adventurer' in the limelight, doing what others do not do (see also Elsrud, 2001, p. 603). The adventure is usually practised in an area separated from others in both time and space, as the adventure story must be built upon its uniqueness and contrast with other 'non-adventure' moments in time and space (Simmel, 1971). The means of supplying the non-adventurers at home with adventure narratives of travel are also increasing. Not only are there photos to take, there are also postcards, diaries or books to write or articles to sell supplying the non-adventurous audience at home with adventure narratives before or after homecoming (Andersson-Cederholm, 1999). In the last 10 years or so, the backpacker circuit has also seen a new development which can possibly change the view on travelling quite drastically. The growth of internet cafes in backpacker areas around the world makes adventure narration to those at home much easier. However, the internet may also increase the risk of a demystification of the adventure and maybe also reduce travellers' feelings of having taken *time* and *space* for own (re)creation.

The Adventuress – the Illegitimate Child of Conflicting Discourses

As noted at the beginning of this chapter, a semantic approach to the adventure topic reveals the inappropriateness of female adventurous acting. This could perhaps be written off as a sign of old sins, but the perspective is still stressed in a critical reading of contemporary media texts and in interviews. A way to understand how such a view upon female adventurous acting has emerged is to focus on her location, caught between two discourses as I have argued above. While one gives her the right to narrate adventurous identity stories, the other robs her of her femininity if she does.

As a female of late or postmodernity, she is allowed, even expected, to enter and explore what life offers including arenas previously regarded as masculine. However, she may find that her 'freedom' of late modernity conflicts with an older and 'modern' discourse giving men the sole right to the adventure. The adventuress, a 'lesser' adventurer, is what emerges when you mix the modern masculine adventurer with the 'makeability' promised to all in late modern or postmodern time spaces. The following will approach these two discourses and identify both of them as present and narrated in texts and tales on backpacking.

The New Adventurer – a Woman in the Making

Our futures, as men and women, are said to be 'open'. No longer are we born into a given set of life circumstances. Numerous scholars, perhaps the most salient in current sociological understanding being Bauman (1991, 1997), Giddens (1984, 1991) and Beck *et al.* (1995) describe our time in the world as a time of 'wandering' about both in thoughts and in space and as a time of individual 'reflexivity'. Common to these scholars is the notion that the authority of traditional institutions such as religion, extended family systems and local community dependency has lost its explanatory power. No longer is the number of individual options said to be limited by a restricting God or a restraining tradition in which children are expected to take over the fate of their parents, be it through adopting similar living conditions, locations or professions. The new world is a world emphasizing the individual, his choices and actions. It is also a world of many 'truths' in which the individual is expected, often single-handedly, to monitor the options reflexively and choose the right action, an expectation causing opportunities as well as uncertainty and anxiety. The identity of a person has accordingly become a 'project' demanding continuous remodelling and reflexive monitoring of the 'truths' at hand at any given time (Giddens, 1991).

Although advocates of late or postmodern 'reflexivity' do

acknowledge the 'anxiety', 'ambivalence' and 'discontent' lurking in the backwaters of this development, the criticism from Furlong and Cartmel (1997) points at the importance of differentiating between the theoretical concepts and lived experience. To begin with, it is important to stress the 'situatedness' of these conditions. There are millions of people around the world who would contest such a description. Poverty, starvation, feudal systems and other, often gendered inequalities, outside what is often described as the 'West', make universal claims that the individual has freedom to act, or even reflect, seem almost ridiculous. Even inside the 'West', such explanatory models should be made with care. As Furlong and Cartmel (1997) point out, to many people the idea of freedom of action is a belief, not a reality (see also Davies, 2001). Young people learn that they can make their own future and identity with the consequence that they also blame themselves when failing, even though their misfortunes often are caused by unjust and unequal structures which still exert authority over the individual. What I am arguing here is that theoretical constructs, no matter how much they help us to understand current conditions, do not correspond to the equivalent expectations of everyday life.

There is a naturalness about the landscape of narratives through which people of post-industrial societies learn that they must and can make their own individual choices in staking out their life tracks and actions. Young people are expected to make active choices regarding future education and jobs. They are told they have the possibility of becoming whatever they want to become, while seldom being informed that matters such as skin colour, sex, class or family background may comprise a serious threat to their freedom of choice (Furlong and Cartmel, 1997). This mundane and seldom opposed discourse, suitably described by Ziehe's concept 'makeability', has influenced the travellers in this research project too (Ziehe, 1991; see also Fornäs, 1995). Very much in line with the claims above, the adventurous women are navigating what they experience as a world of options, and in the process entering areas which were earlier dominated by men, such as the independent journey. Lacking statistical evidence, it would not be right to claim that there are as many women as men travelling 'adventurously', in this case meaning 'solo', 'independently', 'off-the-beaten-track' and 'risky'. Evidently, it would be equally wrong to claim that there are as many men as there are women travelling 'adventurously'. However, there are, as anyone entering the backpacker trail will notice, plenty of female adventurous travellers. In the first decade of the 21st century, these 'adventuresses' are navigating the peripheral areas that comprise the backpacker circuit.

These women, almost without hesitation, describe their journey as an 'identity project', as a possibility to gain 'strength', 'independence' and 'freedom'. Adventure reinforces the identity statements. As in interviews with men, it is regarded as a way to make something interesting out of their lives. Less explicit, yet often present, is the belief that the adventurous journey, if successful, will grant the travellers a higher status after homecoming (see also Munt, 1994; Desforges, 1998, 2000; Elsrud, 2001, 2004). Many of them are, however, also struggling with another voice, robbing them of the 'freedom' to engage in such activities wholeheartedly – the old adventure narrative.

The Masculine Adventurer – a Man of Yesteryear?

As noted above, the adventure comes into being by being demarcated from the non-adventure in time and space. The adventurer must likewise be demarcated from the non-adventurer, being defined by what it is not (see Mills, 2002, p. 72). Glancing at history and discourses of colonial times, there have been at least two hegemonic discourses upon which the adventurer can build an adventure narrative. The adventurer's traits, through colonial history, have been the 'antithesis of the stereotypical feminine qualities' (Mills, 2002, p. 72), thriving on assigned masculine qualities such as mobility, change, strength, risk and courage (see also Mills, 1991; Clifford, 1992; Pratt, 1992; Beezer, 1993; Blunt, 1994; Elsrud, 2001, 2004).

Even if the discursive efforts to exclude women from the adventurous acts were effective and successful, one problem remained for the male adventurer, having left home time and home space in a quest for expressive individuality. There were the 'other' men – local residents – who had to be kept at a distance in order to act out one's adventure narrative. Some researchers into colonial writing (and acting) have described this obstacle as one of the reasons why the adventurer has become such a masculine character. In order to distance the white male from the male of, for instance, India or Africa, an exaggeration of masculine features was stressed. 'Character traits such as strength and fortitude in the face of adversity were deemed important as one of the ways of making clear demarcations between white masculinity and "native" males', states Mills (2002, p. 70). Typical colonial texts describing the (masculine) adventure must therefore be understood as acts of differentiation, where white men of mobility and change are not only separated from white (and coloured) women of believed passivity and domesticity but also from any threat posed by men of colour or location.

Some time has passed between the 'struggle' of the adventurous colonial white man and the travelling 'off-the-beaten-track' self-acclaimed 'adventurer' of today's backpacker circuit. Space has changed too and has in some cases lost a sought-after 'primitive' character.

Opportunities for 'exploring' unknown territory have lessened (see Winter, Chapter 3; Ford and Havdra, Chapter 4; and Pocock, Chapter 5, this volume) although being the 'first white' in a particular context is still often stressed by interviewed backpackers regardless of sex. Yet cultural narratives such as the ones describing travel as adventurous and adventure as – normally – an act of masculinity seem to remain intact, despite efforts by many women to contest its very essence. Tickets to backpackers are sold with erect penises as logos (see Egeland, 1999 for a more thorough analysis of the gendered messages in Kilroy's advertising), and travel magazines such as the Swedish *Vagabond* (1996) make special editions about female solo travellers portraying them as oddities in the (male) travel circuit. From interviews with both men and women, a picture emerges of the adventure being a masculine preoccupation while females in general travel differently. Also, if they do travel differently they are seldom 'ordinary' females. Still, many of the women do intentionally or unintentionally narrate adventure stories, and the following will address the different routes they can take to avoid being 'stigmatized' for acting in ways that are inappropriate to gendered expectations.

Transformations: the Masculine Adventuress?

One detectable strand in the interviews is that of the female traveller not being very feminine at all. In these cases, the female transforms herself into a 'tomboy'. This issue comes to mind, for example, when a female traveller says that she prefers to team up with male travellers as they are more like her. It also appears when female travellers explain that they avoid female company or when female travellers describe their childhood as a time with the boys or playing with boys' toys. The 'tomboy package' is often encouraged by myths of a disagreeable or unpleasant femininity, also expressed by travellers not describing themselves as tomboys. Common examples are myths describing travelling women as conspiratorial and men as open to contact. These stories enhance the opposition between the outgoing, active male and the inert and passive female. Such bipolar constructions seldom suit the complexities of reality. Downgrading women and/or what one considers being feminine may actually be an effective tool to upgrade one's own identity and actions. Expressed awareness about the faults of one's 'own kind' raises the aware person above the 'ignorant' rest. When effective, criticism distances the criticizer from the criticized and places him or her in a superior position/group. From this perspective, the adventuress is not really an adventuress. She is an adventurer.

The Non-adventurous 'Adventuress'

Not all travellers find the adventure worth striving for. Some of the mainly young female interviewees regarded the journey as hard enough without any extra risks added, real or constructed. To these travellers, staying 'on the beaten track' was important and safe, as were avoiding some of the local food and rough living conditions. Adventure was sometimes stressed as foolish and often described as something men engage in. However, not only non-adventurous travellers claimed that they were not adventurous. Some rather 'adventurous' women still saw adventure as a male practice. One example is presented by a 21-year-old German traveller temporarily living on a Thai island with a boyfriend who was a local resident. She emphasized many times in the interview that she was not the adventurous type and that adventures were by definition masculine. Yet she appeared as such to other backpackers who spent quite a bit of time over dinners in the restaurant where she was working analysing her situation, and often arriving at the conclusion that she was either brave or stupid. Thus, some female travellers who do act adventurously according to common backpacker definitions of what it is to be adventurous, see the adventurous acts in others but not in themselves. More often than not, the sex of the actor will define whether or not the act is adventurous, pointing at the constructive character of 'adventurism'. The consequence this reasoning has on the status of the adventuress is nevertheless that she is best off not existing and erased from vocabulary. If she still appears in the backpacker circuit, one can always pretend to ignore her.

The Emancipated Adventuress

There are other responses and other travellers who practise a different criticism of femininity that does not necessarily downgrade women. At stake here is the stereotypical images of femininity, which to some extent restricts women's lives. Some of the interviewees certainly saw their journeys as a way of strengthening their identities to where they would stand above the stereotypical norms placed on women by society. These travellers said they had left make-up, fashion and consumerism behind, as well as feelings of insecurity and dependence upon men. An example is Sara, a 24-year old Australian traveller who said women are 'victims' of society as all they care about 'is if you look beautiful'. She explicitly said that her own journey made her braver and more mature to the point where she felt she could go home and stand up against the pressures that victimized women. It is very likely that adventurous acting enhances the feeling of having escaped restrictions of home. The border-transcending nature of the adventure may be just the context needed to stimulate and encourage opposition and the questioning of (gender) norms. From this perspective, the journey definitely seems like a state of 'liminality' in which many women experience time and room for an upgrading of femininity or of an erasure of the traditional dichotomy between male and female where they both become as one. In any case, the adventuress becomes equal to the adventurer.

The Playful Adventuress

Other travellers practise another way of questioning stereotypes and threatening the old masculine adventure discourse. These are the playful 'adventuresses' who keep the adventure trail warm, but do it with their mind partly elsewhere. The adventure is there to be manifested and experienced, but it is masculine and has to be ridiculed. These travellers told of their own attempts to come across as adventurous and 'off-the-beaten-track' travellers with a clear tone of irony and sarcasm. They spoke ironically of their efforts, as fresh backpackers, to buy new clothes in India hoping they would appear as more adventurous and experienced backpackers. They talked about the inspiration they had found in books such as *The Beach*, yet laughed at the immaturity they felt present in the very same story. In addition, they spoke with irony about such efforts as being masculine and ridiculous.

Downe (1999) has successfully and pertinently shown that female irony and joking can work simultaneously as a way 'to cope with' and as a challenge and resistance towards injustice or unfavourable situations. Clearly irony is a process of distancing oneself from the act (of 'self' or 'other') as opposed to being an ignorant prisoner of action. These travellers are not what Goffman (1959) would call 'duped' by the act. Rather, they are reflexive to an extent where most acts seem like play rather than reality. Therefore, these travellers can continue on an adventure quest while their irony distances them from the foolishness often ascribed to the adventure act. In Cohen and Taylor's (1992, p. 52) words, the ironic traveller is busy 'creating a zone for self', through expressing awareness of and distance from the acts of others.

Irony in this case implies a power relationship. Risking being interpreted as the unworthy (female) intruder into a masculine adventure practice, the ironic female places herself above the ridiculed act of the 'other', or in the case of self-irony above the ridiculed act of the 'other' located within and adapted by the ironic self (Melucci, 1996, pp. 135–137). Consequently, to laugh at one's own efforts is, in addition to distancing oneself from them, also an act of hostility in disguise. The self-irony or laughter neutralizes the aggression directed at the 'other', socialized into the 'self'. The playful and ironic adventuress can actually both have her cake and eat it – she can continue the ridiculous adventure while being immune to the criticism directed at it.

Editing the Adventure Narrative

Within my data, there are four identifiable and common responses to the tensions that exist between the hegemonic masculinity of adventure narratives, and the beliefs that life is a 'makeable' project. Evidently there are signs of both conformation and contestation to the old adventure narratives in these responses. I shall begin here with a short recapitulation of the responses that stress conformity before moving on to a more thorough discussion about the responses I see as more of a challenge to the (masculine) adventure narrative.

Two of the responses to the idea that the adventure is a masculine preoccupation carry little, if any, 'emancipatory' power, the 'tomboy' narrative and the 'non-adventure' narrative. The 'tomboy' narrative, in which women describe themselves as not women and accredit other women with negative qualities, does have the effect of placing the narrator in a favoured position above her sisters-in-travelling. These women avoid subordination by adapting to masculine standards (see Lalander and Johansson, 2002, pp. 153–154). As such, their efforts can be interpreted as acts of personal resistance towards hegemonic masculinity, in that it lifts the narrator above the downtrodden, but it occurs at the cost of stigmatizing other women. Unquestionably, however, the consequence of this is an emphasis of the old adventure discourse in that it stresses the superiority of the masculine adventurer while actually downgrading not only femininity but women in general. The non-adventure narratives work to the same effect. In summary then, these narratives are examples of compliance with structures and as such they do not come as a surprise. The other responses addressed in this chapter are, on the other hand, more interesting to investigate as they do appear to be examples of strategies which will propose a future challenge to structures of inequality outside as well as within travel contexts.

Challenging the Adventure Discourse

This analysis has revealed two ways of resistance to the old adventure discourse, one rather 'diplomatic' and one much more aggressive and threatening. The former is the effort to get a 'piece of the action' while leaving the men to continue what they are already doing. This is the response described above as a critique of the stereotype femininity and as an effort to emancipate the adventuress, i.e. to free her from her negative burden. These 'adventurous' women are travelling alongside 'adventurous' men, without questioning the men or the adventure, but rather demanding a piece of the cake themselves. They want to walk the adventure trail in a serious and sincere effort to prove to themselves – and the world – that they can do it too, as competent women rather than lesser men (as in the 'tomboy' narratives). Their critique is not directed against the adventure discourse as much as it is directed, as mentioned above, at the stereotyped femininity of home. At the same time, there is an indirect critique of any claims that the adventure is masculine, in that women are capable of adventurous acting too. Through their action, these women hope to gain either a femininity or a 'neutral' position unburdened of traditional expectations on gender. As 'freed', these women edit the adventure discourse from its masculinity, making adventure into something both men and women can do.

I see a larger threat to the discourse proposed by the latter, which is the effort to ridicule the masculine adventurer – as well as the feminine – by jokes and irony, consequently threatening those who have previously set the adventure standards. Under attack from irony – the mischievous twin of reflexivity – no-one, regardless of sex, can continue to practise adventure undisturbed. The emperor has definitely been robbed of his clothes. The discourse is threatened in that the categories which construct it are exposed, unveiling the power structure hidden behind its 'naturalness'. In Downe's (1999, p. 73) words, their irony 'highlights the absurdities of otherwise unquestioned situations', thereby exposing as well as challenging oppressive systems.

The ironic narrator is, despite her success in gaining power, also a victim of the very language (and action) she ridicules. Rorty (1989) may give us another perspective of the irony present among the travellers in his conviction that the ironic is worried about having been initiated in the 'wrong tribe, taught to play the wrong language game. She worries that the process of socialization which turned her into a human being by giving her a language may have given her the wrong language, and so turned her into the wrong kind of human being' (Rorty, 1989, p. 75). The ironic narrator feels homeless. Using Bauman's reasoning, we may be talking about a person who has penetrated and unmasked the categories with which we order language and life. He states (1991, p. 1):

> To classify means to set apart, to segregate ... To classify, in other words, is to give the world a *structure*: to manipulate its probabilities; to make some events more likely than some others; to behave as if events were not random, or to limit or eliminate randomness of events ... Language strives to sustain the order and to deny or suppress randomness and contingency. An orderly world is a world in which 'one knows how to go on'.

The irony present in this material is not only a defence against subordination and a way to take charge over the right to define, but also a sign of a rather sorrowful state of not belonging, or wanting to belong in a category. While quite efficient as a tool for gaining power in interpersonal relationships, irony may still leave the subject with the unpleasant feeling of not belonging anywhere and not knowing how to. The traveller, using irony to mock both other adventurers and her adventurous self, will most likely find it very difficult to let herself be carried away by the act.

Regardless of the positive or negative consequences of irony, it is interesting to note that the method as such is quite common among many of the female interviewees in this project. Perhaps this female irony is also a sign of what Felski (1995) addresses as an exclusion of female activity in theories and narratives of modernity which are instead products of hegemonic masculinities (see Connell, 1995) and masculine interpretations. This is most probably also the case with the theories and discourses concerned with masculine 'adventurism', built at least partly on a belief that women by 'nature' are less mobile and prone to change and more caring and inbound. These have been carried through the history of theoretical development in the hands of such influential historical figures as Freud, Marx or Simmel (see Felski, 1995) to more present-day theorists on 'adventure' or 'heroism' (for instance, Scheibe, 1986; Featherstone, 1995). It has been hard to see the woman in theories of male heroic life, not only when she has been busy elsewhere but also when she has been there. A female traveller practising what many still understand to be a masculine adventure may have to turn to irony when she realizes the practice does not belong to her. If a female traveller feels she is forced into categories, which do not suit her experiences, wants and needs, as a woman and as an adventurous traveller irony comes 'naturally' and as a sign of efforts to cope with a life in the 'wrong tribe'.

Conclusion

This research clearly shows that most travellers, when they start their journey, regard it as time and space for experiencing 'freedom', or in other words the cherished possibility to create new exciting identity stories. This creativity we can call identity play, and the practices are in many cases identity statements, expected to remain with the traveller and render status even after homecoming. Many travellers, hoping to explore the unexplored and travel roads not travelled (by 'travellers'), will to their disappointment find that the road to adventure is rather crowded these days. Travellers on a quest for individualism are no exceptions to the rule that many people telling similar stories and manifesting similar narratives do eventually form a structure (Simmel, 1971). The adventure discourse (and the narratives it gives rise to) is one such structure of thought brought from home – a home pregnant with adventure stories in socialization agents, in media and conversation – and renegotiated among the travellers on route.

One of the main arguments here is exactly the renegotiations of the old adventure discourse brought to the fore by the opposing makeability discourse making women believe they have equal rights to and in previously masculine arenas. The existence of opposing structures of thought in a given context is by no means unproblematic, and a gender perspective makes it even less of a clear-cut case. This chapter has dealt not only with similarities found in the backpacking practice, but also with the differences which appear once the focus is turned towards contesting statements, anomalies and other deviations from the common narratives that help structure experiences.

Evidently similarities are found in relation to the presence and awareness of the survival of the masculine narrative of adventure. Had that been all there was, this analysis could only have concluded that this was a victory of structure over agency. However, this was not the case, as the acts of resistance, the rewriting of the adventure narratives, showed. Although some of the responses presented here have opposed categorization on an individual level, they have remained applicable on a structural level. Declaring yourself a 'tomboy' in order to escape categorization often involves negating the feminine, and such a response, together with the 'non-adventurous female' response, would lead to the practice of adventure remaining strongly gendered and biased towards the masculine. Other statements have been oppositional on both individual and structural levels. The victory of the female adventuress, making adventure into a statement about a strong femininity unburdened by the stereotypical femininity of home, promises an adventure which is genderless. Most threatening, however, is the use of irony which ridicules the very essence of the masculine act, as such ridicule only serves to undermine and diminish the act of adventure itself and, thus diminished, the adventure is no longer worth pursuing.

Understanding these different ways, as well as others, to approach persistent discourses, which encroach upon, in this case, female inventiveness and emancipatory action in travelling is important not only to understand backpacking but in all areas where women have been excluded – in theory or practice. Without question, the discrepant and different female narratives presented here call for a future awareness of the fact that women are just as individual as men, a fact which has to a large extent remained unexplored due to the past research focus on masculine activities (see Felski, 1995).

The second important point supports theories which claim that it is hegemonic, rather than patriarchal, circumstances that constrict the lives of many women. Contrary to perspectives in which women appear solely as victims of oppression, this chapter stresses the complexity of power relations. Travelling women are sometimes active as oppressors and at keeping the old masculine adventure tale alive, through reducing the female adventure act, or even the femininity of the acting woman. The power of hegemony is thus manifested in tales and acts of both genders. This is, however, not an either–or case where some women are only oppressing and other women are being oppressed. Negating women as a group is a sign of hegemonic masculinity and male norms being present. Women claiming other women do not belong in the adventure trail, nor possess the right characteristics, are victims too – to the 'male in the head' (Holland *et al.*, 1998). In Mead's (1934) words, we might conclude that this can be expected as long as the 'generalized other', occupying the individual 'mind', remains to some extent a man in narratives of travel. The male in the head needs to be identified and his voices, when oppressive, need opposition regardless of which sex they speak through. Yet one important question remains unanswered. This chapter has presented data gathered from a number of women and men narrating similar adventure stories, expressing similar beliefs in the adventure as a way to express identity; yet similar acts may not always lead to similar consequences for the actor. As Desforges (2000) notes, the journey may be seen as an investment in symbolic capital to be used after homecoming, yet he also noted that for some women, homecoming after such journeys sometimes resulted in negative responses, indicating that while travel may be a way to rewrite the self, homecoming may show just how persistent the old masculine discourse still is.

References

Adams, K.M. (2001) Danger-zone tourism: potentials and prospects for tourism in tumultuous times. In: Teo, P., Chang, T.C. and Ho, K.C. (eds) *Interconnected Worlds: Tourism in South-east Asia*. Pergamon Press, New York, pp. 267–281.

Andersson-Cederholm, E. (1999) *Det Extraordinäras Lockelse: Luffarturistens Bilder och Upplevelser*. Arkiv Förlag, Lund.

Bauman, Z. (1991) *Modernity and Ambivalence*. Polity Press, Cambridge, UK.

Bauman, Z. (1997) *Postmodernity and its Discontents*. Polity Press, Cambridge, UK.

Beck, U., Giddens, A. and Lash, S. (1995) *Reflexive Modernization: Politics, Tradition and Aesthetics in the Modern Social Order*. Polity Press, Cambridge, UK.

Beezer, A. (1993) Women and 'adventure travel' tourism. *New Formations* 21, 119–130.

Blunt, A. (1994) *Travel, Gender and Imperialism: Mary Kingsley and West Africa*. The Guildford Press, London.

Bourdieu, P. (1984) *Distinction*. Routledge and Kegan Paul, London.

Clifford, J. (1992) Traveling cultures. In: Grossberg, L., Nelson, C. and Treihler, P.A. (eds) *Cultural Studies*. Routledge, London, pp. 96–116.

Cohen, S. and Taylor, L. (1992) *Escape Attempts – The Theory and Practice of Resistance to Everyday Life*. Routledge, London.

Connell, R.W. (1995) *Masculinities*. Polity Press, Cambridge, UK.

Davies, K. (2001) New times at the workplace – opportunity or angst? The example of hospital work. In: Soulsby, M.P. and Fraser, J.T. (eds) *Time. Perspectives at the Millennium*. Bergin & Garvey, Westport, Connecticut, pp. 189–202.

Desforges, L. (1998) 'Checking out the planet': global representations/local identities in youth travel. In: Skelton, T. and Valentine, G. (eds) *Cool Places: Geographies of Youth Culture*. Routledge, London, pp. 175–192.

Desforges, L. (2000) Travelling the world: identity and travel biography. *Annals of Tourism Research* 27, 926–945.

Downe, P.J. (1999) Laughing when it hurts: humor and violence in the lives of Costa Rican prostitutes. *Women's Studies International Forum* 22, 63–78.

Egeland, H. (1999) På Vandring – Identitetsutveckling Sett i Lys av 'Back-packing'. *Nordisk Samhällsgeografisk Tidskrift* 29, 73–81.

Elsrud, T. (1998) Time creation in travelling: the taking and making of time among women backpackers. *Time and Society* 7, 309–334.

Elsrud, T. (2001) Risk creation in traveling – backpacker adventure narration. *Annals of Tourism Research* 28, 597–617.

Elsrud, T. (2004) *Taking Time and Making Journeys: Narratives on Self and the Other Among Backpackers*. University of Lund Department of Sociology, Lund, Sweden.

Featherstone, M. (1995) *Undoing Culture: Globalization, Postmodernism and Identity*. Sage, London.

Felski, R. (1995) *The Gender of Modernity*. Harvard University Press, Cambridge, Massachusetts.

Fornäs, J. (1995) *Cultural Theory & Late Modernity*. Sage Publications Ltd, London.

Frederick, B. and Hyde, V. (1993) Introduction. In: Frederick, B. and McLeod, S. (eds) *Women and the Journey: the Female Travel Experience*. Washington State University Press, Pullman, Washington, pp. xvii–xxxiii.

Furlong, A. and Cartmel, F. (1997) *Young People and Social Change – Individualization and Risk in Late Modernity*. Open University Press, Buckingham, UK.

Giddens, A. (1984) *The Consequences of Modernity*. Polity Press, Cambridge, UK.

Giddens, A. (1991) *Modernity and Self-identity: Self and Society in the Late Modern Age*. Polity Press, Cambridge, UK.

Goffman, E. (1959) *The Presentation of the Self in Everyday Life*. Anchor, New York, USA.

Goffman, E. (1967) *Interaction Ritual*. Anchor, New York.

Haraway, D.J. (1991) *Simians, Cyborgs, and Women*. Free Association Books, London.

Hillman, W. (1999) Searching for Authenticity in Touristic Experience: Female Backpackers in North Queensland. Unpublished MSc thesis, James Cook University, Townsville, Australia.

Holland, J., Ramazanogly, C., Sharpe, S. and Thomson, R. (1998) *The Male in the Head. Young People, Heterosexuality and Power*. The Tufnell Press, London.

Keller, E.F. (1985) *Reflections on Gender and Science*. Yale University Press, New Haven, Connecticut.

Lalander, P. and Johansson, T. (2002) *Ungdomsgrupper i Teori och Praktik*. Studentlitteratur, Lund, Sweden.

Lightfoot, C. (1997) *The Culture of Adolescent Risk-taking*. The Guilford Press, New York.

Mead, G.H. (1934) *Mind, Self and Society*. University of Chicago Press, Chicago, Illinois.

Meethan, K. (2001) *Tourism in Global Society. Place, Culture, Consumption*. Palgrave, Basingstoke, UK.

Melucci, A. (1996) *The Playing Self: Person and Meaning in the Planetary Society*. Cambridge University Press, Cambridge, UK.

Mills, S. (1991) *Discourses of Difference: an Analysis of Women's Travel Writing and Colonialism*. Routledge, London.

Mills, S. (2002) Adventure and gender. In: Foster, S. and Mills, S. (eds) *Women's Travel Writing: an Anthology*. Manchester University Press, Manchester, UK.

Munt, I. (1994) The 'other' postmodern tourism: culture, travel and the new middle classes. *Theory, Culture and Society* 11, 101–123.

Pratt, M.L. (1992) *Imperial Eyes: Travel Writing and Transculturation*. Routledge, London.

Riley, P. (1988) Road culture of international long-term budget travelers. *Annals of Tourism Research* 15, 313–328.

Rorty, R. (1989) *Contingency, Irony and Solidarity*. Cambridge University Press, Cambridge, UK.

Scheibe, K.E. (1986) Self-narratives and adventure. In: Sarbin, T.R. (ed.) *Narrative Psychology*. Praeger, New York, pp. 129–151.

Simmel, G. (1971) *On Individuality and Social Forms*. The University of Chicago Press, Chicago, Illinois.

Skeggs, B. (1997) *Formations of Class & Gender*. Sage, London.

Swain, M.B. (1995) Gender in tourism. *Annals of Tourism Research* 22, 247–266.

Uriely, N., Yonay, Y. and Simchai, D. (2002) Backpacking experiences: a type and form analysis. *Annals of Tourism Research* 29, 519–537.

Vagabond (1996) No. 2, Stockholm.

Veijola, S. and Jokinen, E. (1994) The body in tourism. *Theory, Culture and Society* 11, 125–151.

Widerberg, K. (1995) *Kunskapens kön: Minnen, Reflektioner och Teori*. Norstedts, Stockholm.

Ziehe, T. (1991) *Zeitvergleiche: Jugend in kulturellen Modernisierungen*. Juventa, Weinheim/Munich, Germany.

10

More Than Just a Tourist: Distinction, Old Age and the Selective Consumption of Tourist Space

Caroline Oliver

University of Cambridge

Well, its not real here is it? It's living in unreality.
(Barbara, long-term migrant)

What is it like? What do you do?
These questions are often asked of you.
When retirement is on the way,
How do you plan to fill your day?
What are the drawbacks? What are the perks?
Do you get bored? Do you miss your work?
All our pensioner friends say with one voice:
'What do we do? We have a surfeit of choice!'

Far away from the cold, wind and rain
We have chosen Tocina in Southern Spain.
As we enjoy breakfast on our balcony,
We watch the sun rise out of the sea.
Then to the beach for a quick morning swim,
An invigorating way for the day to begin.
Free from stresses of the technological race,
Our life proceeds at a leisurely pace.
We shop, cook, eat and perform our chores,
As our needs are much the same as before.
While Elmer tracks the market's gyrations,
Heidi still writes science dissertations.
Elmer's hobby is marquetry, Heidi's acrylic art,
And in petanque and Players Club we both take part.
                                     ('Retirement' by Elmer and Heidi Swanson)

Introduction

The above poem, written by two seasonal migrants to the Costa del Sol living in a state akin to 'permanent tourism', demonstrates how migrants both adhere to *and* distance themselves from dominant images of tourism in their narratives of identity. The poem at once portrays their new home as tourist-like; a sunny and relaxing 'Shangri-La' site of leisure, whilst simultaneously stressing the continuation of existing non-tourist modes and activities in maintaining the 'normality' of their lives. This chapter will argue that migrants, living in conditions where elements of tourism are negotiated on a daily basis, are more selective than is perhaps apparent, and are implicitly involved in a strategic consumption and rejection of discourses of tourism. This is judged according to how well particular images support their over-riding narratives of themselves as 'positive agers'. The retirees, adjusting to a non-work-oriented identity, utilize images associated with place in their stories of ageing, in which Spain is espoused as providing the appropriate conditions for ageing well in contrast to elsewhere. Ideas of freedom, warmth, anonymity, communality and travel, as well as enabling possibilities for activity and personal development within the particular site of Spain, are employed because they inform a narrative of ageing well. Yet, this only goes so far. Centrally, residents use the distinction of themselves as migrants *not* tourists to confirm their same stories of ageing in a desired form. These refutations are based on an idea that certain putative features of living life as a tourist would equate to ageing badly. The lack of structure, the pressure to 'enjoy', associations of temporariness, dependency, inactivity and the 'herd-like' nature of tourists resonate strongly with elements that migrants would like to avoid in their negotiations of ageing.

My analysis draws on participant observation amongst permanent and seasonal Northern European retired migrants (all names are pseudonyms) in Tocina a town of moderate size at the east end of the Costa del Sol. The migrants live in houses, apartment blocks or urbanizations (self-contained mini-villages). Some of the latter were built originally as retirement complexes, but are now used as holiday lets. To outsiders, there is little to distinguish tourists from migrants, and motivations, expectations and behaviour also overlap on a number of levels (Gustafson, 2002). Yet, this is not to say that there is not a significant *felt* difference, espoused vehemently at times by migrants. If they are at all tourists, they assert, it is only at certain times and for particular motivations. The rest of the time, the tourist figure is utilized as a negative pole for contrast in migrants' self-conceptions. These complexities suggest that the expansion of retirement migration into tourist sites complicates the simplistic and binary divisions between visitors and hosts typical of much tourist research (Smith, 1989). It also renders the theoretical dichotomy between tourists and migrants open to revision, to account for the interplays and overlaps between these forms of mobility (Williams and Hall, 2000; O'Reilly, 2003).

Traditionally, migrants' disdain for tourists may be conceptualized as a matter of distinction (Graburn, 1989); the assertion of class status through style. Yet I argue that migrants' distancing (and at times adoption) of the tourist mode exists because some narratives of tourism speak loudly and resonate strongly with both the ideals and the fears of ageing. Such orientations derive from a cultural shift involving a reinterpretation of ageing, marking a move towards 'positive ageing', associated with different norms of age-related behaviour (Featherstone and Hepworth, 1995; Blaikie, 1999). The traditional 'ages and stages' model of old age (Hepworth, 2000) has dissolved in the face of expectations to create new roles outside of work and experience, and new possibilities in leisured retirement (Blaikie, 1999). In particular, tourism offers possibilities of fulfilling the aspirations to age well.

In using tourism to express ideals about ageing, migrants complicate the dominant model of Urry's *The Tourist Gaze* (1990a) which portrays tourism as a visual cultural construction of various sites. Notwithstanding the contributions of Urry's thesis, criticisms have been raised mainly because of the thesis' tendency to homogenize the diversity of tourist experience (Macleod, 1999). However, if we adopt the research stance Shields advocates, 'into the culturally mediated reception of representations of environments, places or regions which are afloat in society as "ideas in currency"' (1991, p. 14), it is overwhelmingly clear that even with respect to a place as symbolically loaded as the 'Costa', environments are felt and perceived in a variety of different ways. This chapter shows how attention should be paid to the strategic consumption of certain produced images according to the agendas and life course positions of particular individuals, as Urry's updated edition of *The Tourist Gaze* (2002) observes.

After describing the area and people under study, I introduce the phenomenon of retired migrants in Spain and consider the ambiguous position they inhabit in this space (Gustafson, 2002). Secondly, I show how inhabiting a tourist space infuses the narratives of migrants' experiences in a positive way. These narratives are often animated by oppositions to the condition of negative ageing, imagined and located far away in the place of origin. Yet the positive experience of tourism is not total. Finally, I reveal how they *reject* other facets of the tourist experience. Infusing their narratives are stories ridiculing the omnipresent tourists, which distance the migrants from them (see also O'Reilly, 2000; Gustafson, 2002) and deny any similarity.

Tocina – the Zone of Leisure

Tocina is a hive of tourist activity, yet one that some say has a pleasant 'Spanish' atmosphere. Given the irresponsible development of other sites, the onus has fallen upon Tocina, and Freila, a nearby inland white village (*pueblo blanco*), to offer more 'authentic' versions of Spanish towns, and to draw the tourists away from other overdeveloped coastal areas. Yet, in Tocina, the expanse of hotels and apartments, a characteristic feature of mass tourism, sprawls beyond the main town, and grows year by year. Walk through in the height of summer, and you will be jostled by the crowds of tourists. Standing at the end of the marble effect *paseo* (promenade) one sees a number of rocky coves with beautiful sandy bays, as well as a large expanse of man-made beach at the far extremes of the town. Thirty-odd years ago this was a fishing beach, with maybe only one shack for refreshment. Now, it is backed by six or seven *merinderas* (fish restaurants) selling enticing *mariscos, espetos y paella* (seafood, grilled sardines and paella). Sprouting up in the hills behind is a mini-town of self-enclosed holiday villages, complete with decorative water features and swimming pools. They are owned by a growing contingent of seasonal or permanent Northern European migrants or by Spaniards as second homes. They merge into an area of apartment blocks, or mock-pseudo-Andalucían houses, which give way to the more 'traditional' town. Beyond this is an area comprised of some English bars and shops, revealing the entrenchment of a social infrastructure of English conveniences as well as neon-lit nightlife activity for those brave enough (see Andrews, Chapter 11, this volume).

Such a vista confirms the ingrained idea in the Northern European cultural repertoire of the Costa as a liminal leisure zone. Shields (1991) demonstrates how, historically, liminal zones of leisure and relaxation were located in the coastal resorts of the UK. Over time, from the 1960s onwards, such places of 'permissive atmosphere' (Shields, 1991, p. 73) in which one experiences a break from everyday routines and proper behaviour have been relocated to the Mediterranean. In Andalucía, tourist developments have significantly transformed the social and spatial geography, and the economy, once agriculture dependent, it is now service driven. The population is now unevenly distributed, concentrated in urban centres and coastal areas, which are enormously swollen during summer months (Salmon, 1992). In the competition of land use for agriculture or tourism, it is clearly the tourist industry that is dominant. The landscape is marked by an abundance of large, private houses surrounded by large white-washed walls and iron gates, nestled alongside apartment blocks and *urbanizaciones* (urbanizations – bounded off communities of houses), interspersed by coastal marinas and beach developments. As Ryan points out, the hasty development results in 'a tourist complex which could be located on any part of the Mediterranean coastline, so indistinguishable is it from its counterparts' (Ryan, 1991, p. 99), and there are certainly examples around Tocina. Amongst migrants, however, there is currently a strongly felt need to prevent the site from disintegrating into a 'non-place' (Augé, 1995), exhibiting nondescript and disembedded features with little reference to the particular geographical site (Rojek, 1995; see Oliver, 2002).

As a result of the success story of tourism, these coastal zones are specifically designated in local government's policy and practice as leisure zones. The development of the town is aimed at providing an environment for tourist purposes, much like the construction of shopping centres in the UK as social spaces of consumption and leisure for families (Sibley, 1995). Tocina is a geographically specific site devoted entirely to the service industry, replete with semiotic and symbolic content which point towards the luxuries found within such a 'paradise'. Culturally, of course, such postmodern and post-industrial sites evoke fearful reactions, suggesting a direct link between the environment and the behaviours of those inhabiting them. J.G. Ballard describes the Costa del Sol in a novel as 'a zone as depthless as a property developer's brochure' (1996, p. 16), where 'unreality thrived on every side' (p. 17). According to the central character in the novel, 'steeped in sun and sundowners, wandering the golf greens by day and dozing in front of their satellite television in the evening, the residents of the Costa del Sol lived in an eventless world' (Ballard, 1996, p. 33). In the face of this dystopic image, how are inhabitants supposed to engage in any meaningful life? Moreover, how do they develop a sense of self in such an environment? To begin to answer these questions, it is necessary to introduce the people who inhabit a site that is so symbolically loaded in our cultural imaginings.

Old Age Migrants or Residential Tourists?

> Sometimes we go down to Tocina and sit and watch all the Spanish people. We can pretend to be tourists for a while too.
>
> (Edie, village dweller)

In introducing the migrants in this study, it is necessary to point out how they are, without doubt, a mixed bunch. They are mainly Northern European nationals (although a small number are from North America). Whilst it would be misleading to portray any allusions to homogeneity for the diversity between migrants is the most striking factor, one or two relevant points should be noted. First, although many are seasonal migrants (see Gustafson, 2002), a significant number permanently live in the area, and think of Spain as their home, at least until ill health necessitates a revision of that view. Secondly, the majority of Northern

European migrants have retired to the Costa. They are part of a growing band of 'woopies' (well off older persons) enjoying the benefits in retirement accrued through working lives (King *et al.*, 2000).

Given the new impetus of ageing well, novel ways of living up to the imperative are sought out. One means of realizing this is through travel, tourism and retirement migration. A growing number of older people are opting to move from original places of residence to live amongst their peers. This is evidenced in the proliferation of age-segregated societies/retirement communities. In such societies, there is now scope for the assertion of new age-based identities, where older people live permanently 'like other people vacation' (Van den Hoonaard, 1994, p. 23). The phenomenon has repercussions for the location and function of tourist spaces as Blaikie points out:

> Since the mid-1970s, the phenomenon of summers spent lounging on the beach has all but disappeared in the wake of cheap package deals to Continental Europe. Not only have the holiday hordes been displaced to the costas, but also the archetypal 'oldie' at play is now to be found enjoying long-stay winter breaks in the Mediterranean, dressed in department-store light casual wear.
>
> (Blaikie, 1999, pp. 166–167)

Of course, this means that permanent migrants coexist with short-term tourists at times and their shared inhabitancy of a leisure zone rests on somewhat similar motives. Indeed, the reasons and motivations for travel (whether to holiday or retire) do not at first sight appear to differ enormously and often overlap, as the following arrival narratives show:

> We came for holidays first, then eventually for retirement.
>
> (Gerald, lives in a village)

> We put all our stuff in storage and decided to tour around Europe in a camper-van. We never made it to see half of what we had planned!
>
> (Vincent and Carol, urbanization dwellers)

> The climate is the most important thing to make me stay.
>
> (Bob, urbanization dweller)

> We came for culture. We travelled the world and ended up exploring Europe.
>
> (Jed and Sheena, American urbanization dwellers)

> I did the Shirley Valentine thing. I left a note on my husband's pillow and disappeared.
>
> (Barbara, hill-village resident)

The need for escape, freedom, regeneration, self-realization, communication and happiness through tourism (Krippendorf) is equally as salient for migrants as for tourists. Yet according to most existing typologies, migrants are not tourists. Not wishing to indulge in exhaustive analyses of definitions of tourists, it is none the less worth noting that the tourist–migrant distinction largely rests on the idea that tourism implies people's movement 'outside their normal place of residence' (Urry, 1990a, p. 2) and that the tourist experience is 'in some sense a contrast with everyday experiences' (Urry, 1990a, p. 11). It is an impermanent, temporary change of location because, as Graburn expresses, 'we cannot properly vacation at home' (1989, p. 23). This condition is clearly not met by permanent migrants, living in the area. Furthermore, as Chambers writes:

> To travel implies movement between fixed positions, a site of departure, a point of arrival, the knowledge of an itinerary. It also intimates an eventual return, a potential homecoming. Migrancy, on the contrary, involves a movement in which neither points of departure nor those of arrival are immutable or certain. It calls for a dwelling in language, in histories, in identities that are constantly subject to mutation.
>
> (Chambers, 1994, p. 8)

However, one may question the validity of such accounts for contemporary complexities (see Williams and Hall, 2000). Certainly in this case, migrants resemble tourists in several ways. For example, in the work–leisure dichotomy that characterizes tourists as non-workers (Urry, 1990b), migrants, indulging in leisure, are like tourists. In addition, in the 'host–guest' dichotomy (Smith, 1989), migrants are neither strictly hosts nor guests, but fall somewhere in between (see Gustafson, 2002 and O'Reilly, 2003 for a further discussion of the ambiguous position of migrants). On one hand, migrants regularly conceive of themselves as guests in Spain (O'Reilly, 2000), at times adopting this theme as moralizing discourse out of respect for local ways. Yet some feel that their guest status limits their engagement. Bill, for instance, ruefully told of how he felt condemned to a superficial mode. He said, 'I find it difficult to make friends [with Spanish people], as much as I'd like, the tourist infrastructure is too ingrained, and with others we can't find much in common to talk beyond bar conversation'. Yet, on the other hand, they are also subject to the same disruptions as native 'hosts' entrapped in the gaze, particularly because they consider Spain their 'home' (O'Reilly, 2003). For instance, many migrants, particularly in the village, told me how upsetting it was to have tourists peer through the windows of their 'typically' Spanish houses (see Fig. 10.1). Clearly Rojek and Urry's assertion that 'living in a tourist honeypot is akin to being a prisoner in the panopticon' (1997, p. 7) should no longer be exclusively applied to native hosts.

Migrants also sometimes express a sense of being 'in-between'; neither tourists, nor working, and engaged in leisure as a way of life (see Gustafson, 2002). This ambiguous position is captured in one instance,

Fig. 10.1. A tourist looking through the windows of a house in the village.

when one couple, Reg and Janet, announced that they were going back to England. When I inquired as to the reason for their visit, I was met with silence, followed by Reg, instructing his wife Janet to 'tell the girl'. Janet seemed embarrassed and said, 'We're going there because we're leaving for a holiday, a cruise. I mean *a holiday*', she said correcting herself, 'that sounds so stupid doesn't it?' She felt the need to justify their decision to take a break from a holiday site, pointing out, 'Well, we could have cancelled it, but we would have lost our deposit'. Another couple said to me, 'It's not like being on holiday here ... well, I suppose it is compared to England'. The migrants' ambiguous position as leisured retirees in a holiday zone raises the interesting question as to how far tourist images are used to construct their own narratives of life and their ability to 'age well'. First, I examine the ways that positive images of Spain are consumed to support this narrative. Then I turn to an analysis of how more negative connotations inherent in the tourist experience are distanced from to support the same story.

'Just Another Boring Day in Paradise'

Whilst the importance of narrative in understanding ageing is increasingly recognized in analytical terms, for migrants in Spain it takes on a heightened significance. Not only are migrants growing old but they have to represent themselves anew, in new locations and amongst new social groupings. For these migrants, I suggest a crucial feature in their narratives is a strategic employment of myths of 'place' to support stories of positive ageing. As Massey points out, '... geographical specificity, and the meanings and symbolisms which people attach to places, and how these can – and should-be struggled over, are all important issues' (1994, p. 118). As a consequence, there has been a shift towards a reinterpreted notion of 'place' as a significant factor in constituting diverse identities. In practice, this means acknowledging that fluid and adapting identities (in place of the monolithic and fixed conceptions of the modernist era) are constructed with reference to metaphorical spaces and/or specific sites and places.

As Blaikie points out, tourist zones have long been deemed appropriate sites for ageing well. With reference to the UK, he notes there has been a 'conflation of positive ageing and seaside living' (1997, p. 629). Similarly, in the wider Western cultural redressing of negative images of old age, positive images of warmth and community (as used in tourism) have been also associated with the period of old age. For instance, the use of 'sunshine' buses (Fennell *et al.*, 1988) and the naming of units in residential homes after vistas of nature and community (see Oliver, 1999) demonstrates how 'good' old age is associated with pleasant images.

In the Northern European consciousness, Spain in particular is synonymous with a whole series of positive or romantic 'place myths' (Lash and Urry, 1994). Such images and myths represent Spain as a comfortable and familiar place (O'Reilly, 2000) known through prior holidaying (Rodríguez *et al.*, 1998) where one can do what one desires, an anthem echoed in positive ageing discourse (Oliver, 2006b). It is constructed as having 'always' been the site for tourism, right from the beginnings of mass charter tourism in Europe in the 1960s and 1970s. In an analysis of the marketing of holiday destinations to older people, Chaney similarly points out how institutional forms of ageing 'use a form of presentation that casts novelty within the reassurance of tradition' (1995, p. 211). All the more perhaps, following long-term geographical relocation, older people seek to construct familiarity in new, strange surroundings (see Reed and Roskell Payton, 1996) and, in Spain, the prior image of familiarity facilitates this process. Many people convey how living in Spain is an extension of either long holidaying periods in Spain, or a mere continuation of an expatriate lifestyle. In the perpetuation of ideals of continuity, one man pointed out, for instance how it was like 'England in the sun'.

The construction of Spain as a site for experiencing good ageing is repeated through wider cultural discourses of the Mediterranean. Central is the idea that ageing is not hidden in Spain, and that older people still assume central positions in the mainstream of communities. For example, the image of the 'old lady in black' is often used in constructions of the region, such as in postcards. Furthermore a recent development for tourists in the village has involved the construction of a kiosk with coin-activated mechanical models of two older women of the village, 'Carmen' and 'Dolores' talking of 'the good old days'. This visibility of older people is not confined to images, but is also consistently reaffirmed in personal narrative (see O'Reilly, 2000). At one club, one woman commented to a group she was having coffee with that, 'its beautiful here. The Spanish families all come down to the beach and line up in the fish restaurants. They know how to take care of the old here.' As the listeners murmured in agreement, she continued, 'It's how it used to be in England, but they don't do that anymore'. On another occasion, an almost identical scene was celebrated, emphasizing the way the elderly in Spain are 'not packed off in a corner', but completely involved in family life.

It is important to note that positive touristic images are used oppositionally to state the shortcomings of contexts from which migrants came. Karen O'Reilly points out that migrants construct a 'bad Britain' discourse, painting a negative picture of the UK as 'depressing and depressed' (2000, p. 164). This theme was echoed in my own fieldwork, as one man for example described, 'everything in Britain is falling apart'. However, the good/bad dichotomy is extended to the experience of ageing, so that certain types of ageing experience are discursively located in particular places. For example, one woman expressed her satisfaction in Spain, asserting, 'I shall never leave Spain unless in a wooden coat. I would be bored and cold in England.' Another pointed out how in her native Florida, all the older people would be 'bored silly and lined up in rocking chairs'. The subtext is that one is entertained and comfortable in Spain, whilst images of boredom, coldness, greyness and pervasive disorder are linked to the home country. Therefore, the contents of stories of home are not simply negative images of the home country, but rather strongly linked to the fears and worries of ageing; to be bored, cold and alone are worries that can then be located far away geographically in England, or wherever. Alternatively, ideas of freedom, warmth, anonymity, communality, travel, as well as enabling possibilities for activity and personal development within the particular site of Spain are employed because they inform a narrative of ageing well.

The ease with which the tourist experience slips into the 'good ageing' experience is demonstrated by many accounts which particularly emphasize travel and leisure as a means of self-realization. Migrants often refer to their home as 'paradise', in which they seek experiences which 'cater to their desire for learning, nostalgia, heritage, make-believe and a closer look at the Other' (Boissevain, 1996, p. 3). Craik points out, '... tourism has come full circle, revitalising the educative and enlightenment role of early tourism as a training – or finishing school – for travellers' (1997, p. 118). Similarly, here, travel is deemed to broaden the mind, to inform and to educate. The narrative of mobility is employed to present certain positive traits in the individual against a negative image of stasis and stagnation in old age, and the mobility of lifestyle is not put on hold when living there. Much club life is organized around tourist trips and visits to different sites in Spain and Andalucía. Many of these had a 'cultural bent', the tourist experience intertwined with learning and education, incorporating historical facts, archaeological insights or architectural explanations. The consumption of this sort of tourism meets the ethos of the Third Age (Laslett, 1989) offering positive material for self-identification as 'learners' rather than a negative image of themselves read in other experiences of tourism as pure consumers.

The diversion and entertainment of holiday life are used in narrative to fend off a negative image of humdrum everyday life (as is imagined to be the experience in the home country). Rather when the home environment is a leisure environment, daily activities unsurprisingly mirror those undertaken in the tourist experience. For instance, Gerald, a man in his late 70s, goes swimming every day, with another woman living on the seafront, suggesting 'the sea is my personal swimming pool!' Following retirement, leisure and its management fills attention, and gives roles and sources of identity in the absence of work.

In particular, the anonymity of the tourist zone is also exploited in migrants' narratives. The idea that 'one could be who one wanted to be' (found also by King *et al.*, 2000; O'Reilly, 2000; and explored in Oliver, 2006a) was repeated to me on innumerable occasions. Many migrants pointed out how the move had facilitated a 'new start', allowing them the possibility to live away from the over-riding work emphasis of the UK. Moreover, the creativity of identity is facilitated by the constant flow of a tourist 'audience' offering a never-ending source of company and short-term friendship to migrants whilst encouraging a certain spilling over of 'the tourist mode' into migrants' experience. In tourist–migrant interactions, the typical introductory question of 'what do you do?' is replaced by 'how did you get here?', which prompts a telling of arrival narratives. The major discontinuity of the move in migrant's lives is akin to a 'career break' (as described by Humphrey, 1993, p. 166), a defining moment of one's life. Almost every month, there is at least one personal story recounting a migrant's move in the English-language monthly magazines. The stories generally explain how the migrant was seduced or 'fell in love' with Spain. Not only do these tales create narratives of belonging, they also continue the production of place-imaginings because they are also read by visiting tourists.

Images of freedom and lack of everyday life constraints associated with holiday time are also employed by migrants. For example, ideals of communality emphasized in tourist propaganda (particularly for older people – see Chaney, 1995; Ylänne-McEwen, 2000) are adopted, with a relaxing of rules associated with making acquaintances. The *'communitas'* found regularly in the liminal tourist experience is also a condition common in older persons' experiences. For instance, Dawson points out in his study of older people's clubs in Ashington, north-east England, that community is 'a potent topic of interest amongst elderly people', with the construction of *communitas* a regular feature of club life (2002, p. 23; and see Okely, 1990). Many migrants assert that it is easier to make friends in Spain, so much so that some people had to find techniques to limit acquaintances (Oliver, 2006a).

Finally, the perceived relaxing of time management governing holidays is utilized as particularly relevant to this stage of the life course. The sense that in Spain, life is less hurried and less urgent, is evident in many produced images, for instance, a headline for a property supplement describes, 'The rhythm of life in Andalucía may change, but the melody is still sweet. In southern Spain it is still possible to choose the pace at which you want to live your life' (O'Kelly, 1999, p. iv). This is emphasized in contrast to the perceived capitalist work orientation (or as the poem described 'technological race') of the UK. Whilst I do not have space to do full justice to migrants' negotiation of time in the tourist space (see Oliver, 2006b), it is worth noting that there is some benefit from the coexistence with tourists, who exist temporarily within a liminal zone (Graburn, 1989). The sensation of a slow down of linear time in tourist zones has direct parallels with other constructed temporal worlds in the environments of older people, for example in day centres or residential establishments (Hazan, 1980; Hockey, 1990; Huby, 1992). Clearly, the tourist mode is enjoyed for its certain parallels with the benefits of good ageing.

'Tourists, Go Home!' Distancing from Tourism in Age Definition

'Tourists, go home!' exclamation on a poster.
(enlarged from a postcard in a long-term migrant's hallway)

To go into the town in summer? I'd rather go to hell. In summer I hide'.
(Elizabeth, long-term migrant)

As much as certain produced images are applicable to the good ageing experience, I also argue that images are *reflexively* consumed and made meaningful by certain people at certain times. In the particular situational context of the migrants, then, certain touristic images and behaviours are equally *rejected* if they do not correspond to the individual's ideas of ageing well. In fact, despite the part adoption of some features of a tourist lifestyle as previously explored, the suggestion that migrants are at all like tourists is likely to be met with strong refutation (O'Reilly, 2000; Gustafson, 2002). There is rather a strong backlash against tourists and consequent regulation of migrants' own behaviours. This (selective) distancing from tourists is prompted by a need to distinguish themselves because, as O'Reilly suggests, migrants have been located in popular mythology in the same stereotypical space as tourists (O'Reilly, 2000, 2003). Migrants have to fight against a mass of stereotypes that sees them as lazy hedonists, drunken hooligans, colonialists or criminals (O'Reilly, 2000). It is worth interrogating further the implications of these stereotypes in the light of the desired self-images of the migrants. In particular, I suggest that a number of features identified as endemic to mass tourism have connotations far removed from particular ideals of good ageing. To live like a tourist provokes anxiety because it has resonance with the imagined experience of living as a person ageing 'badly' – being inactive, denied individuality, dependent, inauthentic and transient (not belonging) and temporary. In many narratives then, a distancing from a tourist lifestyle occurs; the tourist is instead used as a pole by which one may assert and measure an alternative (more positively ageing) identity.

The first threat to positive ageing represented in living a tourist lifestyle is the possibility of paternalistic control, regulation and loss of autonomy. Whilst the positive employment of leisure for self-actualization has credence in our cultural imaginings, equally (as demonstrated in the J.G. Ballard novel) the mass production of leisure is fearfully viewed as stripping the individual of autonomy and independence. Wesley-Burnett and Rollin (2000) explore how in fictional images of dystopia, 'anti-leisure' becomes the site for mindless entertainment, immoderation and extremes. Similarly, Shields (1989) points out that in constructed geographies of leisure and consumption (for instance in shopping malls), the requisite security also introduces extreme surveillance, of almost Orwellian overtones (Sibley, 1995). Now, whilst mass touristic zones offer comfort and security, the flip-side is that they also bring these negative features of 'anti-leisure', with an associated reduction in autonomy and independence of those living with them. In Tocina, many urbanizations are under 24 hour surveillance, offering all-night lighting, security guards and vigilantes to patrol the plots. These forms of security are viewed disparagingly by some migrants, however, because they can also undermine independence, of particular importance at this stage of the life course when those exact ideals are potentially under threat. For some migrants, therefore, the evaluation of the main semi-touristic urbanization in Tocina was as a 'holiday camp', 'toy-town' and 'a rabbit hutch'. These images invoke childhood and dependency; in short, polar opposites to ideals of good ageing.

Within the urbanizations themselves, the long-term residents however adopt 'responsible' roles *vis à vis* tourists to position themselves away from the dependency of the tourists. They define themselves as 'in charge', for instance by running urbanization committees and enforcing rules at the swimming pools. Will, a key player in the urbanization *comunidad* (community), told me, 'Problems arise from tourists and tour-operators. Psychologically people undergo a change of character to go on holiday, even to get on the airplane. We've had to insist emphatically on a number of rules, that nobody reserves space at the pool, there's no ball game, flippers, so we preserve the tranquillity.' Furthermore, migrants act in some ways as authority figures to the tourists. They have visible tasks as mediators between Spanish and tourists (Gustafson, 2002), for instance as translators at the clinics, or by giving lectures about elements of local history (again confirming their ambiguity as in this case they reproduce images for tourists).

The tourists may be seen as conformist, especially considering that many organized tours (particularly in winter) are comprised of groups of older people who follow itineraries planned by tourist agencies. Lash and Urry (1994) point out that holidays, particularly in the 20th century became very regulated, a fact typified by the holiday camp phenomenon. Routine is superimposed (Pimlott, 1947), with visitors told when to do things and what to do. This factor is even more evident in older people's holiday experiences. Chaney (1995) for example points out how tour operators adopt a comparable 'authoritative paternalism' when marketing to older clients. In reality, this translates to companies making life 'easy', in which everything is done for the tourists. Such a stance is in direct contrast to migrants' ideals, in which most of them overwhelming defined themselves as being 'different' and 'un-typical' individuals (Oliver, 2006a). Rather, migrants' narratives often emphasize the hardiness of character they have had to develop to overcome the obstacles of living in another country. Their self-identities rest on qualities that they do not see exemplified in a tourist lifestyle.

O'Reilly (2000) points out how tourists were figures of fun and objects of ridicule, and sometimes this was born out in my research. I suggest such a narrative functions *de facto* to position the migrants as more autonomous and more responsible. On one occasion, for instance, the chairperson of a club was telling a story to a newly interested potential resident, which reduced tourists to naïve and rather ridiculous figures. She was explaining how she lived further up the coast, 'away from tourists'. She began telling a story of how some tourists in her town had got on the bus ahead of her. For a good few minutes, the tourists and bus driver were engaged in a long misunderstanding. The tourist couple repeatedly asked in English how much the trip would cost. The increasingly frustrated bus driver, getting more and more annoyed, was asking, '*a dónde vais?*' (where are you going to?) to which the tourists repeatedly asked in English, 'how much?' In this particular story, the tourist is held up as a ridiculous and helpless individual, far removed from migrants' narratives of overcoming challenges in the adaptation to life in a different environment. The inability of a tourist to communicate and 'know the ropes' parallels the dependency of very old age.

Another parallel of tourism with undesired ageing is the possibility of inactivity. The majority of tourists arrive in the long, hot summer months which, by necessity, induce periods of inactivity. The excessive heat of the Mediterranean summer induces behaviours opposed to ideals of good ageing, and as such represents a threat to self-esteem. For many tourists to the Costa, the week's break to 'recharge the batteries' is about little more than catching up on sleep, dozing off mid-afternoon whilst sunbathing. Certainly for residents, these aspects of tourism, if taken to extremes, can be considered dangerous to their lifestyle. For, as demonstrated for example in the proverb and title of a book on leisure, 'the devil makes work for idle hands' (Clarke and Critcher, 1985), idleness is seen as morally threatening. Judy, for instance, felt very depressed that her summer months had been spent in lethargy. The heat got to her, and she felt useless and fed up. The inactivity and lack of direction on the part of tourists is seen as at best, a stance to be adopted in moderation, and, at worst, a threat to be kept at bay. Thus when tales of activity were recounted in narratives, it was often in opposition to an undisclosed 'other' who had slipped into a 'tourist' lifestyle (also noted by King *et al.*, 2000; Gustafson, 2002). Those people, 'the undesirables' as Bob, an American, explained, 'came in with mass tourism'. He continued, 'they sit around and get drunk all day.'

Whilst on one hand, the freedom and hedonism associated with a leisure lifestyle is enjoyed some of the time, much work is done to dispel the image that migrants live a permanent holiday. Judy, greatly involved in voluntary work, explained to me when we first met how 'we don't sit around here and drink gin and tonics all day'. One day I was introduced to two tourists visiting their newly migrated friends at a club. When they asked me what I was doing, the man replied to me, 'I can tell you everything you need to know, I'll write it for you … I've only been here a week but that's long enough to see what life here is about. Drink, siesta, drink, siesta, drink, that's what!' Such images strike not just at the heart of the self-image of migrants but they relate also to the fears of boredom and monotony in ageing (as demonstrated in the subtext of the introductory poem). To be involved in a repetitive and unvarying routine is to demonstrate an undesired version of ageing, worlds removed from the positive, active and interesting lifestyle migrants desire. One evident means of distancing from this putative inactivity of tourism is to adopt a work ethic to the pursuit of leisure. Sandra pointed out, 'I like to keep busy. If I feel bored, mind you I never *do* feel bored, I just zoom off somewhere'. Another woman said, 'What would I get done if I sat around like that lot all day?' (it was unclear whether the 'lot' were tourists or badly ageing migrants) 'I'd never get anything done'. Whilst I pointed out earlier that the unstructured time governing leisure spaces can be welcomed at this stage of the life course, it is equally clear that there are downsides if one permanently wastes time. In fending off this feeling, one migrant expressed, 'You have to have a project, otherwise you get lost, then you seek out others who are lost ... then, oh well, its really sad'.

Distancing from the tourist experience also occurs because it jeopardizes migrants' status as belonging. The coexistence of seasonal tourists and migrants can be disruptive to feelings of long-term communality and belonging. For instance, Eva felt antipathy towards tourists, which arose from sharing space in a block of flats originally designated as a retirement community. She was disturbed by the implications of only having two other permanent residents in the unit, especially in winter. She explained:

> It's a shame all this letting, it's always done through agents so you have no idea of who is here. Nobody's got any interest in looking after the place, they do as they please when they are here, the kids playing in the lift all day long.

Furthermore, the transience and lack of long-term presence of tourists diminishes them to anonymous and dehumanized figures in relationships with locals, principally because they are not there long enough to make their mark. Pi-Sunyer argues that whilst tourism commoditizes culture, native hosts also begin to dehumanize tourists, and relate to strangers less as humans than as nuisances or resources (Pi-Sunyer, 1989). Reflecting tourism's necessary consequence of creating a 'we–they' opposition between visitors and native hosts (Nogués-Pedregal, 1996), migrants also feel that tourism has brought a potential threat to their own status. Whilst before mass tourism, as Jim, an American pointed out, migrants were seen as 'distant cousins', now they are seen as 'walking credit cards'. Negative feelings of transience are risked by authorities' classifications of large numbers of foreigners in Spain as 'residential tourists' (*turistas residenciales*) rather than permanent and legitimate members of society.

Having gained insight from living in Spain long term, foreign residents instead perceive tourists as falsely duped into believing inauthentic experiences. Recent assertions suggest that the quality of tourism has degenerated, becoming an experience which is pre-fabricated and constructed through the 'gaze' and exemplified in 'pseudo-events'. For migrants, foreign tourists' attempts to capture 'the sights' and signs associated with 'Spain' including the 'slice of real Spanish life', are seen as evidence of this. For example, one long-term

British resident in Freila exploded angrily to me about an American tourist she saw shaking an old Spanish woman dressed in black up and down and explaining how 'perfect' she was. The older woman did not speak English, and had no idea what the tourist was saying. The tourist was seen by the migrant to violate locals in their pursuit of what was deemed as a false sign of authenticity. The migrants, on the contrary, imply that as a result of living there they achieve real authenticity, consuming the 'authentic' rather than an 'illusion' (Bourdieu, 1984). Claims of *real* authenticity are asserted, in contrast to the tourists' ill-fated attempts to seek it (Gustafson, 2002; Verlot and Oliver, 2005). This can be in apparently insignificant ways, whether by referring to Juan, the bakery delivery boy as 'like a son' or having good relations with the gardener in the urbanization. Others demonstrate a real engagement in local people's lives, although this is harder to achieve.

In drawing to a close, I end with part of a recent correspondence I had with a seasonal migrant, Jim. He explained to me why migrants strongly deny the tourist status. He wrote:

> The likes of me are not tourists,
>
> 1) We are property owners here
> 2) We pay a local tax in addition to our urbanization dues
> 3) We pay a wealth tax
> 4) We can vote in local elections
> 5) We have Spanish Bank Accounts and Credit Cards
> 6) We have Spanish NIE fiscal numbers and cards
> 7) We stay here for up to 181 days a year
>
> TOURISTS DO NOT HAVE OR DO THESE THINGS!
>
> I am sure there are many other differences, like we don't spend so much time on the beach, eat fish and chips, drink vast quantities of booze, and we do have responsibilities like we have to maintain our properties and gardens.
>
> Yes, maybe we can be a bit snobbish about certain types of tourists, particularly the booze cruise types which frequent the Islands, Torremolinos and Benidorm in high season. ...

In Jim's correspondence, he emphasizes that in contrast to tourists, migrants are active, responsible and, as demonstrated by reference to a number of material and symbolic markers, belong in Spain. In defining migrants' self-identity, it is clear that the tourist status is denied, yet here it is employed to show exactly what they are *not*.

Ambiguous Positions and Selective Distinction

Urry suggests that the consumption process of tourism is about meeting the anticipated expectations of imaginings of sites, constructed through advertising and the media. Most importantly, these, he points out, 'relate very clearly to complex processes of social emulation' and competition between classes (1990a, pp. 13–14). We could use this line of thought to explain these migrants' behaviours. After all, one could easily posit that migrants' sometime contempt for tourists and touristic behaviour is evidence of processes of distinction. It is widely accepted that tourism has long held negative connotations, labelled as an insidious disease, detestable and disgusting (Ryan, 1991). Unsurprisingly an 'anti-tourist' mentality has developed, in which tourists avoid other tourists and claim to not be tourists themselves (Crick, 1989). Are migrants merely revealing the same 'rhetoric of moral superiority' when talking of tourists (MacCannell, 1976)? Surely their expression of negative opinions is simply a means of marking out class and status positions *vis à vis* a tourist mass. In tourists' choices to 'set off in their Renault 5 or Simca 1000 to join the great traffic jams of the holiday exodus … cram their tents into overcrowded campsites, fling themselves into the prefabricated leisure activities designed for them by the engineers of cultural mass production' (Bourdieu, 1984, p. 179), they reveal their lack of taste. Are not migrants exacting identical processes of status distinction through their claims of distance and alternative styles of consumption?

There is no doubt that the reactions of migrants can be interpreted according to this line of thought. Yet, to conclude, I suggest their actions are worth probing somewhat more. In particular, it is interesting to ask what is it *exactly* about the features of tourists, moreover what are the *particular* factors in tourist processes that are, at times, so abhorrent? When probing such, it is clear that matters of distinction work in interaction with other concerns. What I have argued is that some features of tourism demonstrate aspects of lifestyle that, at particular points of the life course, take on heightened significance for self-definition. Inactivity, for example, or dependence, or transience are more pressing issues for people existentially negotiating those concerns as they grow older.

Moreover, the interpretation of these processes as a means of distinction would suggest that rejection of certain types of tourism is wholesale and total; a choice either for mass tourism or its complete avoidance. Yet, as this chapter reveals, not *all* aspects of mass tourism are distanced from. What I suggest is rather that there is a process of selection of images in narratives (which range from positive employment to 'running a mile from') and that this is entirely relative to personal circumstances. Rather than consumption being merely a process of social signification assumed to be undertaken with an eye to the rest of the social milieu (Campbell, 1995), I suggest that selective tourist consumption equally reveals personal concerns. Indeed, the partial selection and partial rejection of some aspects of the tourist lifestyle are managed as far as they support the personal story of existentially negotiating ageing. It should not be assumed that in consumption it is only the case that, 'actions are necessarily oriented to others' (Campbell, 1987, p. 117). Clearly this is often the case, but there is also a need to explore how consumption is negotiated according to existential and personal ideals of well-being. Exactly which images are consumed, and which are not, are in this case related to concerns about ageing well. The individual stage in the life course colours and influences the attitude migrants have towards tourism and tourist pursuits, and also has evident ramifications for disposing those individuals to perceive places in different ways.

Acknowledgements

Thanks to Elmer and Heidi Swanson for the reproduction of the poem. I would also like to thank Andy Dawson, Jenny Hockey, Marc Verlot and the editors for their helpful suggestions on this text.

References

Augé, M. (1995) *Non-places: an Introduction to Anthropology of Supermodernity*. Verso, London.
Ballard, J.G. (1996) *Cocaine Nights*. Flamingo, London.
Blaikie, A. (1997) Beside the sea: visual imagery, ageing and heritage. *Ageing and Society* 17, 629–648.
Blaikie, A. (1999) *Ageing and Popular Culture*. Cambridge University Press, Cambridge, UK.
Boissevain, J. (1996) Introduction. In: Boissevain, J. (ed.) *Coping with Tourists. European Reactions to Mass Tourism*. Berghahn, Oxford, pp. 1–26.
Bourdieu, P. (1984) *Distinction: a Social Critique of the Judgement of Taste*. Routledge and Kegan Paul, London.
Campbell, C. (1995) The sociology of consumption. In: Miller, D. (ed.) *Acknowledging Consumption. A Review of New Studies*. Routledge, London, pp. 96–126.
Chambers, I. (1994) *Migrancy, Culture, Identity*. Routledge, London.
Chaney, D. (1995) Creating memories. Some images of aging in mass tourism. In: Featherstone, M. and Wernick, A. (eds) *Images of Ageing. Cultural Representations of Later Life*. Routledge, London, pp. 209–224.
Clarke, J. and Critcher, C. (1985) *The Devil Makes Work. Leisure in Capitalist Britain*. MacMillan, London.
Craik, J. (1997) The culture of tourism. In: Rojek, C. and Urry, J. (eds) *Touring Cultures. Transformations of Travel and Theory*. Routledge, London, pp. 113–136.
Crick, M. (1989) Representations of international tourism in the social sciences: sun, sex, sights, saving and servility. *Annual Review of Anthropology* 22, 461–481.
Dawson, A. (2002) The mining community and the ageing body: towards a

phenomenology of community. In: Amit, V. (ed.) *Realising Community. Concepts, Social Relationships and Sentiments*. Routledge, London, pp. 21–37.

Featherstone, M. and Hepworth, M. (1995) Images of positive aging: a case study of *Retirement Choice* magazine. In: Featherstone, M. and Wernick, A. (eds) *Images of Aging. Cultural Representations of Later Life*. Routledge, London, pp. 29–47.

Fennell, G., Philippson, C. and Evers, H. (1988) *The Sociology of Old Age*. Open University Press, Milton Keynes, UK.

Graburn, N. (1989) Tourism: the sacred journey. In: Smith, V. (ed.) *Hosts and Guests. The Anthropology of Tourism*, 2nd edn. The University of Pennsylvania Press, Pennsylvania, pp. 21–36.

Gustafson, P. (2002) Tourism and seasonal retirement migration. *Annals of Tourism Research* 29, 899–918.

Hazan, H. (1980) *The Limbo People. A Study of the Constitution of the Time Universe among the Aged*. Routledge, London.

Hepworth, M. (2000) *Stories of Ageing*. Open University Press, Buckingham, UK.

Hockey, J. (1990) *Experiences of Death. An Anthropological Account*. Edinburgh University Press, Edinburgh, UK.

Huby, G. (1992) Trapped in the present: the past, present and future of a group of old people in East London. In: Wallman, S. (ed.) *Contemporary Futures. Perspectives from Social Anthropology*. Routledge, London, pp. 36–50.

Humphrey, R. (1993) Life stories and social careers: ageing and social life in an ex-mining town. *Sociology* 27, 166–178.

King, R., Warnes, T. and Williams, A. (2000) *Sunset Lives. British Retirement Migration to the Mediterranean*. Berg, Oxford.

Krippendorf, J. (1984) *The Holiday Makers: Understanding the Impact of Leisure and Travel*. Heinemann, London.

Lash, S. and Urry, J. (1994) *Economies of Signs and Space*. Sage, London.

Laslett, P. (1989) *A Fresh Map of Life: The Emergence of the Third Age*. Macmillan, Basingstoke, UK.

MacCannell, D. (1976) *The Tourist: a New Theory of the Leisure Class*. Schocken Books, New York.

Macleod, D.V.L. (1999) Tourism and the globalisation of a Canary Island. *Journal of the Royal Anthropological Institute* 5, 443–456.

Massey, D. (1994) *Space, Place and Gender*. Polity, Cambridge, UK.

Nogués-Pedregal, A.M. (1996) Tourism and self-consciousness in a South Spanish coastal community. In: Boissevain, J. (ed.) *Coping with Tourists. European Reactions to Mass Tourism*. Berghahn, Oxford, pp. 56–83.

O'Kelly, V. (1999) The rhythm of life in Andalucía may change, but the melody is still sweet. In: *Property in Southern Spain supplement in Sur in English*. October 1–7.

Okely, J. (1990) Clubs for le troisième âge: communitas or conflict. In: Spencer, P. (ed.) *Anthropology and the Riddle of the Sphinx: Paradoxes of Change in the Life Course*. Routledge, London, pp. 194–210.

Oliver, C. (1999) Ordering the disorderly. *Education and Ageing* 14, 171–185.

Oliver, C. (2002) Killing the golden goose? Debates about tradition in an Andalucían village. *Journal of Mediterranean Studies* 12, 169–189.

Oliver, C. (2006a) Imagined communitas: older migrants and aspirational mobility. In: Amit, V. (ed.) *Going First Class? New Approaches towards Privileged Movement and Travel*. Berghahn, Oxford, in press.

Oliver, C. (2006b) *Old Age Travellers. Paradoxes of Positive Ageing in Retirement Migration to Spain*. Routledge, London.

O'Reilly, K. (2000) *The British on the Costa-del-Sol. Transnational Identities and Local Communities*. Routledge, London.

O'Reilly (2003) When is a tourist? The articulation of tourism and migration in Spain's Costa del Sol. *Tourist Studies* 3, 301–317.

Pimlott, J.A.R. (1947) *The Englishman's Holiday*. The Harvester Press, Sussex, UK.

Pi-Sunyer, O. (1989) Changing perceptions of tourism and tourists in a Catalan resort town. In: Smith, V. (ed.) *Hosts and Guests. The Anthropology of Tourism*, 2nd edn. The University of Pennsylvania Press, Pennsylvania, pp. 187–201.

Reed, J. and Roskell Payton, V. (1996) Constructing familiarity and managing the self: ways of adapting to life in nursing and residential homes for older people. *Ageing and Society* 16, 543–560.

Rodríguez, V, Fernández-Mayoralas, G. and Rojo, F. (1998) European retirees on the Costa del Sol: a cross-national comparison. *International Journal of Population Geography* 4, 183–200.

Rojek, C. (1995) *Decentering Leisure: Rethinking Leisure Theory*. Sage, London.

Rojek, C. and Urry, J. (1997) Transformations of travel and theory. In: Rojek, C. and Urry, J. (eds) *Touring Cultures. Transformations of Travel and Theory*. Routledge, London, pp. 1–19.

Ryan, C. (1991) *Recreational Tourism. A Social Science Perspective*. Routledge, London.

Salmon, K. (1992) *Andalucía: an Emerging Regional Economy in Europe*. Consejería de Economía y Hacienda, Spain.

Shields, R. (1989) Social spatialization and the built environment: the West Edmonton Mall. *Environment and Planning D: Society and Space* 7, 147–167.

Shields, R. (1991) *Places on the Margin: Alternative Geographies of Modernity*. Routledge, London.

Sibley, D. (1995) *Geographies of Exclusion. Society and Difference in the West*. Routledge, London.

Smith, V. (1989) Introduction. In: Smith, V. (ed.) *Hosts and Guests. The Anthropology of Tourism*, 2nd edn. The University of Pennsylvania Press, Pennsylvania, pp. 1–19.

Urry, J. (1990a) *The Tourist Gaze. Leisure and Travel in Contemporary Societies*. Sage, London.

Urry, J. (1990b) The 'consumption' of tourism. *Sociology* 24, 23–35.

Urry, J. (2002) *The Tourist Gaze*, 2nd edn. Sage, London.

Van den Hoonaard, D.K. (1994) Paradise lost: widowhood in a Florida retirement community. *Journal of Aging Studies* 8, 121–132.

Verlot, M. and Oliver, C. (2005) European consciousness amongst expatriates in Belgium and Spain. In: Wildemeersch, D., Bron, M. and Stroobants, V. (eds) *Active Citizenship and Multiple Identities in Europe*. Peter Lang Verlag, Frankfurt, Germany, pp. 259–277.

Wesley-Burnett, G. and Rollin, L. (2000) Anti-leisure in dystopian fiction: the literature of leisure in the worst of all possible worlds. *Leisure Studies* 19, 75–90.

Williams, A. and Hall, C. (2000) Tourism and migration: new relationships between production and consumption. *Tourism Geographies* 2, 5–27.

Ylänne-McEwen, V. (2000) Golden times for golden agers: selling holidays as lifestyle for the over 50s. *Journal of Communication*, Summer, 83–99.

Consuming Pleasures: Package Tourists in Mallorca

11

Hazel Andrews

Centre for Tourism, Consumer and Food Studies, Liverpool John Moores University, UK

Introduction

This chapter is concerned with the processes of consumption as they are manifest in Palmanova and Magaluf and in situating the semiotic aspects within a framework that accords the tourists active roles in their consumption practices and extends those practices beyond the visual.

This chapter is about the consumption practices of British tourists holidaying in Palmanova and Magaluf, Mallorca. It is based on ethnographic fieldwork conducted over a period of 8 months in 1998 and 1999. In terms of consumption, there are three key themes to emerge from the work. One is the connection between consumption and the creation or affirmation of identity. The second relates to the way that the production of space informs patterns of consumption and vice versa. The third theme is concerned with the characteristics of the consumption practices.

By an examination of the processes of spatial production, the processes of consumption and their relationship, the nature of tourist consumption moves beyond the subject–object dualism that has tended to characterize the study of consumption in tourism, most notably in the concept of 'the gaze' (Urry, 1990).

The chapter will begin by laying some theoretical foundations. First, it will outline the connection between identity and consumption. This will be followed by an overview of the treatment of consumption in the tourism literature. Thirdly, there will be a consideration of Lefebvre's (1991) *The Production of Space* which will provide a framework for the following ethnography, and enable the relationship between space and consumption practices to be examined.

©CAB International 2006. *Tourism Consumption and Representation:*
Narratives of Place and Self (eds K. Meethan, A. Anderson and S. Miles)

Theoretical Background

The narrowness of economic definitions of consumption has been challenged (see Jackson, 1993; Douglas, 1996) and allowed consumption to be considered in terms of broader meanings. It has been suggested that the interest by anthropologists in the study of consumption has developed, in part, because of the extension of its understanding beyond economic considerations. Thus, it 'has rapidly expanded to mean anything from the popular appropriation of state services to the literal translation of ingestion in traditional Hinduism' (Miller, 1995, p. 283). The move away from an understanding of consumption in purely economic terms has opened up a path for an analysis that does not rely on the demand for goods being solely equated with price. Rather, goods have a symbolic value and a lived association. Thus meanings are ascribed to goods and objects, and it is these meanings that link the practice of consumption with creations and recreations of identity.

Thus far it is clear that consumption is not merely concerned with the sale and purchase of products in monetary terms. What is clear is that items are bought, or rejected, for symbolic reasons that convey messages about the person actively engaged in their consumption or rejection.

What the above examples illustrate is that consumption is a process in which choices are exercised that serve to convey information about the people involved in that consumption activity. Therefore, the idea of engagement links consumption practices to process. Consumption requires the exercise of choices in which the consumer has an active role (Jackson, 1993). For example, an examination of the alterations made to some kitchens on a north London housing estate showed that the occupants were engaged in an active and creative process (Miller, 1997).

The idea of the consumer being involved in active decision making about consumption practices and the attendant connection with choice suggests two things. First, there is a suggestion of freedom, which links to the second aspect, that of democracy – an ideology that has freedom of choice as a basis. It is up to the individual what they wish to consume. Exercising choice is an exercise in freedom. However, there is a tension between the ideas of freedom and choice and the observation that there is no means of escape from the self-perpetuating capitalist system drawn attention to by Baudrillard (1988).

To summarize the arguments so far we need to consider three key aspects. First, the definition of consumption is no longer cast only in terms of economic activity, but has been broadened to include a range of practices in which goods and services are understood to be imbued with more than a monetary value. It is with this broad definition that the present work is concerned.

The second aspect is that practices of consumption can be linked to ideas about identity. This occurs at different levels involving constructions of identity on an individual level as well as a means to social solidarity. They can be seen as reinforcing an understanding of self-identity in the way that Bourdieu (1979) describes working-class eating habits, and also by acts of resistance defining as much who one is not as well as who one is, as Douglas (1996) contends. In both scenarios, the consumer is involved in a process, actively making decisions. This links to the third point that politicizes consumption as it is often cast within a rubric of freedom and democracy, but that the nature of the system that allows these ideals requires contrary workings in order to ensure its own survival. The next stage of this theoretical underpinning is a brief overview of the way in which consumption has been considered in the tourism literature.

Tourism and Consumption

Debates concerning consumption in the anthropology and sociology tourism literature, where they have occurred at all, have tended to centre on the idea of commoditization, in particular the commoditization of whole cultures or cultural artefacts belonging to 'peripheral' peoples seen to be ripe for exploitation by the advanced Western capitalist societies (O'Rourke, 1987; Bell and Lyall, 2002).

Tourism consumption has often been linked to the commoditization of host communities and cultures and paid little attention to the practice of consumption by the tourists (Boissevain, 1996). Predominantly, the arguments have focused on visual consumption, most notably by MacCannell (1976) and Urry (2002). In Urry's argument, the basis of the tourist experience is visual, in which people look at and consume particular objects: which act as signifiers of place, and mark them off as distinct.

However, it would be inaccurate to leave tourists' consumption activities at this point. The problem with the concept of the gaze is that it is not possible to reduce tourist experiences to that of merely gazing. People do more than look at objects of difference on holiday. This is not to deny the importance of semiotic contributions to understanding what is happening in tourist resorts; it does, however, leave aside other senses and the embodiment of the tourist experience (Veijola and Jokinen, 1994). In addition, an emphasis on the gaze renders the tourist experience as pre-determined and static, a subject–object dualism, rather than as a process in which the tourists are fully engaged.

The Production of Space

The emphasis on the visual nature of tourism consumption puts space as a container in which pre-determined activities take place. In this respect, space is one-dimensional, fixed and static. However, space also incorporates the dispositions of those who inhabit it, even if these are short-lived periods. Furthermore, the space will have been thought about and arranged by the 'power broker' elements of society, i.e. those that map on to physical space ideas about space. Therefore, rather than a subject–object split between self and space as other, Lefebvre's theory in the *Production of Space* (1991) provides a framework that allows the different 'fields of space' (Merrifield, 1993) to come together and to be considered together. Thus rather than a dialectic of space, there is a triad of space (Lefebvre, 1991, p. 39), which Soja (1996) refers to as a 'trialectic'. The point being that one aspect should not be privileged above either of the others as all three inform the process of the production of space and all three inform each other in an ongoing process of the production and consumption of space.

The three elements to space that the triad outlines are: (i) spatial practices; (ii) representation of space; and (iii) spaces of representation (sometimes translated as representational space).

The first *spatial practice* refers to the 'facts' of space – or its physical or natural form. It is linked to the production and reproduction of specific places and spatial ensembles. As such, an area may be developed specifically for the testing of nuclear weapons or as a site of leisure on a peripheral geographic area. Thus, an area is understood or perceived to be a site of a particular economic activity and thus becomes a reflection of economic relations.

The second aspect of *representations of space* refers to formal abstractions. It is mental or conceived space. This is the space of the professionals, of planners, policy makers, scientists and designers. Here space is constructed and formalized around ideological discourses on space that is manifest in symbolic works, for example maps. This space is imposed and 'the most significant point here is that of bureaucratic management, that is, attempts to control direct or mediate the dominant form of spatial practice' (Meethan, 2001, p. 37).

The third aspect, *spaces of representation*, is concerned with the world of sensory phenomena (Merrifield, 1993). This is social or cultural space, a discourse of space, and the embodiment of the other two aspects, i.e. how space is directly lived through symbols. For Lefebvre, it is the space in which resistance to the hegemony of spatial practice and representations of space can be acted upon as he links it to 'the clandestine or underground side of social life' (Lefebvre, 1991, p. 33). It is through this lived experience of space that changes can be wrought, and thus it is these spaces that 'provide the focus for identity' (Meethan, 2001, p. 37).

Moving specifically to tourism, the Lefebvrian triad allows an understanding of the processes that inform the production of tourist spaces. Spatial practices are those aspects that determine or identify a space as a site for tourism. Secondly, the representations of space deal with the way in which those sites are then presented in tourism images and the creation of place myths. The space of representation is the direct experience of the tourists. Lefebvre avoids placing one point of the trialectic as more important than the others. However, the main concern here is with the way in which the resorts of Palmanova and Magaluf are encoded and the consumption practices mediated, and then with how these fit or not with the tourists' practices of consumption.

Mallorca

Mallorca is in the north-west Mediterranean off the east coast of the Spanish peninsula. It is the largest island of the Balearic archipelago. Tourism development began at the start of the 20th century, with growth well underway by the 1950s and 1960s. Mass tourism was firmly established by the mid-1970s.

Tourism is the main source of income in the Balearics. In 1996, it accounted for 58% of gross domestic product (GDP) and generated a figure of 700,000 million Spanish pesetas or approximately £3 billion per annum. By 1995, 6 million of the 8 million annual visitors to the Balearics visited Mallorca (Bardolet, 1996).

Palmanova and Magaluf are in the municipality of Calvià located in the south-west of the island and were the first areas to witness tourism development, with two hotels in place by 1930. In 1996 Calvià was the richest municipality in Spain and one of the richest in Europe, with money being derived mainly from tourism (Selwyn, 1996, p. 96). Calvià receives visitor numbers in the region of 1.6 million per annum (Selwyn, 1996, p. 97). There are six coastal resorts: Palmanova and Magaluf are two, the others are: Illetes, Peguara, Portals Nous and Santa Ponça. In addition, there are two historical towns inland: Calvià itself and Capdella.

Magaluf and Palmanova are predominatly 'British' resorts in that the majority of tourists derive from the United Kingdom. The other resorts also have their own national flavour, for example Peguara is associated with Germans, and Santa Ponça is seen as Irish. The tourists to Magaluf and Palmanova can also be characterized as mainly white, heterosexual and 'working class'.

The two tourist destinations are in a distinctly bounded area, and although they are different places it is difficult to ascertain exactly where the border lies between the two. The resorts themselves are bounded inland by a motorway running between Palma in the east and Andraitx in the west, and on the coast quite naturally by the sea. Over the past decade, the local authority has undertaken a number of improvements such as the introduction of a one-way system specifically designed to reduce the use of motor vehicles in the two resorts (Pallicer, personal communication, 1997).

Magaluf

In Magaluf, it is possible to walk for about 1.5 km without having to stop to cross a road. What you see is shop after shop selling a wide range of goods such as postcards, wine, porcelain, glass, jewellery and souvenirs of Mallorca. Interspersed with these are pubs, amusement arcades, nightclubs and food outlets which sell predominantly 'fast' food.

The resort's main road is Punta Balena, which is infamous for the 'rowdy' behaviour of some of the tourists. Many establishments are packed together on both sides of the road, and the number of souvenir shops, for example, gives an impression of variety, abundance and choice, but in fact there is little to choose between them in terms of price or commodity. Goods are often displayed on stands outside the shop; the space in between the two banking facilities appears at either end of the road, enabling the tourists, regardless of what direction they enter from, to change money. Opposite the turn into the road at its top (Punta Balena is on a hill that peaks just before the road ends) is a Burger King.

Palmanova

Palmanova exhibits some of the characteristics of Magaluf, but it is considered by many of the tourists who stay there to be slightly more 'upmarket', with some people referring to the 'badly behaved' tourists in Magaluf as 'animals'. Certainly, Palmanova is less noisy at night and, probably due to the smaller number of clubs, has fewer people on the streets. It is also different in other ways.

For example, the main road of the resort is only built up on one side, with the other being open to the sea. It allows a view across the Bay of Palma; on a day free from heat haze it is possible to see Arenal on the other side.

In comparison with Magaluf, Palmanova is less densely developed. This is especially true of the eastern end of the resort where restaurants with names such as Tabù and Le P'tit Bistro rub shoulders with those more British in character (such as The Willows and Natalies Snack Bar) which would fit in well with the environment of Magaluf.

One of the most expensive restaurants on this road is Ciros. It stands at the end of a stretch of the promenade. After this point, the view of the sea is obscured and there is a concentration of commercial outlets in an enclosed space. Situated at the point where the promenade resumes is a McDonalds restaurant which overlooks the beach. Its terrace area features metallic seats and tables. Like the benches along the promenades in Magaluf and Palmanova, which are also metallic, during hot days the seats become very hot and uncomfortable and allow for only short periods of rest or inactivity.

The purpose of the foregoing descriptions is to provide an understanding of the setting, the physical space within which the consumption practices take place. What it demonstrates is that there is a relationship between the physical nature of space and the consumption practices that occur within it. The openness of Palmanova is more conducive to relaxed and measured activities that may invite more expenditure. The density of Magaluf reflects a 'more for your money ideal' that is present in the bargains and deals on offer.

Representations of the Spaces of Palmanova and Magaluf

Spaces, or sites of consumption, can be imbued with myth, which contributes to informing their sense of place (Shields, 1991). The creation of place myths or associations with place has been explored by a number of authors. The creation of Brighton as a seaside resort and its association with 'dirty' weekends served at one time to make it a site for the conduct of extramarital affairs (Shields, 1991). More recently, its image has developed as a cultural centre including heritage and art with the idea that it is an economically successful town; masking high unemployment and social deprivation (Meethan, 1996).

Palmanova and Magaluf are landscapes characterized by signs of Britishness. On a surface level as well as a deeper symbolic level, there is an overt display of ethnicity. Overwhelmingly it is British but, within that, statements of being English, Scottish and Welsh also exist. Therefore, one encounters advertisements for British food and drink: the fry-up (both English and Scottish), roast beef and Yorkshire pudding, fish and chips, Boddingtons and Tetley's (which can be purchased as an imperial pint), and in some cases there are invitations to spend pounds sterling. The food and drink can be enjoyed in cafe-bars, sometimes British owned or run, which refer directly and indirectly to their British origins – for example The Dudley Tavern, Scots Corner, The Red Lion and Sospan Fach to name but a few. Menus are written in English, although by law they must also appear in Spanish, and sometimes they also appear in other languages, for example French and German. In addition, the sheer volume of British visitors ensures that English appears as the dominant language added to by the broadcasting of British sporting fixtures. It is even possible to catch up with news from home by reading a British daily newspaper or watching Sky TV news. Videos playing on numerous TV screens are not uncommon.

The main attraction is sun, sea and sand, but there are a number of activities in which tourists can participate. These include day trips ranging from visiting a pearl factory, through scenic island tours, to horse riding and going to markets. There is also the nightlife in both Palmanova and Magaluf. There is paragliding, diving, rides on an inflatable banana and amusement arcades. There is an emphasis on fun. There are fun pubs, fun badges and fun through the TV comics. In addition, it is possible to hire a scooter under the banner 'we rent fun'. In such a context, it would not seem unreasonable to suggest that fun itself is a primary object of consumption.

The majority of tourists arrive on a package that has been organized by one of the leading British tour operators: Thomsons, Airtours or First Choice. In their role as provider of the package, their influence has begun before the actual holiday takes place in that, through the provision of brochures, they provide the image which informs peoples' expectations, and feeds into their cognitive understanding of where they are going to. As Dann notes it is '[t]he images [that] define what is beautiful, what should be experienced and with whom one should interact' (Dann, 1996a, p. 79). He goes on to contend that tourism is a language which must be learnt, requiring a process of socialization. The tour operator is key in orchestrating the socialization process involved in the resort through the likes of welcome meetings and the organized bar crawls. In the former, the tour operators use 'devices' of hospitality, for example the welcome drink when the tourists first arrive at their accommodation, in an attempt to turn the stranger tourist into a friendly customer (Andrews, 2000). This is continued in the bar crawls, which are discussed below.

The extent to which the operator dominates and mediates the landscape the tourists find themselves in is suggested in the following example. The majority of hotels provide some form of entertainment for the tourists. This runs during the course of the day, with in-house entertainers encouraging people to join in games. In the evening, the entertainment is usually, for example, a guest comedian or singer. During the summer of 1998, in one hotel dominated by one British tour operator, the advertising of the evening entertainment extended a welcome to the entertainer not by the destination, or hotel, but by the tour operator itself; indeed she had been 'specially flown in'. This also provides us with an example of how one particular spatial arena is used, and it is to a more detailed examination of space I now wish to turn.

Boundaries

The feeling of enclosure that the boundaries to Palmanova and Magaluf provide is added to by the relationship to areas outside of them being limited or discouraged. Opportunities do of course exist to leave the resorts: car hire, local buses and organized excursions by boat or coach. However, the local bus service tends to be unreliable and overcrowded. The services link to either other tourist resorts or the capital Palma, and, as such, are in part crowded because of their use by tourists.

It may be the case that many people have no desire to leave the resorts; everything they need is supplied in the location, often within the confines of their hotel. It is also the case that some people have no understanding of the wider context in which they are situated having not heard of inland tourist attractions such as Valldemossa. Indeed, one tourist asked me 'Is Mallorca an island?' and in response to an affirmative answer 'Is Palma on the mainland then?' The sense of disorientation that some tourists feel about where they are encourages them to look for guidance from the familiar face of the tour operator representatives (rep or reps), someone presumed to have inside knowledge of the destination and thus able to assume an authoritative role.

To leave the resorts outside the guidance of the tour operator is not actively encouraged. In some welcome meetings conducted by tour operators, people are warned against using the local bus service because of pickpockets. Welcome meetings do have the purpose of providing people with practical information, for example expected codes of dress for dinner and taking care in the sun, but their main function is for the commission-earning rep to sell excursions. Under pressure to meet sales targets, the reps must find ways to ensure that people will buy trips from them, e.g. the excursions to the weekly leather market at Inca in the centre of the island. People are not advised of the local train service, but are advised that the local buses to the market will be overcrowded, the number of buses from the market will be few and people will be faced with having to get an expensive taxi back to the resort. Therefore, do not undertake the journey independently, but book the organized excursion. Another example might be found in the island's two water amusement parks. For one, the entrance ticket can be bought from the rep but for the other, on the other side of the Bay of Palma, it cannot. People are warned off from visiting the latter because: (i) it is a difficult journey involving two buses (which is true); and (ii) it is (allegedly) full of Germans.

What we might conclude from this is that the framing of the resorts and the potential difficulties (real or imagined) of leaving them, a lack of understanding on behalf of some tourists as to where they are, and a reliance on tour operators concerned with profit margins, renders the space itself as all-consuming; and lays the ground for patterns of consumption practices. The next section furthers the analysis of the characteristics of consumption by examining more symbolic representations and the tourists' lived experiences of the two resorts.

Magaluf and Palmanova: Spaces of Representation

The signs of 'Britishness' that pervade the resorts contradict the notion that a holiday relies on the visual consumption of difference. Rather than signs of difference, the tourists are confronted with signs of familiarity, not just in the names of cafe-bars and the language spoken, but also in the food and drink available. The food that is chosen to be eaten serves to confirm a sense of national identity (Andrews, 1999). The possibility to spend pounds sterling and drink known branded drinks and eat 'traditional' British foods, including North Sea cod, British milk, British bread, bacon and sausages, heightens a sense of national identity because their availability and signposting mark them as distinct from Mallorcan or Spanish fare. Such items are consumed against a backdrop in which tourists have been warned not to drink the local water, be aware of pickpockets and to avoid the Germans.

The cooked breakfast is by far the most popular meal. It is marked as British as it is often advertised alongside representations of the Union Jack. It is liked for its cheapness, quick preparation and as a source of comfort. One bar owner told me 'It is just comfort food. People don't have time to cook the breakfast at home so they eat it here, it's the only place they get it apart from their mother's.' This view was confirmed by several tourists 'we've been having the fried breakfast, we don't have time at home'. That the breakfast was seen as something 'owned' by the British was exemplified in the complaints about its content and cooking in some hotels. One woman commented 'the food in the hotel is very good ... but the only thing is they [Spanish hotel staff] don't know how to cook bacon' and another male tourist told me 'the toast is lacking in texture and the bacon and sausages are not like the English versions'.

Therefore, the ingestion of food that is seen to be British serves to reinforce a national identity. It also links the places of Magaluf and Palmanova with a sense of Britishness (albeit a particular kind of Britishness) as not only does food act to create social solidarity it also acts to keep out other groups. In the case of the cooked breakfast, consisting mainly of pork produce, Jewish and Muslim sectors of British society, for example, are excluded. Consumption practices also inform a sense of class identity.

Class Identity

Although Palmanova and Magaluf run into one another, they are quite different resorts in terms of atmosphere due in part to what is available in both and also the physical nature of the space. The myth of Magaluf as 'Shagaluf' and the actuality of its emphasis on night clubs and drinking mean that it tends (in the summer months especially) to be dominated by young, single people, whereas Palmanova attracts older people and those with families. This is not an exclusive division rather a general observation, but it does help to illustrate the attachment of class and age to consumption practices.

One family staying in Magaluf consisting of parents and two teenage boys were unusual in that the adults were both professionals. One was an architect and the other a court officer. The holiday was unusual for them in that they normally holidayed in the south of France. Friends had been horrified and amused when they found out about the change in destination that year. Although they had undoubtedly enjoyed their holiday, with the hotel exceeding their expectations 'it's not as tatty as we first thought it would be', they had found the resort 'wonderfully tacky' and had been disappointed by the lack of Spanish culture and the dominance of the English language.

In another case, the mother in a family of two adults and a young adult daughter also staying in Magaluf told me that she found the language (profanities are widely used) shocking and that 'they [the other tourists] are a different class of people'. At the time, we were all watching an England football fixture. The mother explained that they had come on the holiday for her daughter to celebrate her degree, she assured me that 'normally she [the daughter] wouldn't have anything to do with such people, she wouldn't normally entertain them, she would want someone educated like herself'. Thus although the woman recognized a form of camaraderie in participating in supporting the England team and their consumption of that experience, at the same time she distinguished herself from the other tourists by indicating that her own lifestyle and class were in fact different.

The creation of a sense of social solidarity is also manifest in the way in which tourists are cajoled into participating in the evening entertainment that is offered in hotels and night clubs. A common feature is to ask people where they are from. This can take the form of a national origin, e.g. England, Scotland, Wales, Ireland; a regional origin, e.g. The North, South-east or Midlands; and also by city, e.g. Liverpool, London, Newcastle, Birmingham. Generally, people are asked to cheer in response to the site of origin as it is stated. People, but men in particular, further show their allegiance to the home world in the wearing of shirts taken from the football kit of their favoured team, including national outfits. Although it does not necessarily follow that the support of a football team is connected with the home place, it is nevertheless the case that in the context of Palmanova and Magaluf, the Newcastle kit, for example, was sported by those who hailed from that area. Further, there was a pub The Geordie Pride, that clearly appealed to this sense of identity as it was internally draped with Newcastle football colours and memorabilia. The attempt to involve the audience in the entertainment proceedings was also a way in which there were attempts to exert power over their consumption activities. The next section will deal with the question of control.

Consumption as Control

There is a feeling that the movement through the spaces of Magaluf and Palmanova is forced, especially in the former. There are few options to turn off roads once on them, and then only to other roads with more shops. The provision of little to gaze upon other than commodities means one is forced to look. Some tourists expressed a sense of restriction in Magaluf. One woman staying in Palmanova but who had previously visited Magaluf commented 'Magaluf has got dirty now. You go to the end here and then into Magaluf and it's stuffy and noisy.' Another couple told me 'We don't like Magaluf. We went up there and just thought we want to get out. It's noisy and enclosed somehow.' Although these comments are made by middle-aged and retired people staying in Palmanova, the feeling of enclosure was also experienced by younger tourists staying in Magaluf. One male in his 20s told me 'it takes a bit of time to find your way around … there is a feeling of enclosure around Punta Balena which makes it feel hotter, there is a lack of air circulating'.

Notions of enclosure are linked to being hemmed in, kept safe and controlled. Being funnelled through a space in which many of the activities undertaken are mediated adds to the sense of an exertion of power over the tourists by the tour operators. This is often undertaken in the guise of fun, and is particularly evident in the way that some of the bar crawls organized by tour operators are conducted. The bar crawls are a means to show tourists around Magaluf (although the bars used are selected on the basis of financial transactions between the bar and the tour operator). They are also a means for people to meet other people in a party atmosphere, and they are liked for this reason. However, they are also used as a means to facilitate further economic exchange between tour operators and tourists as the reps use them as a method to 'befriend' the tourists by showing themselves to be like-minded people.

The way in which power is exerted over the tourists is in the guise of fun, as playing games also forms part of the outing. For example, all the males must be called Fred, and all the females Wilma (sometimes these are substituted for other couple names); all drinks must be held in either the left or the right hand, as ordered by the rep. The names and which hand the drinks are to be held in are changed throughout the bar crawl. To be caught not playing by the rules incurs a penalty. This is usually to down the current drink in one, and then buy another. The reps also play the games and, if caught out, must pay the penalty, thus showing themselves to be like the tourists. It is also the reps who control the games and administer the penalties. Not playing the game leads to punishment which itself has attendant possibilities of being humiliated. Further, the stripping of the individual of their own name on the one hand reinforces an idea of social solidarity, we are all one; but, on the other hand, removes individual identity. On entering the gladiator school, Spartacus is advised not to ask the names of his inmates. The reason for this is that knowing someone's name implies intimacy and friendship that would make it impossible to kill one's opponents in a contest (Kubrick's 1960 film *Spartacus*). In this case, the tourists lose their own identity; they are part of a mass. In addition, Magaluf has a reputation of being a place to seek casual sexual relationships; bar crawls go some way to facilitating this process. There is an emphasis on getting drunk and an understanding that many of the tourists are looking for a sexual encounter. Indeed, the swearing of one bar crawl oath included a promise 'to get drunk, be sick, drink some more, pull, shag on the beach and eat a kebab'. The gender demarcation made by assigning names such as Fred and Wilma facilitates a heterosexual encounter which is 'normalized' and enforces the idea that Magaluf is a space in which other forms of sexuality are excluded. It also lays the ground for the encounter to be momentary, as the implication is that there is no need to know the real name of the other person involved in the experience.

That acts of consumption are controlled or directed is a feature or characteristic of the nature of consumption in Palmanova and Magaluf. The cramming and layering that exist in both resorts have the effect of heightening or intensifying the holiday experience. Another dimension to the consumption practices is that of speed, which will be explored next.

Consumption and Speed

The appearance of fast food outlets and the feeling of the need to move on – to look at another shop, not to linger on seats, to participate in some form of activity (particularly in Magaluf) – suggests that there is a 'nowness', an urgency, about the experience; there is much more to do or see and a limited time to do it in. For the majority of the tourists, their holiday lasts only 2 weeks, for some only 1 week or 10 days. Thus there is a limited period of time in which activity must take place and of course a limited time for them to be parted with their money.

The connection between the pressure to consume and to do so quickly is mirrored in another set of games, this time played in a hotel as part of the evening's entertainment. Not only does it pick up on the theme of speed but it also again links us back to the notion that consumption practices are controlled and contrived. Three adult males are in competition with each other. The first part of the game is that they must run round the audience kissing as many people as possible in a set period of time. The winner is the one who achieves the most kisses. The second part of the game involves having sangria poured into their mouths. Taking turns, each man sits down, with his top off, and head thrown back, mouth open. A cloth is placed around his neck, and the entertainer holds the jug of sangria up and starts pouring directly into the mouth non-stop. The contestant must keep swallowing. The winner is the one who keeps swallowing for the longest. The last game is to sing a song or nursery rhyme whilst gargling water.

No one is compelling the contestants to participate, although there is a degree of coercion. The representation is one of force in that someone else is pouring the drink in. Masculinity is at stake, and there is a reward for consuming the most, whether drink or people, by kissing them, with the added impetus in the latter of speed; the faster you can get around the more kisses are gained. The gargling is different, however. Here there is prohibition; you are not permitted to consume until you have fulfilled an obligation, i.e. to sing a song – the challenge of course also being the point of the game.

The suggestion of a connection between consumption and prohibition illuminates the tension that is attached to the activities and consumption practices of tourists in the two resorts. The young male tourist who had described Magaluf as feeling enclosed had previously said that one of the attractions of the holiday was the sense of freedom, that there were fewer restrictions on people than in the UK.

One aspect to consider is that the 'myth' of the holiday will bring people into contact with sites of difference and that here there will be freedom. In Magaluf and Palmanova, people are brought into contact with signs of the home world. Although in some ways this is an appropriation of Spanish land to appear like home, to appear familiar, it is underlain by a difference. Quite simply, it is Spain and then overlain by a difference in the form of the words of the tour operators' warnings. In effect, the tourists are caught between feelings of similarity and feelings of disorientation in which they can easily lose their way. Dann notes 'the tourism industry attempts to effect the balance between the need to control its clients on the one hand, while giving the impression of granting them unrestricted freedom on the other' (1996b, p. 101). The ontological insecurity that this tension brings about inculcates a sense of dependency. The bar crawls are one such example; the tourists who exercise the choice to participate in the outings are relying on the tour operator to show them a good time and in this the 'highlights' of Magaluf, rather than discovering these features for themselves. This has the effect of making the tourists childlike, and it is this characteristic of the consumption practices I now turn toward.

Babies and Breasts

The idea of playground, the emphasis on games and having fun are not concomitant with the serious world of adult work. The tourists are in effect rendered to a child-like state; a point perhaps not unnoticed by at least one tourist who when asked why he was wearing a bib replied ''cos I'm a big baby', and perhaps also not unrecognized by souvenir makers who produce bottles of alcohol with a teat on the end. The tourist as baby or child has its needs met, its fears ameliorated, and like babies they can cram it all in, and spew it all back up again without reproach. Dann (1996b) has observed that the balance between the impression of freedom and the control exerted by tour operators is more successful when the tourist is treated as a child. This goes *some way* to understanding one of the dominant symbols in Magaluf and Palmanova: the breast.

Babies are dependent creatures. A symbol of this dependency is the breast. It is a source of comfort for a baby not just in providing nourishment and satisfying hunger. Breastfeeding is about bonding between mother and child, and the softness and warmth of the breast are also sources of comfort. The overt presence of breasts in the two resorts alongside advertisements for food proclaiming that it is 'cooking like mum' expounds the theory that the tourists are engaged in a child-like state or are being appealed to as if they are children.

The breast is a dominant feature in the landscapes of Magaluf and Palmanova. Topless sunbathing is ubiquitous, breasts are common features on postcards, and women are often called upon during evening entertainment games to 'get their tits out for the boys'. An example of this occurs in another game played at the adult night of *Pirates Adventure* – a night club-style entertainment show. As part of the game, the contestants are required to fetch certain items from the audience: a pair of boxer shorts, a £20 note and a topless girl. Once on stage, the latter are required to display their breasts, often on more than one occasion, for the gratification of the males in the audience.

So, what might the apparent importance of the breast be attributed to? There is something about the display and consumption of women within a nexus of male domination that perhaps should not be overlooked. Clearly some of the games played and the imagery is suggestive of this. For example, one postcard shows under the heading of Spanish Barbecue the same pair of breasts through stages of a suntan from pale to very brown. The suggestion is that the breast, and by extension the woman, is like meat to be processed and eaten. However, the breast is also symbolic of nourishment, comfort, warmth and intimacy. Its ubiquitous presence is a constant reminder or reassurance of these features. In this respect, the breast also becomes a symbol of power.

Another two postcards illustrate this point. One depicts a man buried up to his head in sand, extreme thirst clear in his expression. Two breasts appear in the left-hand corner dangling above him. Are they being withheld? He is powerless to reach them and yet the end to his suffering lies so near. Here his desire will never be satiated. The other postcard shows two real breasts, and a cartoon woman, topless herself, holding a cartoon baby that leans towards the breasts. Here there is more hope, but still the baby is being denied nourishment.

The depiction in the postcard of the head poking above the sand renders the male powerless, and there appears little that he can do to alleviate his uncomfortable position. This could be interpreted as reflecting the fate of the tourists. However, finding themselves in an environment in which the promise of 'freedom' appears to be illusory in place of a rather controlled and constrained experience finds many of the tourists (again in some respects rather like children) kicking against these. Fighting and vandalism (smashed up hotel rooms and damage to cars and street signs) are not uncommon.

However, perhaps the most noticeable act of resistance is that of vomiting. Many of the bars have a faint smell of vomit, and in the early hours (and later) of the morning it is not unusual to see people being sick following a drinking session. Thus there is display of having consumed much, and further that it can be wasted because in the holiday environment money is not a problem. In this respect, the vomiting is conformist, it is what might be expected, a sign of a good night out and a display of the fun consumed. However, the act of vomiting is the body reacting to what it does not like in the gut, forcing it out. In this situation, they have reached the gut because more and more has been crammed in. One interpretation here is that it demonstrates a rejection of the attempts to control the holiday experience; a resistance to the demands made to consume ever more products in a confined space, which the body both is and represents.

Conclusion

The analysis of tourists' consumption practices in Palmanova and Magaluf has demonstrated that the tourist experience is not based entirely on the visual consumption of signs of difference. It also involves activities requiring other bodily functions, for example eating and drinking. Three key themes have been identified. The first is the way in which practices of consumption are used to create and affirm a sense of identity. The second is concerned with the way in which the production of space influences consumption practices, which in turn feed into the production of that space as a site of consumption. The third is a consideration of the characteristics of the consumption practices in the two resorts.

Lefebvre's 'triad' of space was used to try to understand the different components that make up the consumption experiences in Magaluf and Palmanova. In the first place, the resorts are perceived to be sites of leisure with the attendant idea of freedom. Encoded on to this space are on the one hand indicators that this is Spain, which is unknown, potentially threatening, and thus requires caution, and on the other hand signs of Britishness. It is these signs of Britishness that are used to make appeals to the tourists by those deemed to have an inside knowledge of the place – the tour operators. Therefore, the tourists are told about the dominance of other nationalities in other resorts, with the implication that it is probably best to stay in the familiar world of the fry-up and White Horse Pub rather than venture unaccompanied into the unknown. The acknowledgement of a British identity (used here in a very broad sense) is manifest in the digestion of food recognized as 'traditionally' British, the spending of pounds sterling, in some cases, and the consumption of British television programmes.

Whilst being kept safe, entertainment is provided, that like the games often played with small children, seeks to socialize the tourists or influence them into a particular way of being. They are reminded to obey the rules of the game – in this case consumption – and that they need to be quick about it because they only have a limited time to part with their money.

The spatial characteristics and layout of Palmanova and Magaluf work to enforce these ideas. As Simmel noted, the attributes of a city in terms of its diversity and variety developed the characteristics of the urbanite. 'The psychological foundation, upon which the metropolitan individuality is erected, is the intensification of emotional life due to the swift and continuous shift of external and internal stimuli' (1950, p. 325). In the spaces of Palmanova and Magaluf, there is much crammed in; numerous shops selling a variety of products with little to differentiate between them. In turn, the tourists are shown to have little to differentiate them when in the participation in bar crawls they are allocated a single name for their gender.

Such activities also speak about the way that the consumption practices are used to construct and affirm identities. In the case of the bar crawls, the message is one of coupling along conventional gender lines, which serves to confirm the destinations as sites for heterosexual activities and holidays. The demarcation and demand for British food further serve to embody notions of a particular national identity whilst excluding other sectors of British society. At the same time, some tourists seek to distinguish themselves from others based on the differences between the two resorts. In addition, the excursion to Andraitx reminds all participants of their place in the world as they are shown the fruits of two different forms of consumption practice: one characterized by bargains and a feeling of claustrophobia and the other by a symbol of wealth and freedom in the form of yachts.

The notion that the capitalist system is self-perpetuating, controlling and from which there is no escape has been explored by Baudrillard (1988). The nature of the physical spaces of Palmanova and Magaluf would seem to work towards confirming such ideas. The role of the tour operator also appears to work in a direction of leading the tourist towards ever more sites and opportunities of consumption in which the tour operator stands to gain.

The leadership provided by the tour operators and the actual participation in the games played has the effect of placing the tourists in a childlike position. They are encouraged to be free, to indulge, but within a restrictive framework. In the bar crawls, the tourists are encouraged to drink a lot of alcohol. The more they drink and become inebriated, the harder it is for them to follow the rules and so they are punished. To translate this into a broader picture, if the tourists were left to their own devices they may well not stay within the realms of the tour operator.

The examples of some consumption practices in Magaluf and Palmanova highlight some tensions that exist around consumption in general. The ability to consume goods and services is often linked to ideas of freedom and politically then to democracy. The pressure to consume that is evident in Palmanova and Magaluf in the form of the work of the tour operators and the space itself, its physical layout and inscription appear to work against these ideals. In addition, there is an association between choice and individuality and variety. Again the homogeneity that appears in many of the commercial outlets in the two resorts, and the removal of individual names in the games played on the bar crawls, serve to contradict these associations.

Finally, many tourist destinations rely on the creation of place myths for their success. Among these myths are ideas of culture and heritage, neither of which is a feature in the conventional sense of the places here. What therefore needs to be added to a compendium of tourism's mythologies is the promotion of unfettered practices of consumption.

References

Andrews, H. (1999) We are what we eat. *Focus* number 32. Tourism Concern, London, pp. 4–5.

Andrews, H. (2000) Consuming hospitality on holiday. In: Lashley, C. and Morrison, A. (eds) *In Search of Hospitality: Theoretical Perspectives and Debates.* Butterworth Heinemann, Oxford, UK, pp. 235–254.

Bardolet, E. (1996) *Balearic Islands General Information.* IBATUR Conselleria de Turisme Govern Balear.

Baudrillard, J. (1988) *Selected Writings.* Polity Press, Cambridge, UK.

Bell, C. and Lyall, J. (2002) *The Accelerated Sublime. Landscape, Tourism and Identity*. Praeger, London.

Boissevain, J. (ed.) (1996) *Coping with Tourists. European Reactions to Mass Tourism*. Berghahn, Oxford.

Bourdieu, P. (1979) *Distinction. A Social Critique of the Judgement of Taste*. Routledge, London.

Dann, G. (1996a) The people of tourist brochures. In: Selwyn, T. (ed.) *The Tourist Image. Myths and Myth Making in Tourism*. John Wiley and Sons, Chichester, UK, pp. 61–81.

Dann, G. (1996b) *The Language of Tourism: a Sociolinguistic Perspective*. CAB International, Wallingford, UK.

Douglas, M. (1996) *Thought Styles. Critical Essays in Good Taste*. Sage, London.

Jackson, P. (1993) Towards a cultural politics of consumption. In: Bird, J., Curtis, B., Putnam, T., Robertson, G. and Tickner, L. (eds) *Mapping the Futures: Local Cultures, Global Change*. Routledge, London, pp. 207–228.

Kubrick, S. (1960) director of *Spartacus*.

Lefebvre, H.i (1974, 1991) *The Production of Space*. Nicholson-Smith, D. (transl.). Blackwell, Oxford, UK.

MacCannell, D. (1976) *The Tourist, A New Theory of the Leisure Class*. Macmillan Press, London.

Meethan, K. (1996) Place, image and power: Brighton as a resort. In: Selwyn, T. (ed.) *The Tourist Image. Myths and Myth Making in Tourism*. John Wiley and Sons, Chichester, UK, pp. 179–196.

Meethan, K. (2001) *Tourism in Global Society. Place, Culture, Consumption*. Palgrave, Basingstoke, UK.

Merrifield, A. (1993) Place and space: a Lefebvrian reconciliation. *Transactions of the Institute of British Geographers NS* 18, 516–531.

Miller, D. (1995) Consumption studies as the transformation of anthropology. In: Miller, D. (ed.) *Acknowledging Consumption. A Review of New Studies*. Routledge, London, pp. 264–295

Miller, D. (1997) Consumption and its consequences. In: Mackay, H. (ed.) *Consumption and Everyday Life*. Sage, London, pp. 13–63.

O'Rourke, D. (1987) *Cannibal Tours* (film). O'Rourke and Associates, Canberra.

Selwyn, T. (1996) Tourism culture and cultural conflict: a case study from Mallorca. In: Fsadni, C. and Selwyn, T. (eds) *Sustainable Tourism in Mediterranean Islands and Small Cities*. MED-CAMPUS in Euromed Tourism Project, Malta, pp. 94–114.

Shields, R. (1991) *Places on the Margin. Alternative Geographies of Modernity*. Routledge, London.

Simmel, G. (1950) The metropolis and mental life. In: Wolff, K. (ed.) *The Sociology of Georg Simmel*. Collier Macmillan, London, pp. 324–349.

Soja, E.W. (1996) *Thirdspace. Journeys to Los Angeles and Other Real and Imagined Places*. Blackwell, Oxford, UK.

Urry, J. (1990) *The Tourist Gaze. Leisure and Travel in Contemporary Societies*. Sage, London.

Urry, J. (2002) *The Tourist Gaze*, 2nd edn. Sage, London.

Veijola, S. and Jokinen, E. (1994) The body in tourism. Theory culture and society. *Critical Explorations in Critical Social Science* 11, 125–151.

12

Narratives of Sexuality, Identity and Relationships in Leisure and Tourism Places

Annette Pritchard and Nigel Morgan

Welsh Centre for Tourism Research, University of Wales Institute, Cardiff, UK

Introduction

Despite increased calls for academic writing to address contemporary sexualities in analyses of the complexities and fluidities of spaces, differences and power relations, the voices and lived experiences of women and gay men continue to remain marginalized in tourism research. This is surprising when one considers the impacts which queer theory, gay and lesbian studies, and feminism have had in other fields and disciplines. For instance, the landscape of contemporary social history has been transformed in recent years because many of the 'new' generation of researchers have been feminists interested in gender (Cannadine, 2000). In contrast, tourism studies have been particularly slow to engage with feminist philosophies and practices which challenge 'historically masculine ways of thinking and knowing through the binary oppositions of man/woman, culture/nature, mind/body, work/leisure' (Fullagar, 2002, p. 58). As a result, the field lacks a critical conceptualization of the psychological, social and cultural dimensions of the multiple expressions of masculinities and femininities and the range of sexual identities. Tourism's lack of conceptual maturity in this area is in contrast to the cognate fields of leisure and sports studies, where the roles of gender and, to a lesser extent, sexuality, as axes of social difference are more established (Aitchison, 2000; Scraton and Flintoff, 2002). In view of tourism's reluctance to engage in any meaningful way with feminist research, it less surprising that the challenges posed by paradigms such as queer theory – which 'brings together with it a radical deconstruction of all conventional categories of sexuality and gender' (Plummer, 2005, p. 359) – are yet to be even recognized.

There is, however, an emergent literature that is beginning to explore the leisure and tourism experiences of the gay male and lesbian communities (see Clift *et al.*, 2002), and extant research has examined a range of issues. These include: the relationships between holidays and gay male identities (Hughes, 1997, 1998, 2000); the sexual behaviour of gay men in tourism spaces (Forrest and Clift, 1998); the touristification of gay spaces (Pritchard *et al.*, 1998); and motivations of gay male and lesbian tourists (Clift and Forrest, 1999; Pritchard *et al.*, 2000a). Significantly, with some exceptions (see Pitts, 1999; Skeggs, 1999; Pritchard *et al.*, 2000b, 2002; Miller, 2002), much of this work in tourism has focused on male rather than female sexual identities and experiences. As a result, once again, the tourism academy is marginalizing women, despite the fact that the gay male and lesbian communities are heterogeneous, culturally diverse groups of men and women (Greene, 1997). Certainly, any discussion which assumes some homogeneous homosexual community occludes the voices of those who define themselves as lesbians, bisexual, transsexual or queer, and subsumes a range of sexual identities into the masculine gender-neutral 'norm' – a theme we explore in detail below.

This chapter seeks to explore how the dynamics of sexualities, genders and identities – key expressions of cultural politics – are played out in the liminal places of tourism and leisure environments, focusing in particular on the case of Manchester's Gay Village. As we shall see, engagement with cultural politics is dependent (at least in part) on the extent of one's visibility in such public spaces. These spaces enable all of us, differentially empowered and socially positioned, to participate in the creation of our own sexual and gendered identities; indeed, sexuality and gender are as innately bound up with space as with the body. Mitchell (2000, p. 217), drawing on feminist theory, has noted that there is 'an intimate relationship between the social construction (and policing) of space, the cultural construction (and policing) of gender and the ways we comport ourselves, the experiences we have …'. Whilst heterosexuality dominates public space, homosexuality has been confined to the private and has struggled to claim or mark social spaces. It is these contested social relationships, identities, territories and spaces that are our focus in this chapter. In order to explore sexuality and spatial narratives, we briefly revisit work on the socio-cultural construction of leisure and tourism spaces, describing how they are constantly subject to confrontation and challenge as power, identity, meaning and behaviour are construed and negotiated according to socio-cultural dynamics. Despite these continual renegotiations, however, we suggest that such spaces remain overwhelmingly heterosexual and androcentric. Moreover, our discussion of the emotional geography of gay and lesbian places contends that, whilst they may offer many gay men emotional and psychological empowerment away from the disciplining heteronormative gaze, the masculinist power dialectics that characterize their socio-cultural construction are not equally empowering for those who define themselves as lesbian, bisexual, transsexual or queer.

The Socio-cultural Construction of Leisure and Tourism Places

Today we conceptualize leisure and tourism landscapes (and the places of which they are composed), not as fixed, objective artefacts, but as symbolic, mutable and culturally constructed mixtures of representation and form. As a result of the 'cultural turn' in the social sciences, we now understand place (unlike the Cartesian conception of it as an objective, physical surface) to be a site, not only which we physically inhabit, but also which all of us actively construct (see Hubbard *et al.*, 2004). How space is socially constructed, how people invest meanings in space, together with the discourses and power which structure, control and dominate spatial relations have become hot topics for debate across a range of research fields. Such scholarship means that space is now seen as an active ingredient in the 'constitution and reproduction of social identities and social relations' that are vital to 'the production of material and symbolic or metaphorical spaces' (Valentine, 2001, p. 7). Indeed, one writer has recently described space as possibly the 'final frontier in socio-political thinking' (Osborne, 2002, p. 235). Still other scholars challenge researchers to explore, via the concept of third space, the identification process, arguing that 'the complexity, ambiguity and multidimensionality of identity … [reflects] the way that class, gender and 'race' [to which we would add sexuality] cross cut and intersect in different ways at different times and places' (Smith, 1999, p. 21). Such explorations of space and identity must also confront the powerful psychological and ideological meanings of space, described by Olwig (1993, p. 312) as 'the stuff of poetry more than science', since spaces mean different things to different people at different times and represent, reinforce, idealize and naturalize relations of gender and sexuality.

The cultural turn has also been reflected in the conceptualization of leisure and tourism places, spaces and sites as political and contested socio-cultural constructions. In tourism research, this theme, whilst still recent, gathered pace during the 1990s, and discourses in tourism have now begun to emphasize the interplay between tourism, landscape, representation and social structures, experiences and identities (e.g. Ashworth and Dietvorst, 1995; Ringer, 1998; Crouch, 1999; Aitchison *et al.*, 2000). Much of this work explores how space, place and landscape are sites where dominant discourses and wider hegemonic socio-cultural relations are resisted, contested or affirmed. For instance, Valentine (1993) and Pritchard *et al.* (1998) demonstrated that public leisure space is masculinized and heterosexually dominated. Similarly, Edensor and Kothari (1994) and Aitchison (1999b) have critiqued the role of gendered representations of heritage in the creation of gendered spaces and places in cultural tourism. Yet, despite such scholarship, there remains much to do, and researchers have still fully to 'acknowledge that the synergy between gender relations and spatial relations is a major contributor to leisure relations' (Aitchison, 1999a, p. 19) – a point that has equal resonance in terms of the relationships between sexuality, spatial relations and tourism relations. Scraton and Watson's (1998, p. 123) comment that tourism studies have largely failed to investigate '... the complexities of space ... as a site for the maintenance and reproduction of complex power relations' remains sharply pertinent.

Of course, cultural and feminist geographers have long argued that there are no politically neutral spaces, and they have focused on the ways in which places are heterosexualized (Valentine, 1993, 1996; Ashworth and Dietvorst, 1995; Bell and Valentine, 1995; Duncan, 1996; Aitchison, 1999a), gendered (Valentine, 1989; Rose, 1993) and racialized (Segal, 1990; Cohen, 1995; Anderson, 1996). A number of cultural and feminist geographers have noted that landscapes are often gendered in that they are portrayed and represented in feminine and sexualized terms (Rose, 1993; Lewes, 2000), allowing both landscape and woman to be burdened with men's meaning and interpreted by masculinist discourse. Gender is thus demonstrably critical to the construction of space and, indeed, it has been said that spaces and places are 'both shaped by, and a shaper of, gender in a gender–space dialectic' (Aitchison and Reeves, 1998, p. 51). Thus, many feminist scholars have demonstrated how built environments (from the intimate place of the home to the public spaces of shopping centres) routinely subject women to confinement and control. In such everyday spaces, experiences and interactions are gender segregations established, maintained and reinforced (see McDowell, 1997). The problems of claiming female spaces must therefore be seen in the context of a society where the architectural construction of space is highly gendered (Booth *et al.*, 1996) and where public space has been traditionally characterized as male space. Women's use of space is constructed by patriarchal discourses (Valentine, 1989) and by practices that encourage women to restrict themselves to designated, supposedly safe spaces (Butler, 1990; Valentine, 1992; Gardner, 1995). Whereas to be an adult male is to occupy space clearly, to have a physical presence in the world (Connell, 1983), most women learn that their bodies are expected to occupy less space than men's and that they do not belong in many public places – that many such spaces are not for them.

It is important to recognize that this lack of female visibility and power in public space is configured in diverse and complex ways, and that sexuality, gender, race and social class combine to create layers of oppression. In such ways, discourses intersect, so that some identities (white, male, middle-class, heterosexual) are construed as more powerful than others. As a result, space is not only androcentric but also heterosexual: as Valentine (1996, p. 146) has discussed, 'the street ... is not an asexual place. Rather, it is commonly assumed to be "naturally" or "authentically" heterosexual.' Public space is a place where heterosexual men and women can publicly express their identities through intimacy, such as holding hands or kissing, whereas gay men and lesbians are often made to feel uncomfortable or unsafe when displaying such behaviour (Taylor and Jamieson, 1997; Stanko and Curry, 1997). As space is constantly contested, however, the heterosexual nature of the street is by no means fixed; rather it is subject to continual challenge. Myslik (1996), for instance, has discussed the development of spaces that have become identified inside and outside the gay community as gay spaces. As we will see below, such gay male and lesbian spaces are often empowering places, providing a sense of community and territory and, as such, they become sites of cultural resistance with tremendous symbolic meaning. They are also subject to heterosexual attack (physical, verbal or visual) and active encroachment which leads to the dilution and erosion of gay and lesbian spaces and identities (Pritchard *et al.*, 2000b). In such heterotopias (spaces of difference, multiplicity and conflicting performances), we can therefore witness geographies not only of control and discipline but also of resistance and fulfilment (Foucault, 1986).

Embodiment, Sexuality and Space

If material and imagined space is the location for tourism and leisure encounters, it is through our bodies that we experience, know and make sense of such places and personal interactions. The body is also the ultimate site of control and resistance, and it has emerged in 21st century consumer culture as *the* significant symbolization of self. It is a key metaphor for identity, and the media, advertising and fashion industries, amongst others – including leisure and tourism – all contribute to the discourses within which we manage and locate our own bodies (Evans and Lee, 2002). The body symbolizes the self; it connects us with other people and places but it can also mark us as different and 'out of place' (Cresswell, 1996). The corporeal is therefore the ultimate basis for spatial exclusion and inclusion since whether we are perceived as white or black, young or old, female or male, able-bodied or disabled determines others' responses to us and, at every scale from individual to nation, dictates what different bodies can or cannot do (Valentine, 2001). The body is the site where our personal identities are constituted and social knowledges and meanings inscribed, and there are many ways in which bodies may be 'sexualized'. As Stephens (2002) notes, bodies may be biologically sexed as either male or female, they may be seen to exhibit certain gendered behaviour (and thus be sexualized in terms of their masculinity or femininity), or they may be seen as sexualized because they engage in heterosexual or homosexual practices. In this sense, while sex and gender may seem inextricably linked, they are two separable and culturally constructed social status characteristics. As Swain (1995, p. 258) argues, gender is:

[A] system of culturally constructed identities, expressed in ideologies of masculinity and femininity, interacting with socially structured relationships in divisions of labour and leisure, sexuality and power between women and men.

The fixity of gender, sexuality and identity has been questioned as researchers have explored how the same individual may both experience and represent her or his femininity or masculinity differently in different contexts and in relation to different people (Pink, 2001). This emphasis on the plural rather than the binary nature of gendered and sexual identities, and thus on multiple femininities and masculinities (Moore, 1994), means we need to consider differences *among* as well as *between* female and male bodies and to confront the assumption that sex, gender and sexuality are universal, essentialist and definable experiences. Of course, whilst sexuality is embodied, it is also '… inherently *spatial* – it both depends on particular spaces for its construction and in turn produces and reproduces the spaces in which sexuality can be … forged' (Crouch, 2000, p. 175). Moreover, liminal zones such as tourist resorts, hotels and night-time leisure spaces are closely identified with pleasure, desire, sex and sexuality (Pritchard and Morgan, 2006). It is in these places that we see people actively engaged in (re)creating their sexual selves and performing their sexual identities, which are themselves often entwined with contested social spaces. At the same time, the dominant discourses of sexuality have constructed heterosexual relationships, behaviours and performances in these places as the norm, and homosexual relationships and activities as deviant and transgressive.

However, travel and leisure allow opportunities to resist and revise dominant gender and sexual narratives (Wearing, 1998). Certainly, spaces of pleasure and leisure create possibilities of alternative identities of self through what Fullager (2002, p. 65) has elsewhere characterized as the 'movement of release, of letting go in order to be open to difference through an experience of desire… '. Desire is a deeply embedded, affective and unconscious imperative, which mediates our travel relationships and experiences in culturally specific ways; yet, in tourism studies, conceptualizations of desire have focused on individual motivation as opposed to a motivation to move 'towards that which is different, unknown and other to the self ' (Fullager, 2002, p. 57). This chapter will now turn to discuss how the body, desire and difference are encountered in leisure spaces which are characterized by 'alternative' desires, sexualities, and masculine and feminine subjectivities. More specifically, it will reflect on how gay men, and particularly on how lesbian women, negotiate the material and metaphorical space that is Manchester's Gay Village.

Place, Sexualities and Identities: Narratives from the North-west of England

Leisure and tourism have been described by Crouch (2000, p. 63) as 'encounters ... with other people, with material space, with one's imagination, ideas, metaphors of place ...'. We established above that visibility and 'legitimacy' in public spaces are critically tied to cultural politics and to the recognition of 'rights' – dictating who is publicly included or excluded from the democratic social world – who is one of 'us' or one of 'them'. At the same time, in the heteronormative and androcentric public spaces of the city, 'encounters with "difference" are being read not as pleasurable and part of the vitality of the streets, but rather as potentially threatening and dangerous' (Valentine, 2001, p. 199). City spaces, are negotiated spaces where decisions are made about group visibility, recognition and legitimacy (Keith, 1995; Zukin, 1995, 1996) and, as with all negotiations, some groups are more powerful than others and thus more able to claim and dominate both physical and social spaces. In such an environment, gay men, lesbians, bisexuals and transsexuals have been socially and spatially marginalized, regulated and segregated, derided, feared, and identified as immoral, transgressive and threatening. Even those spaces which have been claimed and marked as 'gay and lesbian territories' are uneasy spaces, continually contested and threatened. For example, Manchester's Gay Village (one of the UK's biggest and most well known gay and lesbian scenes outside of London) has become an increasingly 'degayed' territory as a result of its commercialization. As a result, gay men, lesbians, bisexuals and transsexuals have become ever more alienated from a place in that city they once claimed as their own, a place in which their sexuality could be safely affirmed (Pritchard *et al.*, 1998).

Whilst heterosexuals have frequented the Village from the outset, their visibility in its bars and clubs had historically been quite low key. However, greater tensions surfaced in the later 1990s when the commercial success of the Village prompted an influx of a new generation of bars and clubs which began to attract a more aggressive and confrontational heterosexual clientele. A number of studies (e.g. Pritchard *et al*., 1998; Skeggs, 1999) subsequently contended that the Village was becoming seen as 'a gay theme park', with its non-heterosexual clientele subject to verbal, visual and sometimes physical abuse. Clearly, the nature of the Village was changing, with many of its clubs being increasingly patronized by hen parties and heterosexual voyeurs and, for many gay men and lesbian women, this degaying of the Village has made it a less safe environment, becoming a place where they are now targeted because of their sexuality. Most of the lesbians interviewed in the study of Pritchard *et al*. (2002) described the presence of large groups of heterosexual men in the Village as increasingly threatening and aggressive, and talked of being made to feel uncomfortable about their sexuality in a place they once regarded as largely 'safe and welcoming'. Many discussed their experiences of being subjected to persistent male sexual advances and a sexualizing male gaze – their narratives endorsing the continuing acceptability for men to gaze at, comment on and approach and touch women's bodies in public spaces (Young, 1990). As one woman commented:

> The thing that annoys me is being approached by straight lads who won't take no for an answer. You're in the Village, sitting at a table with a group of friends and a group of straight guys come over saying 'Can I buy you a drink?' We say 'you're wasting your time', they say, 'oh no, we're just buying you a drink' and we say 'we've heard all the lines, go away'.
>
> (cited in Pritchard *et al*., 2002, p. 115)

This is a male gaze that also subjects other non-heterosexuals in the Village, such as transsexuals and transvestites, to mockery and approbation, as one lesbian related:

> I was standing outside the door on Saturday night and there was a really fabulous drag queen walking down the street with a couple of gay male friends and this group of eight straight people went up to them, laughing at them and then got out a camera, wanting their picture taken with them, it was like being at a freak show. I come here because I enjoy it here and feel safe here and I don't want to have to go out there and have photos taken of my friends because they look freakish to other people.
>
> (cited in Pritchard *et al*., 2002, p. 115)

This was not an isolated incident, and another woman commented how:

> There were a number of occasions when we were walking down Canal Street and we got abuse from straight people. We'd feel unsafe walking there because there would be loads of men with bottles in their hands just waiting for something to happen. It created the environment where you didn't want to be in the Village anymore. In fact, I took six months out from the Village after that.
>
> (cited in Pritchard *et al*., 2002, pp. 114–115)

Interestingly, however, the women's uneasy relations and negotiations with space and identity in the Village were by no means restricted to the area's heterosexual male clientele (see also Pritchard *et al.*, 2000a). In fact, these studies highlight that lesbians identified gay men's attitudes and behaviours as a significant source of their unease in the Gay Village. In some respects, the attitudes of gay men towards lesbians were perceived as more threatening and offensive than those of 'straight' men, suggesting that previous discussions of gay space have not only tended to eschew gender but also unwittingly to obscure gay men's oppression of lesbians. The female participants in the studies of Pritchard *et al.* (2000b, 2002) considered that gay men exhibited the same patriarchal attitudes towards lesbians as 'straight' men. Many lesbians felt that their relationships with gay men in the Village were difficult and that the men were not supportive of their presence in what they regarded as their territory. Whilst the women wanted to be 'made to feel as welcome in the men's scene', this was not the case – with many gay men's attitudes reported to range from indifference to outright intimidation. One lesbian described how she thought gay men off-putting and pretentious when lesbians occupied 'their space' – 'the way they carried themselves, the way they acted, very camp when they don't need to be'. Many similar comments highlighted an underlying competitiveness between the men and women that seems characteristic of territorial challenges. 'They [gay men] look at you. They look you up and down and puff their cheeks out as if to say, "God, not another one" … especially if you look better than them. They don't like being beaten on things like that' (participants cited in Pritchard *et al.*, 2002, p. 116).

Such studies, though limited in scale and scope, suggest that the liminal space that is Manchester's Gay Village is an essentially male space and (with one exception at the time of writing which we will discuss below), provision for lesbians tends to be limited to the occasional 'lesbian night' in venues that are essentially catering for gay men. As one of the female interviewees said:

> The men have got their fetish nights, they've got all their hell fire and fist nights, they've got their seedy bars, their nice cruisy bars, dance bars, they've got everything they want. Because it's always been known as the Gay Village, they've got all the variety there. They've always got something to pick from. We have one women's bar.
>
> (cited in Pritchard *et al.*, 2002, p. 113)

In attempting to explain the general invisibility of lesbian spaces in the gay scene (in the UK and elsewhere), some authors (e.g. Skeggs, 1999) have pointed to the fact that, in comparison with most lesbians, gay men are more likely to have easier access to different forms of legitimate capital, which can be spatialized. This seems highly plausible given prevailing gendered socio-economic imbalances (Beeghley, 1996) but is only a part of the explanation, and the extent and nature of women's 'territorial aspirations' are highly ambiguous and contested. Rothenberg (1995, p. 168) has suggested that 'a specifically gay female entertainment spot is unlikely to establish itself ... unless there is already a protective gay male population in the area', and Cassells (1993) has argued that women place more importance on relationships and that they do not seek to compete for or to control space in the same way as men. Yet, it seems to us that such essentializing arguments once again seem to confine women, by their gender, to the world of the personal and the private, to the realm of relationships instead of the public sphere of the street and territorial contestation. In fact, Forsyth (1997) has recently suggested that many lesbians are indeed engaged in creating public lesbian spaces, attempting to reposition the feminine away from the confines of the domestic as the place of identity. This is a slow process, however, and the wider commercial sector in Manchester's Gay Village continues to regard dedicated lesbian venues as unsustainable, despite the popularity of lesbian events and nights. Yet many of the women interviewed in the study of Pritchard *et al.* (2002) commented that they had long wanted to participate in the Village's social scene and talked of their differing needs and their desire for female-only venues. As one commented:

> I think people are waking up to the fact that we do have an identity other than the gay-man identity within the Village. We do need to be catered for, there is a market out there for us and we are willing to participate in it.
>
> (Pritchard *et al.*, 2002, p. 113)

This relative invisibility of lesbians in Manchester's Gay Village confirms the continued strength of heteropatriarchy in public leisure spaces, defined by Valentine (1993, p. 396) as 'a process of sociosexual power relations, which reflects and reproduces male dominance'. This is further endorsed by those women who commented that potential customers will 'stay at home thinking that they've not really got a place to go' when there are no regular, defined and recognized lesbian venues (cited in Pritchard *et al.*, 2002, p. 112). Since most of these women considered many of the bars to be full of gay men who 'never really want to integrate with the women [but] ... generally prefer to have their own space', it is unsurprising that, prior to the opening of a lesbian-oriented bar, they felt they had little claim to the Village. When Vanilla opened in 1998 as a 'contemporary women's bar', it was the only lesbian venue in the Village and the first 7 days a week venue in the UK. Once it opened, the bar took on an increasingly important role for these women, becoming a friendly and safe territory; a place where women could socialize and escape the pressures faced outside, even in the rest of the Village. As its owner was keen to stress:

> If you know anything about the women's scene, which we obviously do, then you're aware that there's also a lot of professional women out there that [sic] want their own space ... I've worked on the gay scene for a long time, worked in the café/bar restaurant scene for the last 12 years and I'm a gay woman myself, and I'm sick of not being catered for.
>
> (cited in Pritchard *et al.*, 2002, p. 113)

The importance of such a 'sanctuary' in the Village should not be underestimated, particularly in a context where many of the women interviewed in these two studies talked of their unease in 'mixed gay venues':

> I know I can come in here on my own and I will know the bar staff and at least one other member of the clientele. It's nice to come in here, have a quiet cup of coffee or a beer and be in familiar surroundings. I could go somewhere else in the Village and it may be very male orientated or it may be a straight or a mixed crowd and I wouldn't feel at ease. This place is everything you want it to be.
>
> (cited in Pritchard *et al.*, 2002, p. 117)

In claiming this female space, the bar's staff and customers felt that, not only were they creating a safe haven to escape the prejudices experienced both outside and inside the Village, but that they also created one of 'the most gay' spaces in the Village. As one customer commented: 'that's what's good about Vanilla. ... On the whole, this place is more gay than any of the other places in the Village because it's not as appealing.' Another elaborated:

> There's no reason to come in here unless you're lesbian. Straight girls are not interested so therefore the straight men don't come in. The gay men only come in with their friends. You have more of a guarantee when you come in here that you're going to have more of a gay night than anywhere else.
>
> (cited in Pritchard *et al.*, 2002, p. 117)

Not only did the bar soon develop into a sanctuary for many lesbians, but there was also clearly a sense of territorial competition in the marking of a space for and by women. Here, Vanilla provided an opportunity to reverse the dominant gendered narrative of the Village as a place where men are only allowed in on women's terms. In the words of one of the women:

> I talked before about the male domination. ... Vanilla is my space and if men want to come in they have to be accompanied by women. It's a complete turn around and it's no hassle in here, just easygoing.
>
> (cited in Pritchard *et al.*, 2002, p. 117)

Conclusions

As the above discussion of the complex relationships within Manchester's Gay Village suggests, contemporary sexualities are social performances that are subject to struggle, conflict, contestation and embracement. Moreover, space is vital to the expression and development of both gender and sexuality, and is itself subject to constant challenge. We discussed at the beginning of the chapter how the hard-won territory of the Gay Village, once a safe space for the expression and development of multiple sexualities and identities, is under challenge. Just as the heterosexual dominance of public spaces is always subject to continual revision, sometimes leading to the creation of gay and lesbian spaces, so too are those resultant gay and lesbian spaces themselves the subject of heterosexual contestation. Manchester's Gay Village could thus be seen as a heterotopia – a counter site offering resistance to dominant heterosexual geographies of control and discipline, yet, at the same time given the fluid nature of space; this space is also subject to processes promoting the re-colonization of non-heterosexual space. All spaces are being continually constructed, renegotiated and reinvented. Studies in Manchester's Gay Village suggest that gay men and lesbians have become increasingly alienated from the area by what could be termed 'a heterosexual invasion' of the Village. This has threatened the 'sanctity' of the Village and led to the objectification of both gay men and lesbians, now increasingly the subject of 'straight' attention, ridicule and threat, and objects of the heterosexual gaze.

There is no denying that gay and lesbian spaces have emotional and psychological importance as empowering places in a 'straight' world, and such spaces remain hotly contested. However, in the case of the Manchester Gay Village, from the outset, this space was never as empowering for lesbians as for gay men. Here and elsewhere, the spatial opportunities for the expression of lesbian identities are more limited and fragile because of the patriarchal power dialectics characterizing the socio-cultural construction of such public space. In such heterotopias, gender remains a significant constructor of social space and, of course, gender itself is constructed in and through those spaces. In this way, we have seen here how the production and politics of gender and sexuality in social life are entwined with the rights and abilities of men and women to create and define the structures and spaces through which their lives are lived. The women interviewed in the studies discussed here clearly have territorial ambitions in the Village – their own space is important to them, it confirms their place in the Village and it supports the development of their social networks in an often hostile, hetero-patriarchal world. We have also seen, however, how that space has been exceptionally difficult to claim, since the more powerful and established gay male communities of the Village have not particularly welcomed the women. Here then, lesbian relationships with gay men emerge as often difficult and uneasy; fraught with tension frequently derived from lesbians and gay men's competitive use of the same space. The women identified patriarchal attitudes towards the Village's public spaces, which they saw as essentially male spaces. Yet, where it has been claimed, the rare phenomenon of lesbian space provides opportunities for women to challenge the male domination of the environment. The lesbian club, Vanilla, in essence, provides a sanctuary for women from what they see as not only a very hetero-patriarchal, but also a homo-patriarchal world. Ironically, this bar is considered by the women to be the 'gayest' space in the Village since 'straight' consumers have no interest in it and gay men enter only on the women's terms.

Clearly, there is a pressing need for many more explorations of the relationships between gender, sexuality and space. Here, in this chapter, we have argued that our small-scale studies suggest that any analysis of sexuality, identity and space that ignores gender is at best incomplete, and at worst misleading. The leisure and tourism academy must thus incorporate feminine, masculine and transsexual voices if it is not to remain partial and unrepresentative, since leisure and tourism studies have too often silenced other experiences by subsuming the plurality of voices into some unstated masculinized norm. For many researchers, this need to embrace, articulate and reflect multiple identities and voices remains an unrecognized challenge because as white, middle-class men they are the self, the same, the norm against which others are measured, they have 'no class, no race, no gender ... [they are] the generic person' (Kimmel, 1996, p. 4). Ironically, this has also had the effect of concealing heterosexual and masculine leisure and tourism experiences from fuller examination as researchers have shied away from foregrounding the self as the research subject in their obsession to research their other. The role and influence of heterosexuality deserve a much wider exploration than hitherto, and sexuality needs to be investigated as a shaper of both heterosexual and non-heterosexual leisure identities. Thus, in the coming years, not only does the academy need more nuanced conceptual and methodological approaches to the study of sexualities, but it must also embrace the diversity and plurality of currently marginalized voices.

References

Aitchison, C. (1999a) New cultural geographies: the spatiality of leisure, gender and sexuality. *Leisure Studies* 18, 19–39.

Aitchison, C. (1999b) Heritage and nationalism: gender and the performance of power. In: Crouch, D. (ed.) *Leisure/Tourism Geographies: Practices and Geographical Knowledge*. Routledge, London, pp. 59–73.

Aitchison, C. (2000) Poststructural feminist theories of representing others: a response to the 'crisis' in leisure studies' discourse. *Leisure Studies* 19, 127–144.

Aitchison, C. and Reeves, C. (1998) Gendered (bed)spaces: the culture and commerce of women only tourism. In: Aitchison, C. and Jordan, F. (eds) *Gender, Space and Identity. Leisure, Culture and Commerce*. Leisure Studies Association, Brighton, UK, pp. 47–68.

Aitchison, C., MacLeod, N.E. and Shaw, J. (2000) *Leisure and Tourism Landscapes: Social and Cultural Geographies*. Routledge, London.

Anderson, K. (1996) Engendering race research: unsettling the self–other dichotomy. In: Duncan, N. (ed.) *Bodyspace: Destabilizing Geographies of Gender and Sexuality*. Routledge, London, pp. 197–211.

Ashworth, G. and Dietvorst, A. (eds) (1995) *Tourism and Spatial Transformations*. CAB International, Wallingford, UK.

Bell, D. and Valentine, G. (eds) (1995) *Mapping Desire: Geographies of Sexualities*. Routledge, London.

Beeghley, L. (1996) *What Does Your Wife Do? Gender and the Transformation of Family Life*. Westview Press, Oxford.

Booth, C., Darke, J. and Yeandle, S. (eds) (1996) *Changing Places: Women's Lives in the City*. Paul Chapman Publishing, London.

Butler, J. (1990) *Gender Trouble: Feminism and the Subversion of Identity*. Routledge, London.

Cannadine, D. (2000) *Class in Britain*. Penguin Books, London.

Cassells, F. (1993) Quoted in Rothenberg, T. (1995) Lesbians creating urban social space. In: Bell, D. and Valentine, G. (eds) *Mapping Desire: Geographies of Sexualities*. Routledge, London.

Clift, S. and Carter, S. (eds) (2000) *Tourism and Sex: Culture, Commerce and Coercion*. Pinter, London.

Clift, S. and Forrest, S. (1999) Gay men and tourism: destinations and holiday motivations. *Tourism Management* 20, 615–625.

Clift, S., Luongo, M. and Callister, C. (eds) (2002) *Gay Tourism: Culture, Identity and Sex*. Continuum, London.

Cohen, C. (1995) Marketing paradise, making nation. *Annals of Tourism Research* 22, 404–421.

Connell, R.W. (1983) *Which Way is Up? Essays on Sex, Class and Culture*. Allen and Unwin, Sydney.

Crang, M. (1998) *Cultural Geography*. Routledge, London.

Cresswell, T. (1996) *In Place/Out of Place: Geography, Ideology and Transgression*. University of Minnesota Press, Minneapolis, Minnesota.

Crouch, D. (ed.) (1999) *Leisure/Tourism Geographies: Practices in Geographical Knowledge*. Routledge, London.

Crouch, D. (2000) Places around us: embodied lay geographies in leisure and tourism. *Leisure Studies* 19, 63–76.

Davies, K. (1997) Embodying theory: beyond modernist and postmodernist readings of the body. In: Davis, K. (ed.) *Embodied Practices: Feminist Perspectives on the Body*. Sage, London.

Duncan, N. (1996) Sexuality in public and private spaces. In: Duncan, N. (ed.) *Bodyspace: Destabilizing Geographies of Gender and Sexuality*. Routledge, London, pp. 127–145.

Edensor, T. and Kothari, U. (1994) The masculinisation of Stirling's heritage. In: Kinnaird, V. and Hall, D. (eds) *Tourism: a Gender Analysis*. Wiley, Chichester, UK, pp. 164–187.

Evans, M. and Lee, E. (eds) (2002) *Real Bodies: a Sociological Introduction*. Palgrave, Hampshire, UK.

Forrest, S. and Clift, S. (1998) Gay tourist space and sexual behaviour. In: Aitchison, C. and Jordan, F. (eds) *Gender, Space and Identity*. Leisure Studies Association, Brighton, UK, pp. 163–176.

Forsyth, A. (1997) 'Out' in the valley. *International Journal of Urban and Regional Restructuring* 21, 38–62.

Foucault, M. (1986) Of other spaces. *Diacritics* 16 (Spring), 22–27.

Fullagar, S. (2002) Narratives of travel: desire and the movement of the feminine subjectivity. *Leisure Studies* 21, 57–74.

Gardener, C.B. (1995) *Passing-by*. University of California Press, Berkeley, California.

Greene, B. (ed.) (1997) Ethnic and cultural diversity among lesbians and gay men. *Psychological Perspectives on Lesbian and Gay Issues*, Vol. 3. Sage, Thousand Oaks, California.

Hubbard, P., Kitchin, R. and Valentine, G. (eds) (2004) *Key Thinkers on Space and Place*. Sage, London.

Hughes, H. (1997) Holidays and homosexual identity. *Tourism Management* 18, 3–7.

Hughes, H. (1998) Sexuality, tourism and space: the case of gay visitors to Amsterdam. In: Tyler, D., Robertson, M. and Guerrier, Y. (eds) *Managing Tourism in Cities: Policy, Process and Practice*. Wiley, Chichester, UK, pp. 163–178.

Hughes, H. (2000) Holidays and homosexuals: a constrained choice? In: Robinson, M., Long, P., Evans, N., Sharpley, R. and Swarbrooke, J. (eds) *Reflections on International Tourism. Expressions of Culture, Identity and Meaning in Tourism*. Business Education Publishers, Sunderland, UK, pp. 221–230.

Keith, M. (1995) Ethnic entrepreneurs and street rebels: looking inside the inner city. In: Pile, S. and Thrift, N. (eds) *Mapping the Subject: Geographies of Cultural Transformation*. Routledge, London, pp. 355–370.

Lewes, D. (2000) *Nudes from Nowhere: Utopian Sexual Landscapes*. Rowman and Littlefield, Lanham, Maryland.

McDowell, L. (1997) *Capital Culture: Gender at Work in the City (Studies in Urban and Social Change)*. Blackwell, Oxford, UK.

Miller, C. (2002) Better living through circuitry: lesbians and circuit parties. In: Clift, S., Luongo, M. and Callister, C. (eds) *Gay Tourism: Culture, Identity and Sex*. Continuum, London, pp. 214–230.

Mitchell, D. (2000) *Cultural Geography. A Critical Introduction*. Blackwell, Oxford, UK.

Moore, H. (1994) *A Passion for Difference: Essays in Anthropology and Gender*. Polity Press, Oxford, UK.

Myslik, W.D. (1996) Renegotiating the social/sexual identities of place: gay communities as safe havens or sites of resistance. In: Duncan, N. (ed.)

Bodyspace. Destabilizing Geographies of Gender and Sexuality. Routledge, London, pp. 156–169.

Olwig, K. (1993) A sexual cosmology: nation and landscape at the conceptual interstices of nature and culture; or what does landscape really mean? In: Bender, B. (ed.) *Landscape. Politics and Perspectives*. Berg Publishers, Oxford, pp. 307–343.

Osborne, R. (2002) *Megawords*. Sage, London.

Pink, S. (2001) *Doing Visual Ethnography*. Sage, London.

Pitts, B.G. (1999) Sports tourism and niche markets: identification and analysis of the growing lesbian and gay sports tourism industry. *Journal of Vacation Marketing* 5, 31–50.

Plummer, K. (2005) Critical humanism and queer theory: living with the tensions. In: Denzin, N. and Lincoln, Y.S. (eds) *The Sage Handbook of Qualitative Research*, 3rd edn. Sage, London, pp. 357–374.

Pritchard, A. and Morgan, N. (2006) Hotel Babylon? Exploring hotels as liminal sites of transition and transgression. *Tourism Management* (in press).

Pritchard, A., Morgan, N.J., Sedgley, D. and Jenkins, A. (1998) Reaching out to the gay tourist: opportunities and threats in an emerging market segment. *Tourism Management* 19, 273–282.

Pritchard, A., Sedgley, D. and Morgan, N.J. (2000a) Exploring issues of space and sexuality in Manchester's gay village. In: Robinson, M. *et al.* (eds) *Reflections on International Tourism. Expressions of Culture, Identity and Meaning in Tourism*. Business Education Publishers, Sunderland, UK, pp. 225–238.

Pritchard, A., Morgan, N.J., Sedgley, D., Khan, E. and Jenkins, A. (2000b) Sexuality and holiday choices: conversations with gay and lesbian tourists. *Leisure Studies* 19, 267–282.

Pritchard, A., Morgan, N.J. and Sedgley, D. (2002) In search of lesbian space: the experience of Manchester's gay village. *Leisure Studies* 21, 105–124.

Ringer, G. (ed.) (1998) *Destinations: Cultural Landscapes of Tourism*. Routledge, London.

Rose, G. (1993) *Feminism and Geography. The Limits of Geographical Knowledge*. Polity Press, Cambridge, UK.

Rothenberg, T. (1995) Lesbians creating urban social space. In: Bell, D. and Valentine, G. (eds) *Mapping Desire: Geographies of Sexualities*. Routledge, London.

Scraton, S. and Flintoff, A. (2002) *Gender and Sport: a Reader*, Routledge, London.

Scraton, S. and Watson, B. (1998) Gendered cities: women and public leisure space in the 'postmodern city'. *Leisure Studies* 17, 123–137.

Segal, L. (1990) *Slow Motion. Changing Masculinities, Changing Men*. Virago, London.

Skeggs, B. (1999) Matter out of place: visibility and sexualities in leisure spaces. *Leisure Studies* 18, 213–232.

Smith, S. (1999) Society space. In: Cloke, P., Crang, P. and Goodwin, M. (eds) *Introducing Human Geography*. Arnold, London.

Stanko, B. and Curry, P. (1997) Homophobic violence and the self 'at risk': interrogating the boundaries. *Social and Legal Studies* 6, 513–532.

Stephens, K. (2002) Sexualized bodies. In: Evans, M. and Lee, E. (eds) *Real Bodies: a Sociological Introduction*. Palgrave, New York, pp. 29–45.

Swain, M. (1995) Gender in tourism. *Annals of Tourism Research* 22, 247–266.

Taylor, I. and Jamieson, R. (1997) 'Proper little mesters': nostalgia and protest masculinity in de-industrialised Sheffield. In: Westwood, S. and Williams, J. (eds) *Imagining Cities: Scripts, Signs, Memory*. Routledge, London, pp. 152–178.

Valentine, G. (1989) The geography of women's fear. *Area* 21, 385–390.

Valentine, G. (1992) Images of danger: women's sources of information about the spatial distribution of male violence. *Area* 24, 22–29.

Valentine, G. (1993) Hetero(sexing) space: lesbian perceptions and experiences of everyday spaces. *Society and Space* 11, 395–413.

Valentine, G. (1996) (Re)negotiating the heterosexual street. In: Duncan, N. (ed.) *Bodyspace. Destabilizing Geographies of Gender and Sexuality*. Routledge, London, pp. 146–155.

Valentine, G. (2001) *Social Geographies: Space and Society*. Pearson, Harlow, UK.

Wearing, B. (1998) *Leisure and Feminist Theory*. Sage, London.

Young, I.M. (1990) *Justice and the Politics of Difference*. Pittsburgh University Press, Pittsburgh, Pennsylvania.

Zukin, S. (1995) *The Culture of Cities*. Blackwell, Oxford, UK.

Zukin, S. (1996) Space and symbols in an age of decline. In: King, A.D. (ed.) *Re-Presenting the City: Ethnicity, Capital and Culture in the 21st Century Metropolis*. Macmillan, Basingstoke, UK, pp. 43–59.

13

Modernist Anthropology, Ethnic Tourism and National Identity: the Contest for the Commodification and Consumption of St Patrick's Day, Montserrat

Jonathan Skinner

The Queen's University Belfast, UK

> Evidence of the Irish is everywhere – from the bright green shamrock stamped on the visitor's passports, to the names of the places like Kinsale, Cork Hill and Galway, to the Irish accents in the native's speech. And, of course, the surnames, Ryans and Sullivans and names beginning with 'O' are common. In a predominantly black population, taken out of context, these names are somewhat humorous: a visitor might encounter a Rastafarian man with waist-length 'dreadlocks' who will proudly proclaim that his name is Ras O'Reilly.
>
> (Solomon, 1984, p. 46)

Introducing Travel, Writing and Anthropology

Solomon is a travel writer who was writing about his visit to Montserrat, a British Overseas Territory in the Eastern Caribbean. He was describing what he considered to be a pervasive Irish influence found *on* the island and *in* the islanders, an all-encompassing Hibernian haze. For Solomon, Montserrat is '[a] wee bit o' Ireland in the Caribbean', the title of his article. For him, Montserrat – including the Montserratians – is an unusual island tourist attraction, an island which capitalizes upon a strong semiotic and symbolic likeness to Ireland. Montserrat is often billed as 'The Emerald Isle of the Caribbean' or 'The Other Emerald Isle' by travel writers (Anonymous, undated; Strong, 1981), tourists, the Montserrat Tourist Board and visiting anthropologists such as the American John

©CAB International 2006. *Tourism Consumption and Representation: Narratives of Place and Self* (eds K. Meethan, A. Anderson and S. Miles)

Messenger (1994). The island is also marketed as 'The Way The Caribbean Used To Be' (Montserrat Department of Tourism, 1993) as the island's tourist industry tries to distinguish Montserrat from the many other Caribbean islands, each with their similar suns, seas and sands.

'Talk about "sure and begorra" meeting "no problem", Montserrat' (Sylvan, 1994, p. 15): this island is an emerald, an-other emerald, a blackened emerald; and the islanders are Irish, British, colonial – and nothing if not comical 'Black Irish' (see Solomon, 1984; Fallon, 1993). It is a place of oddities, the 'humorous' side of ethnic tourism, Ras O'Reilly the Irish Rasta for instance. This reaction, turning an experience or an encounter into a comical moment, is a coping strategy for visitors forced to deal with what for them is the unexpected, the unusual, the unfamiliar. According to student American anthropologist Susan Laffey (1995, pp. 35–36), they reveal in the travel writings 'the racist assumptions of Euro-American travel writers and their audiences' – the mutually exclusive categories of Irish culture and black skin – which transform 'Montserratian people into a Euro-American ethnic fantasy'. Both the island and the islanders have been exoticized, commoditized and turned into an 'ethnic tourism' spectacle and destination, an example of unmentionable racism which can be read between the writers' lines (see Leach, 1984; MacCannell, 1992, p. 170).

These collectivized representations of Montserratians can have a profound effect upon the islanders, 10,000 descendants of African sugar slaves. For them, culture and ethnicity have become commodities: in this new world economy, Montserratian celebrations of St Patrick's Day and their Black Irish self-representations are used to attract new visitors to the island, just like iconic Scottish figures such as the bagpiper and kiltwearer, both of which have become petrified stereotypes which have turned 'Scotland the Brave' into 'Scotland the Brand' (McCrone *et al.*, 1995) and now 'Scotland the Bland' (Skinner, 2001). The issue, then, in this chapter is what effect outsiders are having upon the identity of Montserratians. A large number of Montserratians, such as the poet and writer E.A. Markham for instance, now see themselves as African West Indians as well as Irish – as African but different, as special West Indians.

The historian of Ireland and the Irish Diaspora, Donald Akenson (1997, pp. 180–181) has commented favourably upon these contemporary identity politics taking place on Montserrat:

> [i]f ever there was a place that needed the invention of a robust historical tradition, it is Montserrat, and Messenger's Hibernicist vision is a valuable gift from outside. [...] At its best, the Hibernicist invention has the potential of doing for Montserrat what the various invented traditions did for Great Britain: hold the people together until they find themselves their own history.

The 'metonymic event' indirectly referred to is what I describe and detail as a change in cultural viewpoint, one which has changed the annual 1-day religious observance of St Patrick's Day into a 6-day festival with competing Irish and African slave themes, and one which is not quite so innocuous. Following an introduction to the representation of Montserrat, this chapter goes on to present and consider two St Patrick's Day events as they were consumed by two anthropologists (Messenger and myself). The chapter then situates these accounts in the literature of tourism's commoditization of culture. Throughout this chapter I shall be drawing correspondences and contrasts between tourism and anthropology, disciplines which both exhibit an imperialistic and colonial gaze (see Nash, 1989), neither of which should be allowed to run rampant.

Messenger's Hibernicism and the Institutionalization of St Patrick's Day

The American anthropologist John Messenger (1967, 1973, 1975) 'discovered' this Hibernicism on Montserrat in the late 1960s and early 1970s during 7 weeks' fieldwork and created the 'Black Irish' ethnic category for a loosely specified number of Montserratians. In Messenger's (1975, p. 281) key article, 'Montserrat: The Most Distinctively Irish Settlement in the New World', he describes Montserrat in the following way:

> Montserrat is known as the 'Emerald Isle of the Caribbean', where live the 'Black' or 'Montserrat Irish', a population reflecting over two centuries of genetic and cultural exchange between Irish and Africans.

More controversially, Messenger (1975, p. 295) continues:

> Most of Montserrat culture today is an amalgam of African retentions, European and regional borrowings, and internal innovations, of which Irish retentions and reinterpretations with African forms make up but a limited portion. The Irish heritage is manifested in the phenotypes of the islanders [...] in the place names and surnames [...]. Irish 'cultural imponderables' – motor habits, linguistic patterns, musical styles, systems of values, and codes of etiquette – are as prevalent as African ones among the Black Irish. They are difficult to describe in their subtlety, but can be 'sensed' by researchers who have resided for long periods in both peasant Ireland and the region of Africa from which most of the slaves were taken.

Messenger's 'sensed' ideas and interpretative (*verstehen*) research (see also Messenger, 1994, p. 13) from the 1960s and 1970s have been avidly picked up by his sympathetic audience of 'Irish-leaning' scholars, the travel writers and tourist industry on and off Montserrat, as well as many local Montserratians themselves. Whilst the traces and echoes of Ireland and the Irish can be found throughout the island and are not in dispute, the nature, nurture and condemnation of the 'Black Irish' construct is a debate which still engulfs the island and islanders (see Fergus, 1992).

My anthropological use of the traditional and grounded ethnographic practice of participant observation, however, reveals that St Patrick's Day activities are an example of how tourism influences the consumption of local cultural practices and affects their production (invention) as a 'non-tradition' (Errington and Gewertz, 1995, p. 94, after Hobsbawm and Ranger, 1983). In academic terms, there is a reflexive anthropological critique in my account as I treat, after Foucault, modern-day Montserrat as a discursive place, one where Messenger's 'Hibernicism' – a form of myth–legend–hystoria (cf. Showalter, 1997) of Black (Irish) Montserrat – and the travel writing and tourist industry surrounding Montserrat perhaps equate to a version of Said's (1991) 'Orientalism' – an intertextual edifice of second order analyses, an 'ideological fiction – mind forg'd manacles' (Said, 1991, p. 328).

Messenger (1994) has written about St Patrick's Day in detail in his article 'St Patrick's Day in "the other Emerald Isle"'. Appearing in the journal *Eire–Ireland*, the article maintains a critical stance towards many Montserratians, is disparaging of their activities, and patronizes their intellectual endeavours, all from its own rather sketchy and dubious vantage point. The article begins by sketching over Messenger's (1994, p. 13) previous publications and ideas about Montserrat, paying attention to the vestiges of Ireland on the island and to the Irish tradition manifested in a 'Caucasoid phenotype' amongst approximately 'a thousand "Black" or "Montserrat Irish" [...] located in the north of Montserrat, mostly descendants of marriages between Irish and slaves and mostly Protestant'. This dramatic assertion is followed by comments about how the Montserrat 'Irishry' found in specific families has been adopted and adapted by non-'Montserrat Irish' to become a 'stage Irishry [...] acting out Irish stereotypic behaviour for the delight of Irish-American tourists and their favour, and to the dismay of Irish visitors' (p. 14).

According to Messenger, St Patrick's Day has long been celebrated by the Catholic Church on the island. In 1985, however, this religious day-long celebration for St Patrick became a 6-day long festival associated with the village St Patrick's in the south of the island. Messenger (1994, p. 15) refers to this change as the result of a 'revitalization movement' on the island which began in the 1960s with a concerted attempt 'to engender national consciousness and pride in Montserrat culture'. His published work thus became bound up in a local ideological shift from colonial resistance to burgeoning (pan-African) nativism.

Messenger (1994, p. 16) defines the struggle for St Patrick's Day as one between 'advocates of the economic and psychological benefits of the festival, Afrocentric elitists, and the Catholic clergy and congregation'. Essentially, however:

> the institutionalization of St. Patrick's Day was [most strongly influenced by the] Afrocentric West Indian elitists who wished to shift the focus of the celebration from Ireland and the worship of the saint to slave resistance and emancipation, even though the Carnival traditionally served the latter end.
> (Messenger, 1994, pp. 15–16).

He goes on to disparage the evidence for the Afrocentric commemoration of St Patrick's Day, namely, for him, some unpublished sketchy historical records noting that there was a failed conspiracy attempted on the planters by their slaves on 17 March 1768 (see English, 1930). Messenger (1994, p. 16) treats English's account as the record of a legend, and an 'untrustworthy legend' at that. He also accuses the Afrophiles on the island of 'counter-racism' and of attempting to 'discredit' his writings about the Irish connection. It is clear that Messenger is referring to Sir Howard Fergus as one of the key Afrophiles when Messenger (1994, p. 17) follows his criticisms with a quote from Fergus (1993, p. 4) taken from 'The Official St. Patrick's Day Programme 1993':

> This is a predominantly black country, the African retentions and reinterpretations in our culture are unmistakable [...]. This is why the celebration of St. Patrick's Day is different here from the festivities of diasporic Irish cells in North America and elsewhere. [...] [T]he day as celebrated now is a secular concept, the creation of local students of history blessed with national consciousness and insights into the role of development in history.

Sir Fergus is the sole university lecturer on Montserrat, Deputy Governor and a historian and poet of Montserrat. It was Fergus (1994, pp. 73–76) who campaigned for the establishment of the St Patrick's Day commemorations after uncovering historical material about the failed uprising and the execution of nine ring-leaders; as he (Fergus, 1992, p. 43) notes, it was not until 1971 that 'local scholars rediscovered the day'.

Fergus's (1994, p. 75) perspective on the rebellion past and its connection with the present-day St Patrick's Day and sense of Montserratian national pride and identity differs dramatically from that of Messenger:

> The participation in the abortive uprising registered in blood the slaves' love of freedom and unsettled the whites somewhat. It was not until 1985 that the slaves who were involved came to be regarded as national freedom-fighters for their attempt, and Montserratians began to celebrate St. Patrick's Day annually as a public holiday. This came about after a few nationalist scholars popularized the event by staging cultural activities around the theme on the date and canvassed John Osborne's government to recognise the day officially.

Fergus's (1994, p. 76) history of St Patrick's Day on Montserrat can be found in his history of the island. There he reiterates his commemoration argument for St Patrick's Day on Montserrat:

> This author [Fergus] had an occasion recently to warn against incipient distortion in the significance and celebration of the holiday. It was, in his view, beginning to resemble the style in which the Irish diaspora in the United States celebrate St. Patrick's Day. The holiday was intended to honour our slave ancestors who bravely essayed to overthrow their oppressive European overlords – and these were English, Scottish, and Irish.

In other words, for Fergus (1994, p. 265), the recent commemoration of St Patrick's Day is a vital part of Montserrat's 'cultural awakening' which began late in the 1970s. In this vein, Fergus (1994, p. 266) concludes his history of Montserrat with the following words:

> The decision in 1985 to make St. Patrick's Day a national holiday and to celebrate Montserratian heroes past and present with activities rooted in creole culture, is contributing to the development of a national and cultural identity. [...] Montserrat can be colonial in constitution, if it thinks it has to be, without being crassly colonial in identity and mentality.

The importance of the nationalists' institutionalization of St Patrick's Day cannot and should not be underestimated by investigating scholars. It is far more than a historical tribute to the past. It has present-day psychological implications: the historical fact of slave resistance and struggle in the past ameliorates thoughts about the horrors and complicities of the slave system in the present. Though Messenger casts doubt upon the veracity of this rebellion, it has been substantiated by Fergus through Colonial Office research, and has been corroborated by the work of Akenson (1997), Skinner (1997) and Mullin (1992, p. 223), especially, who has pointed out the significance of the St Patrick's Day rebellion as one of the first major slave conspiracies in the Caribbean.

Two St Patrick's Day Festivities Consumed and Considered

According to Messenger (1994, pp. 18–22), the St Patrick's Day celebrations in 1993 lasted for a week. There were 16 major events, with five of them taking place on 17 March. The week began with a calypso competition in the St Patrick's Village Community Centre. Consistent with his critical approach to this revitalization cult on Montserrat which is displacing and destroying local traditions and culture, Messenger (1994, p. 18) notes that this calypso competition was the first time that it was held outside of Carnival celebrations at Christmas time: it was to be 'the first of several borrowed events'. This critical stance taken by Messenger is one which views culture as something discrete and unchanging, an approach which contrasts with my understanding of culture as a diffuse and mobile mix of practices and knowledges. Messenger laments both the cultural change itself and the appropriateness of the change. Comparing Messenger's St Patrick's Day in 1993 with the St Patrick's Day I witnessed in 1995 (Saturday 11 March to Saturday 18 March), there were only two additional events in the 1995 programme. Furthermore, the 1995 programme began with a 'Roman Catholic Dinner' – West Indian food served, serenaded with Irish folk songs. However, 'The Official St. Patrick's Day Programme 1995' (James, 1995) contains the same tensions running through the messages which Messenger found in 1993: the Governor continues to express a desire for St Patrick's Day to be used as a way of forging closer ties between Ireland and Montserrat; the Chief Minister of the island still uses St Patrick's Day to celebrate local community; and Sir Fergus again memorializes St Patrick's Day as a commemoration of achievement and human spirit for martyrs to freedom.

On the second day of the week, Messenger (1994, p. 18) notes that the Annual Dinner was held with Irish folk songs played to the diners. On Sunday 12 March 1995, I observed a formal 'semi-classical concert' in the capital's University Centre, and an informal and local Cultural Concert in the St Patrick's Community Centre at which the only other off-island visitors were two American Catholics – 'one-eighth Irish' themselves – who had been 'attracted to a vacation which celebrated Irish ancestry'.

Day three of the 'festival' for Messenger consisted of dawn Masses in St Patrick's and St Anthony's Churches followed by a brunch in the Community Centre. In the late afternoon, the University Centre hosted a 'Cultural Concert' of short plays, songs, poetry readings and music played by string and masquerade bands (masqueraders are masked dancers who dance Irish heel–toe jigs to African styles and rhythms). In the evening, an 'Oldy Goldy Party' was put on, playing music for some of the elderly expatriates (out of a total of approximately 300 'residential' tourists), tourists and Montserratians. The third day of the festivities in 1995 was the Tuesday, missing the Monday, and was scheduled to have been the annual 'St Patrick's Lecture', to be given by Dr Howard Fergus. Unfortunately, it was cancelled.

Days four and five of the St Patrick's Day programme in 1993 consisted of first a National Heroes Day, and second a Calypso Day with an evening pub crawl. The intention was to have a broadcast through the day of biographies of six outstanding 20th century Montserratians including the politician who 'piloted the move to institutionalize St. Patrick's Day, and the leading local West Indian historian' (Messenger, 1994, p. 20). The broadcast was delayed by a day. Messenger was indirectly referring to Fergus because he explains later that the following night the same historian gave a lecture about the arts and culture on Montserrat, drawing upon his forthcoming history of the island. The following day, a calypso contest took place in the Shamrock cinema, followed by a pub crawl which went to 'rum shops displaying shamrock emblems to guide revellers to "approved premises"' (Messenger, 1994, p. 20).

On the Wednesday night (1995), a number of expatriates and tourists were bussed around the island by the Montserrat Tourist Board, visiting bar after bar on their island pub crawl. At the same time, a second Cultural Concert was held at the University Centre, a family show consisting of a children's steel band, school story tellers, and local dancers and singers – including calypsonians singing slave rebellion and Irish-orientated calypsos. The following day, there was an arts and crafts Street Fair in the capital, Plymouth, and in the evening there was another Tourist Board-sponsored 'pub crawl' and an impromptu calypso competition in a local bar which lasted for three-quarters of an hour before disintegrating. The tourist drinkers were escorted by members of the Montserrat Tourist Board who do not drink with them and apologize for their behaviour when they move on. Though attracted by the opportunity to celebrate St Patrick's Day, when the white tourists arrive on the island, they find themselves repelled by the revelation that many of their black co-revellers are commemorating a failed slave insurrection. Tourist escapism is mollified by such local antipathies.

St Patrick's Day 1993 was 'an around-the-clock celebration' beginning with morning masses and ending with an all-night jump-up party, all staged in Irish colours. The first main event was a symbolic 'Freedom Run' from the capital to St Patrick's Village. This was followed by a bicycle race from the village to the capital, Plymouth. St Patrick's then held a 'Slave Feast' of local delicacies ranging from 'goat water' stew to fried 'mountain chicken' (giant frogs). Arts and crafts were sold at the village Community Centre, and a local cricket match was played throughout the day. There was meant to have been a carnival-like 'Pageant Parade' leaving from the capital, but it never happened, contributing to Messenger's (1994, p. 22) overall comment that this extended St Patrick's Day commemoration was turning into a 'faltering festival'.

In many respects, St Patrick's Day 1995 was a similar affair, with a Freedom Run in the morning, Slave Feast at lunchtime, an all-day Cricket Match and dancing in the streets till early into the next morning. Throughout the day, guided hikes (EC$45) were also organized by the Tourist Board for tourists to visit local nature sites. The local media ran the usual features leading up to the festivities to encourage participation in the St Patrick's Day festivities and ask for islanders to exercise restraint and courtesy towards the tourists, to promote the island and help build a 'meaningful tourism trade' (Anonymous, 1995a, p. 4). After the St Patrick's Day week, however, the same media were critical of the festivities, referring to them as a 'flop' (Anonymous, 1995b).

During the St Patrick's Day week, I talked to several villagers and they told me that their surnames – Irish, Allen, O'Donahue, Galloway, Maloney – prove that they have a *genetic* connection with Ireland. Interestingly, Messenger notes at the end of his article that the Black Irish of Montserrat, found in the north of the island, were not involved in the 1993 festivities, and certainly I neither saw nor heard *from* them or *of* them in 1995. Messenger (1994, p. 22) also notes that his respondents who participated in the festivities 'were only peripherally concerned with whether its significance was Afrocentric or Hibernophilic; they were mostly concerned with enjoying themselves'. This was true also for the 1995 festivities. On the night of St Patrick's Day, the half-mile street running through the village was jam-packed full of Montserratians socializing and dancing to soca and masquerade music.

Messenger (1994, pp. 22–23) notes that high school education on Montserrat bears the 'imprimatur of the government', namely 'the Afrocentric version of the festival', and yet the local historical perception of this newly institutionalized set of festivities remains diverse for all the Afrocentric (Fergus) and Hibernophilic (Messenger) scholarship. Roman Catholics in Plymouth and the south were, of course, more committed to the religious interpretation of the celebration, and they showed the most knowledge – although it was incomplete, often distorted and even false, to paraphrase Messenger – of the Irish connection and St Patrick himself. For example, when one woman from St Patrick's Village was asked why she was wearing the Irish national colours, she replied that they symbolized the '*green* flash' sometimes seen at the moment the *orange* sun sets in the sea and leaves behind once *white* clouds in the sky above. Another villager, of Afrocentric bent, claimed that the slave rebellion of 1768 was successful and led to the immediate emancipation of the slaves which had been being both celebrated and commemorated today. These various interactions and local understandings of St Patrick's Day were similar to those I came across in 1995. Missie Blake, for example, was convinced that Montserratians were commemorating Montserrat's national freedom-fighters who, under the leadership of a slave called Patrick, had successfully led an anti-English/colonial rebellion in 1768 which had emancipated both the oppressed slaves and the oppressed Irish on the island.

Tourism, 'Material Culture' and the Commoditization of St Patrick's Day

This chapter is more than just a critiquing of Messenger's anthropological research methods (7 weeks participant observation, 'sensed' and hence unverifiable interpretative anthropology), findings ('Black Irish' ethnic category and Irish 'motor' habits on Montserrat) and publications (condescending 'Black Irish' and St Patrick's Day articles). This extended ethnographic examination of St Patrick's Day festivities and their contested significance bears some resemblance to other anthropological debates regarding the theoretical and methodological approaches to the host–guest interaction. The debate has become polarized around reactions to Davydd Greenwood's (1977) article 'Culture by the pound: an anthropological perspective on tourism as cultural commoditization'. He asks the question 'can culture be considered a commodity' and answers it with reference to the Alarde public ritual and festival held by the people of Fuenterrabia, the Spanish Basque country, an annual recreation of the town's victory over a siege by the French in 1638. Greenwood (1989, p. 180) suggests that this 350-year-old ritual is an invented tradition. It is different, then, from an invented tradition such as St Patrick's Day which has been recreated as part of a modern revitalization movement.

Greenwood (1989, p. 173) articulates local concerns, namely that 'local culture is being treated as a commodity *sui generis*'. He laments the sense of anomie which came to this public collective expression of solidarity in which citizens of the wards of Fuenterrabia come together in traditional costume. This public performance has always been performed *by* and *for* the citizens, an inaccessible 'sacred history' (Greenwood, 1989, p. 176), unadvertised and taking place in a plaza so small that it could not cater for many onlookers. In 1969, the municipal government proposed that the Alarde should take place twice on the same day so that tourists and more members of the town could see the festivities. The consequences of this suggestion were that the people involved in the re-enactment reacted first by 'being up in arms', followed by an indifference to the occasion. In effect, the authority's decision made explicit their attempts at commoditizing local culture, of selling it by the pound, of turning a ritual into an inauthentic and 'meaningless' performance for money.

Though the St Patrick's Day festivities are not a re-enactment on the same scale as the Alarde, nor are they an invented tradition with a long history, they are festivities which the local authorities such as the Montserrat Tourist Board and the Montserrat Government are trying to commoditize. These organizations are opposed by those whom Messenger refers to as 'Afrophiles' who originally pressed for the 'institutionalization' of St Patrick's Day. In both Messenger and Greenwood's case studies, the anthropologist is presenting their traditional critique on modernization. Their 'culture politics' is to view the commoditization of culture on Montserrat and in Fuenterrabia as a form of ethnic tourism, an alienating and objectifying process.

Culture, once an identity marker, has now become a trademark or brand, Picard (1995, p. 60) writes wistfully. In his overview of tourism and culture research on Bali, one which we can also apply to many other locations, Picard (1995) picks out the critics of tourism such as Hanna (1972) who believes that tourism needs culture but that tourism also destroys culture, as well as the proponents of tourism such as McKean (1973) who argues that tourism has done much to stimulate and revive Balinese interest in their cultural heritage and artistic creativity. Picard sides neither with the spoiling nor the renewing of Balinese culture theses. Picard argues that tourism is *a part of* culture, not *apart from* culture and that, as such, the investigator's concerns should lie with the various conceptualizations and mobilizations of culture.

Picard's case study is pertinent to the recent touristification and commoditization of Montserrat because of the influence external researchers have had upon Balinese identity. It serves as a warning. Picard (1995, p. 47) refers to Bali as a 'living museum', a human species Galapagos island, a place and a people which now appear to have a 'touristic vocation'. The end-product cultural display has been scripted ever since the Dutch orientalists viewed – and subsequently actively maintained and preserved – their new colonial territory at the start of the 20th century. Their approach resulted in the policy of active conservation of Balinese culture, the 'Balinization of Bali' (*Balisering*) as Bali's inhabitants were instructed in how to remain authentically Balinese, a premodern example of Hindu–Javanese civilization. Picard's (1995, p. 48) history of the colonization and touristification of Bali continues by noting that visiting artists and 'culture and personality' school anthropologists working on Bali at the start of the last century were producing canvases and academic studies which 'comforted' the colonial policy by selecting and preserving the artistic and ceremonial manifestations of the culture. Their preservation of Balinese culture inadvertently 'invented' (see Wagner, 1981) culture in an Escher-like style. These anthropological involutions have now imprisoned the Balinese in 'a cultural image promoted by the marketers of Bali as a tourist paradise. In as much as they are expected to display evidence of their Balinese-ness, the Balinese [now] run the risk of becoming [semiotic] signs of themselves' (Picard, 1995, p. 61).

Euro-American tourism, British colonialism and American anthropology on Montserrat are starting to produce similar effects. Montserratian heritage is increasingly commoditized and packaged to suit the tourist. In other words, Laffey's initial analyses and fears are being borne out: Montserratians are becoming signs of themselves, living Black Irish lives inculcated by alien projections (the anthropologists, the travel writers, the tourists). The island is fortunate, however, in that it has a number of historians and Afrophiles like Sir Fergus who are able to counter the off-island influences which buffet the island. It is Fergus who counters the Black Irish myth/legacy, presses for the commemoration of Montserratian historical figures, questions the colonial emblems found around the island, and guards an indigenous history of the people and the place.

On an optimistic note, Picard (1995, p. 57) writes that McKean and several other Bali scholars believe that:

> the Balinese have learnt to distinguish their cultural performances according to the audience for whom they are intended, with the consequence that the meaning of a Balinese cultural performance is not affected by its being performed for a tourist audience.

This means that in terms of the production of culture, the Balinese reserve one sphere for internal consumption and one sphere for external consumption. These spheres depend upon the nature of the audience such that the same Balinese dance can simultaneously be watched as a spectacle and enacted as a ritual. This is possible, I would suggest, only if the performers have a high degree of cultural self-confidence and self-assurance. Currently on Montserrat, the St Patrick's Day festivities are played out more for indigenous consumption than for exogenous consumption. The commoditization of St Patrick's Day festivities has not yet become dominated by guest expectations as opposed to host traditions, but there is every danger that this trajectory will develop. Montserratians have, however, moved on from Akenson's initial comment above about the need for Messenger's Hibernicism, a vision which they probably never needed nor desired to prop up their historical and cultural consciousness.

Drama, Performance and Consumption

> The West, it appears, is a place organized as a system of commodities, values, meanings, and representations, forming signs that reflect one another in a labyrinth without exits.
>
> (Mitchell, 1992, p. 300)

According to Mitchell, in his account of World Fairs, Orientalism is a concept akin to the idea of the world-as-exhibition, a part of a machinery of commerce which places everything into a system of signification. Both are handmaidens of colonialism. As Prakash (1992, p. 382) states, 'the Third World is [...] a signifier of cultural difference [...] rapidly appropriated and commodified as cultural surplus'. The Caribbean, in particular, is one of these regions which is subjected and signified by tourism. The dark fantasies surrounding orientalism and colonialism are also brought together by the Marxist post-structuralist Robert Young (1995, p. 173) whose theoretical position necessitates his comment that 'capitalism is the destroyer of signification'. By this, he (p. 173) means that the system of meaning is debased by capitalism, reduced 'to a Jakobsonian system of equivalences, to commodification through the power of money'. This *reductio ad semiotica* takes place to the detriment of both the consumer and the consumed. Critics of the influence of tourism consumption rail against the Americanization of Cuba (Schwartz, 1997, p. 75), for example, of meaningless tourist performances which have no connection with reality such as the sun dance of the aboriginal Siboney Indians which has no basis in Cuban history. Tourism has deracinated the cultures of the Caribbean – Paradise Lost 'n' Sold – resulting in homogenized heritage quays in every port, and an inauthenticity in every entertainment drama: Jamaican reggae defining a region; Trinidadian Carnival diffused through the Lesser Antilles; Greek plate-breaking; and African limbo finishing off the nightly voodoo ceremonies in Haitian hotels (see Patullo, 1996, pp. 178–198). These tourism critics take, I suggest, an anti-globalization stance, a modernist position in sympathy with sharp distinctions between indigenous and alien practices, authentic and inauthentic festivities. For them, the world is 'populated by endangered authenticities' (Clifford, 1988, p. 5).

The St Patrick's Day festivities on Montserrat are an interesting example of cultural change, one which is increasingly influenced by the tourist. They have not yet reached the point where they have been completely commoditized – a condition where 'social relationships are wholly shaped by the dictates of market exchange' (Nash, 1996, p. 24). It is still an island festivity for islander consumption. Yet the islanders' consumption patterns and consumption understandings have been shaped by an alien anthropologist and by the market forces of the tourist industry. Significantly, many of the tourists to Montserrat are Montserratians themselves who either migrated from the island during the recent volcanic natural disaster, or whose parents and grandparents left the island for employment throughout the 20th century. Every year an 'Annual Pilgrimage' is held in July/August for returning Montserratians, the 'Paradise Regained Millennium Pilgrimage' in 2000, for example. Montserratians of the Diaspora also return during the Christmas/New Year fortnight of celebrations, as well as for the St Patrick's Day week of festivities. The St Patrick's Day example of tourism consumption, then, of cultural and ethnic tourism, could be declared an example of indigenous narratives of place and people, even if the festivities are 'defined by the identification of its audience' (Abram, 1997, p. 45). Unlike on Bali, on Montserrat, the indigenous–exogenous distinction is not clear-cut; Montserratian islanders have not had to distinguish between insider and outsider festivities (cf. Crain, 1996); nor have the St Patrick's Day festivities on the island reached the stage when the participants' motivations are guided solely by the island's visitors whether visiting Montserratian or not.

According to Nash (1996, p. 24), Greenwood's Alarde festival remains the benchmark publication for examinations into the commoditization of culture. Reading Greenwood results in theoretical calibration (see Wilson, 1993; Wood, 1993; Watson and Kopachevsky, 1994; Nash, 1995; Boissevain, 1996, pp. 13–14). For me, what is significant about Greenwood's (1989, pp. 181–185) account as a point of articulation is that he revised his words and stance in an 'Epilogue' in the second edition of Valene Smith's (1989) *Hosts and Guests* edited volume. There he moderates his initial stance by first briefly situating and interpreting the Alarde in its political context of Basque nationalist expression rather than semiotic-induced anomie; and secondly, by pointing out that the 'objectification of local culture via tourism' (p. 183) can in fact stimulate rather than stultify local culture. From this, I make my point, *contra* Messenger and Greenwood, that the anthropologist's position should be more neutral and objective in their research. Unfortunately, Greenwood's revision does not sit well with the earlier sections in his chapter which remain the same. Greenwood now views the tourist cultural performances as middle-class culture dramas, pseudo-tragedies. His critics, Wood and Wilson, are thus right to take on his work: an 'ethnographic time-trap' (Wilson, 1993, p. 37) of interpretative anthropology which lacks longitudinal verification; an example of a researcher open to the ethnographic persuasions of a few political respondents but closed to the idea that his own 'cultural politics' might also be bound up in a construction of the present, that if tourism cannot be conceptualized outside of culture then nor can the culture-broker's discipline of anthropology itself.

Wood's (1993, p. 66) social construction/postmodern approach to tourism focuses upon 'the complex ways tourism enters and becomes part of an already on-going process of symbolic meaning and appropriation'. For me, anthropology is also a key determinant both *of* and *in* this process, particularly so in a world where tin miners in Bolivia fashion Carnival masks based upon article clippings (Van den Berghe, 1980), and Montserratians construct their identity and ethnicity by reading travel writers who in turn have read and drawn from the work of an American anthropologist. Both tourism and anthropology are 'dialogic constructions' (Wood, 1993, p. 67) in dialogue with local cultures; tourism – with its 'imperialist nostalgia' (Rosaldo, 1993, p. 71), i.e. 'the way the Caribbean used to be' on Montserrat – most notably, changes both the tourist self and the native self by forcing the developing world location to serve as a mirror of Western fantasies (cf. Bruner, 1991); often the natives' self changes as they are made aware of more powerful and wealthy people, such as the case of the tourist disruption of Chambri male hierarchy during initiation in Papua New Guinea (Errington and Gewertz, 1995). Anthropology collects, represents and synthesizes local cultures, comparing them directly through participant observation, or indirectly through ethnographic comparison. In both tourism and anthropology, there is the danger of dominance, misrepresentation and objectification of indigenous people and practices. The problem then, to return to Said's 'Orientalism' – equivalent to Messenger's Hibernicism, so reported and fostered by travel writers – is that the dialogue is not an equal exchange but is one which favours the sojourner.

Conclusion

This chapter has been an ethnographic consideration of the institutionalization of St Patrick's Day which became a national holiday on Montserrat in 1985 (commemoration), as well as a tourist product (celebration) – both contested and contesting consumption narratives tied to anti-colonial/nationalist discord and an anthropologically induced identity crisis on the island. The 'contest' for the commoditization of St Patrick's Day is predominantly between narratives of a place and a people constructed by the Montserrat Tourist Board, Sir Howard Fergus and Professor John Messenger. This chapter has also explored the nature of tourism and anthropology, activities which have contributed to the objectification and the commoditization of people and places in general. Both are immersed in the cultural politics of a place and a people, and are involved in an uneven 'exchange' of experience and information.

Tourism has and always will be about the consumption of signs. It is about consuming places (Urry, 1995) and peoples. Tourists, then, are like anthropologists: indeed, both tourists and anthropologists are patrons of culture. The consumption of Montserrat place and Montserratian people by tourist and indigenous selves has been shown to be especially diverse. The congeries of meanings range from the Afrocentrism of the Afrophiles to Messenger's Black Irish and 'modernistic' anthropology, from Missie Blake's emancipationary commemoration to the Montserrat Tourist Board's profitable and tolerable pub crawl and other tourist promotions, and to my own anthropology of 'anthropology' – to parody Wood's (1993, p. 68) reflexive 'development of "development"' position.

My conclusion, then, leads us to a diversity of potential consumed meanings, rather like the 'avenues of meanings' (Barthes, 1988, p. 173) available to the reader of a text. MacCannell, Patullo, Greenwood and other Modernist tourism scholars, with whom I would include Messenger, distinguish between front and back regions, authentic and inauthentic cultural performances, real Carnival versus appropriated festivities and 'jump-up' on the streets of Montserrat. These scholars lament and protest the deracination of culture, its westernization. However, the *roots* of Carnival – and culture – are more like *routes* in their history of mobility and fluidity. Carnival's history is hybrid and lies in European Catholic culture and Trinidadian mimicry exported and imported to other islands (Montserrat) and continents (where expatriate West Indians hold Carnivals in Canada and Britain). Furthermore, *contra* the traditional anthropological observed discreteness of cultural practices, and the modernist fears of homogenization, contemporary anthropologists of the 'global cultural economy' such as Appadurai (1990) ('mediascapes' and 'ethnoscapes') and Hannerz (1996) ('transnational connections') are finding fluidity and diffusion, and disjuncture and difference in what they consider to be a new dynamics of indigenization.

From 1971 (historical discovery) to 1985 (national institutional-ization) and 1993/5 (anthropological investigation), St Patrick's Day has been propelled forwards to become a key feature of the annual cycle of events on Montserrat, for local and returning Montserratians, and (residential) tourists. Fergus and other Afrophiles seek to turn St Patrick's Day into an anchor event in the deep history of the island. As this chapter has noted, there is a danger that much of the tension between tourist celebration and local commemoration will eventually be lost in favour of the former, leaving behind an entertaining and humorous event. In the 1920s, the inhabitants of the Duke of York islands in Papua New Guinea instituted a national commemoration of Reverend George Brown's arrival in 1875. As Errington and Gewertz (1995, p. 78) lament, this serious celebration of the arrival of Christianity to the islanders has now become a humorous pastiche, a Jubilee re-enactment with 'auto-orientalized' views of native life. St Patrick's Day has definitely lost its 'original' celebration of Christianity's arrival and colonization of the island. Presently, the meaning of this national holiday is torn between the cultivation of Irish symbols and emblems on Montserrat as a celebration of some 'staged [Irish] authenticity' (cf. MacCannell, 1989, pp. 98–99), and an ironic resistance of these colonial emblems – ironic in the sense that Ireland is usually associated with anti-colonialism. The future, one can only hope, will not be one of a continued caricaturization of Montserrat in which the words of Solomon and Messenger are internalized into a Montserratian 'auto-orientalized view' (Errington and Gewertz, 1995, p. 78) which eventually becomes an accurate self-representation.

References

Abram, S. (1997) Performing for tourists in rural France. In: Abram, S., Waldren, J. and Macleod, D. (eds) *Tourists and Tourism: Identifying with People and Places.* Berghahn, Oxford, UK. pp. 29–50.
Akenson, D. (1997) *If the Irish Ran the World: Montserrat, 1630–1730.* McGill-Queen's University Press, London.

Anonymous (undated) Montserrat: no elevator, Doris Day, 'Montserrat – the Emerald Isle. *Sunday San Juan Star*, pp. 1–4, Caribbean Travel Section, no other references available.

Anonymous (1995a) Good manners. Editorial. *The Montserrat Reporter* XI(11), 17 March, p. 4.

Anonymous (1995b) St. Patrick's Day celebrations flop. *The Montserrat Reporter* XI(12), 24 March, front and back pages.

Appadurai, A. (1990) Disjuncture and difference in the global cultural economy. In: Featherstone, M. (ed.) *Global Culture: Nationalism, Globalization and Modernity*. Sage Publications, London, pp. 295–310.

Barthes, R. (1988) Textual analysis: Poe's 'Valdemar'. In: Lodge, D. (ed.) *Modern Criticism and Theory – A Reader*. Longman, London, pp. 172–195.

Boissevain, J. (1996) Introduction. In: Boissevain, J. (ed.) *Coping with Tourists: European Reactions to Mass Tourism*. Berghahn, Oxford, UK, pp. 1–26.

Bruner, E. (1991) The transformation of self in tourism. *Annals of Tourism Research* 18, 238–250.

Clifford, J. (1988) *The Predicament of Culture: Twentieth Century Ethnography, Literature and Art*. Harvard University Press, Cambridge, Massachusetts.

Crain, M. (1996) Contested territories: the politics of touristic development at the shrine of El Rocio in Southwestern Andalusia. In: Boissevain, J. (ed.) *Coping with Tourists: European Reactions to Mass Tourism*. Berghahn, Oxford, pp. 27–55.

English, T. (1930) Records of Montserrat. Unpublished manuscript, Montserrat Public Library.

Errington, F. and Gewertz, D. (1995) *Articulating Change in the 'Last Unknown'*. Westview Press, Oxford.

Fallon, J. (1993) 'The Black Irish', findings of the Florida Unity Conference Group about Montserrat's Irish–African connection. *Irish Echo*, 27 July–3 August, p. 18.

Fergus, H. (1992) *Montserrat – Emerald Isle of the Caribbean*. Macmillan Caribbean Guides, London.

Fergus, H. (1993) St. Patrick's Day – the Montserratian concept. *The Official St. Patrick's Day Programme 1993*, p. 4

Fergus, H. (1994) *Montserrat: History of a Caribbean Colony*. Macmillan Caribbean, London.

Greenwood, D. (1977) Culture by the pound: an anthropological perspective on tourism as cultural commoditization. In: Smith, V. (ed.) *Host and Guests: the Anthropology of Tourism*. University of Pennsylvania Press, Philadelphia, Pennsylvania, pp. 129–138.

Greenwood, D. (1989) Culture by the pound: an anthropological perspective on tourism as cultural commoditization. In: Smith, V. (ed.) *Host and Guests: the Anthropology of Tourism*, 2nd edn. University of Pennsylvania Press, Philadelphia, Pennsylvania, pp. 171–185.

Hanna, W. (1972) Bali in the seventies. Part I: cultural tourism. *American Universities Field Staff Reports, South-east Asia Series* 20, 1–7.

Hannerz, U. (1996) *Transnational Connections: Culture, People, Places*. Routledge, London.

Hobsbawm, E. and Ranger, T. (eds) (1983) *The Invention of Tradition*. Cambridge University Press, Cambridge, UK.

James, G. (ed.) (1995) *The Official St. Patrick's Day Programme 1995*. George James Publishing, Montserrat.

Laffey, S. (1995) Representing Paradise: Euro-American Desires and Cultural Understandings in Touristic Images of Montserrat, West Indies. MA Anthropology Thesis, Texas University, Austin.

Leach, E. (1984) Glimpses of the unmentionable in the history of British social anthropology. *Annual Review of Anthropology* 13, 1–23.

MacCannell, D. (1989) *The Tourist – A New Theory of the Leisure Class*. Schocken Books Inc., New York.

MacCannell, D. (1992) *Empty Meeting Grounds: the Tourist Papers*. Routledge, New York.

McCrone, D., Morris, A. and Kiely, R. (1995) *Scotland – the Brand: the Making of Scottish Heritage*. Edinburgh University Press, Edinburgh.

McKean, P. (1973) Cultural Involution: Tourists, Balinese, and the Process of Modernization in an Anthropological Perspective. PhD dissertation, Brown University.

Messenger, J. (1967) 'The Black Irish' of Montserrat. *Eire-Ireland* II(1), 27–40.

Messenger, J. (1973) African retentions in Montserrat. *African Arts* 6(4), 54–57.

Messenger, J. (1975) Montserrat: the most distinctively Irish settlement in the new world. *Ethnicity* 2, 281–303.

Messenger, J. (1994) St. Patrick's Day in 'The Other Emerald Isle'. *Eire-Ireland* Spring, 12–23.

Mitchell, T. (1992) Orientalism and the exhibitionary order. In: Dirks, N. (ed.) *Colonialism and Culture*. University of Michigan Press, Ann Arbor, Michigan, pp. 289–317.

Montserrat Department of Tourism (1993) *Holiday Montserrat – The Way The Caribbean Used To Be: an Official Tourist Guide of the Montserrat Department of Tourism 1993/94*. West Indies Publishing Ltd, St John's, Antigua.

Mullin, M. (1992) *Africa in America: Slave Acculturation and Resistance in the American South and the British Caribbean, 1736–1831*. University of Illinois Press, Chicago.

Nash, D. (1989) Tourism as a form of Imperialism. In: Smith, V. (ed.) *Host and Guests: the Anthropology of Tourism*, 2nd edn. University of Pennsylvania Press, Philadelphia, Pennsylvania, pp. 37–54.

Nash, D. (1995) Prospects for tourism study in anthropology. In: Shore, C. and Ahmed, A. (eds) *The Future of Anthropology: Its Relevance to the Contemporary World*. The Athlone Press, London, pp. 179–202.

Nash, D. (1996) *Anthropology of Tourism*. Pergamon, Oxford, UK.

Patullo, P. (1996) *Last Resorts: the Cost of Tourism in the Caribbean*. Cassell, London.

Picard, M. (1995) Cultural heritage and tourist capital: cultural tourism in Bali. In: Lanfant, M., Allcock, J. and Bruner, E. (eds) *International Tourism: Identity and Change*. Sage Publications Ltd, London, pp. 44–66.

Prakash, G. (1992) Writing post-orientalist histories of the third world: Indian historiography is good to think. In: Dirks, N. (ed.) *Colonialism and Culture*. University of Michigan Press, Ann Arbor, , Michigan, pp. 353–390.

Rosaldo, R. (1993) *Culture and Truth: the Remakings of Social Analysis*. Routledge, London.

Said, E. (1991) *Orientalism*. Penguin, London.

Schwartz, R. (1997) *Pleasure Island: Tourism and Temptation in Cuba*. University of Nebraska Press, London.

Showalter, E. (1997) *Hystories: Hysterical Epidemics and Modern Culture*. Picador, London.

Skinner, J. (1997) Impressions of Montserrat: a Partial Account of Contesting Realities on a British Dependent Territory. PhD dissertation, University of St Andrews, UK.

Skinner, J. (2001) Tourism, heritage and community. In: Skinner, J., Di Domenico, C., Law, A. and Smith, M. (eds) *Scotland's Boundaries and Identities in the New Millennium*. University of Abertay Press, UK, pp. 163–169.

Smith, V. (1989) Preface. In: Smith, V. (ed.) *Host and Guests: the Anthropology of Tourism*, 2nd edn. University of Pennsylvania Press, Philadelphia, Pennsylvania, pp. ix–xi.

Solomon, A. (1984) Montserrat – a wee bit o' Ireland in the Caribbean. *Travel-Holiday* October, 44–47.

Strong, V. (1981) Montserrat – the Emerald Isle. *Virgin Islander* June, 41–43.

Sylvan, R. (1994) Fantasy island – Montserrat has Irish roots. *The Montserrat News* IV(30), 11 November, p. 15; reported from *The Miami Herald*.

Urry, J. (1995) *Consuming Places*. Routledge, London.

Van den Berghe, P. (1980) Tourism as ethnic relations: a case study of Cuzco, Peru. *Ethnic and Racial Studies* 3, 375–392.

Wagner, R. (1981) *The Invention of Culture*. The University of Chicago Press, London.

Watson, G. and Kopachevsky, J. (1994) Interpretations of tourism as commodity. *Annals of Tourism Research* 21, 115–137.

Wilson, D. (1993) Time and tides in the anthropology of tourism. In: Hitchcock, M., King, V. and Parnwell, M. (eds) *Tourism in South-east Asia*. Routledge, London, pp. 32–47.

Wood, R. (1993) Tourism, culture and the sociology of development In: Hitchcock, M., King, V. and Parnwell, M. (eds) *Tourism in South-East Asia*. Routledge, London, pp. 48–70.

Young, R. (1995) *Colonial Desire: Hybridity in Theory, Culture and Race*. Routledge, London.

Selling Celtic Cornwall: Changing Markets and Meanings?

14

Amy Hale

St Petersburg College, Florida, USA

Cornwall may be one of the most complex and misunderstood regions of the UK. It is the domestic holiday capital of Britain, and as such has a variety of 'images' from which to draw in order to attract different and segmented markets. In the popular imagination, Cornwall is a land of sun, sea, surf and caravan parks, and it is predominantly these features which have drawn British tourists to Cornwall since the rise of the seaside holiday in the 1950s. For the more upscale, the image may include second or holiday homes in attractive hamlets. Young visitors to Newquay, on Cornwall's north coast, come for the surfing and the nightlife. The amazing success of the Eden Project, essentially a plant-based theme park set in former china clay pits in St Austell, has helped to promote Cornwall as a destination for garden enthusiasts. Of course, Cornwall is also the land of King Arthur, megalithic monuments, Iron Age hillforts and ancient holy wells, all of which appeal to the Celtic enthusiast for one reason or another. Increasingly, economic strategists in Cornwall have been promoting the quite striking remains of Cornwall's industrial past, particularly the stacks of the tin and copper mines of the mid-Cornwall area around Redruth and Camborne, known as the Great Flat Load. The importance of this area can be judged by the fact that in early 2005, the UK government formally nominated areas of Cornwall and also parts of east Devon as a UNESCO World Heritage Site (http://www.cornish-mining.org.uk/).

Aside from these tourist 'packages' listed above, there are other Cornwalls still. There is a hunter's Cornwall, a sailor's Cornwall, a literary Cornwall, an art lover's Cornwall. All of these exist against a backdrop of changing internal and external perceptions of Cornwall's

©CAB International 2006. *Tourism Consumption and Representation: Narratives of Place and Self* (eds K. Meethan, A. Anderson and S. Miles)

ethnic status within the UK, and at a time when that ethnicity is becoming central to how Cornwall is marketed. A great deal has been written about how Cornwall has been constructed as a tourist destination. Much of the literature has been quite critical, claiming in essence that tourism, even 'cultural' or 'heritage' tourism, continually short-changes the Cornish, misrepresents Cornish culture and is an economic disservice to the Cornish economy (Deacon *et al.*, 1988; Williams, 1993, pp. 159–163).

In the past 10 years, heritage and tourism operators have worked to integrate Cornish ethnicity into their attractions and their goods. Often this is done with a broader reference to Cornwall's Celtic past. What constitutes Cornwall's Celtic past (and Celtic present) has been contested from both inside and outside the territory. Nevertheless, what is certain is that as discourses concerning Cornish ethnicity have been articulated over the past 150 years, they have often been set within the emerging construction of Celtic ethnicity (see Hale, 1997). Of course, the contemporary logic behind this strategy is to gain economic, social and perhaps political benefits by promoting to visitors a sense of Cornish difference. However, what is also happening is that themed attractions which previously would not have been considered representative of 'Celtic' Cornwall are now able to hop on the Celtic bandwagon. As a result, the very nature of how Celtic Cornwall is perceived is changing.

Within the UK, Celtic revivals have occurred simultaneously both inside and outside Celtic regions. Within the Celtic regions, the revival takes the form of cultural and socio-political movements related to the discourses of ethnicity and identity. Outside the Celtic regions, interest in Celtic matters tends to be spiritually and aesthetically motivated. Examples of this can be found in the peaks of esoteric Celtic spirituality which developed in England and peaked during the 1920s, 1960s and presently. These can include Neo-Paganism, Wicca, Neo-Druidism and Celtic Christianity (see Bowman, 1996). There may be a political dimension to the Celtic revivals outside of the Celtic territories as well. As Malcolm Chapman has argued, people who embrace and identify with Celtic culture, either spiritually or in a broader lifestyle sense such as those New Age travellers who often try to emulate premodern and 'Celtic' ways of living, often have a political sense which is predominantly oppositional in nature, and are characterized by left wing and green concerns (Chapman, 1992). Naturally, all of the above statements are generalizations.

The Celtic craze which began in the mid-1990s has been unprecedented in scope and scale, with more people having access to more types of 'Celtic' goods and materials than ever before. Simply put, mass marketing, availability and better links between artists and consumers have made Celtic books and goods more accessible in an international marketplace. Furthermore, placed in the context of globalization and the mainstreaming of identity politics, the effects of the most recent Celtic revival have also been more tangible in terms of political devolution in Scotland and Wales, and economic regeneration strategies based on culture such as those which have been so successful in Ireland.

There is no doubt that Cornwall's 'Celticity' is being asserted more vigorously than at any time in the past. There is a much greater general interest in Cornwall's Celtic 'heritage', and also in promoting and understanding Cornwall's persisting cultural difference. There have been strategic policy advantages in adopting this approach. In 2000, after a long campaign, Cornwall's differences from Devon, both cultural and in terms of economic disparity, allowed for the two regions finally to be statistically separated, allowing Cornwall deservedly to achieve Objective One status from the European Union. Objective One is one of the most significant regeneration programmes given to the most underperforming regions of the European Union. During the debates leading up to this statistical separation from Devon and in the time period just after Objective One status was gained, a new round of strategy building and policy making emerged in Cornwall which promoted Cornwall's cultural and ethnic differences as an economic asset in a much more systematic and positive way than had previously occurred. Most often, this difference was expressed under somewhat essentialist discourses relating to 'Celticity', and was justified by recourse to the Cornish language, religion, history and expressive behaviour (see Hale, 2002).

However, in Cornwall, contextualizing this 'Celticity' is still in a sense quite murky as the 'Celtic heritage' of Cornwall continues to carry a variety of meanings to people both inside and outside the territory. This is despite a more widespread practice within Cornwall understanding Celtic as a term that is somehow descriptive of Cornish ethnicity and particular expressions or demonstrations of that ethnicity. There is a wide range of products and services in Cornwall that are being marketed as 'Celtic'. The observation has been made many times that Celtic, like sex, sells. However, in Cornwall, marking or labelling something as 'Celtic' cannot be done in a completely arbitrary manner. It must have a meaning (or meanings) for specific audiences which are tacitly accepted.

Celtic Goods and Services

The range of products in Cornwall which can even be tangentially described as 'Celtic' is quite astonishing. They can make some sort of visual reference to 'Celtic' tradition through knotwork designs, or they can refer to the linguistic category of Celtic by some use of the Cornish language. Although it is possible that many Celtic goods were at one time produced exclusively or primarily for the tourist market, that is no longer the case, as people have a range of reasons for purchasing these products.

Some items will appeal to the general Celtic enthusiast, who can fall into several categories. For instance, this person may be someone who is interested in Celtic spirituality in some way or is involved in Cornish cultural activism. They may be a visitor, or they may be a Cornish native. These items include the very popular range of St Justin Celtic knotwork jewellery, Celtic clocks, moulded miniature versions of Cornish standing crosses with knotwork on them, T-shirts, flasks, wall-hangings, calendars, all of which are produced as well as sold in Cornwall. With these products, the range of buyers is greater and the meanings here are more negotiable. Someone wearing a Celtic knotwork brooch could be either a Methodist from mid-Cornwall celebrating her Cornish heritage, or a Wiccan from Suffolk visiting Cornish megalithic monuments or holy wells on a religious pilgrimage, or a woman from Wisconsin who is descended from Cornish miners. In any case, the interpretation of the piece and the meanings ascribed may be radically different and possibly conflicting.

Some products or services which employ a 'Celtic' marketing strategy are appealing much more to sympathy with specifically Cornish ethnicity, and most often will use the Cornish language as their marker of 'Celticity'. Examples include Cornish language mugs, tea towels, postcards and businesses using 'Kernow' (the Cornish language name for Cornwall) such as *Kernow Cabs* in St Austell. Partially as a result of pressure from Cornish nationalists, English Heritage has adopted a token use of the Cornish language on the main interpretive signs at their Cornish sites. A limited number of Cornish pubs, such as the *Driftwood Spars* in St Agnes, also use some Cornish in their welcome signs and internally for decorative purposes. Although these gestures can be interpreted as politically motivated, there is also an economic rationale behind this strategy, one which is becoming more central to Cornwall's economic development. Studies from the Highlands and Islands have indicated that visitors will often enjoy seeing another language in use, even if they do not understand it, because it enhances the experience of cultural difference that they expect and seek out while on holiday (Pedersen, 2000). Indicating this 'difference' through the Cornish language has become more important in recent years in marketing Cornwall as a place with a distinctive cultural identity. As a result, the use of Cornish on places and products has an external, as well as an internal value (Cornwall Enterprise, 2000).

Some companies will simply use the word 'Celtic' in their titles or on their products, with the hopes that the reference to a Cornish origin will be clear. Some such as *The Celtic Wool Shop* and *Celtic Legends* in Tintagel are obviously playing off of that village's association with King Arthur, but perhaps in the case of 'Celtic Wool' also appealing to associations of 'Celtic' with goods which are handcrafted, also enforcing notions of 'traditional' Celtic industry (see Hale and Thornton, 2000). St Austell Brewery's Celtic Ale which uses the slogan 'From the Land of Legend' identifies itself as a Cornish product, but also draws on associations of Celtic peoples, and Cornwall itself perhaps being somehow more 'legendary' and 'other-worldly'. In these cases, there is a secondary semantic interpretation of 'Celticity' which reinforces beliefs about certain essentialist qualities of what a Celtic product should be or represent. Other choices of the word Celtic for marketing purposes are not nearly so deep and multi-faceted. Some businesses clearly use 'Celtic' primarily to identify themselves as Cornish or Cornish-based businesses, such as Celtic Engineering Services (saw sharpening and repair), Celtic Colours Screen Printing, Celtic Contracting Services, Celtic Fencing and Celtic Glass and Glazing. Here the product or service has no other association with established constructions of 'Celticity' aside from location or possibly ethnicity.

A number of Celtic items in Cornwall are marketed specifically for a youth or subcultural market. Some products are made specifically for surfers, such as Celtic surfboards which feature knotwork designs, neo-tribal jewellery, both permanent and henna tattoos which sometimes blend Maori and Celtic designs, and surfing boots called 'Celtic', which are manufactured in Cornwall. There is also a line of surfing gear which features the Cornish language on fleeces, along with bilingual washing instructions. As Alan Kent has shown, there is a persistent connection between 'Celtic' and youth or subculture in Britain (Kent, 2001). In Cornwall, this may be most evident within surfing culture. Celtic goods for surfers may reinforce both the associations of 'Celtic' with 'nature' or perhaps even Celtic Atlantic landscapes near the ocean, and also with notions of 'tribalism'. Kent also notes how Celtic surfing goods reinforce 'Cornishness' for young surfers, and how surf style in itself is beginning to mark young people outside Cornwall as 'Cornish' (Kent, 2001).

Celtic Tourism

That there are multiple readings and markets for Celtic goods and Celticity in general in Cornwall is certainly not a phenomenon limited to the Duchy; surely it happens in all the Celtic territories. In fact, multiple interpretations are somewhat to be expected. However, because Cornwall's 'Celticity' is a contentious issue for so many reasons, not the least of which politically, 'Celtic' as a marketing strategy is not always employed where perhaps you would most expect it. Ever since the early days of the Great Western Railway, Cornwall's Celtic 'difference' has been employed as a selling point – a 'home away from home' where well-off English tourists could literally experience the exotic without having to experience the discomfort of actually travelling abroad (Payton and Thornton, 1995). However, there is a distinction (if only semantic) between selling 'Cornish difference' and promoting the 'exotic Celticism' of Cornwall and the Cornish, where 'Celtic' becomes equated with primitive and superstitious.

It is rather interesting that the Cornwall Tourist Board has not adopted a cohesive Celtic tourism strategy even though they acknowledge that it may be profitable to do so. The main reason is that because the term 'Celtic' has had so many contested meanings in itself, they have been afraid to exploit the term. The root of this concern comes from two sources. The first is the broader academic debate over what 'Celtic' actually means. Different disciplines have somewhat different criteria for defining Celtic cultures (Sims-Williams, 1998). Many British archaeologists today do not believe that the Iron Age peoples of Britain and Ireland were actually known as Celts, although they shared some material, social and cultural similarities with named Celtic populations on the continent. For that reason, many archaeologists are wary of the term 'Celtic' altogether in describing material remains. On advice from the Cornwall Archaeological Unit, the Tourist Board became concerned about promoting certain sites to tourists as 'Celtic'; how can they label Iron Age settlements and even later medieval sites as 'Celtic' if there were never Celts there.

The other area of disquiet surrounds the other defining measure of 'Celticity'; the Cornish language. Although promoting contemporary manifestations of Celticity (such as language classes or traditional Cornish music events) was another avenue the Tourist Board could have chosen, the infighting surrounding different forms of revived Cornish have made it difficult even to use Cornish to any significant degree on their literature because of the fear of complaints from various factions.

Then, there are the difficulties of marketing Celtic Cornwall as a tourist product, especially when that very 'Celticity' is an assertion of persisting ethnic and cultural difference from England. As previously stated, the bulk of tourists to Cornwall every year are from the rest of the UK. Research shows that many visitors return because of pleasant memories of holidays taken in Cornwall as children (Cornwall Tourist Board, 2000). In short, Cornwall is a traditional holiday destination for much of Britain. So, how would one manage a strategy promoting cultural difference from England when much of England thinks of Cornwall as, in a sense, home? The result could be alienating to say the least.

However, there is a great demand for 'Celtic' tourist destinations from people from the European continent and the USA. One solution is for Cornwall to devise multiple marketing strategies as they have done in Scotland. The film *Braveheart* alone resulted in an increase of interest in overseas tourism, but tourism officials in Scotland found that the reasons that these visitors were interested in Scotland were quite different from those of visitors from the UK. Overseas visitors were interested in Scottish history, landscape and culture, while only three in ten UK visitors were motivated by those features (*The Times*, 5 October 1995). This resulted in two somewhat opposing advertising campaigns: one for overseas, specifically for France and Germany, promoting Scottish cultural difference and a unique history; the other for the rest of the UK promoting the arts, shopping and watersports. This multi-streamed approach could be a potentially successful strategy for Cornwall. However, because much of Cornwall's overseas tourism marketing is actually funded jointly with the neighbouring county of Devon, they often employ a unified strategy which does not include promoting Celtic difference to any great degree.

There are some in Britain who do appreciate Cornwall's Celticity, both past and present, but this group also presents a problem for tourism officials. People who are interested in Celtic spirituality, either Neo-Pagans or people with an interest in Celtic Christianity, will often visit Cornwall as a site of pilgrimage. In 1994, John Lowerson identified Cornwall as a place of pilgrimage for many English 'Celtophiles', citing Malcolm Chapman's analysis of the persistent attraction to Celtic 'otherness', particularly as it has been constructed as mystical, supernatural and spiritual (Lowerson, 1994, p. 128; see also Chapman, 1992). In addition, there is a connection with the continuing popular belief that megalithic monuments such as those found in abundance in Cornwall were part of a Celtic mystery tradition. Lowerson writes of the current interest among those interested in Celtic spirituality in visiting holy wells, standing stones and other megalithic monuments, saint's ways and stone crosses (Lowerson, 1994, p. 134). He also notes Cornwall's attraction as a Celtic tourist destination:

> In the spectrum of modern Celticism, Cornwall has come almost to represent a British Tibet; distant, valued by others and threatened by an occupying territory ... It might serve to describe the impact of the neo-Celtic tourist on Cornwall as it tries to cope with an identity some of its residents have helped to create and a spiritual hunger which threatens its ascribed isolation.
>
> (Lowerson, 1994, p. 135)

Clearly not everyone is comfortable with this phenomenon, and not everyone wants to exploit it. First, the New Age interpretation of Celtic Cornwall has been rejected by some as an imposition of a romantic ideal generated by 'outsiders' which is at odds with native constructions of Cornwall's difference which are anything but mystical and other-worldly (Deacon, 1997, p. 21). Another problem is a lack of understanding about precisely who these visitors are and how to assess their impact at the sites they visit. This is beginning to change, however, as bodies such as the Cornwall Archaeological Unit and English Heritage are working with local and national Pagan groups to evaluate the stress caused by visitors at certain sites, and consider how best they can be maintained. Substantial research on spiritual or religious tourism in Cornwall has not yet been conducted, but this is not unusual as this is often an under-researched area in tourism studies. Boris Vukoni'c notes that while religion is a persistent motivating factor in world tourism, it is not often the focus of sustained research, except perhaps in obvious areas such as Jerusalem or the Vatican (Vukoni'c, 1996, p. 55).

Many 'Celtic pilgrims' to Cornwall are viewed unfavourably by the general public, councillors and also possibly the tourist industry, and this may be a reason why they are not more actively sought after. There is a perception that many of these spiritual visitors are New Age travellers, and therefore undesirable due to a perceived lack of disposable income, as well as a fear in the community that they may disturb or destroy ancient sites (Earle *et al.*, 1994, pp. 130–131). It is true that New Age travellers do migrate to Cornwall during certain times of the year, and that many of them do have an interest in Celtic cultures and in Pagan spirituality. However, as Lowerson notes, the interests of New Age travellers 'offer(s) an odd compatibility with contemporary urban, middle-class lifestyles' (Lowerson, 1994, p. 131). In fact, probably the majority of spiritual tourists in Cornwall are not New Age travellers – they could be neo-Druid university students from France, Pagans from Atlanta or Anglicans from London. Importantly, Lowerson also notes that this type of spiritual tourism often depends on relative affluence, which may go against conventional perceptions of the purchasing power of these particular spiritual tourists. Celtic Christians are another growing market within Cornish tourism. Cornwall's legacy of saints is of particular interest to this group, and their lives and holy sites often form the basis for pilgrimage routes. Nevertheless, there is an argument that, like Paganism, contemporary Celtic Christianity has it roots in Anglican reform, and does not reflect any form of Christianity which was or is practised by Celtic peoples.

An interesting case study for Celtic-based spiritual tourism is the total solar eclipse which took place on 11 August 1999 and the types of visitors it drew. This event may have been the single biggest disaster in the marketing of Cornwall. The initial estimates of visitors who would come to Cornwall to witness this event were so high that Cornish officials panicked about clogged roads, water and sewage shortages and a lack of food. Instead of an event to be marketed internationally, it was turned into a crisis by the Cornwall County Coucil who hired a retired military officer to plan Cornwall's response. Nevertheless, before all of the bad publicity hit, concert and event promoters invested in music festivals that were supposed to be the most spectacular events of the

20th century. When the frightened crowds opted to watch the eclipse on television, a score of local, national and international promoters and vendors lost everything.

The 1999 solar eclipse was a missed opportunity in so many ways, but one angle was the potential for an influx of spiritual tourism motivated in part by the belief that people wanted to witness this event in a Celtic place, and have a 'Celtic' experience. People did come for this reason, but not as many as anticipated, and a number of spiritually based festivals had to shut down half way through due to lack of funds. Newspapers and websites promoted the special significance of this event to Pagans, many of whom came from throughout Britain and beyond to festivals and organized rituals at a number of megalithic sites in Cornwall, most notably at Boscawen Un, the Men an Tol in west Cornwall and the Hurlers on Bodmin Moor. There is no doubt that the particular spiritual interest in this event was intimately linked to perceptions of Cornwall's 'Celticity', which provided an added impetus for people to make the pilgrimage. There was a set of esoteric, almost millennial beliefs linked with the Cornish eclipse worldwide that claimed that the time and place of this eclipse was so significant that it would herald the second reign of King Arthur (Mason, 1999; www.ping.be/the-dba/eclip/Pages/11–11.html). As might be expected, most of this marketing was 'underground', on websites or in speciality publications. Local councillors did not want to promote this angle too heavily for fear that less savoury types of people might come to visit.

However, there were some companies and individuals who were aware of this market and attempted to capitalize on it. St Justin, for instance, designed a number of Celtic/Eclipse motif items. 'Celtic Eclipse' T-shirts were sold at the Royal Institution of Cornwall gift shop, among other places. Special postcards were printed linking the eclipse with ancient monuments, and were visually implicated as Celtic with knotwork. Still, eclipse organizers led by the County Council clearly did not promote this aspect. In fact, early on, several officials in the press denounced the possible proliferation of 'hippies and weirdos' who would come for this spiritual event.

There is one kind of 'Celtic' tourism which seems less controversial, and is embraced as the 'right' kind of Celtic tourism by officials. This is the increasing trend in family research and heritage holidays, particularly from North America and Australia. Many visitors come to Cornwall each year to peruse the County Records Office, the Cornwall Family History Society and various libraries for genealogical purposes. Although this may not overtly seem to be a form of Celtic tourism, some of these visitors are increasingly seeing themselves as part of a wider 'Celtic diaspora'. Some Cornish Americans or Cornish Australians become quite involved in pan-Celtic activities at home, such as organizing or participating in Celtic festivals. Many of them have a great interest in Celtic revivalist activities in Cornwall, such as the Cornish Gorseth (an annual ceremony held in the Cornish language which honours Cornish achievement) and the Cornish language. While visiting Cornwall, they provide a market for 'Celtic' goods such as tartans and jewellery. In fact, many of these goods have an export market as well. Cornovi Creations, who markets the most popular form of Cornish tartan, does a reasonable trade exporting Cornish kilts for weddings all over the world, and St Justin Pewter visits major gift trade shows in North America.

Yet the Cornish diaspora is being targeted as the primary market for Cornwall's industrial heritage as well. The Cornish diaspora, particularly those from the USA, has become more politicized in the past 15 years, and have shifted their interests from solely genealogical pursuits to taking an interest in the economic and cultural well-being of modern Cornwall. Initially many Cornish descendants were interested in Cornwall's industrial remains because so many Cornish were descended from rock miners. However, greater communication with Cornish activists, particularly Gorseth members who foster connections with the diaspora through Cornish societies internationally to promote Cornish causes, have increased their interest in Cornwall beyond genealogy related to mining. As a result, Cornish Americans in particular have developed more of an understanding of distinctively Cornish ethnicity, instead of considering the Cornish to be English, and they are taking an interest in a range of topics once under the rubric of Celtic Cornwall, including language, Celtic dance and music events, and the Gorseth ceremony which inducts a number of international members each year. This has created a conflation of what used to be two rather separate interests in this emerging market, as the formerly 'constructed as premodern' Celt meets industry in Cornwall.

As yet, however, although the market for the 'industrial Celt' exists for Cornwall, it is nascent and not yet fully realized as such by strategists, and for the most part iconography and images of the two Cornwalls, Celtic and industrial, remain separate. If Cornwall is successful in its bid to have the mining regions recognized as a UNESCO World Heritage Site, it will be interesting to observe to what degree images and signifiers of Celtic Cornwall, such as the Cornish language, are integrated with the tourist marketing of industrial sites, as even the tourist phenomenon the Eden Project has tipped its hat to Celtic Cornwall. This plant-based attraction aspires to merge science and art through fostering a greater understanding of how plants are used by people all over the planet. The attraction has been criticized for not featuring enough culturally Cornish content. However, it has worked to rectify this by offering occasional Cornish language classes to staff members and interested visitors, and by programming Cornish language, dance and music events. On 19 August 2001 Eden hosted the

Forbidden Fruits Festival, a sort of pan-Celtic dance and music event featuring traditional Cornish and Breton acts. Although a Cornish–English bilingual Eden website is probably not just around the corner, Eden programmers are recognizing that there is at least a political motivation for incorporating some aspects of Cornish Celticity into their attraction.

Conclusions

Clearly the markets for Celtic goods and tourism in Cornwall are varied and have the potential to expand. Joep Leerssen has commented that a study which reduces Celticism and Celtic identities to a result of the dynamics of polar oppositions such as centre–periphery, self–other or colonized–colonizer relationships is neglecting the intricate responses that people have to history and the overall struggle to self-define (Leerssen, 1996, p. 17). The multiple Celtic identities within Cornwall exemplify these intricacies, especially as they are currently developing in new directions away from polarized expressions of exotic otherness to include vigorous images of modernity and industrialism that have been previously rejected by Celtic revivalists and other Celtic enthusiasts. The challenge for those marketing Celtic Cornwall will be to present a focused and uncluttered image of Cornwall to a variety of markets as Cornwall continues to shape and refine its overall brand image.

References

Bowman, M. (1996) Cardiac Celts: images of the Celts in paganism. In: Harvey, G. and Hardman, C. (eds) *Paganism Today*. Thorsons, London, pp. 242–251.

Chapman, M. (1992) *The Celts: the Construction of a Myth*. Macmillan, London.

Cornwall Enterprise (2000) *A Framework Strategy for Tourism in Cornwall: Delivering Distinctive Difference*. Cornwall Enterprise, Truro, UK.

Deacon, B. (1997) 'The hollow jarring of the distant steam engines': images of Cornwall between West Barbary and the delectable Duchy. In: Westland, E. (ed.) *Cornwall: Cultural Constructions of Place*. Patten Press, Penzance, UK, pp. 7–24.

Deacon, B., George, A. and Perry, R. (1988) *Cornwall at the Crossroads*. Cornwall Economic and Research Group, Redruth, UK.

Earle, F., Dearling, A., Whittle, H., Glasse, R. and 'Gubby' (1994) *A Time to Travel?: an Introduction to Britain's Newest Travellers*. Enabler Publications, Lyme Regis, UK.

Hale, A. (1997) Rethinking Celtic Cornwall: an ethnographic approach. In: Payton, P. (ed.) *Cornish Studies 5*. University of Exeter Press, Exeter, UK, pp. 85–89.

Hale, A. (2002) Creating a Cornish brand: discourses of traditionality in Cornish economic regeneration strategies. In: Kockel, U. (ed.) *Culture and Economy: Contemporary Perspectives*. Ashgate, London, pp. 164–170.

Hale, A. and Thornton, S. (2000) Pagans, pipers and politicos: constructions of Celtic in a festival context. In: Hale, A. and Payton, P. (eds) *New Directions in Celtic Studies*. University of Exeter Press, Exeter, UK, pp. 97–107.

Kent, A.M. (2001) Celtic Nirvanas: constructions of 'Celtic' in contemporary British youth culture. In: Harvey, D.C., Jones, R., McInroy, N. and Milligan, C. (eds) *Celtic Geographies*. Routledge, London, pp. 208–228.

Leerssen, J. (1996) Celticism. In: Brown, T. (ed.) *Celticism*. Rodopi, Amsterdam, pp. 1–20.

Lowerson, J. (1994) Celtic tourism: some recent magnets. In: Payton, P. (ed.) *Cornish Studies: Two*. University of Exeter Press, Exeter, UK, pp. 128–137.

Mason, J.E. (1999) Solar Eclipse 1999 – Final Quest for the Holy Grail. www.greatdreams.com/eclipse.htm

Payton, P. and Thornton, P. (1995) The Great Western Railway and the Cornish Celtic revival. In: Payton, P. (ed.) *Cornish Studies, Three*. University of Exeter Press, Exeter, UK, pp. 83–103.

Pedersen, R. (2000) The Gaelic economy. In: Hale, A. and Payton, P. (eds) *New Directions in Celtic Studies*. University of Exeter Press, Exeter, UK, pp. 152–166.

Scottish Tourism Hit (1995) *The Times* (London). 5 October 1995.

Sims-Williams, P. (1998) Celtomania or Celtoscepticism? *Cambrian Medieval Celtic Studies* 36, 1–35.

Vukoni'c, B. (1996) *Tourism and Religion*. Pergammon, Oxford, UK.

Williams, M. (1993) Housing the Cornish. In: Payton, P. (ed.) *Cornwall Since the War*. Dyllansow Truran, Redruth, UK, pp. 157–180.

Creating the Tourist Destination: Narrating the 'Undiscovered' and the Paradox of Consumption

15

Richard Voase

University of Lincoln, UK

Introduction

This chapter seeks to discuss three phenomena within the field of tourism. First, the manner in which discourse shapes and defines perceived tourist realities is examined, drawing on the perspective of Foucault. Secondly, the supposed desire of the tourist to uncover the authentic is considered, for which the work of MacCannell provides the principal theoretical background. Thirdly, the response of the business discipline of marketing to the need to create and extend the tourist destination is considered. The intention is to demonstrate, by means of theoretical argument, that conventional marketing wisdom, itself a discourse, runs contrary to what can be learned about fashionable consumption from definitive media discourses relating to the authentic, thus creating a paradox of consumption. A further paradox arises within the discourse of the pursuit of the authentic, in that the supposedly authentic can only be shown to be demonstrably real by comparison with the inauthentic or overfamiliar: the two are linked in symbiosis. It will be suggested in conclusion, first, that discourses about tourism, in particular those circulated by cultural intermediaries and ideologically dependent on fashionability and novelty, have a salient role in shaping perceived realities. Secondly, it is suggested that business-based product extension strategies for tourist destinations, prescribed from conventional marketing theory, should be treated with caution when applied to destinations whose principal selling proposition is an invitation to explore and discover.

©CAB International 2006. *Tourism Consumption and Representation: Narratives of Place and Self* (eds K. Meethan, A. Anderson and S. Miles)

Foucault and Discourse

I will begin by attempting to summarize aspects of Foucault's thinking on discourse, and power relationships, in four points. First, in Foucault's thinking, the role of the author is severely diminished. Foucault does not believe in an absolute subject in the Cartesian sense, and for this reason he sees the author as circulator rather than an initiator of discourse. Preferring to speak of an 'author-function', he posits the theoretical possibility of a culture in which discourses circulate without any need for an author (Foucault, 1979, pp. 19, 23, 28, 32). Secondly, an 'archive' of discourses can be considered to exist, whose contents are available for circulation in any particular place, time or epoch. These discourses may be circulated in accordance with sets of discursive pre-conditions, for which Foucault coins the term 'discursive formation' (Foucault, 1972, pp. 31–39, 126–131). What is said or written, by whom and to whom and when and where, depends on the operation of these discursive pre-conditions (Foucault, 1979, p. 29). Thirdly, the circulation of discourse is also a means by which extant power relations are rehearsed and re-established, by means of 'examination' (Foucault, 1977, pp. 184–192). In other words, in any discursive exchange, the discursive pre-conditions permit certain questions to be put, and certain responses to be proffered. Fourthly, Foucault diagnoses the condition of contemporary society (see Kendall and Wickham, 1999, p. 4) in terms of the 'grand metaphor' (Bauman, 1992, p. xvi) of panopticism:

> Our society is one not of spectacle, but of surveillance; under the surface of images ... the play of signs defines the anchorages of power ... (we are) in the panoptic machine invested by its effects of power, which we bring to ourselves since we are part of its mechanism.
>
> (Foucault, 1977, p. 217)

Hollinshead (1999, p. 8) has argued the case for applying Foucault's insights to the understanding of the practitioner-world of tourism, outlining a worthy purpose as:

> ... (to register) ... how individual managers, developers, researchers in tourism and travel quickly engage in small and large games of cultural, social, environmental and historical cleansing, as they promote and project some sociopolitical universes and chastise or omit other possible contending worldviews.

and that

> ... in terms of the *relations of power*, Foucauldian analysis could conceivably ... (make) ... visible what managers and developers in tourism really do and privilege through their everyday talk and deeds.
>
> (Hollinshead, 1999, p. 9)

In response to Hollinshead's invitation, I feel it would be useful to relate and analyse an incident from my pre-academic life as a practitioner in destination marketing. Employed in the early 1980s at a seaside resort which at the time was bucking decline (Voase, 1995, chapter 12), I once met a travel journalist writing for *The Guardian*, a newspaper of the liberal intelligentsia. She was on an English Tourist Board-sponsored familiarization visit to destinations which were considered to be adopting a novel approach. On meeting, it emerged that she was not staying in the resort, but in an isolated village in the rural hinterland. Her next port of call was to be another isolated village; and she then proposed to depart. I pointed out that her chosen stopover was a tiny hamlet with no facilities for tourists. She replied that a bed-and-breakfast had opened up and it was quite charming. An attempt to explain what had been done to reverse the decline in visits to the seaside resort, and why it had worked, was met with a glazed look and the repeated question, 'But what are you doing that is new?' I had sudden inspiration: a new Harbour History Exhibition had opened. 'History'. At the mention of the word, a pencil was produced, and a notepad. 'Where is it? Let me see it. Isn't it wonderful?' (it was tiny). However, apart from that tiny exhibition, that resort, for that journalist, written about in that newspaper, for that readership, did not exist. Never mind that she had walked past (and ignored) two crowded beaches on a hot sunny day. The region was defined in terms of a small exhibition of maritime history and a one-room bed-and-breakfast in the rural back-of-beyond. In terms of Foucault's panoptic metaphor, she was the apparent overseer, and the apparent author; but was herself the overseen, disciplined by the discursive requirements of the story which she was to write to conform to a narrative of place which circulated around liberal middle-class dinner tables.

For me, this event was a proverbial 'moment of truth'. Embodied within that exchange of examination and confession were three manifestations of what in Foucault's thinking is a contingent outcome of the interaction of power and knowledge (Foucault, 1980). First, there was an incompatibility between the discursive pre-conditions by which it was possible to write about tourism in that newspaper, for that readership, and the observable reality. Secondly, clearly evident in those discursive pre-conditions is the transcendence of the individual and the simultaneous rejection of the collective and the commodified (see Urry, 1988, p. 42). Thirdly, clearly present is the hegemonic power of the past, 'history', as a badge of cultural worth (see Thrift, 1989). What was powerfully evident to me, in retrospect and in the Foucauldian sense, was the absence of authorship. Not only could the journalist 'not write' the 'real' story, the idea of doing so did not occur to her. In the Foucauldian sense, the 'story' was already waiting in the archive, pre-formed by discursive pre-conditions. Having first responded to the journalist's examination in terms of a Cartesian subject, I had turned mid-stream into a 'subjected'; the mention of history was for me, at that time, an instinctive rather than reflexive move. Heritage, representing history in its commodified form, had become common linguistic currency around the mid-1970s and was to become, during the 1980s, a heritage industry in its own right. For me, the introduction of the discursive term 'history' was to submit to that hegemony, and it worked: it was better to see the resort mentioned in the resultant newspaper article as the location of a tiny history exhibition, and its accommodation defined by an isolated bed-and-breakfast establishment in the rural hinterland, than not mentioned at all. As Fairclough observes:

> ... the 'right to speak' and 'ability to understand' as well as the right to draw upon 'the corpus of already formulated statements' are unequally distributed across social groups ... I would want to suggest that structures are reproduced or transformed depending on the state of relations, the 'balance of power', between those in struggle in a particular sustained domain of practice, such as the school or workplace.
>
> (Fairclough, 1992, pp. 48, 58)

A term which Foucault eschewed (1972, p. 38) but which is arguably of considerable relevance is that of *ideology*. Louis Althusser, Foucault's teacher, developed the concept from its Marxist origins via the work of Gramsci, and pointed to the ubiquity of ideologies in everyday life: when one least considers oneself to be influenced by ideologies, that is likely to be the point at which they are at their most powerful (Althusser, 1992). Thus, the mention of the word 'history' creates a set of discursive pre-conditions which include one set of possibilities and exclude others. Discourses are vehicles for ideologies (Purvis and Hunt, 1993, p. 476), ideologies are vehicles for power (Fairclough, 1989, p. 2) and, in a postmodern world in which 'the past' is regarded as the repository of good taste amongst cultural intermediaries (Urry, 1990), its mere mention nullifies the need for any alternative agenda. There is and was, however, another interesting dimension to the discursive approach of the journalist in the anecdote. Her repeated question was, 'But what are you doing that is *new*?' 'History' was the ideologically laden response, but her request was, in fact, for *novelty*. This leads to a consideration of some recent writings of MacCannell, who, citing the travel writings of Stendhal, observes that the motive of Stendhal's character, a Mr L____, is *to have something new to say*. The nub of MacCannell's argument is that tourists seek to construct their own narrative of their experience and it is the unexpected, rather than the extraordinary, which is the raw material (MacConnel, 2001, pp. 32, 34, 36 see also Elsrud, Chapter 9, this volume). This neatly leads to the second theme of this chapter, which aims to understand the tourist's apparent pursuit of the authentic by means of what shall be termed the 'discourse of the undiscovered'.

The Discourse of the 'Undiscovered'

There is a whole genre of travel and tourism literature dedicated to the 'undiscovered' (see also Ford and Havrda, Chapter 2, and Winter, Chapter 3, this volume). The titular prefix is typically 'undiscovered', 'secret' or ' hidden'. The discursive construction of two examples of such literature will be examined shortly but, before that, two other bodies of theory are to be introduced. The first is a model for the development of international holiday-taking, developed by the Henley Centre for Forecasting (1992, pp. 25–27; see also Voase, 1995, p. 163). This model seeks to categorize tourists into four different types but, unlike some of the categorizations formulated in the early years of the study of tourism as a discipline, its key variable is the passage of time, and the effects that increased travel maturity, wealth and time availability bring. Thus individuals and whole cultures whose lives as international tourists begin as 'bubble travellers' will to some extent, with the passage of time, evolve into 'idealized pleasure seekers' whose increased maturity facilitates the self-organization of certain kinds of short-haul trips. For example, a UK overseas holiday-maker may acquire the capability of booking a *gîte* holiday in France, but will remain a bubble traveller when visiting long-haul non-European destinations.

The second body of theory is drawn from MacCannell (1976, pp. 41–42), namely his theorized 'trajectory of discovery' (1976, pp. 101–102). MacCannell suggests that tourists are engaged in a perpetual quest for the authentic. Because few tourists can understand cultural sites without assistance, key sites are marked out and interpreted so that they can be recognized for what they are. However, the very act of marking and interpreting leads the tourist to believe that, somehow, these sites have been staged for their benefit. Convinced that there must be something really authentic to discover behind the sites which are staged, they embark on a trajectory in pursuit of the as yet undiscovered. MacCannell illustrates this by means of a metaphor derived from Erving Goffman. Presented with a staged spectacle front stage, tourists become convinced that the authenticity which they seek exists somewhere backstage.

These two theoretical positions enjoy the ring of common sense about them. However, in Foucauldian terms, if the second-order judgements behind these positions are questioned (see Kendall and Wickham, 1999, pp. 13–14), i.e. if the assumptions behind the two positions are examined, the results are revealing. First, the Henley Centre position was based on the assumption that wealthy, time-rich, mature travellers will seek to assume greater control of their own travel arrangements. This was based on the notion that individualism, identified as a growing cultural trait in the Britain of the 1980s (Mort, 1988; Henley Centre for Forecasting, 1989, p. 20; see also Meethan,

Chapter 1, this volume), would continue to manifest itself in consumer behaviour. Indeed it does, but the point has been well made that niche holidays offered by niche tour operators, however aggressively promoted as individualistic products, are in technical terms little different from the mass-market products from which their producers attempt to distinguish them (Munt, 1994). They are, after all, package holidays. Similarly, MacCannell's proposition makes sense in terms, first, of certain kinds of tourist who seek out the authentic, including authentic social relationships with the natives of the place visited; and, secondly, in terms of the general inquisitiveness of the human species. However, it would be mistaken to assume that these second-order judgements are generic to all tourists. Aldous Huxley memorably observed, in his essay entitled *Why Not Stay At Home*, that tourists in the Piazza of St Mark, Venice, are 'a gloomy-looking tribe' who only appear to lighten up when enjoying each other's company (1992, p. 13). Similarly, Boorstin cites the words of a British consul in Italy, writing in 1865:

> The Cities of Italy … (were) deluged with droves of these creatures, for they never separate, and you see them forty in number pouring along a street with their director – now in front, now at the rear, circling round them like a sheepdog …
>
> (Boorstin, 1963, p. 96)

More recently, Holloway has applied the term 'tourist daze' to the kinds of tourist who, dragooned into beholding sites and sights with which they enjoy no rapport, have little or no idea where they are or why they are there (Holloway, 1995; see also Boorstin, 1963, p. 99; Voase, 2002, p. 250). It is easy for the reader, whether lay or academic, to accept as given the second-order judgements of the Henley Centre and MacCannell positions, but it requires only a moment's reflection to realize that the mass of tourists are neither personally inquisitive nor bent on taking control of their travel arrangements. The point is well made by Munt that the discursive content of promotional materials for niche tours typically adopts an aggressively oppositional stance with respect to mass-market travel, yet the niche customers themselves are as similar to one another in terms of discourse and dress codes as are those who buy mass-market packages (1994, pp. 114–115). It is suggested that there exists a discursive link between the familiar and the hidden, and the next section aims to reveal this, by reference to two promotional publications.

'Hidden Holland' and 'Hidden England'

Hidden Holland

This brochure was published by the Netherlands Board of Tourism in association with *The Guardian* (1997), and distributed with a Saturday weekend edition of that newspaper, whose primary readership is the liberal intelligentsia. The invitation, in the banner headline on the front page, is to read about 'Hidden Holland'. The image on the front cover is of ... a bicycle. The double-page spread on pp. 2–3 includes a large and impressive picture of ... tulip fields. The illustrations on pp. 4–5 are of ... windmills (albeit windmills depicted in a 16th century painting by Avercamp). The illustrations on both subsequent double-page spreads are of ... canals. The first and obvious observation is that these sights are not exactly hidden territory for anyone with an ounce of knowledge about Holland. Nevertheless, the opening copy on p. 2 is oppositional toward the notion that Holland should be known through the stereotypically obvious. Under the heading, 'Out of Amsterdam', it begins as follows:

> Blame Max Bygraves if you will, but tulips and Amsterdam seem to be as much as anyone in Britain knows about the Netherlands. That's not to say that Amsterdam isn't deservedly popular for weekend breaks. But there's so much more to see: historical towns and grand museums that date back to the golden age of the Dutch Republic during the 17th century when its merchants grew rich on international trade and invested heavily in fine art and fine houses. The countryside may be flat, but it's a soothing landscape of bulb fields, Friesian cows, dykes and polders.

Discursively, the publication uses the well-known sites of Holland as an introduction to the notion that there is another level of authenticity, backstage, which is waiting to be discovered by the discerning, liberal, intelligent visitor. Despite its disparaging opening regarding what it assumes to be the dazed tourist's view of Holland, the illustrations which anchor the copy are precisely those stereotypical motifs. It can be said that the discourse of the undiscovered links the 'authentic' back regions with the 'staged' front regions in a kind of symbiosis. The invitation to the liberally intelligent reader is to demonstrate cultural competence by pursuing the supposed authenticity of the back regions. The complementary assumption is that the culturally competent reader will find mention of tulips and Amsterdam as welcome as the mention of the name of Max Bygraves, i.e. in their view, passé, overfamiliar and middle-brow. So, the invitation to discover is accompanied by the assumed rejection of the marked and interpreted site, *and* of the kind of tourism which seeks out such sights without embarking on a tasteful trajectory of discovery. So it can be posited that the back regions depend on the front regions; but if the relationship is one of authentic symbiosis, it needs to be shown that the front regions are dependent on the back. I will return to this point shortly, after the second example.

Hidden England

This is a publication of the English Tourism Council (2002). The front cover is a composition of photographs which are not wholly indexical, i.e. they are not readily recognizable as named tourist sites in England. However, their connotative message is unmistakcable. A Georgian folly, situated in parkland, overlooks a lake; bicycles lean against a red postbox; a sculptured stone lion, wearing a crown, stands on a balustrade; a wild rose displays its five, open petals; and a wooden doorway, located in a timber-and-brick cottage, is surrounded by climbing shrubs in bloom. These may not be named sites, but as signifiers in syntagmatic relationship they point with clarity to a common signified: this is England, or rather, the 'merrie' version of it. The p. 2 copy lacks the aggressive style of *Hidden Holland* but still draws heavily on front regions as an introduction to back regions:

> There are some places whose beauty and importance have earned them a place in every guide book to England. But we also know of many fabulous hidden gems tucked away throughout the land. In this colourful guide, we have devised 10 routes that uncover a blend of both, from cathedral cities and stately Royal palaces to ancient battle sites, hidden abbeys and the unexplored wilds of our stunning and remote national parks ...

(English Tourism Council, 2002, p. 2)

Such is the perceived power and potential of the discourse of the undiscovered that, at the time of writing, two national campaigns are using it as their main motif. The French National Tourist Board in London, the *Maison de la France*, announced its intention some years ago to direct promotional efforts toward the UK market in terms of the supposed 'individualism' and 'taste for authenticity' of key sectors of the British outbound market (Duval Smith, 1996). At the time of writing, a series of advertisements is appearing in the British quality press issuing the invitation to 'Uncover Hidden France'. Simultaneously, staff are being recruited to a pilot project, based in Cumbria, England, for a 'Hidden Britain Centre' which will aim to develop tourism to lesser known locations within rural Cumbria. This project is said to have been inspired by a British tourist authority initiative known as 'Hidden Britain', with the intention of applying a similar model over the whole country. The question arises, however, as to how the status of the hidden is affected once its hidden status is lost; and, in particular, how the integrity of the front regions may be dependent on the continued existence of 'undiscovered' back regions. The suggested answer to this question begins with the application of the work of Bourdieu, in respect of the taste conflicts by which groupings within the middle class seek to define themselves.

Tourism as a Field of 'Symbolic Struggle'

The issue to be addressed is how the discourse of tourism, as written about by journalists who occupy a particular class position in terms of education, qualifications and cultural adaptation within society, represents the perspective of that class rather than apparent realities. Bourdieu's research revealed the way in which taste is used by fractions of the middle class as a weapon in a symbolic struggle (1984). The struggle is in essence one of taste versus money, where the cultured salariat compensate for their relative lack of economic power by flaunting their cultural capital. The cultured salariat are a growing faction within the middle class, termed by Bourdieu the *new petite bourgeoisie*, and identifiable as creative workers in such fields as the media, advertising, governmental and quasi-governmental organizations, education, and so on: in other words, in knowledge industries which involve the transmission of information, opinion and values. For this reason, Bourdieu also calls them the new cultural intermediaries. This middle-class grouping equates rougly to what British sociologists have referred to as the service class (Urry, 1988, pp. 40–41; Thrift, 1989, p. 21; Frow, 1993, pp. 257–262; Butler, 1995).

To link this service class and their cultural role to the subject matter of this chapter, a sequence of linkages needs to be summarized. The service class, upwardly mobile but weakly formed as a class and in search of class credentials, a pedigree if you like, have been cogently linked by Thrift with the growth of interest in heritage and the countryside (1989). Urry has made the point that the service class predilection for the historic and natural has led to the reversal of valuations placed on domestic regions worthy of tourist visitation, exalting the unspoiled and natural, and simultaneously condemning the supposed vulgarities of the collective and contrived (1988, p. 42). To use Bourdieu's term, aspects of the *habitus* of the service class have been mediated and in part adopted by other groups within society. Munt has argued that the service class predilection for individuated, non-contrived tourist experience has reached hegemonic levels, because tourism, like other fields of consumption, has become a battleground for the symbolic struggle (1994). It could be added that tourism makes a very suitable battleground because, in a world where global manufacturing has led to a convergence of styles – for example, the convergence of car designs in recent years – in tourism, it is still possible (almost) to do something completely individual. In this symbolic struggle, the active rejection of the contrived and commodified is as much a part of the act of consumption as the seeking out of the individual and the tasteful: they are in symbiotic binary opposition. The service class are upwardly mobile in their mission to acquire cultural capital; and, as they acquire it, they place distance between themselves and their less cultured origins. As Bourdieu puts it, in words chosen to echo those of St Paul, it is 'a shame, horror, even hatred of the old Adam' (1984, p. 251).

Two different examples have been chosen to illustrate acts of symbolic violence. In these cases, it is argued, they are unconscious discursive acts emanating from the service class *habitus* and the ideology which informs it. The first is from a travel feature about Greece, which appeared in a British provincial newspaper of tabloid character: not, please note, and with all due respect to its readers, a newspaper of the intelligentsia. Writing under the title, *An isle of hidden gems: find real Greece beneath tourist tat*, the journalist includes these observations:

> The influence of the lengthy French and Venetian occupations has rubbed off on Corfu Town ... peeling window-shutters that are nearly falling off; washing lines, laden with laundry, zig-zagging across narrow alleys; faded pinks, greens, yellows and greys. 'I wish they'd clean it up a bit', one clueless Brit said. [...] Along the way are villages of the real Corfu, whose inhabitants grow their own food, make their own wine, and welcome you. On buses you share seats with people going to and from work, or seeing relatives. We went to Corfu's water park, Aqualand, with a local firm. But the unfathomably laid-back owner, Michalis, forgot to book us on the bus [...] This confirmed to us that, although Thomson's excursions are more expensive, they are worth the peace of mind. A rep is available 24 hours a day – you know you are in safe hands.
>
> (Hawcroft, 2001)

The paradox which is evident within this piece results, it is suggested, from a collision between two discourses and the ideologies embedded in them. The first discourse is constituted by the invitation to reject the obvious, and embrace the authentic: unmanicured environments, sharing transport with locals. To criticize the authentic is to be dismissed as 'clueless'. However, this is transcended by a second discourse, which can be termed the discourse of consumerism. The same relaxed lifestyle which allows the built environment to slide into a state of characterful poor repair is also the cause of bungled sightseeing arrangements. However, on this occasion, the result is far from characterful. The injunction is to rely on the tour operator as a pair of safe hands. Corfu is thus revealed as a theatre space in which, despite talk of mingling with welcoming locals, there is a sharp divide between the gazers and the gazed-upon: all are inside the panoptic machine.

The second example is a letter to a newspaper by the father of a young man who, tragically, was killed in an incident, in which he was apparently uninvolved, while touring in central Africa. In attempting to come to terms with the death of his son, the correspondent poses the rhetorical question, was it folly to take risks by travelling in possibly dangerous areas? He answers his own question by suggesting that a 'wonderful tradition of adventure' (itself an ideological concept) is justifiably attractive and exciting. However, the correspondent does not stop there:

> I would hate to think that, as a result of these tragedies, young travellers now retreated into the bland and mediocre. We could insist that we exposed our young men and women to nothing more challenging and threatening than Disneyland or a Club Med holiday; that in our attempts to ensure 100 per cent security, we offered fifth-rate experiences.
>
> (Dalton, 1999)

Discursively, this offers a different kind of insight into the relationship between the front and back region, involving the deployment of symbolic violence. Arguably the writer had set out to construct a meaning for the death of his son, rather than to label the holiday choices of the majority as 'bland', 'mediocre' and 'fifth-rate'. However, in order to make his point, this is what he does. Discursively, so it would appear, it is insufficient to argue for the free-standing value of adventurous travel. Comfortable tourism has to be demonized, in order for adventure to be seen in a favourable and justified light (see also Elsrud, Chapter 9, this volume).

It appears therefore that the relationship between the front and back region is one of authentic symbiosis. The back regions need the front regions to act as portals as much as the front regions need the back regions in order to get themselves mentioned. It has been argued that the service class, or to use Bourdieu's term, the new cultural intermediaries, are ideologically drawn to the back regions on grounds of personal taste, and out of the compelling need to find something new to write about. Therefore, front regions are dependent on the existence of back regions because, without them and their role as definers of taste, and sources of novelty, there is nothing left to say. 'The obvious' offers neither novelty, nor news.

The Tourist Historic City and the Paradox of Consumption

In this, the final part of the chapter, an attempt is made to link these insights to the creation and extension of the tourist destination. The chosen example is the City of York, one of England's best known historic cities. In 1994, York City Council commissioned a report from a firm of consultants to advise on action needed to secure the city's future as a tourist destination. Their report recommended that a new major visitor attraction be created, referred to variously as an 'icon' and a 'must-see' attraction, in order to secure the future of the already healthy tourist industry in the city (Touche Ross, 1994). This advice is rooted in what I have termed in an earlier note on this topic, the business metaphor (Voase, 1999), i.e. the terminology of manufacturing is applied, metaphorically, to the city-as-tourist-destination. Thus, the city is a 'product', consisting of product attributes such as sights and sites which can be labelled 'resources' (for instance, see Jansen-Verbeke, 1986; Burtenshaw *et al.*, 1991, pp. 202–211). The product has a life cycle (Kotler and Armstrong, 1991, p. 299): just as surely as a model of motor car passes its sales peak and requires investment and relaunch in order to extend the product to a Mark 2 model and beyond, so the tourist product requires investment in order to be extended (Butler, 1980). What has been termed the business metaphor could be described as a structuralist approach: the principles of product evolution are held to be the same, irrespective of the nature of the product. Immediately, something of a problem is apparent. Anecdotally, I remember being told about an orchestra which, during the mid-1980s, appointed its first marketing manager. Addressing the members of the orchestra about his professional intentions for them, the newly appointed official informed them that, in marketing terms, they were no different from a can of beans. Fortunately, marketeers have since moved healthily into their own post-structuralist era but, nevertheless, during the 1980s that sort of thinking, and talking, was not uncommon. The problem with the business metaphor is that it constrains both analysis and prescription within the parameters of the metaphor. Concepts transferred from one discursive domain to another simultaneously transfer the discursive formations of the domain of origin (see Foucault, 1972, p. 59).

It must be said, however, that the creation of major visitor attractions was used during the 1980s to extend the tourist product in some seaside resorts, and to create, or begin to create, the tourist product in industrial cities. This was done with success in many cases. However, York is neither seaside town, nor an industrial city as such, but rather what can be termed, rather clumsily perhaps, a tourist historic city (Ashworth and Tunbridge, 1990). There is a salient difference. The essence of a seaside resort is a certain obviousness, which proclaims itself loud and clear: the beach, the sea, amusements, variety shows. This is mediated through a well-understood system of signification involving cheeky postcards, ludic objects such as sticks of rock and Kiss-Me-Quick hats, fish and chips, donkeys on the beach and so on. The invitation is not to seek out and explore the undiscovered, but to visit and experience the obvious. Similarly, to place a new visitor attraction within a post-industrial city is to create a new, albeit different kind of obviousness: new cultural facility emerges from industrial dereliction. A traditional historic city, however, is somewhat different: a historic environment, dating from periods which (in the case of York) span close to 2000 years, is not 'the obvious' in the same sense. Rather, it is a detailed collection of spatial narratives (Meethan, 1996, p. 324) which invite selective and detailed reading. As levels of tourist interest in York have risen since the 1970s, a range of attractions has emerged to expose, mark and interpret aspects of the city's history (Voase, 1999, pp. 291–292). The problem is that each new attraction is in effect a commodization of an aspect of the city's past, making manifest that which hitherto was hidden. The danger is that additional acts of commodification will propel the city further into becoming a simulacrum of itself. The new cultural intermediaries, on whose discursive mediations continued success depends, would begin to consider that the potential for a (in their terms) fashionable trajectory of discovery was being frustrated. Once the discourse surrounding the city no longer satisfies fashionable requirements as defined by travel writers, long-term problems can be anticipated because, as has been suggested earlier, the influence of such discourses is hegemonic.

So, the structuralist application of the business metaphor is arguably inappropriate in a destination whose essence consists of a multitude of spatial narratives. In practical terms, what is required is qualitative research into the nature of the consumption sought and experienced by visitors to York. The particular research question would concern the extent to which the trajectory of discovery is or is not important. Secondly, and crucially, a study of the discourse surrounding tourism to the city and, preferably, an assessment of its influence on industry intermediaries such as tour operators is needed. At this point, it is perhaps worthwhile to speculate as to what may constitute an alternative strategy to achieve the long-term goal of maintaining the city's attractiveness to tourists. Curiously enough, it is already part and parcel of the regeneration strategies of industrial cities. In attempts to woo fashionability, i.e. to influence the new cultural intermediaries favourably in order that they might favourably influence the wider world, industrial cities have embarked upon policies termed cultural regeneration, around which a whole corpus of literature has arisen (e.g. Bianchini and Parkinson, 1993; Griffiths, 1993; Kearns and Philo, 1993; Lim, 1993; Voase, 1997). Cultural regeneration does not simply involve acquiring cultural facililites, but the industries which are themselves the engines of culture: advertising, fashion, publishing and education. This injection of fashionable industries and the fashionable people who come with them is intended to inject not just new energy into city life, but a body of the cultural intermediaries who will proceed to mediate positive images of their adopted home. The acquisition of new residents engaged in contemporarily thriving work, as opposed to mass tourists whose ephemeral dazed visits can be construed as a cultural drain on a community, rather than a cultural contribution to it, might succeed in fostering a fresh authenticity of social relations. These new social relations, and the supporting facilities which grow up around them, create something more vital than a simulation of a premodern past: an encounter with a vibrant present.

Conclusion

This chapter has sought to demonstrate the linkages between three phenomena. First, the work of Foucault provides both a panoptic metaphor for understanding the nature of the gaze in tourism, and an insight into the salience of discourse in the determination of perceived realities in tourist experience. Secondly, a development of MacCannell's theorized trajectory of discovery reveals a relationship of symbiosis between the familiar and the undiscovered, a relationship which itself has given rise to a genre of tourism discourse. Examples reveal the powerful presence of service-class ideologies in the ways in which these relationships are expressed; frequently this expression takes the form, *selon* Bourdieu, of symbolic violence. Thirdly, these insights reveal the inadequacy of what has been termed the business metaphor, in the form of structurally applied product extension strategies involving the creation of new visitor attractions, to the needs of a tourist destination such as the City of York. Rather, a destination of the kind which invites exploration should ensure there remains something to explore: both for visitors, and for the demands of journalists and travel writers, whose twin cravings are to demonstrate their own good taste, and feed off novelty. As the psychologist William James noted: 'An idea, to be suggestive, must come to the individual with the force of a revelation' (1902, p. 113).

References

Althusser, L. (1992) Ideology and ideological state apparatuses. In: Easthope, A. and McGowan, K. (eds) *A Critical and Cultural Theory Reader.* Open University Press, Buckingham, UK, pp. 50–58.

Ashworth, G. and Tunbridge, J. (1990) *The Tourist-Historic City.* Belhaven, London.

Bauman, Z. (1992) *Intimations of Postmodernity.* Routledge, London.

Bianchini, F. and Parkinson, M. (eds) (1993) *Cultural Policy and Urban Regeneration: the West European Experience.* Manchester University Press, Manchester, UK.

Boorstin, D. (1963) *The Image, or What Happened to the American Dream.* Penguin, London.

Bourdieu, P. (1984) *Distinction: a Social Critique of the Judgement of Taste.* Routledge, London.

Burtenshaw, D., Bateman, M. and Ashworth, G. (1991) *The European City: a Western Perspective.* David Fulton, London.

Butler, R. (1980) The concept of a tourist area cycle of evolution: implications for management of resources. *Canadian Geographer* XXIV, 5–12.

Butler, T. (1995) The debate over the middle classes. In: Butler, T. and Savage, M. (eds) *Social Change and the Middle Classes.* UCL Press, London, pp. 26–36.

Dalton, B. (1999) He died, but he lived, letter to *The Guardian*. 5 March p. 21.

Duval Smith, A. (1996) France woos discerning British. *The Guardian* 12 February, p. 11.

English Tourism Council (2002) *Hidden England: a Touring Guide.* English Tourism Council, London.

Fairclough, N. (1989) *Language and Power.* Longman, London.

Fairclough, N. (1992) *Discourse and Social Change.* Polity Press, Cambridge, UK.

Foucault, M. (1972) *The Archaeology of Knowledge.* Tavistock, London.

Foucault, M. (1977) *Discipline and Punish: the Birth of the Prison.* Reprint 1991. Penguin, London.

Foucault, M. (1979) What is an author? *Screen* 20, 13–33.

Foucault, M. (1980) *Power/Knowledge.* Gordon, C. (ed.) Harvester Wheatsheaf, London.

Frow, J. (1993) Knowledge and class. *Cultural Studies* 7, 240–281.

Griffiths, R. (1993) The politics of cultural policy in urban regeneration strategies. *Policy and Politics* 21, 39–46.

Hawcroft, S. (2001) An isle of hidden gems: find real Greece beneath tourist tat. *Hull Daily Mail 21* July, p. 17.

Henley Centre for Forecasting (1989) *Leisure Futures.* Henley Centre, London.

Henley Centre for Forecasting (1992) *Inbound Tourism: a Packaged Future?* Henley Centre/NEDO, London.

Hollinshead, K. (1999) Surveillance of the worlds of tourism: Foucault and the eye-of-power. *Tourism Management* 20, 7–23.

Holloway, C. (1995) The tourist as streetwalker: gaze or daze? *The Urban Environment: Tourism.* Conference paper. South Bank University, London.

Huxley, A. (1992) Why not stay at home. In: Venter, M. (ed.) *The Spirit of Place: an Anthology of Travel Writing,* Oxford University Press, Oxford, UK, pp. 13–16.

James, W. (1902) Varieties of Religious Experience, lectures 4 and 5. Cited in Augarde, T. (ed.) (1992) *Oxford Dictionary of Modern Quotations.* Oxford University Press, Oxford, UK.

Jansen-Verbeke, M. (1986) Inner-city tourism: resources, tourists and promoters. *Annals of Tourism Research* 13, 79–100.

Kearns, G. and Philo, C. (eds) (1993) *Selling Places: the City as Cultural Capital, Past and Present.* Pergamon, Oxford, UK.

Kendall, G. and Wickham, G. (1999) *Using Foucault's Methods.* Sage, London.

Kotler, P. and Armstrong, G. (1991) *Principles of Marketing*, 5th edn. Prentice-Hall, Englewood Cliffs, New Jersey.

Lim, H. (1993) Cultural strategies for revitalizing the city: a review and evaluation. *Regional Studies* 27, 589–595.

MacCannell, D. (1976) *The Tourist: a New Theory of the Leisure Class.* Schocken Books, New York.

MacCannell, D. (2001) Tourist agency. *Tourist Studies* 1, 23–37.

Meethan, K. (1996) Consuming (in) the civilised city. *Annals of Tourism Research* 23, 322–340.

Mort, F. (1988) Boy's own? Masculinity, style and popular culture. In: Chapman, R. and Rutherford, J. (eds) *Male Order: Unwrapping Masculinity.* Lawrence & Wishart, London, pp. 143–209.

Munt, I. (1994) The 'other' postmodern tourism: culture, travel and the new middle classes. *Theory, Culture and Society* 11, 101–123.

Netherlands Board of Tourism/*The Guardian* (1997) Hidden Holland. Enclosure to *Guardian Weekend*.

Purvis, T. and Hunt, A. (1993) Discourse, ideology, discourse, ideology, discourse, ideology … *British Journal of Sociology* 44, 473–499.

Thrift, N. (1989) Images of social change. In: Hamnett, C., McDowell, L. and Sarre, P. (eds) *The Changing Social Structure*. Sage, London, pp. 12–42.

Touche Ross (1994) *Tourism Strategy for York*. Touche Ross, London.

Urry, J. (1988) Cultural change and contemporary holiday-making. *Theory, Culture and Society* 5, 5–26.

Urry, J. (1990) *The Tourist Gaze: Leisure and Travel in Contemporary Societies*. Sage, London.

Voase, R. (1995) *Tourism: the Human Perspective*. Hodder & Stoughton, London.

Voase, R. (1997) The role of flagship cultural projects in urban regeneration. *Managing Leisure: an International Journal* 2, 230–241.

Voase, R. (1999) 'Consuming' tourist sites/sights: a note on York. *Leisure Studies* 18, 289–296.

Voase, R. (2002) Demographic change, climatic change and the 'smart' consumer: influences on tourism in the western Europe of the 21st century. In: Voase, R. (ed.) *Tourism in Western Europe: a Collection of Case Histories*. CABI, Wallingford, UK, pp. 243–253.

Index